P9-DVI-337

LITERATURE OF

Asia

TRADITIONS IN WORLD LITERATURE

National Textbook Company
a division of NTC/CONTEMPORARY PUBLISHING GROUP
Lincolnwood, Illinois USA

Cover Illustration: Fine Shira-Punu Mask, Asian Art
Christie's, London
Christie's/SuperStock

ISBN (student edition): 0-8442-1157-5 (hardbound); 0-8442-1158-3 (softbound)
ISBN (teacher's edition): 0-8442-1331-4 (softbound)

Acknowledgments begin on page 252, which is to be considered an extension of this copyright page.

Published by National Textbook Company,
a division of NTC/Contemporary Publishing Group, Inc.
4255 West Touhy Avenue,
Lincolnwood (Chicago), Illinois 60646-1975 U.S.A.
© 1999 NTC/Contemporary Publishing Group, Inc.
All rights reserved. No part of this book may be reproduced,
stored in a retrieval system, or transmitted in any form or by any means,
electronic, mechanical, photocopying, recording, or otherwise,
without prior permission of the publisher.
Manufactured in the United States of America.

Library of Congress Cataloging-in-Publication Data

Literature of Asia.
        p. 272   cm. 23 (Traditions in World Literature)
        Includes index.
        ISBN 0-8442-1157-5 (hard). — ISBN 0-8442-1158-3 (soft). —
        ISBN 0-8442-1331-4 (Teacher's Edition).
        1. Oriental literature (English). 2. Oriental literature (English)—History and
criticism. 3. Oriental literature—Translating—History and criticism. 4. Authors,
Oriental—Biography. I. Series.
PR9415.L57 1998
895—dc21   98-44317
                                                                              CIP
                                                                              AC

90 QB 0 9 8 7 6 5 4 3 2 1

Contents

CHINESE LITERATURE

JAPANESE LITERATURE

INTRODUCTION

A HUMANIZED WORLD: AN APPRECIATION OF CHINESE LYRICS

Ling Chung

> "Fair, fair," cry the ospreys
> On the island in the river.
> Lovely is this noble lady,
> Fit bride for our lord.
> —from "Kwan Chu," translated by Arthur Waley

The most famous collection of Chinese poetry, *Shih Ching* ("Book of Songs"), which is supposed to have been compiled by Confucius around 500 B.C., starts with a wedding song, "Kwan Chu." This poem begins with the echoing of the birds on an island to celebrate a happy marital union in the human world. This poem anticipates a dominant thematic aspect of the Chinese lyric tradition for more than two thousand years thereafter: the harmonious relationship between man and nature, and among men.

The relation between man and nature in Chinese poetry has often been misinterpreted by the Western world. There are no figures equivalent to Odysseus, Coleridge's Ancient Mariner, or Byron's Childe Harold. When these Western heroes find themselves in lofty mountains or on the vast sea, they are exiled into a hostile and challenging world. When a Chinese hermit-poet finds himself alone in nature, however, he is utterly at peace with his environment because he believes that man and nature are one. This difference in the relationship between man and nature in the cultures of China and of the Western world is often the cause of misinterpretation in translation. Gary Snyder, for example, is an excellent translator, with his knowledge of Chinese language and literature, his enthusiasm for the Asian style of life, and his poetic rendering of Chinese poetry into English; yet he like other Western translators has distorted the Chinese concept of nature in his translation of a poem by Han-shan. In his version of one of the Cold Mountain Poems (page 131), Snyder translates the Chinese word for *deep* as "rough" to describe the mountain trail, *round stone* as "sharp cobble," *cold* as "icy," *lone* as "bleak," an onomatopoeia of the light, cool wind as "whip, whip," *blows* as "slaps" to describe the wind, and *descending thickly* as "whirled and tumbled" to describe the snow. These deliberate, crucial changes of natural images result in a different picture of nature. In Snyder's version nature is aggressive: it whips the hermit, slaps his face, and tends to bury him with snow. The original poem, however, presents the traditional poetic image of a hermit sitting in the snow, appreciating in tranquility the natural beauty that surrounds him.

W. B. Yeats in his poem "Lapis Lazuli" describes a Chinese mountain scene, carved on lapis lazuli, which depicts two hermits, a servant carrying a musical instrument, and a bird. Yeats imagines the hermits looking down on a tragic scene below them. One asks the other to play a mournful melody, and their spirits are refreshed by the music: "Their ancient, glittering eyes are gay."

Actually, in Chinese poetry and art rarely is a mountain hermit such a heroic figure that he can completely transcend the tragedy of mankind and achieve an immovable gaiety. Even a Chinese Buddhist monk, supposed to have achieved the state of Nirvana, or eternal bliss, will not stare at the wretched world with gaiety, but more likely, with compassion. These heroic hermits of Yeats are distorted pictures, because Yeats has imposed his own notions about life and nature on his interpretation of the Chinese mind. A genuine picture of Chinese hermits and their relation with nature can be found in Li Po's "On Hearing Chün the Buddhist Monk from Shu Play His Lute" (p. 136). In this poem the music, man's mind, and nature are blended into one. In the second couplet, a figure of speech has brought together the artificial music and the natural music, the song of the pines. In the third couplet man's music and that of nature become fused in even more poetic images. This couplet, amplified by the classical allusions, can be paraphrased as follows:

> The melody like the tone Flowing Stream played by the great ancient musician Po-ya, cleanses the heart of a traveler; its final notes fade into the sound of temple bells which is vibrated by the fallen frost.

The music played by man is likened to that of a mountain stream; and the bell's song, caused by the fallen frost, merges with the music of man. When the music ceases in the last couplet, the perspective is shifted to a panorama of a serene, autumnal landscape:

> And I feel no change though the mountain darkens
> And cloudy autumn heaps the sky.

This device of shifting the perspective fuses man's consciousness and the man-made music into a timeless universe.

A great portion of Chinese lyrics are songs written on simple, personal themes. They are songs expressing love for natural beauty and peaceful rural life, and expressing warm thoughts for the members in the family, for the homeland and the country. The tone may be intensified when the poet is agitated because of suffering brought on by wars, famines, and corrupted bureaucracy, or because of the inevitable tragic transiency of human life. There is also a certain degree of artifice and sophistication in some of the narrative poetry and love lyrics.

In ancient China, the Confucian gentry would require a poet to go through a pattern of life: that is, to take the imperial examinations, become an officer to serve the emperor and the people, succeed in a career and acquire fame. At the same time, the Taoist-Buddhist's belief always urges the poet to enjoy a tranquil and leisurely life in the mountains and countryside. The majority of Chinese poets incline to the latter, because they regard it either as a Utopian form of life worth pursuing or an escape from the tumult of political intrigue. Po Chü-i's "Chu-ch'ēn Village" (p. 146), manifests this inclination. Tu Fu in his "A Hearty Welcome" (p. 139) depicts how a scholar-farmer-poet would enjoy an impractical, yet aesthetic, life: watching the flying gulls, drinking wine with friends, and writing poetry. Furthermore, in a society generally dominated by Confucianism, certain human relations are emphasized, especially those between emperor and subject, father and son, husband and wife, between friends, and between brothers. Chinese poetry of all ages has devoted considerable attention to short lyrics expressing the sorrow caused by separation from the beloved one. Li Po's "Parting at a Wine-Shop in Nan-king" (p. 137) and Tu Fu's "Remembering My Brothers on a Moonlight Night" (p. 138) express this theme.

In Chinese poetry great generals and warriors are praised because of their valor and military strategy, but war itself is not glorified. On the contrary, it is frequently condemned. In *Shih Ching* there are many anti-war folk songs written by anonymous poets. Tu Fu, the greatest humanist among Chinese poets, and also one of the greatest humanists who ever lived, witnessed the climactic blooming of the T'ang Dynasty as well as its decline after A.D. 755. The ceaseless disasters—the wars, deaths, famines, and plagues—that befell him, his family, and the Chinese people, inspired him out of his compassion to sing in a tone of suppressed anger against evil and corruption. In "A Song of War-Chariots" (p. 141), he first gives a very vivid picture of new recruits marching out of a city, and of families running with the army, crying and tugging at the sleeves of the drafted young men. Then his vision shifts to the vast land of China, barren because of the war and taxation. The poem ends with a striking and pathetic scene—ghosts of the old dead and the new dead mingling in the remote border land. Witter Bynner's translation is certainly touching, but the sound effect of an onomatopoeia is missed in the translation: "Ch'iu Ch'iu" in the last line, a mixture of the sound of rain and the ghosts, intensifies the protest of the dead and of a furious universe.

The degree of sophistication is slight in the love songs among the traditional folk lyrics. Love songs from *Shih Ching* are still naïve, straight forward, and autobiographical. Gradually after about A.D. 100 the image of a lovelorn woman is isolated and becomes a popular topic. The poet will assume a situation for such a lovelorn woman—either her husband has gone away to war, to trade, or to another woman. The psychology of this woman will be carefully described either in a direct dramatic monologue or in detailed elaboration of the background scenery as a foil for the interior movement in the woman's psychology. Li Po, the greatest romantic genius in Chinese poetry, not only writes on weighty subjects such as the grandeur of nature and the tragic passing of human life in the stream of time but also excels in assuming the pose and psychology of a woman. In "A Song of Ch'ang-kan" (p. 136), he has successfully recreated the tone of a girl naïve and deeply in love. His "A Sigh from a Staircase of Jade" (p. 135) is a highly sophisticated poem. The original merely presents an artistic, objective picture, while Witter Bynner in his translation has put down all the implicit meanings which are only suggested in the original such as "cold," "she lingered," "behind her closed casement, why is she still waiting." This type of sophisticated artistry, which flourishes from about A.D. 900 on, is an important formalistic aspect of Chinese poetry.

READING TRANSLATIONS

Since every language is a unique and complex structure of sounds and meanings, translation cannot be a simple matter of subtituting a word from one language for a word in another. When a work of literature is being translated, the challenge is even greater. In that case the translator must attempt to create something that is both faithful to the work in the original language but also reads well in the language into which the work is being translated.

Below is a rubái, a quatrain (four-line stanza), by Omar Khayyám in the original Persian. Five English translations of his poetry follow on pages xi and xii. The first and most famous English version of the rubáiyát (plural of rubái) of Omar Khayyám was done by Edward FitzGerald in the 1850s. FitzGerald observes that he frequently "mashed together" Omar Khayyám's quatrains in his translation. An examination of FitzGerald's most famous lines, the quatrain beginning "A Book of Verses underneath the Bough," shows this process at work. In this case FitzGerald has taken two very similar quatrains from the Persian original and collapsed them into one. The other translators have rendered both quatrains. (The Persian passage is the original of the second quatrain of each of the translated pairs.)

گر دست دهذ ز مغز گندم نانی
وز می دومنی ز گوسپندی رانی
با دلبرکی نشسته در ویرانی
عیشی است کی نیست حدّ هر سلطانی

EDWARD FITZGERALD (1879)

A Book of Verses underneath the Bough,
A Jug of Wine, a Loaf of Bread—and Thou
    Beside me singing in the Wilderness—
Oh, Wilderness were Paradise enow!

E. H. WHINFIELD (1883)

Give me a skin of wine, a crust of bread,
A pittance bare, a book of verse to read;
    With thee, O love, to share my solitude,
I would not take the sultan's realm instead!

So long as I possess two maunds of wine,
Bread of the flower of wheat, and mutton chine,
    And you, O Tulip-cheeks, to share my cell,
Not every Sultan's lot can vie with mine.

JUSTIN HUNTLY MCCARTHY (1932)

Give me a flagon of red wine, a book of verses, a loaf of bread, and
a little idleness. If with such store I might sit by thy dear side in some
lonely place, I should deem myself happier than a king in his kingdom.

When the hand possesses a loaf of wheaten bread, two measures of
wine, and a piece of flesh, when seated with tulip-cheeks in some lonely
spot, behold such joy as is not given to all sultans.

ROBERT GRAVES AND OMAR ALI SHAH (1968)

A gourd of red wine and a sheaf of poems—
A bare subsistence, half a loaf, not more—
Supplied us two alone in the free desert:
What sultan could we envy on his throne?

Should our day's portion be one mancel loaf,
A haunch of mutton and a gourd of wine
Set for us two alone on the wide plain,
No Sultan's bounty could evoke such joy.

PETER AVERY AND JOHN HEATH-STUBBS (1979)

I need a jug of wine and a book of poetry,
Half a loaf for a bite to eat,
Then you and I, seated in a deserted spot,
Will have more wealth than in a Sultan's realm.

If chance supplied a loaf of white bread,
Two casks of wine and a leg of mutton,
In the corner of a garden with a tulip-cheeked girl
There'd be enjoyment no Sultan could outdo.

Babylonian
Literature

THE EPIC OF GILGAMESH

One of the oldest surviving literary works in the world, the *Epic of Gilgamesh* was written on clay tablets around 2000 B.C. Its hero is the Babylonian king who ruled the city of Erech (or Uruk), around 2600 B.C. The legendary adventures of Gilgamesh were the inspiration for a series of tales that circulated for several hundred years before they were finally written down. The twelve clay tablets containing the adventures of Gilgamesh would probably have been lost had it not been for the efforts of King Ashurbanipal of Assyria, who established a library at his palace in Nineveh around 650 B.C. It was in the ruins of this library that the *Gilgamesh* tablets were eventually discovered in the mid-1800s, almost 40 centuries after they were written.

The *Epic of Gilgamesh*, like many literary works from the ancient Near East, is filled with a strong sense of the fragility of life and the haunting presence of death. Although the epic includes several episodes that demonstrate the proud triumphs of Gilgamesh, the central episode is the hero's painful quest for everlasting life, a quest that is ultimately hopeless. ■

Translated from the Babylonian and retold by Theodor H. Gaster

Once upon a time there lived in the city of Erech a great and terrible being whose name was Gilgamesh. Two-thirds of him were god, and only one-third was human. He was the mightiest warrior in the whole of the East; none could match him in combat, nor could anyone's spear prevail against him. Because of his power and strength all the people of Erech were brought beneath his sway, and he ruled them with an iron hand, seizing youths for his service and taking to himself any maiden he wished.

At length they could endure it no longer, and prayed to heaven for relief. The lord of heaven heard their prayer and summoned the goddess Aruru—that same goddess who, in olden times, had fashioned man out of clay.

"Go," said he, "and mold out of clay a being who will prove the equal of this tyrant, and let him fight with him and beat him, that the people may have relief."

Thereupon the goddess wetted her hands and, taking clay from the ground, kneaded it into a monstrous creature, whom she named Enkidu. Fierce he was, like the god of battle, and his whole body was covered with hair. His tresses hung long like a woman's, and he was clothed in skins. All day long he roamed with the beasts of the field, and like them he fed on grass and herbs and drank from the brooks.

But no one in Erech yet knew that he existed.

One day a huntsman who had gone out trapping noticed the strange creature refreshing himself beside the herds at the fountain. The mere sight was sufficient to turn the huntsman pale. His face drawn and haggard, his heart pounding and thumping, he rushed home in terror, screaming with dismay.

The next day he went out again into the fields to continue his trapping, only to find that all the pits he had dug had been filled in and all the snares he had laid torn up, and there was Enkidu himself releasing the captured beasts from the toils!

On the third day, when the same thing happened once more, the huntsman went and consulted his father. The latter advised him to go to Erech and report the matter to Gilgamesh.

When Gilgamesh heard what had happened, and learned of the wild creature who was interfering with the labors of his subjects, he instructed the huntsman to choose a girl from the streets and take her with him to the place where the cattle drank. When Enkidu came thither for water she was to strip off her clothing and entice him with her charms. Once he embraced her the animals would recognize that he was not of their kind, and they would immediately forsake him. Thus he would be drawn into the world of men and be forced to give up his savage ways.

The huntsman did as he was ordered and, after three days' journey, arrived with the girl at the place where the cattle drank. For two days they sat and waited. On the third day, sure enough, the strange and savage creature came down with the herd for water. As soon as she caught sight of him the girl stripped off her clothing and revealed her charms. The monster was enraptured and clasped her wildly to his breast and embraced her.

For a whole week he dallied with her, until at last, sated with her charms, he rose to rejoin the herd. But the hinds and gazelles knew him no more for one of their own, and when he approached them they shied away and scampered off. Enkidu tried to run after them, but even as he ran he felt his legs begin to drag and his limbs grow taut, and all of a sudden he became aware that he was no longer a beast but had become a man.

Faint and out of breath, he turned back to the girl. But now it was a changed being who sat at her feet, gazing up into her eyes and hanging intently upon her lips.

Presently she turned toward him "Enkidu," she said softly, "you have grown handsome as a god. Why should you go on roving with the beasts? Come, let me take you to Erech, the broad city of men. Let me take you to the gleaming temple where the god and goddess sit enthroned. It is there, by the way, that Gilgamesh is rampaging like a bull, holding the people at his mercy."

At these words Enkidu was overjoyed; for, now that he was no longer a beast, he longed for the converse and companionship of men.

"Lead on," said he, "to the city of Erech, to the gleaming temple of the god and goddess. As for Gilgamesh and his rampaging, I will soon alter that. I will fling a challenge in his face and dare him, and show him, once for all, that country lads are no weaklings!"

It was New Year's Eve when they reached the city, and the high point of the festival had now arrived, the moment when the king was to be led to the temple to play the role of bridegroom in a holy marriage with the goddess. The streets were lined with festive throngs, and everywhere the cries of young revelers rang out, piercing the air and keeping their elders from sleep. Suddenly, above the din and hubbub, came a sound of tinkling cymbals and the faint echo of distant flutes. Louder and louder it grew, until at last, around a bend in the road, the great procession wound into sight, with Gilgamesh himself the central figure in its midst. Along the street and into the courtyard of the temple it wove its way. Then it came to a halt, and Gilgamesh strode forward.

But even as he was about to pass within there was a sudden movement in the crowd, and a moment later Enkidu was seen standing in front of the gleaming doors, shouting defiance and barring the way with his foot.

The crowd shrank back amazed, but their amazement was tempered with a secret relief.

"Now at last," each whispered to his neighbor, "Gilgamesh has met his match. Why, this man is his living image! A trifle shorter, perhaps, but just as strong, for he was weaned on the milk of wild beasts! Now we shall see things humming in Erech!"

Gilgamesh, however, was by no means dismayed; for he had been forewarned in dreams of what was about to take place. He had dreamed that he was standing under the stars when suddenly there had fallen upon him from heaven a massive bolt which he could not remove. And then he had dreamed that a huge mysterious ax had suddenly been hurled into the center of the city, no man knew whence. He had related these dreams to his mother, and she had told him that they presaged the arrival of a mighty man whom he would not be able to resist but who would in time become his closest friend.

Gilgamesh strode forward to meet his opponent, and in a few moments they were locked in battle, raging and butting like bulls. At last Gilgamesh sank to the ground and knew that he had indeed met his match.

But Enkidu was chivalrous as well as strong, and saw at once that his opponent was not simply a blustering tyrant, as he had been led to believe, but a brave and stout-hearted warrior, who had courageously accepted his challenge and not flinched from the fight.

"Gilgamesh," said he, "you have proved full well that you are the child of a goddess and that heaven itself has set you on your throne. I shall no longer oppose you. Let us be friends."

And, raising him to his feet, he embraced him.

Now Gilgamesh loved adventure and could never resist a hazard. One day he proposed to Enkidu that they go together into the mountains and, as an act of daring, cut down one of the cedars in the sacred forest of the gods.

"That is not easy," replied his friend, "for the forest is guarded by a fierce and terrible monster called Humbaba. Often, when I lived with the beasts, I beheld his works. His voice is a whirlwind, and he snorts fire, and his breath is the plague."

"For shame!" retorted Gilgamesh. "Should a brave warrior like you be frightened of battle? Only the gods can escape death; and how will you face your children when they ask you what you did in the day when Gilgamesh fell?"

Then Enkidu was persuaded, and, after weapons and axes had been fashioned, Gilgamesh went to the elders of the city and told them of his plan. They warned him against it, but he refused to yield, and promptly repaired to the sun-god and implored his aid. The sun-god, however, was reluctant to help him. So Gilgamesh turned to his mother, the heavenly Queen Ninsun, and begged her to intervene. But when she heard of his plan she too was filled with dismay.

Putting on her finest raiment and her crown, she went up to the roof of the temple and addressed the sun-god. "Sun-God," she said, "you are the god of justice. Why, then, have you allowed me to bear this son, yet made him so restless and wild? Now, dear Sun-God, he has taken it into his head to travel for days on long and perilous paths only to do battle with the monster Humbaba! I beg you to watch over him day and night, and to bring him back to me safe and sound!"

When the sun-god saw her tears, his heart melted with compassion and he promised to help the heroes.

Then the goddess came down from the roof and placed upon Enkidu the sacred badge which all her votaries[1] were wont to wear. "From now on," said she, "you are one of my wards. Go forth unafraid and lead Gilgamesh to the mountain!"

When the elders of the city saw that Enkidu was wearing the sacred badge, they relented of their previous counsel and gave Gilgamesh their blessing.

"Since," they said, "Enkidu is now a ward of the goddess, we will safely entrust our king to his keeping."

Eagerly and impetuously the two stalwarts set out on their journey, covering in three days the distance of six weeks' march. At length they came to a dense forest, and at the entrance of the forest there was a huge door. Enkidu pushed it open a trifle and peered within.

"Hurry," he whispered, beckoning to his companion, "and we can take him by surprise. Whenever he wanders abroad Humbaba always bundles himself up in seven layers of garments. Now he is sitting wearing only his vest. We can get him before he goes out!"

But even as he spoke the huge door swung upon its hinges and slammed shut, crushing his hand.

For twelve days Enkidu lay writhing in anguish, and all the while kept imploring his comrade to give up the wild adventure. But Gilgamesh refused to pay heed to his words.

"Are we such puny weaklings," he cried, "as to be put out by the first mishap? We have traveled a long way. Shall we now turn back defeated?

---

1. **votaries:** devoted admirers.

For shame! Your wounds will soon be healed; and if we cannot engage the monster in his house, let us wait for him in the thicket!"

So on they went to the forest and at last they reached the Mountain of Cedars itself—that high and towering mountain on the summit of which the gods held session. Fatigued by the long journey, they lay down beneath the shade of the trees and were soon asleep.

But in the middle of the night Gilgamesh suddenly awoke with a start. "Did you wake me?" he called to his companion. "If not, it must have been the force of my dream. For I dreamed that a mountain was toppling upon me, when all of a sudden there appeared before me the most handsome man in all the world, and he dragged me out from under the weight and raised me to my feet."

"Friend," replied Enkidu, "your dream is an omen, for the mountain which you saw is yon monstrous Humbaba. Now it is clear that even if he falls upon us we shall escape and win!"

Then they turned upon their sides, and sleep fell on them once more. But this time it was Enkidu who woke suddenly with a start.

"Did you wake me?" he called to his companion. "If not, it must have been the force of my dream. For I dreamed that the sky rumbled and the earth shook, and the day grew black and darkness fell, and lightning flashed and a fire blazed, and death poured down. And then, all of a sudden, the glare faded and the fire went out and the sparks which had fallen turned to ashes."

Gilgamesh knew full well that the dream portended ill for his friend. Nevertheless he encouraged him not to give up; and presently they had risen and were deep in the forest.

Then Gilgamesh grasped his ax and felled one of the sacred cedars. The tree fell to earth with a loud crash, and out rushed Humbaba from his house, growling and roaring.

Now the monster had a strange and terrible face, with one eye in the middle, which could turn to stone any upon whom it gazed. As he came storming through the thicket, nearer and nearer, and as the tearing and cracking of branches announced his approach, Gilgamesh for the first time grew truly frightened.

But the sun-god remembered his promise and called to Gilgamesh out of the heavens, bidding him go forth unafraid to the combat. And even as the leaves of the thicket parted and the terrible face bore down upon the heroes, the sun-god sent mighty, searing winds from every quarter of the heavens, and they beat against the eye of the monster until they blinded his vision and he could move neither backward nor forward.

Then, as he stood there, thrashing with his arms, Gilgamesh and Enkidu closed in upon him, until at last he begged for grace. But the heroes would grant him none. They drew their swords and severed the horrible head from his giant frame.

Then Gilgamesh wiped the dust of battle from his brow and shook out the braid of his hair and removed his soiled garments and put on his kingly robe and crown. So wondrous did he appear in his beauty and valor that even a goddess could not resist him, and presently the Lady Ishtar[2] herself was there at his side.

"Gilgamesh," said she, "come, be my lover. I will give you a chariot of gold encrusted with gems, and the mules that draw it shall be swift as the wind. You shall enter our house beneath the fragrance of cedars. Threshold and stoop shall kiss your feet. Kings and princes shall bow before you and bring you the yield of the earth for tribute. Your ewes shall bear twins; your chariot horses shall be chargers; and your oxen shall have no equal."

But Gilgamesh remained unmoved. "Lady," he replied, "you speak of giving me riches, but you would demand far more in return. The food and clothing you would need would be such as befits a goddess; the house would have to be meet for a queen, and your robes of the finest weave. And why should I give you all this? You are but a drafty door, a palace tottering to its ruin, a turban which fails to cover the head, pitch that defiles the hand, a bottle that leaks, a shoe that pinches.

"Have you ever kept faith with a lover? Have you ever been true to your troth? When you were a girl there was Tammuz.[3] But what happened to him? Year by year men mourn his fate! He who comes to you preened like a jaybird ends with broken wings! He who comes like a lion, perfect in strength, you ensnare into pits sevenfold! He who comes like a charger, glorious in battle, you drive for miles with spur and lash, and then give him muddied water to drink! He who comes like a shepherd tending his flock you turn to a ravening wolf, scourged by his own companions and bitten by his own dogs!

"Remember your father's gardener? What happened to *him*? Daily he brought you baskets of fruit, daily bedecked your table. But when he refused your love you trapped him like a spider caught in a spot where it cannot move! You will surely do the same to me."

When Ishtar heard these words she was very angry, and rushed to her father and mother in heaven to complain of the insults which the hero had hurled at her. But the heavenly father refused to interfere, and told her roundly that she had got what she deserved.

Then Ishtar fell to threats. "Father," she cried, "I want you to send against this fellow that mighty heavenly bull whose rampaging brings storms and earthquakes. If you refuse I will break down the doors of hell and release the dead, so that they arise and outnumber the living!"

"Very well," said her father at length, "but remember, whenever the bull comes down from heaven it means a seven-year famine on earth. Have you provided for that? Have you laid up food for men and fodder for beasts?"

---

2. Lady Ishtar: a Babylonian goddess of love and war.

3. Tammuz: a Babylonian god of the flocks who was confined to the afterworld as a companion for Ishtar.

"I have thought of all that," replied the goddess. "There is food enough for men and fodder for beasts."

So the bull was sent down from heaven and straightway rushed upon the heroes. But even as it charged, snorting and foaming in their faces, flaying and thrashing with its mighty tail, Enkidu seized its horns and thrust his sword into the back of its neck. Then they plucked out its heart and brought it as an offering to the sun-god.

Meanwhile Ishtar was pacing up and down upon the ramparts of Erech, watching the fight in the valley below. When she saw that the bull had been vanquished she leaped upon the battlements and let out a piercing shriek.

"Woe betide Gilgamesh," she screamed, "who has dared to hold me in contempt and to slay the bull of heaven!"

At these words Enkidu, wishing to make it clear to her that he too had played his part in the victory, tore off the buttocks of the bull and flung them in her face. "Would that I could lay hands on you," he cried, "and do the same to you! Would that I could tear out your entrails and hang them up beside this bull's!"

Ishtar was now thoroughly put out, and all that she could do was to prepare to give decent burial to the bull, as befitted a heavenly creature. But even this was denied her, for the two heroes promptly picked up the carcass and carried it in triumph into Erech. So the goddess was left with her maidens, absurdly shedding tears over the animal's buttocks, while Gilgamesh and his comrade went striding merrily into the city, proudly displaying the evidence of their prowess and receiving the plaudits of the people.

But the gods are not mocked; whatsoever a man sows, that shall he also reap.

One night Enkidu had a strange dream. He dreamed that the gods were sitting in council, trying to decide whether he or Gilgamesh was the more to blame for the slaying of Humbaba and the heavenly bull. The more guilty, they had ruled, was to be put to death.

For a long while the debate raged back and forth, but when at length they had still not made up their minds, Anu, the father of the gods, proposed a way out.

"In my opinion," he declared, "Gilgamesh is the greater culprit, for not only did he slay the monster but he also cut down the sacred cedar."

No sooner, however, had he uttered these words than pandemonium broke loose, and soon the gods were at sixes and sevens, each roundly abusing the other.

"Gilgamesh?" screamed the god of the winds. "It is Enkidu who is the real villain, for it was he that led the way!"

"Indeed!" roared the sun-god, wheeling sharply upon him. "What right have *you* to talk? It was *you* who hurled the winds into Humbaba's face!"

"And what about *you*?" retorted the other, shaking with anger. "What about *you*? If it hadn't been for you, neither of them would have done these things! It was *you* that encouraged them and kept coming to their aid!"

Fiercely they argued and fiercely they wrangled, their tempers growing hotter by the minute and their voices louder and louder. But before they could come to a decision—Enkidu woke up.

He was now firmly convinced that he was doomed to die. But when he told the dream to his companion it seemed to Gilgamesh that the real punishment was destined, after all, for himself.

"Dear comrade," he cried, the tears streaming down his cheeks, "do the gods imagine that by killing you they will be letting me go free? Nay, good friend, all my days I shall sit like a beggar on the threshold of death, waiting for the door to open that I may enter and see your face!"

For the rest of the night Enkidu lay awake on his bed, tossing and turning. And as he lay, his whole life seemed to pass before him. He remembered the carefree days of old, when he had roamed the hills with the beasts, and then he bethought him of the huntsman who had found him and of the girl who had lured him to the world of men. He recalled also the adventure in the forest of cedars, and how the door had slammed shut on his hands, inflicting upon him the first and only wound that he had ever suffered. And he cursed the huntsman and the girl and the door with a bitter curse.

At last the first rays of the morning sun came stealing through the window, bathing the room in light and playing against the shadows on the opposite wall. "Enkidu," they seemed to be saying, "not all of your life among men has been darkness, and those whom you are cursing were rays of light. Were it not for the huntsman and the girl, you would still be eating grass and sleeping in cold meadows, but now you feed on the fare of kings and lie on a princely couch. And were it not for them, you would never have met with Gilgamesh, nor found the closest friend of your life!"

Then Enkidu knew that the sun-god had been speaking to him, and he no longer cursed the huntsman and the girl, but called down upon them all manner of blessings.

A few nights later he dreamed a second dream. This time it seemed as though a loud cry went up from heaven and earth, and a strange, grisly creature, with the face of a lion and the wings and talons of an eagle, swooped down from nowhere and carried him off. All of a sudden his arms sprouted feathers, and he became like the monstrous being which had assailed him. Then he knew that he was dead and that one of the harpies of hell was speeding him along the road of no return. At last he reached the house of darkness, where dwelt the shades of the departed. And behold, all the great ones of the earth were around him. Kings and nobles and priests, their crowns and robes put aside forever, sat huddled like hideous demons, covered with birdlike wings; and instead of the roasts and bakemeats of old they now ate dirt and dust. And there, on a lofty throne, sat the queen of hell herself, with her faithful handmaid squatting beside her, reading from a tablet the record of every soul as it passed in the gloom.

When he awoke Enkidu related the dream to his companion; and now they knew for certain which of them was doomed to die.

For nine days Enkidu languished upon his bed, growing weaker and weaker, while Gilgamesh watched beside him, torn with grief.

"Enkidu," he cried in his anguish, "you were the ax at my side, the bow in my hand, the dirk in my belt, my shield, my robe, my chiefest delight! With you I braved and endured all things, scaled the hills and hunted the leopard! With you I seized the heavenly bull and came to grips with the ogre of the forest! But now, behold, you are wrapped in sleep and shrouded in darkness, and hear not my voice!"

And even as he cried he saw that his companion no longer stirred nor opened his eyes; and when he felt Enkidu's heart it was beating no more.

Then Gilgamesh took a cloth and veiled the face of Enkidu, even as men veil a bride on the day of her espousal. And he paced to and fro and cried aloud, and his voice was the voice of a lioness robbed of her whelps. And he stripped off his garments and tore his hair and gave himself up to mourning.

All night long he gazed upon the prostrate form of his companion and saw him grow stiff and wizened, and all the beauty was departed from him. "Now," said Gilgamesh, "I have seen the face of death and am sore afraid. One day I too shall be like Enkidu."

When morning came he had made a bold resolve.

On an island at the far ends of the earth, so rumor had it, lived the only mortal in the world who had ever escaped death—an old, old man, whose name was Utnapishtim. Gilgamesh decided to seek him out and to learn from him the secret of eternal life.

As soon as the sun was up he set out on his journey, and at last, after traveling long and far, he came to the end of the world and saw before him a huge mountain whose twin peaks touched the sky and whose roots reached down to nethermost hell. In front of the mountain there was a massive gate, and the gate was guarded by fearsome and terrible creatures, half man and half scorpion.

Gilgamesh flinched for a moment and screened his eyes from their hideous gaze. Then he recovered himself and strode boldly to meet them.

When the monsters saw that he was unafraid, and when they looked on the beauty of his body, they knew at once that no ordinary mortal was before them. Nevertheless they challenged his passage and asked the purpose of his coming.

Gilgamesh told them that he was on his way to Utnapishtim, to learn the secret of eternal life.

"That," replied their captain, "is a thing which none has ever learned, nor was there ever a mortal who succeeded in reaching that ageless sage. For the path which we guard is the path of the sun, a gloomy tunnel twelve leagues long, a road where the foot of man may not tread."

"Be it never so long," rejoined the hero, "and never so dark, be the pains and the perils never so great, be the heat never so searing and the cold never so sharp, I am resolved to tread it!"

At the sound of these words the sentinels knew for certain that one who was more than a mortal was standing before them, and at once they threw open the gate.

Boldly and fearlessly Gilgamesh entered the tunnel, but with every step he took the path became darker and darker, until at last he could see neither before nor behind. Yet still he strode forward, and just when it seemed that the road would never end, a gust of wind fanned his face and a thin streak of light pierced the gloom.

When he came out into the sunlight a wondrous sight met his eyes, for he found himself in the midst of a fairy garden, the trees of which were hung with jewels. And even as he stood rapt in wonder the voice of the sun-god came to him from heaven.

"Gilgamesh," it said, "go no farther. This is the garden of delights. Stay awhile and enjoy it. Never before have the gods granted such a boon to a mortal, and for more you must not hope. The eternal life which you seek you will never find."

But even these words could not divert the hero from his course and, leaving the earthly paradise behind him, he proceeded on his way.

Presently, footsore and weary, he saw before him a large house which had all the appearance of being a hospice.[4] Trudging slowly toward it, he sought admission.

But the alewife, whose name was Siduri, had seen his approach from afar and, judging by his grimy appearance that he was simply a tramp, she had ordered the postern barred in his face.

Gilgamesh was at first outraged and threatened to break down the door, but when the lady called from the window and explained to him the cause of her alarm his anger cooled, and he reassured her, telling her who he was and the nature of his journey and the reason he was so disheveled. Thereupon she raised the latch and bade him welcome.

Later in the evening they fell to talking, and the alewife attempted to dissuade him from his quest. "Gilgamesh," she said, "that which you seek you will never find. For when the gods created man they gave him death for his portion; life they kept for themselves. Therefore enjoy your lot. Eat, drink, and be merry; for *that* were you born!"

But still the hero would not be swerved, and at once he proceeded to inquire of the alewife the way to Utnapishtim.

"He lives," she replied, "on a faraway isle, and to reach it you must cross an ocean. But the ocean is the ocean of death, and no man living has sailed it. Howbeit, there is at present in this hospice a man named Urshanabi. He is the boatman of that aged sage, and he has come hither on an errand. Maybe you can persuade him to ferry you across."

So the alewife presented Gilgamesh to the boatman, and he agreed to ferry him across.

"But there is one condition," he said. "You must never allow your hands to touch the waters of death, and when once your pole has been

---

4. **hospice:** a house of rest for travelers.

dipped in them you must straightway discard it and use another, lest any of the drops fall upon your fingers. Therefore take your ax and hew down six-score poles; for it is a long voyage, and you will need them all."

Gilgamesh did as he was bidden, and in a short while they had boarded the boat and put out to sea.

But after they had sailed a number of days the poles gave out, and they had well nigh drifted and foundered had not Gilgamesh torn off his shirt and held it aloft for a sail.

Meanwhile, there was Utnapishtim, sitting on the shore of the island, looking out upon the main, when suddenly his eyes descried the familiar craft bobbing precariously on the waters.

"Something is amiss," he murmured. "The gear seems to have been broken."

And as the ship drew closer he saw the bizarre figure of Gilgamesh holding up his shirt against the breeze.

"That is not my boatman," he muttered. "Something is surely amiss."

When they touched land Urshanabi at once brought his passenger into the presence of Utnapishtim, and Gilgamesh told him why he had come and what he sought.

"Young man," said the sage, "that which you seek you will never find. For there is nothing eternal on earth. When men draw up a contract they set a term. What they acquire today, tomorrow they must leave to others. Age-long feuds in time die out. Rivers which rise and swell, in the end subside. When the butterfly leaves the cocoon it lives but a day. Times and seasons are appointed for all."

"True," replied the hero. "But you yourself are a mortal, no whit different from me; yet you live forever. Tell me how you found the secret of life, to make yourself like the gods."

A faraway look came into the eyes of the old man. It seemed as though all the days of all the years were passing in procession before him. Then, after a long pause, he lifted his head and smiled.

"Gilgamesh," he said slowly, "I will tell you the secret—a secret high and holy, which no one knows save the gods and myself." And he told him the story of the great flood which the gods had sent upon the earth in the days of old, and how Ea, the kindly lord of wisdom, had sent him warning of it in the whistle of the wind which soughed[5] through the wattles of his hut. At Ea's command he had built an ark, and sealed it with pitch and asphalt, and loaded his kin and his cattle within it, and sailed for seven days and seven nights while the waters rose and the storms raged and the lightnings flashed. And on the seventh day the ark had grounded on a mountain at the end of the world, and he had opened a window in the ark and sent out a dove, to see if the waters had subsided. But the dove had returned, for want of place to rest. Then he had sent out a swallow, and the swallow too had come back. And at last he had sent out a raven, and the raven had not returned. Then he had led forth his kinsmen and his cattle and offered

---

5. **soughed** (soud, suft): made a moaning or sighing sound.

thanksgiving to the gods. But suddenly the god of the winds had come down from heaven and led him back into the ark, along with his wife, and set it afloat upon the waters once more, until it came to the island on the far horizon, and there the gods had set him to dwell forever.

When Gilgamesh heard the tale he knew at once that his quest had been vain, for now it was clear that the old man had no secret formula to give him. He had become immortal, as he now revealed, by special grace of the gods and not, as Gilgamesh had imagined, by possession of some hidden knowledge. The sun-god had been right, and the scorpion-men had been right, and the alewife had been right: that which he had sought he would never find—at least on this side of the grave.

When the old man had finished his story he looked steadily into the drawn face and tired eyes of the hero. "Gilgamesh," he said kindly, "you must rest awhile. Lie down and sleep for six days and seven nights." And no sooner had he said these words than, lo and behold, Gilgamesh was fast asleep.

Then Utnapishtim turned to his wife. "You see," said he, "this man who seeks to live forever cannot even go without sleep. When he awakes he will, of course, deny it—men were liars ever—so I want you to give him proof. Every day that he sleeps bake a loaf of bread and place it beside him. Day by day those loaves will grow staler and moldier, and after seven nights, as they lie in a row beside him, he will be able to see from the state of each how long he has slept."

So every morning Utnapishtim's wife baked a loaf, and she made a mark on the wall to show that another day had passed; and naturally, at the end of six days, the first loaf was dried out, and the second was like leather, and the third was soggy, and the fourth had white specks on it, and the fifth was filled with mold, and only the sixth looked fresh.

When Gilgamesh awoke, sure enough, he tried to pretend that he had never slept. "Why," said he to Utnapishtim, "the moment I take a nap you go jogging my elbow and waking me up!" But Utnapishtim showed him the loaves, and then Gilgamesh knew that he had indeed been sleeping for six days and seven nights.

Thereupon Utnapishtim ordered him to wash and cleanse himself and make ready for the journey home. But even as the hero stepped into his boat to depart Utnapishtim's wife drew near.

"Utnapishtim," said she, "you cannot send him away empty-handed. He has journeyed hither with great effort and pain, and you must give him a parting gift."

The old man raised his eyes and gazed earnestly at the hero. "Gilgamesh," he said, "I will tell you a secret. In the depths of the sea lies a plant. It looks like a buckthorn and pricks like a rose. If any man come into possession of it, he can, by tasting it, regain his youth!"

When Gilgamesh heard these words he tied heavy stones to his feet and let himself down into the depths of the sea; and there, on the bed of the ocean, he espied the plant. Caring little that it pricked him, he grasped it between his fingers, cut the stones from his feet, and waited for the tide to wash him ashore.

Then he showed the plant to Urshanabi the boatman. "Look," he cried, "it's the famous plant called Graybeard-grow-young! Whoever tastes it, gets a new lease on life! I will carry it back to Erech and give it to the people to eat. So will I at least have some reward for my pains!"

After they had crossed the perilous waters and reached land, Gilgamesh and his companion began the long journey on foot to the city of Erech. When they had traveled fifty leagues the sun was already beginning to set, and they looked for a place to pass the night. Suddenly they came upon a cool spring.

"Here let us rest," said the hero, "and I will go bathe."

So he stripped off his clothes and placed the plant on the ground and went to bathe in the cool spring. But as soon as his back was turned a serpent came out of the waters and, sniffing the fragrance of the plant, carried it away. And no sooner had it tasted of it than at once it sloughed off its skin and regained its youth.

When Gilgamesh saw that the precious plant had now passed from his hands forever he sat down and wept. But soon he stood up and, resigned at last to the fate of all mankind, he returned to the city of Erech, back to the land whence he had come.

DISCUSSION QUESTIONS

1. Unlike most legendary heroes, Gilgamesh fails in his quest. Why, then, do you think Gilgamesh emerged as a great epic hero among the ancient Babylonians?

2. What impression of Gilgamesh do you get from the first paragraph? How does Gilgamesh change in the course of the epic? How do you account for this change?

3 What is the purpose of the episode in which Gilgamesh sleeps for six days and seven nights? Why does he deny that he was ever asleep?

4. What view of the gods is presented in this epic? Do they tend to be wise and just, like the God of the Bible or the Koran, or irresponsible troublemakers, like the Greek and Roman gods, or something else entirely? Support your answer.

5. When the *Epic of Gilgamesh* was first discovered, people were amazed at the parallels between this epic and parts of the Bible. If you are familiar with the book of *Genesis* in the Bible, point out some of the similarities.

6. Ancient works of literature often make use of repetition. In the *Epic of Gilgamesh* the statement "that which you seek you will never find" is repeated at three different times. Who are the three speakers? What does this repetition accomplish?

SUGGESTION FOR WRITING

Toward the beginning of the *Epic of Gilgamesh* the main character is said to be "rampaging like a bull." This simile is the first of numerous figures of speech in the epic. Make a chart showing as many similes and metaphors as you can find. Classify them as either animals, clothing and household items, or weapons. Then choose one figure of speech that strikes you as particularly apt and explain what makes it effective.

Hebrew Literature

THE BIBLE

King James Version

The most influential book in the history of Western civilization, the Bible is actually a collection of many books regarded as sacred by Jews and Christians. The Christian Bible is divided into two parts, the Old Testament, containing the history, laws, and literature of the Jews, and the New Testament, containing the life and teachings of Jesus. The Jewish Bible contains only the 39 books of the Old Testament, which were written almost entirely in Hebrew. The selections that follow are all taken from the Old Testament.

The story of Samson comes from the book of Judges, which recounts the deeds of various military leaders known as "judges," who were sent by God to deliver the people of Israel from enemy oppression during a dark and unstable period of Jewish history. The book of Psalms is a collection of sacred songs that were used as the hymn book of the Jews. (The word *psalms* comes from *psalterion,* the stringed instrument that provided accompaniment to these songs.) The book of Ecclesiastes is an example of what is often called "wisdom literature." Using rich poetic language, the unknown narrator of this book, who refers to himself simply as the "Preacher," describes his investigation into the meaning of life.

There have been numerous English translations of the Bible, starting in 1388 and continuing to the present. All of the selections given here are taken from the King James Version, which was first published in 1611. Although many newer translations are available, the King James Version has been so highly regarded over the centuries that it is considered a major work of English literature. ■

THE STORY OF SAMSON

CHAPTER 13

And the children of Israel did evil again in the sight of the LORD; and the LORD delivered them into the hand of the Philistines[1] forty years.

And there was a certain man of Zorah, of the family of the Danites, whose name was Manoah; and his wife was barren, and bare not.

And the angel of the LORD appeared unto the woman, and said unto her, "Behold now, thou art barren, and bearest not: but thou shalt conceive, and bear a son.

"Now therefore beware, I pray thee, and drink not wine nor strong drink, and eat not any unclean thing:[2]

---

1. **Philistines:** ancient people of Palestine who were enemies of the Hebrews.

2. **eat . . . thing:** a reference to the Hebrew dietary laws which prohibit the Jews from eating certain foods.

"For, lo, thou shalt conceive, and bear a son; and no razor shall come on his head: for the child shall be a Nazarite[3] unto God from the womb: and he shall begin to deliver Israel out of the hand of the Philistines."

Then the woman came and told her husband, saying, "A man of God came unto me, and his countenance was like the countenance of an angel of God, very terrible: but I asked him not whence he was, neither told he me his name:

"But he said unto me, Behold, thou shalt conceive, and bear a son; and now drink no wine nor strong drink, neither eat any unclean thing: for the child shall be a Nazarite to God from the womb to the day of his death."

Then Manoah entreated the LORD, and said, "O my LORD, let the man of God which thou didst send come again unto us, and teach us what we shall do unto the child that shall be born."

And God hearkened to the voice of Manoah; and the angel of God came again unto the woman as she sat in the field: but Manoah her husband was not with her.

And the woman made haste, and ran, and shewed her husband, and said unto him, "Behold, the man hath appeared unto me, that came unto me the other day."

And Manoah arose, and went after his wife, and came to the man, and said unto him, "Art thou the man that spakest unto the woman?" And he said, "I am."

And Manoah said, "Now let thy words come to pass. How shall we order the child, and how shall we do unto him?"

And the angel of the LORD said unto Manoah, "Of all that I said unto the woman let her beware.

"She may not eat of any thing that cometh of the vine, neither let her drink wine nor strong drink, nor eat any unclean thing: all that I commanded her let her observe."

And Manoah said unto the angel of the LORD, "I pray thee, let us detain thee, until we shall have made ready a kid for thee."

And the angel of the LORD said unto Manoah, "Though thou detain me, I will not eat of thy bread: and if thou wilt offer a burnt offering, thou must offer it unto the LORD." For Manoah knew not that he was an angel of the LORD.

And Manoah said unto the angel of the LORD, "What is thy name, that when thy sayings come to pass we may do thee honor?"

And the angel of the LORD said unto him, "Why askest thou thus after my name, seeing it is secret?"

So Manoah took a kid with a meat offering, and offered it upon a rock unto the LORD: and the angel did wondrously; and Manoah and his wife looked on.

For it came to pass, when the flame went up toward heaven from off the

---

3. **Nazarite:** among the ancient Hebrews, one who had taken strict religious vows that included abstaining from alcohol and refusing to cut their hair.

altar, that the angel of the LORD ascended in the flame of the altar. And Manoah and his wife looked on it, and fell on their faces to the ground.

But the angel of the LORD did no more appear to Manoah and to his wife. Then Manoah knew that he was an angel of the LORD.

And Manoah said unto his wife, "We shall surely die, because we have seen God."

But his wife said unto him, "If the LORD were pleased to kill us, he would not have received a burnt offering and a meat offering at our hands, neither would he have shewed us all these things, nor would as at this time have told us such things as these."

And the woman bare a son, and called his name Samson: and the child grew, and the LORD blessed him.

And the Spirit of the LORD began to move him at times in the camp of Dan between Zorah and Eshtaol.

CHAPTER 14

And Samson went down to Timnath, and saw a woman in Timnath of the daughters of the Philistines.

And he came up, and told his father and his mother, and said, "I have seen a woman in Timnath of the daughters of the Philistines: now therefore get her for me to wife."

Then his father and his mother said unto him, "Is there never a woman among the daughters of thy brethren, or among all my people, that thou goest to take a wife of the uncircumcised Philistines?" And Samson said unto his father, "Get her for me; for she pleaseth me well."

But his father and his mother knew not that it was of the LORD, that he sought an occasion against the Philistines: for at that time the Philistines had dominion over Israel.

Then went Samson down, and his father and his mother, to Timnath, and came to the vineyards of Timnath: and, behold, a young lion roared against him.

And the Spirit of the LORD came mightily upon him, and he rent him as he would have rent a kid, and he had nothing in his hand: but he told not his father or his mother what he had done.

And he went down, and talked with the woman; and she pleased Samson well.

And after a time he returned to take her, and he turned aside to see the carcass of the lion: and, behold, there was a swarm of bees and honey in the carcass of the lion.

And he took thereof in his hands, and went on eating, and came to his father and mother; and he gave them, and they did eat: but he told not them that he had taken the honey out of the carcass of the lion.

So his father went down unto the woman: and Samson made there a feast; for so used the young men to do.

And it came to pass, when they saw him, that they brought thirty companions to be with him.

And Samson said unto them, "I will now put forth a riddle unto you: if ye can certainly declare it me within the seven days of the feast, and find it out, then I will give you thirty sheets and thirty change of garments:

"But if ye cannot declare it me, then shall ye give me thirty sheets and thirty change of garments." And they said unto him, "Put forth thy riddle, that we may hear it."

And he said unto them, "Out of the eater came forth meat, and out of the strong came forth sweetness." And they could not in three days expound the riddle.

And it came to pass on the seventh day, that they said unto Samson's wife, "Entice thy husband, that he may declare unto us the riddle, lest we burn thee and thy father's house with fire: have ye called us to take that we have? is it not so?"

And Samson's wife wept before him, and said, "Thou dost but hate me, and lovest me not: thou hast put forth a riddle unto the children of my people, and hast not told it me." And he said unto her, "Behold, I have not told it my father nor my mother, and shall I tell it thee?"

And she wept before him the seven days, while their feast lasted: and it came to pass on the seventh day, that he told her, because she lay sore upon him: and she told the riddle to the children of her people.

And the men of the city said unto him on the seventh day before the sun went down, "What is sweeter than honey? and what is stronger than a lion?" And he said unto them, "If ye had not plowed with my heifer, ye had not found out my riddle."

And the Spirit of the LORD came unto him, and he went down to Ashkelon, and slew thirty men of them, and took their spoil, and gave change of garments unto them which expounded the riddle. And his anger was kindled, and he went up to his father's house.

But Samson's wife was given to his companion, whom he had used as his friend.

CHAPTER 15

But it came to pass within a while after, in the time of wheat harvest, that Samson visited his wife with a kid; and he said, "I will go in to my wife into the chamber." But her father would not suffer him to go in.

And her father said, "I verily thought that thou hadst utterly hated her; therefore I gave her to thy companion: is not her younger sister fairer than she? take her, I pray thee, instead of her."

And Samson said concerning them, "Now shall I be more blameless than the Philistines, though I do them a displeasure."

And Samson went and caught three hundred foxes, and took firebrands, and turned tail to tail, and put a firebrand in the midst between two tails.

And when he had set the brands on fire, he let them go into the standing corn of the Philistines, and burnt up both the shocks, and also the standing corn, with the vineyards and olives.

Then the Philistines said, "Who hath done this?" And they answered, "Samson, the son-in-law of the Timnite, because he had taken his wife, and given her to his companion." And the Philistines came up, and burnt her and her father with fire.

And Samson said unto them, "Though ye have done this, yet will I be avenged of you, and after that I will cease."

And he smote them hip and thigh with a great slaughter: and he went down and dwelt in the top of the rock Etam.

Then the Philistines went up, and pitched in Judah, and spread themselves in Lehi.

And the men of Judah said, "Why are ye come up against us?" And they answered, "To bind Samson are we come up, to do to him as he hath done to us."

Then three thousand men of Judah went to the top of the rock Etam, and said to Samson, "Knowest thou not that the Philistines are rulers over us? what is this that thou hast done unto us?" And he said unto them, "As they did unto me, so have I done unto them."

And they said unto him, "We are come down to bind thee, that we may deliver thee into the hand of the Philistines." And Samson said unto them, "Swear unto me, that ye will not fall upon me yourselves."

And they spake unto him, saying, "No; but we will bind thee fast, and deliver thee into their hand: but surely we will not kill thee." And they bound him with two new cords, and brought him up from the rock.

And when he came unto Lehi, the Philistines shouted against him: and the Spirit of the LORD came mightily upon him, and the cords that were upon his arms became as flax that was burnt with fire, and his bands loosed from off his hands.

And he found a new jawbone of an ass, and put forth his hand and took it, and slew a thousand men therewith.

And Samson said, "With the jawbone of an ass, heaps upon heaps, with the jaw of an ass have I slain a thousand men."

And it came to pass, when he had made an end of speaking, that he cast away the jawbone out of his hand, and called that place Ramath-lehi.

And he was sore athirst, and called on the LORD, and said, "Thou hast given this great deliverance into the hand of thy servant: and now shall I die for thirst, and fall into the hand of the uncircumcised?"

But God clave a hollow place that was in the jaw, and there came water thereout; and when he had drunk, his spirit came again, and he revived: wherefore he called the name thereof Enhakkore, which is in Lehi unto this day.

And he judged Israel in the days of the Philistines twenty years.

CHAPTER 16

Then went Samson to Gaza, and saw there a harlot, and went in unto her.

And it was told the Gazites, saying, "Samson is come hither." And they compassed him in, and laid wait for him all night in the gate of the city, and were quiet all the night, saying, "In the morning, when it is day, we shall kill him."

And Samson lay till midnight, and arose at midnight, and took the doors of the gate of the city, and the two posts, and went away with them, bar and all, and put them upon his shoulders, and carried them up to the top of a hill that is before Hebron.

And it came to pass afterward, that he loved a woman in the valley of Sorek, whose name was Delilah.

And the lords of the Philistines came up unto her, and said unto her, "Entice him, and see wherein his great strength lieth, and by what means we may prevail against him, that we may bind him to afflict him: and we will give thee every one of us eleven hundred pieces of silver."

And Delilah said to Samson, "Tell me, I pray thee, wherein thy great strength lieth, and wherewith thou mightest be bound to afflict thee."

And Samson said unto her, "If they bind me with seven green withes that were never dried, then shall I be weak, and be as another man."

Then the lords of the Philistines brought up to her seven green withes which had not been dried, and she bound him with them.

Now there were men lying in wait, abiding with her in the chamber. And she said unto him, "The Philistines be upon thee, Samson." And he brake the withes, as a thread of tow is broken when it toucheth the fire. So his strength was not known.

And Delilah said unto Samson, "Behold, thou hast mocked me, and told me lies: now tell me, I pray thee, wherewith thou mightest be bound."

And he said unto her, "If they bind me fast with new ropes that never were occupied, then shall I be weak, and be as another man."

Delilah therefore took new ropes, and bound him therewith, and said unto him, "The Philistines be upon thee, Samson." And there were liers in wait abiding in the chamber. And he brake them from off his arms like a thread.

And Delilah said unto Samson, Hitherto thou hast mocked me, and told me lies: tell me wherewith thou mightest be bound. And he said unto her, "If you weavest the seven locks of my head with the web."[4]

And she fastened it with the pin, and said unto him, "The Philistines be upon thee, Samson." And he awaked out of his sleep, and went away with the pin of the beam, and with the web.

And she said unto him, "How canst thou say, I love thee, when thine heart is not with me? thou hast mocked me these three times, and hast not told me wherein thy great strength lieth."

And it came to pass, when she pressed him daily with her words, and urged him, so that his soul was vexed unto death;

That he told her all his heart, and said unto her, "There hath not come a razor upon mine head: for I have been a Nazarite unto God from my

---

4. **weavest . . . web:** The web refers to the strings of a loom. Samson is suggesting that Delilah weave his hair into the warp of the loom and fasten it with the pin or peg.

mother's womb: if I be shaven, then my strength will go from me, and I shall become weak, and be like any other man."

And when Delilah saw that he had told her all his heart, she sent and called for the lords of the Philistines, saying, "Come up this once, for he hath shewed me all his heart." Then the lords of the Philistines came up unto her, and brought money in their hand.

And she made him sleep upon her knees; and she called for a man, and she caused him to shave off the seven locks of his head; and she began to afflict him, and his strength went from him.

And she said, "The Philistines be upon thee, Samson." And he awoke out of his sleep, and said, "I will go out as at other times before, and shake myself." And he wist[5] not that the LORD was departed from him.

But the Philistines took him, and put out his eyes, and brought him down to Gaza, and bound him with fetters of brass; and he did grind in the prison house.

Howbeit the hair of his head began to grow again after he was shaven.

Then the lords of the Philistines gathered them together for to offer a great sacrifice unto Dagon their god, and to rejoice: for they said, "Our god hath delivered Samson our enemy into our hand."

And when the people saw him, they praised their god: for they said, "Our god hath delivered into our hands our enemy, and the destroyer of our country, which slew many of us."

And it came to pass, when their hearts were merry, that they said, "Call for Samson, that he may make us sport." And they called for Samson out of the prison house; and he made them sport: and they set him between the pillars.

And Samson said unto the lad that held him by the hand, "Suffer me that I may feel the pillars whereupon the house standeth, that I may lean upon them."

Now the house was full of men and women; and all the lords of the Philistines were there; and there were upon the roof about three thousand men and women, that beheld while Samson made sport.

And Samson called unto the LORD, and said, "O LORD God, remember me, I pray thee, and strengthen me, I pray thee, only this once, O God, that I may be at once avenged of the Philistines for my two eyes."

And Samson took hold of the two middle pillars upon which the house stood, and on which it was borne up, of the one with his right hand, and of the other with his left.

And Samson said, "Let me die with the Philistines." And he bowed himself with all his might; and the house fell upon the lords, and upon all the people that were therein. So the dead which he slew at his death were more than they which he slew in his life.

Then his brethren and all the house of his father came down, and took him, and brought him up, and buried him between Zorah and Eshtaol in the burying place of Manoah his father. And he judged Israel twenty years.

---

5. **wist:** knew.

PSALM 8

O Lord our Lord, how excellent is thy name in all the earth! who hast set thy glory above the heavens.

Out of the mouth of babes and sucklings hast thou ordained strength because of thine enemies, that thou mightest still the enemy and the avenger.

When I consider thy heavens, the work of thy fingers, the moon and the stars, which thou hast ordained;

What is man, that thou art mindful of him? and the son of man, that thou visitest him?

For thou has made him a little lower than the angels, and hast crowned him with glory and honor.

Thou madest him to have dominion over the works of thy hands; thou hast put all things under his feet:

All sheep and oxen, yea, and the beasts of the field;

The fowl of the air, and the fish of the sea, and whatsoever passeth through the paths of the seas.

O Lord our Lord, how excellent is thy name in all the earth!

PSALM 19

The heavens declare the glory of God; and the firmament sheweth his handywork.

Day unto day uttereth speech, and night unto night sheweth knowledge.

There is no speech nor language, where their voice is not heard.

Their line is gone out through all the earth, and their words to the end of the world. In them hath he set a tabernacle for the sun,

Which is as a bridegroom coming out of his chamber, and rejoiceth as a strong man to run a race.

His going forth is from the end of the heaven, and his circuit unto the ends of it: and there is nothing hid from the heat thereof.

The law of the Lord is perfect, converting the soul: the testimony of the Lord is sure, making wise the simple.

The statutes of the Lord are right, rejoicing the heart: the commandment of the Lord is pure, enlightening the eyes.

The fear of the Lord is clean, enduring for ever: the judgments of the Lord are true and righteous altogether.

PSALM 23

The Lord is my shepherd; I shall not want.

He maketh me to lie down in green pastures: he leadeth me beside
    the still waters.

He restoreth my soul: he leadeth me in the paths of righteousness for
    his name's sake.

Yea, though I walk through the valley of the shadow of death, I
    will fear no evil: for thou art with me; thy rod and thy staff
    they comfort me.

Thou preparest a table before me in the presence of mine enemies:
    thou anointest my head with oil; my cup runneth over.

Surely goodness and mercy shall follow me all the days of my life:
    and I will dwell in the house of the Lord for ever.

PSALM 45

My heart is indicting[6] a good matter: I speak of the things which I
    have made touching the king: my tongue is the pen of a ready
    writer.

Thou art fairer than the children of men: grace is poured into thy
    lips: therefore God hath blessed thee for ever.

Gird thy sword upon thy thigh, O most mighty, with thy glory
    and thy majesty.

And in thy majesty ride prosperously because of truth and
    meekness and righteousness; and thy right hand shall teach thee
    terrible things.

Thine arrows are sharp in the heart of the king's enemies; whereby
    the people fall under thee.

Thy throne, O God, is for ever and ever: the sceptre of thy
    kingdom is a right sceptre.

Thou lovest righteousness, and hatest wickedness: therefore God,

thy God, hath anointed thee with the oil of gladness above thy
    fellows.

All thy garments smell of myrrh, and aloes, and cassia,[7] out of the
    ivory palaces, whereby they have made thee glad.

King's daughters were among thy honorable women: up thy right
    hand did stand the queen in gold of Ophir.[8]

Hearken, O daughter, and consider, and incline thine ear; forget
    also thine own people, and thy father's house;

---

6. indicting: composing or dictating something to be written down.

7. cassia: a variety of cinnamon.

8. Ophir: a country famous for its precious stones, possibly in southern Arabia or the eastern coast
of Africa. Its exact location is unknown.

So shall the king greatly desire thy beauty: for he is thy Lord; and
worship thou him.
And the daughter of Tyre[9] shall be there with a gift; even the rich
among the people shall entreat thy favor.
The king's daughter is all glorious within: her clothing is of
wrought gold.
She shall be brought unto the king in raiment of needlework: the
virgins her companions that follow her shall be brought unto
thee.
With gladness and rejoicing shall they be brought: they shall enter
into the king's palace.
Instead of thy fathers shall be thy children, whom thou mayest
make princes in all the earth.
I will make thy name to be remembered in all generations:
therefore shall the people praise thee for ever and ever.

PSALM 95

Oh come, let us sing unto the Lord: let us make a joyful noise to
the rock of our salvation.
Let us come before his presence with thanksgiving, and make a
joyful noise unto him with psalms.
For the Lord is a great God, and a great King above all gods.
In his hand are the deep places of the earth: the strength of the
hills is his also.
The sea is his, and he made it: and his hands formed the dry land.
O come, let us worship and bow down: let us kneel before the
Lord our maker.
For he is our God; and we are the people of his pasture, and the
sheep of his hand. To-day if ye will hear his voice,
Harden not your heart, as in the provocation, and as in the day of
temptation in the wilderness:
When your fathers tempted me, proved me, and saw my work.
Forty years long was I grieved with this generation, and said, "It is
a people that do err in their heart, and they have not known
my ways:
Unto whom I sware in my wrath that they should not enter into
my rest.

---

9. Tyre: an ancient seaport in Phoenicia.

PSALM 98

Oh sing unto the Lord a new song; for he hath done marvellous things: his right hand, and his holy arm, hath gotten him the victory.

The Lord hath made known his salvation: his righteousness hath he openly shewed in the sight of the heathen.

He hath remembered his mercy and his truth toward the house of Israel: all the ends of the earth have seen the salvation of our God.

Make a joyful noise unto the Lord, all the earth: make a loud noise, and rejoice, and sing praise.

Sing unto the Lord with the harp; with the harp, and the voice of a psalm.

With trumpets and sound of cornet make a joyful noise before the Lord, the King.

Let the sea roar, and the fulness thereof; the world, and they that dwell therein.

Let the floods clap their hands: let the hills be joyful together

Before the Lord; for he cometh to judge the earth: with righteousness shall he judge the world, and the people with equity.

ECCLESIASTES 3

To every thing there is a season, and a time to every purpose under the heaven:

A time to be born, and a time to die; a time to plant, and a time to pluck up that which is planted;

A time to kill, and a time to heal; a time to break down, and a time to build up;

A time to weep, and a time to laugh; a time to mourn, and a time to dance;

A time to cast away stones, and a time to gather stones together; a time to embrace, and a time to refrain from embracing;

A time to get, and a time to lose; a time to keep, and a time to cast away;

A time to rend, and a time to sew; a time to keep silence, and a time to speak;

A time to love, and a time to hate; a time of war, and a time of peace.

What profit hath he that worketh in that wherein he laboreth?

I have seen the travail, which God hath given to the sons of men to be exercised in it.

He hath made every thing beautiful in his time: also he hath set the world in their heart, so that no man can find out the work that God maketh from the beginning to the end.

I know that there is no good in them, but for a man to rejoice,
and to do good in his life.

And also that every man should eat and drink, and enjoy the good
of all his labor, it is the gift of God.

I know that, whatsoever God doeth, it shall be for ever: nothing
can be put to it, nor any thing taken from it: and God doeth it,
that men should fear before him.

That which hath been is now; and that which is to be hath already
been; and God requireth that which is past.

And moreover I saw under the sun the place of judgment, that
wickedness was there; and the place of righteousness, that
iniquity was there.

I said in mine heart, God shall judge the righteous and the
wicked: for there is a time there for every purpose and for every
work.

I said in mine heart concerning the estate of the sons of men, that
God might manifest them, and that they might see that they
themselves are beasts.

For that which befalleth the sons of men befalleth beasts; even one
thing befalleth them: as the one dieth, so dieth the other; yea,
they have all one breath; so that a man hath no preeminence
above a beast: for all is vanity.

All go unto one place; all are of the dust, and all turn to dust
again.

Who knoweth the spirit of man that goeth upward, and the spirit
of the beast that goeth downward to the earth?

Wherefore I perceive that there is nothing better, than that a man
should rejoice in his own works; for that is his portion: for who
shall bring him to see what shall be after him?

DISCUSSION QUESTIONS

1. On a scale of 1 (low) to 10 (high) how would you rate Samson's success as a leader and deliverer of his people? Defend your answer.

2. Why does the writer of the Samson story spend so much time on events that occurred before Samson's birth?

3. How does Samson's experience with his wife foreshadow his experience with Delilah?

4. Psalm 8 asks the question, "What is man that thou art mindful of him?" and then provides an answer, describing man's place in a hierarchy of beings. Starting with God, describe this hierarchy in descending order of importance. Why does the psalmist wonder why God is "mindful" of man?

5. Psalm 19 and Psalm 98 are both celebrations of God's creation, and both poems present personifications of the creation. What are these personifications, and what is their intended effect on the reader?

6. What images in Psalm 23 suggest protection and trust? How are the images in the second half of the psalm different from those in the first half?

7. How would you describe the tone and world view expressed in Ecclesiastes 3?

SUGGESTIONS FOR WRITING

1. Samson, who is described by one scholar as a "simpleminded, muscle-bound boy," has fascinated readers over the years because he is an interesting combination of strengths and weaknesses. Do you agree that he is "simpleminded," that stupidity is one of his problems? Write an essay defending your point of view.

2. The book of Psalms and the book of Ecclesiastes are filled with concrete images that are preserved in the King James translation. Some translators, however, have chosen to dispense with these images in favor of direct statements. In Chapter 11 of Ecclesiastes, for example, the King James translators write, "He that observeth the wind shall not sow, and he that regardeth the clouds shall not reap." In the Living Bible translation the passage reads, "If you wait for perfect conditions, you will never get anything done."

   Write a new version of Psalm 23 in which you use no metaphors but rely entirely on direct statements. Then write a brief commentary explaining what is gained and what is lost when the poem is expressed in abstract statements.

HAYYIM NAHMAN BIALIK
(1873–1934)

One of the greatest modern Hebrew poets, Bialik was born in a small Russian town in Ukraine and received a strict religious education. He spent most of his life teaching, publishing, and writing. Although he wrote in a variety of styles and genres, Bialik is known primarily for his fiery poems protesting the exile and persecution of the Jews. In 1903 he published *Songs of Wrath,* which included a poem inspired by the massacres of Jews in Eastern Europe entitled "In the City of Slaughter." This is the poem that first brought him recognition.

With the coming of the Communist Revolution in Russia, Bialik traveled to Germany. He became a strong supporter of the Zionist movement, which sought to establish a permanent homeland for the Jews in the Middle East. In 1924 he moved to Tel Aviv, now located in the country of Israel, where he lived until his death. Bialik was influential in reviving the Hebrew language and translated a large number of literary works into Hebrew. Although he did not live to see Israel become a nation, he is often referred to as the "national poet" of Israel. ■

POEMS

Translated by L. V. Snowman

SUMMER IS DYING

Summer is dying, woven in fine gold,
   Couched on a purple bed
Of falling garden leaves and twilight clouds
   That lave[1] their hearts in red.

5   The garden is deserted, save where a youth
      Saunters, or a maiden walks,
Casting an eye and a sigh after the flight
   Of the last and lingering storks.

The heart is orphaned. Soon a rainy day
10   Will softly tap the pane.
"Look to your boots, patch up your coats, go fetch
   The potatoes in again."

---

1. lave: to wash or bathe.

ON MY RETURN

Here again is the wizened man
    With shrunk and shriveled look,
Shade of dry stubble, wandering leaf
    That strays from book to book.

5   Here again is the wizened hag,
    Knitting socks and fumbling,
Her mouth with oaths and curses filled,
    Her lips forever mumbling.

Our cat is there: he has not stirred
10   From his quarters in the house,
But in his oven dream he makes
    A treaty with a mouse.

The rows of spiders' webs are there,
    As of old in darkness, spread
15   In the western corner, choked with flies,
    Their bodies blown out, dead.

You have not changed, you're antic old,
    There's nothing new I think;
Friends, let me join your club, we'll rot
20   Together till we stink.

DISCUSSION QUESTIONS

1. How would you describe the mood of these two poems? What particular phrases or images contribute to the mood of each poem?

2. In "Summer Is Dying" how do the images used in the first stanza differ from those in the last stanza? What is the effect of this difference?

3. In line 9, what does Bialik mean when he says, "The heart is orphaned"? How does this relate to the changing of the season?

4. In "On My Return" the poet paints an unpleasant picture of the scene of his return. What do you think he is criticizing? What do the animal images (cat, mouse, spiders, flies) contribute to the impact of this poem?

5. In the last line what does Bialik mean by the expression "join your club"? How do the final lines drive home the point of the poem?

SUGGESTION FOR WRITING

Both of these poems deal with a transition, a change in time or place. Select a transition in your life that you feel strongly about. Write a poem or a paragraph dramatizing the contrast between the old time or place and the new one and your feelings about them. You might want to consider a change from one school to another, from one town to another, from one class to another, from one age to another, or from one time of year to another.

KA-TZETNIK 135633

(born 1917)

Born on a farm in Poland, Ka-tzetnik, whose birth name was Yehiel Finer, studied the Hebrew classics and published stories and poems in Yiddish magazines. During World War II he was imprisoned at Auschwitz, a Nazi concentration camp in Poland. A few months after his release, while still in a transit camp, he wrote *Salamandra,* one of the first books published about the Holocaust. For his pseudonym he chose Ka-tzetnik, a Yiddish term used to designate an inmate of a concentration camp. The number 135633 was the one tattooed on the author's arm at Auschwitz.

After the war Ka-tzetnik moved to Israel, where he lives under the personal name Yehiel De Nur. He and his wife Nina, who is his translator, founded the Israeli Movement for Arab-Jewish Cooperation in an attempt to moderate the hostilities between Jews and Arabs in the Middle East. Though suffering from an acute form of post-traumatic syndrome as a result of his experiences at Auschwitz, Ka-tzetnik has continued to write works that recreate the horrific experiences of the death camp inmates. Among them are *Star Eternal, House of Dolls, Phoenix over the Galilee,* and *Shaviti.* The following selection is part of *Star Eternal.* ■

from STAR ETERNAL

Translated from the Hebrew by Nina De-Nur and Chayym Zeldis

FACE TO FACE

Naked march into the night.

Midnight silence of Auschwitz.

You cannot hear a single step from all the bare feet marching on the ground.

You do not know the length of the column in which you march, where it begins, where it ends.

Around you breathe naked human bodies, marching six abreast. Six abreast.

A transport is being led to the Auschwitz "Bath House."[1]

Over your head vaults a star-sprinkled sky. Before your eyes a smoke-stack thrusts skywards. Thick, fatty smoke gushes out.

Sparks beyond count. Sparks scatter and flash across the starry sky, mingle with the stars, and you cannot tell whose light is the brighter.

---

1. **"Bath House":** a term for the gas chamber, a building usually disguised as a bathhouse, used by the Nazis for mass extermination of their victims by means of poisonous gas.

Unnumbered naked bodies. Auschwitz under your bare feet. The column marches towards the smokestack.

Night about you. Auschwitz about you. Death holds your life between his hands—a circular mirror held up to your eyes. You don't see Death in person—not yet. His face is hidden behind the mirror. His breath alone blows on you, the way wind blows on a spark in ashes—

The better to see it go out.

On both sides walk SS Germans,[2] silhouettes of silence mantled in night. You are no longer free to choose your own death. You have already been handed over. Death, your master, is taking you to his abode.

Walking under his long cloak, you scent his smell. You can no longer change places with anyone. He knows your flesh by now. He has seen you. Naked, you come unto him.

No longer are you free to choose your own death. This is—Auschwitz. Already your feet tread the corridor of your death. In a moment, you'll go inside and see him face to face; your lord and master, Death-of-Auschwitz.

Hush. No one here dares breathe a word. Words are no more. Sparks slip out of the smokestack. You squeeze the bit of soap in your fist. Countless feet. Naked feet. You can't hear their steps. Night leads you unto itself. Stars vanish over your head. Nothing is yours anymore. Even your head's hair has been taken away from you. This hair is still worth something, you are shorn of all. Except for a single spark you still carry within you. Death has bought it on the Jew-market. It belongs to him. Soon it will shoot out of the smokestack.

Auschwitz.

What kind of factory has death established here? Of what use to him can be the sparks leaping from the smokestack?

INSIDE

A network of pipes above your head. From the pipes jut shower sprinklers. Row upon row of sprinklers. And in the sprinklers—pores.

From somewhere in among the sprinklers, rusted opaque light drains down, illuminating what is imminent.

The open gate thrusts into the night. Still they keep coming in, an unbroken stream: naked bodies. More and more. Human beings. All of them looking alike. More, still more.

It's getting packed. Bodies, nude and clammy, around you. Naked skin on naked skin. At each contact your body shudders. But as the shudder runs over you, you suddenly thrill to a feeling of reprieve. It wakens a sense of life in you. You still have a body! A body of your own. As if you had it thrust anew into your arms. Never did you love your body so. You feel: fear whetting knife-blades on it. Soon it must grapple with a faceless

---

2. **SS Germans:** members of an elite military corps of the Nazi party, notorious for their calculated brutality.

death. Soon death will make his appearance. Soon you will see him, face to face. He sits on high, inside the sprinkler-pores. Any second now—

All eyes are fixed on the sprinkler-pores overhead.

The gates of the "Bath House" lock. Even night is no more.

Naked bodies enclose your body. Trembling, the way your body trembles. The tremor runs from end to end, like wind through cornstalks in a field. The ends you cannot see, but you can feel the shudder of all the bodies through your own. The gates are sealed. Even night is gone. Nothing but bodies. All bodies are now—your body, just as the death of any body is now—the death of your own.

Inch by inch all bodies turn to stone. A crust of hoarfrost jells over all. Petrified, all.

Necks.

Not a head to be seen. Not a face. Nothing but necks. Necks thrown back. A plateau of necks flung back. Headless.

To start with—a torso; on top of it—shoulders; on top of the shoulders—a neck. And atop the neck—pores. Dark pores.

Sprinkler-pores of the Auschwitz "Bath House."

Rust-clotted light eddies between the necks and the shower-pores. In this light, death hovers. About to swoop.

Necks like cobblestones. Death stomps upon them as on stones of a deserted street. Here he is all by himself. Here he is on his own grounds, alone. This is his abode. Here he casts off his veils and his face shows. Here, in the sealed "Bath House"; here, in this inner sanctum of the Temple of Auschwitz.

And you see him.

Heads flung back to the nape, like chickens' heads in the slaughterer's grip. Mouths wide open. Necks stretched out. To the slaughtering knife on high.

You see his face.

Death's face.

The necks take no breath.

Suddenly—

A wisp of white steam. Unhurrying. Leisurely. Lightly twisting and weaving. Gracefully curling against the sprinkler-pores as if circling a floor in dance. And gone.

The necks take no breath.

Then from the pores swell—drops. Single drops. Pendulous. Pear-shaped. Unfalling. Suspended above the eyes—

The necks take no breath. Petrified.

Suddenly:

Thin, scalding streaks, vapor-encoiled. White-hot whips. A moment—and off they break in midair. Gone.

Once again empty pores, dark and secretive. Shower-pores of the Auschwitz "Bath House."

Suddenly:

Thin, freezing streaks. Biting whips of frost. A moment—and off they break in mid-air. Gone.

Empty pores, dark and secretive. The shower-pores of the Auschwitz "Bath House."

Over again

    again,

       and again,

All at once a wailing shriek comes out:

"Water!!!"

"Water!!!

"Water!!!

Bodies leap up into the air, howling and screaming, tearing their scalps as they would tear hair. Drenched in tears they bawl out their happiness in wild uncontrollable weeping:
"W—a—t—er!!!"
At the walls, fingers pinch their own body; raving mad they scratch and grovel at the blank walls: *Water!!!*
As if corks had all at once blasted from their stoppered throats. All as one, they wail with twisted mouths, weeping and flailing arms gone crazy with joy:
"W—a—t—er!!!"
One, the Know-it-all in every crowd, shouts back at them: "Shut up! Of course it's water! That's all it is—water!"
But not one of them pays him any attention. The mouths sob at him, shrieking insanely: W—a—t—e—r!!!
Until the gates unlock.
Outside, the night foams and bubbles with the mirthsome guffaws of SS Germans; it rolls on the waves of their laughter, breaking over black-horizoned shores. The Germans stand in the dark and look on, the way spectators watch a comedy enacted on a brightly-lit screen—and double up in laughter.
The naked bodies stream out, as if spewed onto an unfamiliar shore. Opposite them, the sparks stream from the smokestack and vanish over the starry sky. Stupefied, they stare at the laughing maws and do not understand—
They don't understand that truly happy were those who got, not water out of sprinklers, but Zyklon[3] cans jetting blue gas into their lungs, instead.

---

3. **Zyklon:** the name of a gas used by the Nazis for the mass extermination of their victims.

They don't understand that truly happy were those who at the very threshold of Auschwitz were turned into these sparks now spraying out of the smokestack opposite—

W—a—t—e—r!

They are alive—

And they go marching, drunk with joy, towards the blocks of the camp called "Auschwitz."

DAWN IN AUSCHWITZ

Backs.

Backs and eyes—

In Auschwitz, everyone tries to draw his back as high up as he can, as if the back were a woolen blanket you could pull over your head to keep warm.

On the narrow backpath running along the blocks.

More than ten thousand shadow-men.

No beginning, no end to them. There is no beginning, no end in Auschwitz. Everywhere around, beyond the walls of barbed wire surrounding your camp, range more camps. No end of camps. Isolated from each other, like stars. A galaxy as yet beyond human ken and exploration. To the right—"B" Camp, to the left—Quarantine Camp. Behind— Women's Camp. In front—the milky way, down which the packed vans roll without cease, without cease, to the crematorium.

And above all—the final hour.

The final hour of the night. Ten thousand pairs of eyes spill out of the blocks every day at this hour, the hour before dawn, into the backpath. Cleanliness. The German loves cleanliness, so now the block orderlies "clean out" the blocks—they are apportioning out the bread rations. Instead of four, they'll cut eight and ten rations from each loaf. The loaves they gain in this way will soon be on their way to the latrine—the camp stock-exchange—to be traded for cigarettes for the Block Chiefs. Four cigarettes to the loaf. And outside, on the backpath running along the blocks, ten thousand and more shadow-men hop a hypnotic jungle dance, foot up, foot down—

The cold earth of Auschwitz sucks through the soles of bare feet the last remains of marrow from the bones.

Eyes—

A river, over which rain whips endlessly, trace enormous, gaping water-eyes. A stream which flows from the railroad platform to the crematorium. Ever the same stream, never the same drops. Drops ever changing, ever new. You see them in their sluggish, silent flow as they look at you with glass-sheened gazes, probing your face for some stir of their own lives which stream by—out of their reach—and see naught. Not even the camp they're passing through.

Eyes—

Eyes that for fifty years struck foundations for generations to come; and eyes of fifteen years, in first beauty of flowering, brimming with sap and vitality, finest of mankind, the crown of creation.

Eyes—of lords of wealth, ruthless tyrants of international trademarts; and eyes of careworn shopkeepers, harassed and cowed, penniless tradesmen whose worries have been handed down to them at birth: where will food for the Sabbath come from? Who will pay the teacher's wages?

Eyes—of seekers, men of science, artists anointed with divine gifts of genius; and eyes of thick-tongued laborers, prayerbooks clasped in blackened, callused hands. Gray as the days of the week, nondescript as the chemicals fructifying our earth.

Eyes—of self-designated lordlings, society's upper crust, whose names by the clash of cymbals were always heralded; yet miserly, insatiable, enviously ill-willed if ever success shone in through another's window. And eyes of men of soul, delicate spirits, noble, modest—the sweet fragrance of our lives.

All along the road, from the Auschwitz railroad platform to the crematorium, these eyes all now beg the answer to one question:

When will the soup ration ever be handed out?

O Night-of-Auschwitz on backs and eyes!

Hour of awful despair and pity.

Enigma of an hour when night wraps in one black robe SS man and campling alike.

Far, far off, lights speed down the main road. You know: each pair of lights—a packed van heading for the crematorium. Many a time you have wished to be taken to the crematorium at night. Better by night than by day. At night you can cry. Never did anyone weep on his way to the crematorium by day. At night, tears come from your eyes.

Awesome mystery of Night-of-Auschwitz, never to be fathomed by mortal man.

Until night is drawn from your lids, like black scabbard slipped from sword. Slowly the chill blade of Auschwitz day gleams bare.

To the west, the red bulbs still glow along the barbed wire—a coral necklace on the flesh of Auschwitz night.

To the east, the new day already shows ashen-gray among the block-roofs, as if the mounds of ash had quit their posts by the crematorium, falling into line here between one roof and the next.

The SS sentry climbs down the watchtower ladder, rung by rung: first, the black boots, then the rifle slung across back. He carries the night with him, folded and shriveled. Like a black crow night roosts on his shoulder. He turns over his post to his *Kamerad*, the day-sentry, who climbs up the ladder, rung by rung: first the hands, white hands, soaking in the new day—your day. Every hunched-up back in Auschwitz now proffers your eyes your own loneliness. Each pair of eyes gazes at you with the pity for a life that once bore your name—

Dawn of Auschwitz on backs and eyes.

"WIEDERGUTMACHUNG"[4]

I

My mother was—my mother.

How can I describe you, Mother?

My mother was the most beautiful of all mothers in the world.

My mother said:

"No! My little boy didn't do this naughty thing . . ." Lovingly she pressed the profiles of my head between her open palms, her fingers long and parted. Her eyes plumbed the depths of my own as she said, "I! I did the naughty thing! Because I am my little boy!"

Afterwards, I was always very careful to behave, because I couldn't bear for my mother to do a naughty thing.

My mother!

Of all mothers in the world mine was the most beautiful.

On her way to the crematorium my mother saw my face. I know it. Because I, too, on my way to the crematorium, saw my mother's face.

Mother, now they want to give me money to make up for you.

I still can't figure how many German marks a burnt mother comes to.

"My little boy couldn't have done this naughty thing . . ."

Mother, I feel your open palms touching the profiles of my head. My eyes sink into yours: Isn't it true, Mother, you wouldn't take money for your little one, burnt?

II

My sister's hair was long and curly, the color of ripe gold. Mother's hands vanished in white-gold foam every time she washed it. Whenever she rinsed it, sheer gold cascaded down my sister's nape like a waterfall all the way to the bottom of the tub.

My mother loved to plait ribbons into her tiny daughter's hair. She would sort them out, singing soft to herself as she did:

"Ribbon green for hair's gold sheen,
Ribbon pink for chocolate skin,
Ribbon blue for the eyes . . ."

My sister's eyes were blue like sky.

Sabbath morning, in front of the house, when the sun met my sister's hair, neighbors at their windows would call:

---

4. **"Wiedergutmachung"**: literally, "setting things right": reparations paid by the West German government to the victims of Nazi persecution or to their families. [German]

"Whose hair is that, little Goldilocks?"

"My mother's," answered my sister.

I loved my sister's hair. She never lifted scissors to it. She said "My mother's . . ."

Before my sister was burned in the crematorium of Auschwitz they shaved off her hair. Seventeen years the golden locks lengthened on my sister's head. Long locks of gold. Seventeen years.

In a shipment of hair, in sacks, or in rectangular bales, tight-pressed like cotton from rich plantations, my sister's hair was sent to Germany. It was unloaded at a factory, to make:

blankets—

soft club-chairs—

upholstery—

Somewhere, in Germany, a young Fräulein now covers herself with a blanket. A single hair of gold, unprocessed, thrusts out of the blanket's weave. The Fräulein stretches out a bare arm, pulls, pulls . . .

"Fräulein! Give me back that hair! It's out of my sister's golden locks . . ."

My sister, now they want to give me money for you. But I don't know how many German marks your curls should bring.

"Whose hair is it, little Goldilocks?"

"My mother's . . ."

Mother, Mother, what do you say—how much is your little Goldilocks' hair worth?

My mother croons to herself:

"Ribbon green for hair's gold sheen,
Ribbon pink for chocolate skin,
Ribbon blue for the eyes . . ."

My sister had eyes like the blue sky.

III

Among tens of thousands of shoes I'd recognize a shoe of yours, Father! Your heels were never crooked.

Father, your step was always straight.

Each day a new mountain of shoes piles up on the compound of the crematorium. Remember when I was little? The first time you let me shine your shoes, I polished them tops and bottoms. Oh how you laughed at me then!

"There is, sonny, a dirty side as well, on which a man must tread. When you're big you'll understand."

Father, I'm big now.

The sun bends over the slope of the tall shoe-mountain, illuminating it for me as with a flashlight:

Shoes!

Shoes without end!

A torn baby-shoe—like an infant's open mouth, eager for the full spoon in mother's hand; a torn baby-shoe—an infant's head, eyes bugging from the shoe-mountain to the sun shining on earth.

Nearby—

A narrow, delicate woman's shoe, high and slender-heeled, brown-scaled. Open on all sides. Several entwined leather straps on top. The gold imprint on the steep arch glitters in the face of the sun.

Nearby—

A lime-spattered workman's shoe. The sun peers into it as into the mouth of a cavern hacked into barren mountain rock.

Nearby—

A mountaineer's shoe, its toe wedged in the side of the mountain, as if the climber had paused in mid-ascent, breathless: "Oh, what a view! . . ."

Nearby—

A leg with a shoe on its foot—prosthesis[5] to the groin. Trouserless, naked to the sun.

Shoes!

Shoes beyond count!

Father, among tens of thousands of shoes I would recognize yours!

Your heels were never crooked—

Father, your step was straight.

IV

How can I take money for my sister the "Field Whore" from you—and not be a pimp?

Give me—

Give me back one single hair of my sister's golden curls!

Give me back one shoe of my father's;

A broken wheel from my little brother's skates;

And a mote of dust that on my mother rested—

---

5. prosthesis: an artificial replacement part for the body.

DISCUSSION QUESTIONS

1. With remarks such as "I still can't figure how many German marks a burnt Mother comes to," Ka-tzetnik ridicules the idea of "reparation" to the Jews. What, if anything, do you think the German government should do for the Jews who were victims of Nazi persecutions?

2. In the section called "Face to Face" Ka-tzetnik uses the word *spark* to signify several different things. Explain how the meaning of the word changes in this section.

3. Ka-tzetnik often speaks of the prisoners of Auschwitz as if they were simply body parts. In the section called "Inside," for example, the prisoners are called "necks," while in "Dawn in Auschwitz" they are repeatedly referred to as "eyes." What effect does the author achieve by referring to the prisoners in this way?

4. Ka-tzetnik recalls several members of his family by describing the remnants that are left after their death. How does he use these remnants to characterize his father and sister?

SUGGESTION FOR WRITING

Imagine that you are a publisher who is planning to publish an illustrated edition of *Star Eternal*. The artist who will do the illustrations needs guidelines about how they should be drawn. Choose one section that you would like to see illustrated. Then write a letter to the artist explaining what should appear in the illustration. Be sure to explain the mood you want to create in the illustration. You might also want to make suggestions about the use of color, if any, and the style of drawing (detailed and realistic or simplified and stark, for example).

AHARON MEGGED

(born 1920)

Born in Poland, Aharon Megged moved to Palestine (now Israel) when he was a child. After completing high school he lived on a fishing kibbutz for ten years. Megged spent several years as a cultural representative in London and then returned to Israel to become a literary editor and journalist. Although he has written several plays, he is best known for his short stories and novels, which include *Israeli Folk, Fortunes of a Fool, Living on the Dead,* and *Anat's Day of Illumination.* Megged's works tend to be gently satirical, and they often focus on the conflict between old Jewish traditions and the "new Jews" of Israel, who strive to break free from these traditions. The following story dramatizes this conflict. ■

THE NAME

Translated from the Hebrew by Minna Givton

Grandfather Zisskind lived in a little house in a southern suburb of the town. About once a month, on a Saturday afternoon, his granddaughter Raya and her young husband Yehuda would go and pay him a visit.

Raya would give three cautious knocks on the door (an agreed signal between herself and her grandfather ever since her childhood, when he had lived in their house together with the whole family) and they would wait for the door to be opened. "Now he's getting up," Raya would whisper to Yehuda, her face glowing, when the sound of her grandfather's slippers was heard from within, shuffling across the room. Another moment, and the key would be turned and the door opened.

"Come in," he would say somewhat absently, still buttoning up his trousers, with the rheum of sleep in his eyes. Although it was very hot he wore a yellow winter vest with long sleeves, from which his wrists stuck out—white, thin, delicate as a girl's, as was his bare neck with its taut skin.

After Raya and Yehuda had sat down at the table, which was covered with a white cloth showing signs of the meal he had eaten alone—crumbs from the Sabbath loaf, a plate with meat leavings, a glass containing some grape pips, a number of jars and so on—he would smooth the crumpled pillows, spread a cover over the narrow bed and tidy up. It was a small room, and its obvious disorder aroused pity for the old man's helplessness in running his home. In the corner was a shelf with two sooty kerosene burners, a kettle and two or three saucepans, and next to it a basin containing plates, knives and forks. In another corner was a stand holding books with thick leather bindings, leaning and lying on each other. Some of his clothes hung over the backs of the chairs. An ancient walnut cupboard with an empty buffet stood exactly opposite the door. On the wall hung a clock which had long since stopped.

"We ought to make Grandfather a present of a clock," Raya would say to Yehuda as she surveyed the room and her glance lighted on the clock; but every time the matter slipped her memory. She loved her grandfather, with his pointed white silky beard, his tranquil face from which a kind of holy radiance emanated, his quiet, soft voice which seemed to have been made only for uttering words of sublime wisdom. She also respected him for his pride, which had led him to move out of her mother's house and live by himself, accepting the hardship and trouble and the affliction of loneliness in his old age. There had been a bitter quarrel between him and his daughter. After Raya's father had died, the house had lost its grandeur and shed the trappings of wealth. Some of the antique furniture which they had retained—along with some crystalware and jewels, the dim luster of memories from the days of plenty in their native city—had been sold, and Rachel, Raya's mother, had been compelled to support the home by working as a dentist's nurse. Grandfather Zisskind, who had been supported by the family ever since he came to the country, wished to hand over to his daughter his small capital, which was deposited in a bank. She was not willing to accept it. She was stubborn and proud like him. Then, after a prolonged quarrel and several weeks of not speaking to each other, he took some of the things in his room and the broken clock and went to live alone. That had been about four years ago. Now Rachel would come to him once or twice a week, bringing with her a bag full of provisions, to clean the room and cook some meals for him. He was no longer interested in expenses and did not even ask about them, as though they were of no more concern to him.

"And now . . . what can I offer you?" Grandfather Zisskind would ask when he considered the room ready to receive guests. "There's no need to offer us anything, Grandfather; we didn't come for that," Raya would answer crossly.

But protests were of no avail. Her grandfather would take out a jar of fermenting preserves and put it on the table, then grapes and plums, biscuits and two glasses of strong tea, forcing them to eat. Raya would taste a little of this and that just to please the old man, while Yehuda, for whom all these visits were unavoidable torment, the very sight of the dishes arousing his disgust, would secretly indicate to her by pulling a sour face that he just couldn't touch the preserves. She would smile at him placatingly, stroking his knee. But Grandfather insisted, so he would have to taste at least a teaspoonful of the sweet and nauseating stuff.

Afterwards Grandfather would ask about all kinds of things. Raya did her best to make the conversation pleasant, in order to relieve Yehuda's boredom. Finally would come what Yehuda dreaded most of all and on account of which he had resolved more than once to refrain from these visits. Grandfather Zisskind would rise, take his chair and place it next to the wall, get up on it carefully, holding on to the back so as not to fall, open the clock and take out a cloth bag with a black cord tied round it. Then he would shut the clock, get off the chair, put it back in its place, sit down on it, undo the cord, take out of the cloth wrapping a bundle of sheets of paper, lay them in front of Yehuda and say:

"I would like you to read this."

"Grandfather," Raya would rush to Yehuda's rescue, "but he's already read it at least ten times. . . ."

But Grandfather Zisskind would pretend not to hear and would not reply, so Yehuda was compelled each time to read there and then that same essay, spread over eight, long sheets in a large, somewhat shaky handwriting, which he almost knew by heart. It was a lament for Grandfather's native town in the Ukraine[1] which had been destroyed by the Germans, and all its Jews slaughtered. When he had finished, Grandfather would take the sheets out of his hand, fold them, sigh and say:

"And nothing of all this is left. Dust and ashes. Not even a tombstone to bear witness. Imagine, of a community of twenty thousand Jews not even one survived to tell how it happened . . . Not a trace."

Then out of the same cloth bag, which contained various letters and envelopes, he would draw a photograph of his grandson Mendele, who had been twelve years old when he was killed; the only son of his son Ossip, chief engineer in a large chemical factory. He would show it to Yehuda and say:

"He was a genius. Just imagine, when he was only eleven he had already finished his studies at the Conservatory, won a scholarship from the Government and was considered an outstanding violinist. A genius! Look at that forehead. . . ." And after he had put the photograph back he would sigh and repeat "Not a trace."

A strained silence of commiseration would descend on Raya and Yehuda, who had already heard these same things many times over and no longer felt anything when they were repeated. And as he wound the cord round the bag the old man would muse: "And Ossip was also a prodigy. As a boy he knew Hebrew well, and could recite Bialik's poems[2] by heart. He studied by himself. He read endlessly, Gnessin, Frug, Bershadsky . . . You didn't know Bershadsky; he was a good writer . . . He had a warm heart, Ossip had. He didn't mix in politics, he wasn't even a Zionist,[3] but even when they promoted him there he didn't forget that he was a Jew . . . He called his son Mendele, of all names, after his dead brother, even though it

---

1. **Ukraine:** a republic in southwest Russia. During World War II Ukraine was occupied by German forces who, according to most estimates, massacred 250,000 Jews.

2. **Bialik's poems:** the poems of Hayyam Nahman Bialik (1873-1934), a modern Hebrew writer who protested the persecution of European Jews and promoted the establishment of a new Jewish homeland in the Middle East. See page 32.

3. **Zionist:** a member of the Zionist movement founded during the nineteenth century to secure the return of Jewish exiles to Palestine (Israel).

was surely not easy to have a name like that among the Russians . . . Yes, he had a warm Jewish heart . . ."

He would turn to Yehuda as he spoke, since in Raya he always saw the child who used to sit on his knee listening to his stories, and for him she had never grown up, while he regarded Yehuda as an educated man who could understand someone else, especially inasmuch as Yehuda held a government job.

Raya remembered how the change had come about in her grandfather. When the war was over he was still sustained by uncertainty and hoped for some news of his son, for it was known that very many had succeeded in escaping eastwards. Wearily he would visit all those who had once lived in his town, but none of them had received any sign of life from relatives. Nevertheless he continued to hope, for Ossip's important position might have helped to save him. Then Raya came home one evening and saw him sitting on the floor with a rent in his jacket.[4] In the house they spoke in whispers, and her mother's eyes were red with weeping. She, too, had wept at Grandfather's sorrow, at the sight of his stricken face, at the oppressive quiet in the rooms. For many weeks afterwards it was as if he had imposed silence on himself. He would sit at his table from morning to night, reading and re-reading old letters, studying family photographs by the hour as he brought them close to his shortsighted eyes, or leaning backwards on his chair, motionless, his hand touching the edge of the table and his eyes staring through the window in front of him, into the distance, as if he had turned to stone. He was no longer the same talkative, wise and humorous grandfather who interested himself in the house, asked what his granddaughter was doing, instructed her, tested her knowledge, proving boastfully like a child that he knew more than her teachers. Now he seemed to cut himself off from the world and entrench himself in his thoughts and his memories, which none of the household could penetrate. Later, a strange perversity had taken hold of him which it was hard to tolerate. He would insist that his meals be served at his table, apart, that no one should enter his room without knocking at the door, or close the shutters of his window against the sun. When any one disobeyed these prohibitions he would flare up and quarrel violently with his daughter. At times it seemed that he hated her.

When Raya's father died, Grandfather Zisskind did not show any signs of grief, and did not even console his daughter. But when the days of mourning were past it was as if he had been restored to new life, and he emerged from his silence. Yet he did not speak of his son-in-law, nor of his son Ossip, but only of his grandson Mendele. Often during the day he would mention the boy by name as if he were alive, and speak of him familiarly, although he had seen him only on photographs—as though deliberating aloud and turning the matter over, he would talk of how Mendele ought to be brought up. It was hardest of all when he started criticizing his son and his son's wife for not having foreseen the

---

4. **rent in his jacket:** In Judaism it is customary for a mourner to rend (tear) a garment.

impending disaster, for not having rushed the boy away to a safe place, not having hidden him with non-Jews, not having tried to get him to the Land of Israel in good time. There was no logic in what he said; this would so infuriate Rachel that she would burst out with, "Oh, do stop! Stop it! I'll go out of my mind with your foolish nonsense!" She would rise from her seat in anger, withdraw to her room, and afterwards, when she had calmed down, would say to Raya, "Sclerosis, apparently. Loss of memory. He no longer knows what he's talking about."

One day—Raya would never forget this—she and her mother saw that Grandfather was wearing his best suit, the black one, and under it a gleaming white shirt; his shoes were polished, and he had a hat on. He had not worn these clothes for many months, and the family was dismayed to see him. They thought that he had lost his mind. "What holiday is it today?" her mother asked. "Really, don't you know?" asked her grandfather. "Today is Mendele's birthday!" Her mother burst out crying. She too began to cry and ran out of the house.

After that, Grandfather Zisskind went to live alone. His mind, apparently, had become settled, except that he would frequently forget things which had occurred a day or two before, though he clearly remembered, down to the smallest detail, things which had happened in his town and to his family more than thirty years ago. Raya would go and visit him, at first with her mother and, after her marriage, with Yehuda. What bothered them was that they were compelled to listen to his talk about Mendele his grandson, and to read that same lament for his native town which had been destroyed.

Whenever Rachel happened to come there during their visit, she would scold Grandfather rudely. "Stop bothering them with your masterpiece," she would say, and herself remove the papers from the table and put them back in their bag. "If you want them to keep on visiting you, don't talk to them about the dead. Talk about the living. They're young people and they have no mind for such things." And as they left his room together she would say, turning to Yehuda in order to placate him, "Don't be surprised at him. Grandfather's already old. Over seventy. Loss of memory."

When Raya was seven months pregnant, Grandfather Zisskind had in his absent-mindedness not yet noticed it. But Rachel could no longer refrain from letting him share her joy and hope, and told him that a great-grandchild would soon be born to him. One evening the door of Raya and Yehuda's flat opened, and Grandfather himself stood on the threshold in his holiday clothes, just as on the day of Mendele's birthday. This was the first time he had visited them at home, and Raya was so surprised that she hugged and kissed him as she had not done since she was a child. His face shone, his eyes sparkled with the same intelligent and mischievous light they had in those far-off days before the calamity. When he entered he walked briskly through the rooms, giving his opinion on the furniture and its arrangement, and joking about everything around him. He was so pleasant that Raya and Yehuda could not stop laughing all the time he was speaking. He gave no indication that he knew what was about to take place, and for the first time in many months he did not mention Mendele.

"Ah, you naughty children," he said, "is this how you treat Grandfather? Why didn't you tell me you had such a nice place?"

"How many times have I invited you here, Grandfather?" asked Raya.

"Invited me? You ought to have *brought* me here, dragged me by force!"

"I wanted to do that too, but you refused."

"Well, I thought that you lived in some dark den, and I have a den of my own. Never mind, I forgive you."

And when he took leave of them he said:

"Don't bother to come to me. Now that I know where you're to be found and what a palace you have, I'll come to you . . . if you don't throw me out, that is."

Some days later, when Rachel came to their home and they told her about Grandfather's amazing visit, she was not surprised:

"Ah, you don't know what he's been contemplating during all these days, ever since I told him that you're about to have a child . . . He has one wish—that if it's a son, it should be named . . . after his grandson."

"Mendele?" exclaimed Raya, and involuntarily burst into laughter. Yehuda smiled as one smiles at the fond fancies of the old.

"Of course, I told him to put that out of his head," said Rachel, "but you know how obstinate he is. It's some obsession and he won't think of giving it up. Not only that, but he's sure that you'll willingly agree to it, and especially you, Yehuda."

Yehuda shrugged his shoulders. "Crazy. The child would be unhappy all his life."

"But he's not capable of understanding that," said Rachel, and a note of apprehension crept into her voice.

Raya's face grew solemn. "We have already decided on the name," she said. "If it's a girl she'll be called Osnath, and if it's a boy—Ehud."

Rachel did not like either.

The matter of the name became almost the sole topic of conversation between Rachel and the young couple when she visited them, and it infused gloom into the air of expectancy which filled the house.

Rachel, midway between the generations, was of two minds about the matter. When she spoke to her father she would scold and contradict him, flinging at him all the arguments she had heard from Raya and Yehuda as though they were her own, but when she spoke to the children she sought to induce them to meet his wishes, and would bring down their anger on herself. As time went on, the question of a name, to which in the beginning she had attached little importance, became a kind of mystery, concealing something preordained, fearful, and pregnant with life and death. The fate of the child itself seemed in doubt. In her innermost heart she prayed that Raya would give birth to a daughter.

"Actually, what's so bad about the name Mendele?" she asked her daughter. "It's a Jewish name like any other."

"What are you talking about, Mother"—Raya rebelled against the thought—"a Ghetto name, ugly, horrible! I wouldn't even be capable of letting it cross my lips. Do you want me to hate my child?"

"Oh, you won't hate your child. At any rate, not because of the name . . ."

"I should hate him. It's as if you'd told me that my child would be born with a hump! And anyway—why should I? What for?"

"You have to do it for Grandfather's sake," Rachel said quietly, although she knew that she was not speaking the whole truth.

"You know, Mother, that I am ready to do anything for Grandfather," said Raya. "I love him, but I am not ready to sacrifice my child's happiness on account of some superstition of his. What sense is there in it?"

Rachel could not explain the "sense in it" rationally, but in her heart she rebelled against her daughter's logic which had always been hers too and now seemed very superficial, a symptom of the frivolity afflicting the younger generation. Her old father now appeared to her like an ancient tree whose deep roots suck up the mysterious essence of existence, of which neither her daughter nor she herself knew anything. Had it not been for this argument about the name, she would certainly never have got to meditating on the transmigration of souls and the eternity of life. At night she would wake up covered in cold sweat. Hazily, she recalled frightful scenes of bodies of naked children, beaten and trampled under the jackboots of soldiers, and an awful sense of guilt oppressed her spirit.

Then Rachel came with a proposal for a compromise: that the child should be named Menachem. A Hebrew name, she said; an Israeli one, by all standards. Many children bore it, and it occurred to nobody to make fun of them. Even Grandfather had agreed to it after much urging.

Raya refused to listen.

"We have chosen a name, Mother," she said, "which we both like, and we won't change it for another. Menachem is a name which reeks of old age, a name which for me is connected with sad memories and people I don't like. Menachem you could call only a boy who is short, weak and not good-looking. Let's not talk about it any more, Mother."

Rachel was silent. She almost despaired of convincing them. At last she said:

"And you are ready to take the responsibility of going against Grandfather's wishes?"

Raya's eyes opened wide, and fear was reflected in them:

"Why do you make such a fateful thing of it? You frighten me!" she said, and burst into tears. She began to fear for her offspring as one fears the evil eye.[5]

"And perhaps there is something fateful in it . . ." whispered Rachel without raising her eyes. She flinched at her own words.

_____

5. **evil eye:** a superstition, still prevalent in the Middle East, that certain individuals can do harm with a malicious glance.

"What is it?" insisted Raya, with a frightened look at her mother.

"I don't know . . ." she said. "Perhaps all the same we are bound to retain the names of the dead . . . in order to leave a remembrance of them . . ." She was not sure herself whether there was any truth in what she said or whether it was merely a stupid belief, but her father's faith was before her, stronger than her own doubts and her daughter's simple and understandable opposition.

"But I don't always want to remember all those dreadful things, Mother. It's impossible that this memory should always hang about this house and that the poor child should bear it!"

Rachel understood. She, too, heard such a cry within her as she listened to her father talking, sunk in memories of the past. As if to herself, she said in a whisper:

"I don't know . . . at times it seems to me that it's not Grandfather who's suffering from loss of memory, but ourselves. All of us."

About two weeks before the birth was due, Grandfather Zisskind appeared in Raya and Yehuda's home for the second time. His face was yellow, angry, and the light had faded from his eyes. He greeted them, but did not favor Raya with so much as a glance, as if he had pronounced a ban upon the sinner. Turning to Yehuda he said, "I wish to speak to you."

They went into the inner room. Grandfather sat down on the chair and placed the palm of his hand on the edge of the table, as was his wont, and Yehuda sat, lower than he, on the bed.

"Rachel has told me that you don't want to call the child by my grandchild's name," he said.

"Yes . . ." said Yehuda diffidently.

"Perhaps you'll explain to me why?" he asked.

"We . . ." stammered Yehuda, who found it difficult to face the piercing gaze of the old man. "The name simply doesn't appeal to us."

Grandfather was silent. Then he said, "I understand that Mendele doesn't appeal to you. Not a Hebrew name. Granted! But Menachem—what's wrong with Menachem?" It was obvious that he was controlling his feelings with difficulty.

"It's not . . ." Yehuda knew that there was no use explaining; they were two generations apart in their ideas. "It's not an Israeli name . . . it's from the *Golah*."[6]

"*Golah*," repeated Grandfather. He shook with rage, but somehow he maintained his self-control. Quietly he added, "We all come from the *Golah*. I, and Raya's father and mother. Your father and mother. All of us."

"Yes . . ." said Yehuda. He resented the fact that he was being dragged into an argument which was distasteful to him, particularly with this old man whose mind was already not quite clear. Only out of respect did he restrain himself from shouting: That's that, and it's done with! . . . "Yes, but we were born in this country," he said aloud; "that's different."

---

6. **Golah:** a term applied to all geographical locations outside Israel where Jews have settled.

Grandfather Zisskind looked at him contemptuously. Before him he saw a wretched boor, an empty vessel.

"You, that is to say, think that there's something new here," he said, "that everything that was there is past and gone. Dead, without sequel. That you are starting everything anew."

"I didn't say that. I only said that we were born in this country . . ."

"You were born here. Very nice . . ." said Grandfather Zisskind with rising emotion. "So what of it? What's so remarkable about that? In what way are you superior to those who were born *there*? Are you cleverer than they? More cultured? Are you greater than they in Torah[7] or good deeds? Is your blood redder than theirs?" Grandfather Zisskind looked as if he could wring Yehuda's neck.

"I didn't say that either, I said that *here* it's different . . . "

Grandfather Zisskind's patience with idle words was exhausted.

"You good-for-nothing!" he burst out in his rage. "What do you know about what was there? What do you know of the *people* that were there? The communities? The cities? What do you know of the *life* they had there?"

"Yes," said Yehuda, his spirit crushed, "but we no longer have any ties with it."

"You have no ties with it?" Grandfather Zisskind bent towards him. His lips quivered in fury. "With what . . . with what *do* you have ties?"

"We have . . . with this country," said Yehuda and gave an involuntary smile.

"Fool!" Grandfather Zisskind shot at him. "Do you think that people come to a desert and make themselves a nation, eh? That you are the first of some new race? That you're not the son of your father? Not the grandson of your grandfather? Do you want to forget them? Are you ashamed of them for having had a hundred times more culture and education than you have? Why . . . why, everything here"—he included everything around him in the sweep of his arm—"is no more than a puddle of tap water against the big sea that was there! What have you here? A mixed multitude! Seventy languages! Seventy distinct groups! Customs? A way of life? Why, every home here is a nation in itself, with its own customs and its own names! And with this you have ties, you say . . ."

Yehuda lowered his eyes and was silent.

"I'll tell you what ties are," said Grandfather Zisskind calmly. "Ties are remembrance! Do you understand? The Russian is linked to his people because he remembers his ancestors. He is called Ivan, his father was called Ivan and his grandfather was called Ivan, back to the first generation. And no Russian has said: From today onwards I shall not be called Ivan because my fathers and my fathers' fathers were called that; I am the first of a new Russian nation which has nothing at all to do with the Ivans. Do you understand?"

---

7. **Torah:** the fundamental laws of Judaism.

"But what has that got to do with it?" Yehuda protested impatiently. Grandfather Zisskind shook his head at him.

"And you—you're ashamed to give your son the name Mendele lest it remind you that there were Jews who were called by that name. You believe that his name should be wiped off the face of the earth. That not a trace of it should remain . . ." He paused, heaved a deep sigh and said:

"O children, children, you don't know what you're doing . . . You're finishing off the work which the enemies of Israel began. They took the bodies away from the world, and you—the name and the memory . . . No continuation, no evidence, no memorial and no name. Not a trace . . ."

And with that he rose, took his stick and with long strides went towards the door and left.

The new-born child was a boy and he was named Ehud, and when he was about a month old, Raya and Yehuda took him in the carriage to Grandfather's house.

Raya gave three cautious knocks on the door, and when she heard a rustle inside she could also hear the beating of her anxious heart. Since the birth of the child Grandfather had not visited them even once. "I'm terribly excited," she whispered to Yehuda with tears in her eyes. Yehuda rocked the carriage and did not reply. He was now indifferent to what the old man might say or do.

The door opened, and on the threshold stood Grandfather Zisskind, his face weary and wrinkled. He seemed to have aged. His eyes were sticky with sleep, and for a moment it seemed as if he did not see the callers.

"Good Sabbath, Grandfather," said Raya with great feeling. It seemed to her now that she loved him more than ever.

Grandfather looked at them as if surprised, and then said absently, "Come in, come in."

"We've brought the baby with us!" said Raya, her face shining, and her glance traveled from Grandfather to the infant sleeping in the carriage.

"Come in, come in," repeated Grandfather Zisskind in a tired voice. "Sit down," he said as he removed his clothes from the chairs and turned to tidy the disordered bedclothes.

Yehuda stood the carriage by the wall and whispered to Raya, "It's stifling for him here." Raya opened the window wide.

"You haven't seen our baby yet, Grandfather!" she said with a sad smile.

"Sit down, sit down," said Grandfather, shuffling over to the shelf, from which he took the jar of preserves and the biscuit tin, putting them on the table.

"There's no need, Grandfather, really there's no need for it. We didn't come for that," said Raya.

"Only a little something. I have nothing to offer you today. . . ." said Grandfather in a dull, broken voice. He took the kettle off the kerosene burner and poured out two glasses of tea which he placed before them. Then he too sat down, and said "Drink, drink," and softly tapped his fingers on the table.

"I haven't seen your Mother for several days now," he said at last.

"She's busy . . ." said Raya in a low voice, without raising her eyes to him. "She helps me a lot with the baby. . . ."

Grandfather Zisskind looked at his pale, knotted and veined hands lying helplessly on the table; then he stretched out one of them and said to Raya, "Why don't you drink? The tea will get cold."

Raya drew up to the table and sipped the tea.

"And you—what are you doing now?" he asked Yehuda.

"Working as usual," said Yehuda, and added with a laugh, "I play with the baby when there's time."

Grandfather again looked down at his hands, the long thin fingers of which shook with the palsy of old age.

"Take some of the preserves," he said to Yehuda, indicating the jar with a shaking finger. "It's very good." Yehuda dipped the spoon in the jar and put it to his mouth.

There was a deep silence. It seemed to last a very long time. Grandfather Zisskind's fingers gave little quivers on the white tablecloth. It was hot in the room, and the buzzing of a fly could be heard.

Suddenly the baby burst out crying, and Raya started from her seat and hastened to quiet him. She rocked the carriage and crooned, "Quiet, child, quiet, quiet . . ." Even after he had quieted down she went on rocking the carriage back and forth.

Grandfather Zisskind raised his head and said to Yehuda in a whisper:

"You think it was impossible to save him . . . it was possible. They had many friends. Ossip himself wrote to me about it. The manager of the factory had a high opinion of him. The whole town knew them and loved them. . . . How is it they didn't think of it . . . ?" he said, touching his forehead with the palm of his hand. "After all, they knew that the Germans were approaching . . . It was still possible to do something . . ." He stopped a moment and then added, "Imagine that a boy of eleven had already finished his studies at the Conservatory—wild beasts!" He suddenly opened eyes filled with terror. "Wild beasts! To take little children and put them into wagons and deport them . . ."

When Raya returned and sat down at the table, he stopped and became silent; and only a heavy sigh escaped from deep within him.

Again there was a prolonged silence, and as it grew heavier Raya felt the oppressive weight on her bosom increasing till it could no longer be contained. Grandfather sat at the table tapping his thin fingers, and alongside the wall the infant lay in his carriage; it was as if a chasm gaped between a world which was passing and a world that was born. It was no longer a single line to the fourth generation. The aged father did not recognize the great-grandchild whose life would be no memorial.

Grandfather Zisskind got up, took his chair and pulled it up to the clock. He climbed on to it to take out his documents.

Raya could no longer stand the oppressive atmosphere.

"Let's go," she said to Yehuda in a choked voice.

"Yes, we must go," said Yehuda, and rose from his seat. "We have to go," he said loudly as he turned to the old man.

Grandfather Zisskind held the key of the clock for a moment more, then he let his hand fall, grasped the back of the chair and got down.

"You have to go. . . ." he said with a tortured grimace. He spread his arms out helplessly and accompanied them to the doorway.

When the door had closed behind them the tears flowed from Raya's eyes. She bent over the carriage and pressed her lips to the baby's chest. At that moment it seemed to her that he was in need of pity and of great love, as though he were alone, an orphan in the world.

DISCUSSION QUESTIONS

1. What would you have done about the baby's name if you had been in Raya and Yehudi's position? Why?

2. What indications are there at the beginning of the story that Grandfather Zisskind relies strongly on traditions?

3. What is the symbolic significance of Grandfather Zisskind's wall clock, which is mentioned several times in the course of the story?

4. How does Grandfather Zisskind's behavior change when he finds out that Raya is about to have a child? How do you explain this change?

5. What does the grandfather mean when he says to Yehuda, "You're finishing off the work which the enemies of Israel began"? How does his repeated phrase, "Not a trace," change meaning in the course of the story?

6. At the end of the story why does Raya regard her baby as an "orphan"?

SUGGESTION FOR WRITING

Select an established tradition that you would like to see preserved. It could be a holiday tradition such as fireworks on the Fourth of July or trick-or-treating on Halloween. Or it could be a special tradition that is observed in your family or community. Imagine that someone or some group is trying to eliminate the tradition. Write an essay defending the tradition and explaining its importance to the participants.

Arabic and Persian Literature

THE KORAN

The Koran is the sacred scripture for the religion of Islam, which is practiced by millions of Muslims throughout the Middle East, in other regions of Asia, and in many parts of Africa. Muslims regard the Koran as the actual words of Allah (God), which were revealed to the prophet Mohammed around 610 A.D. Comprised of laws, moral teachings, and historical accounts, the text is divided into chapters called "surahs." The Koran demands total surrender to the will of Allah and stresses Allah's mercy. It has much in common with the Bible, emphasizing the existence of a single God and introducing some of the same key figures, such as Moses and Jesus. One of the main doctrines set forth in the Koran is the final judgment of the world, with the righteous being rewarded and sinners punished. Rewards and punishments are frequently depicted in vivid detail. ■

Translated from the Babylonian and retold by Theodor H. Gaster

SURAH 81: THE OVERTHROWING

REVEALED AT MECCA[1]

In the name of Allah, the Beneficent, the Merciful.

When the sun is overthrown,
And when the stars fall,
And when the hills are moved,
And when the camels big with young are abandoned,
5   And when the wild beasts are herded together,
And when the seas rise,
And when souls are reunited,
And when the girl-child that was buried alive[2] is asked
For what sin she was slain,
10   And when the pages are laid open,
And when the sky is torn away,
And when hell is lighted,

---

1. **Mecca:** As the birthplace of Mohammed, Mecca is the chief holy city of the Muslims. Today it is one of the two capitals of Saudi Arabia.

2. **girl-child . . . alive:** a reference to the custom practiced by pagan Arabs of burying alive female infants, whom they considered unnecessary.

And when the garden is brought nigh,
(Then) every soul will know what it hath made ready.

15   Oh, but I call to witness the planets,
The stars which rise and set,
And the close of night,
And the breath of morning
That this is in truth the word of an honored messenger,

20   Mighty, established in the presence of the Lord of the Throne,
(One) to be obeyed, and trustworthy;
And your comrade is not mad.
Surely he beheld him on the clear horizon.[3]
And he is not avid of the Unseen.

25   Nor is this the utterance of a devil worthy to be stoned.
Whither then go ye?
This is naught else than a reminder unto creation,
Unto whomsoever of you willeth to walk straight.
And ye will not, unless (it be) that Allah willeth, the Lord of
      Creation.

SURAH 82: THE CLEAVING

REVEALED AT MECCA

In the name of Allah, the Beneficent, the Merciful.

When the heaven is cleft asunder,
When the planets are dispersed,
When the seas are poured forth,
And the sepulchers are overturned,

5   A soul will know what it hath sent before (it) and what left
      behind.
O man! What hath made thee careless concerning thy Lord, the
      Bountiful,
Who created thee, then fashioned, then proportioned thee?
Into whatsoever form He will, He casteth thee.
Nay, but they deny the Judgment.

10   Lo! there are above you guardians,
Generous and recording,
Who know (all) that ye do.
Lo! the righteous verily will be in delight.
And lo! the wicked verily will be in hell;

15   They will burn therein on the Day of Judgment,
And will not be absent thence.

_____

3. he beheld . . . horizon: a reference to Mohammed's vision at Mt. Hira, where an angel descended
   and spoke to him.

Ah, what will convey unto thee what the Day of Judgment is!
Again, what will convey unto thee what the Day of Judgment is!
A day on which no soul hath power at all for any (other) soul. The
(absolute) command on that day is Allah's.

SURAH 112: THE UNITY

REVEALED AT MECCA

In the name of Allah, the Beneficent, the Merciful.

Say: He is Allah, the One!
Allah, the eternally Besought of all!
He begetteth not nor was begotten.
And there is none comparable unto Him.

DISCUSSION QUESTIONS

1. What impression do you think the first two surahs were intended to have on readers or listeners? Why do you think so?

2. What images do the first two surahs have in common? What message do they deliver?

3. What attributes (qualities) of Allah are emphasized in these selections from the Koran?

4. Surah 81 offers a clue about the special reward that awaits the righteous. What is that reward?

SUGGESTION FOR WRITING

Compare the message and the images of Surah 82 to those set forth in the following verses, taken from the fourth chapter of Malachi in the Old Testament:

For, behold, the day cometh, that shall burn as an oven; and all the proud, yea, and all that do wickedly, shall be stubble; and the day that cometh shall burn them up, saith the Lord of hosts, that it shall leave them neither root nor branch.

But unto you that fear my name shall the Sun of righteousness arise with healing in his wings; and he shall go forth, and grow up as calves of the stall.

AL-JAHIZ

(773–869)

Al-Jahiz lived in Basra, Iraq, where he was well known for both his ugliness and his intelligence. The name Al-Jahiz is a nickname meaning "goggle-eyed," a descriptive name that has followed him through the centuries. The grandson of a black slave, he rose from very humble beginnings by the power of his intellect and his immense energy. He read and absorbed an amazing number of books on various subjects, including Greek philosophy and science, and was highly esteemed. It is said that he often rented booksellers' shops so that he could read all night.

Al-Jahiz wrote entertaining books on a variety of subjects, such as misers, etiquette, beauty, and the art of persuasion. His two most famous works are probably *The Book of Animals,* which fills seven volumes, and *The Book of Eloquence.* Although he was learned and well read in scholarly subjects, his works tend to be light-hearted, charming, and filled with amusing anecdotes. The following selection, "Flies and Mosquitoes," is taken from *The Book of Animals.* ∎

from The Book of Animals
FLIES AND MOSQUITOES
Translated from the Arabic by Reynold A. Nicholson

In the fly there are two good qualities. One of these is the facility with which it may be prevented from causing annoyance and discomfort. For if any person wish to make the flies quit his house and secure himself from being troubled by them without diminishing the amount of light in the house, he has only to shut the door, and they will hurry forth as fast as they can and try to outstrip each other in seeking the light and fleeing from the darkness. Then no sooner is the curtain let down and the door opened than the light will return and the people of the house will no longer be harassed by flies. If there be a slit in the door, or if, when it is shut, one of the two folding leaves does not quite close on the other, that will serve them as a means of exit; and the flies often go out through the gap between the bottom of the door and the lintel. Thus it is easy to get rid of them and escape from their annoyance. With the mosquito it is otherwise, for just as the fly has greater power (for mischief) in the light, so the mosquito is more tormenting and mischievous and bloodthirsty after dark; and it is not possible for people to let into their houses sufficient light to stop the activity of the mosquito, because for this purpose they would have to admit the beams of the sun, and there are no mosquitoes except in summer when the sun is unendurable. All light that is derived from the sun partakes of heat, and light is never devoid of heat, though heat is sometimes devoid of light. Hence, while it is easily possible to contrive a remedy against flies, this is difficult in the case of mosquitoes.

The second merit of the fly is that unless it ate the mosquito, which it pursues and seeks after on the walls and in the corners of rooms, people would be unable to stay in their houses. I am informed by a trustworthy authority that Muhammad son of Jahm said one day to some of his acquaintance, "Do you know the lesson which we have learned with regard to the fly?" They said, "No." "But the fact is," he replied, "that it eats mosquitoes and chases them and picks them up and destroys them. I will tell you how I learned this. Formerly, when I wanted to take the siesta, I used to give orders that the flies should be cleared out and the curtain drawn and the door shut an hour before noon. On the disappearance of the flies, the mosquitoes would collect in the house and become exceedingly strong and powerful and bite me violently as soon as I began to rest. Now on a certain day I came in and found the room open and the curtain up. And when I lay down to sleep, there were no mosquitoes and I slept soundly, although I was very angry with the slaves. Next day they cleared out the flies and shut the door as usual, and on my coming to take the siesta I saw a multitude of mosquitoes. Then on another day they forgot to shut the door, and when I perceived that it was open I reviled them. However, when I came for the siesta, I did not find a single mosquito and I said to myself, 'Methinks I have slept on the two days on which my precautions were neglected, and have been hindered from sleeping whenever they were carefully observed. Why should not I try today the effect of leaving the door open? If I sleep three days with the door open and suffer no annoyance from the mosquitoes, I shall know that the right way is to have the flies and the mosquitoes together, because the flies destroy them, and that our remedy lies in keeping near us what we used to keep at a distance.' I made the experiment, and now the end of the matter is that whether we desire to remove the flies or destroy the mosquitoes, we can do it with very little trouble."

DISCUSSION QUESTIONS

1. Al-Jahiz seems to accept the reasoning of Muhammad, son of Jahm, when he concludes that flies must eat mosquitoes. Do you find Muhammad's experiment and conclusions convincing? If not, why not? Can you think of a better way to find out the truth?

2. What are the fly's "two good qualities," according to Al-Jahiz?

3. This essay, which was written to glorify the fly, is similar to several ancient fables in which an insignificant creature proves its worth, such as Aesop's tale of the lion and the mouse. Usually such stories have a moral. Do you think that this essay has a moral, either directly stated or indirectly suggested?

SUGGESTION FOR WRITING

Choose an animal that is often detested, such as the snake, rat, spider, alligator, shark, or bat. After doing some research, write an essay entitled "In Defense of the _____," in which you present the good qualities of that animal. Your defense should be based on actual facts. (If you have had first-hand experience with any of these animals, you may use your personal observations as evidence too.)

OMAR KHAYYÁM
(1050–1123)

An astronomer to the Persian royal court and one of the most notable mathematicians of his time, Omar Khayyám lived in Nishapur (now in Iran). Although he was highly respected and led a secure and comfortable life, he constantly wrestled with the mysteries of human existence. He is remembered today as the author of the famous *Rubáiyát,* a poem expressing his spiritual doubts. The outlook on life he expresses is both skeptical and compassionate. He basically endorses a philosophy of *carpe diem* (Latin "seize the day"), urging his readers to live for the moment. The poem was written in one of the most common forms of Persian verse, the *rubai,* or quatrain, a stanza of four lines. *Rubáiyát* is the plural of *rubai.*

The tremendous popularity of *The Rubáiyát of Omar Khayyám* among English readers is due to the famous translation of Edward FitzGerald (1809-1883). FitzGerald did not exactly translate the poem but rather paraphrased it, seeking to capture its spirit rather than its exact pattern of images. FitzGerald did not even paraphrase the poem quatrain by quatrain but blended various parts, creating an essentially new work of literature. The Argentine writer Jorge Luis Borges once said that the encounter between the Persian poet and the Victorian Englishman produced "an extraordinary poet who does not resemble either of them." ■

from THE RUBÁIYÁT OF OMAR KHAYYÁM

Translated from the Persian by Edward FitzGerald

1

Wake! For the Sun, who scattered into flight
The Stars before him from the Field of Night,
    Drives Night along with them from Heav'n and strikes
The Sultàn's Turret with a Shaft of Light.

7

Come, fill the Cup, and in the fire of Spring
Your Winter garment of Repentance fling;
    The Bird of Time has but a little way
To flutter—and the Bird is on the Wing.

12

A Book of Verses underneath the Bough,
A Jug of Wine, a Loaf of Bread—and Thou
    Beside me singing in the Wilderness—
Oh, Wilderness were Paradise enow![1]

---

1. **enow:** enough.

13

Some for the Glories of This World, and some
Sigh for the Prophet's[2] Paradise to come;
   Ah, take the Cash, and let the Credit go,
Nor heed the rumble of a distant Drum!

14

Look to the blowing Rose[3] about us—"Lo,
Laughing," she says, "into the world I blow,
   At once the silken tassel of my Purse
Tear, and its Treasure on the Garden throw."

15

And those who husbanded the Golden Grain,
And those who flung it to the winds like Rain,
   Alike to no such aureate Earth are turned
As, buried once, Men want dug up again.

16

The Worldly Hope men set their Hearts upon
Turns Ashes—or it prospers; and anon,
   Like Snow upon the Desert's dusty Face,
Lighting a little hour or two—is gone.

17

Think, in this battered Caravanserai[4]
Whose Portals are alternate Night and Day,
   How Sultàn after Sultàn with his Pomp
Abode his destined Hour, and went his way.

19

I sometimes think that never blows so red
The Rose as where some buried Caesar bled;
   That every Hyacinth the Garden wears
Dropped in her lap from some once lovely Head.[5]

---

2. the Prophet: Mohammed.

3. blowing Rose: blossoming rose.

4. Caravanserai: a large inn where caravans stopped for the night.

5. Hyacinth . . . Head: In Greek mythology Hyacinth, a beautiful youth, was accidentally slain by the god Apollo, who caused a flower (the hyacinth) to grow from his blood.

20

And this reviving Herb whose tender Green
Fledges the River-Lip on which we lean—
    Ah, lean upon it lightly! for who knows
From what once lovely Lip it springs unseen!

21

Ah, my Belovèd, fill the Cup that clears
Today of past Regrets and future Fears:
    Tomorrow!—Why, Tomorrow I may be
Myself with Yesterday's Sev'n Thousand Years.[6]

22

For some we loved, the loveliest and the best
That from his Vintage rolling Time hath prest,
    Have drunk their Cup a Round or two before,
And one by one crept silently to rest.

24

Ah, make the most of what we yet may spend,
Before we too into the Dust descend;
    Dust into Dust, and under Dust, to lie,
Sans[7] Wine, sans Song, sans Singer, and—sans End!

27

Myself when young did eagerly frequent
Doctor and Saint,[8] and heard great argument
    About it[9] and about; but evermore
Came out by the same door where in I went.

28

With them the seed of Wisdom did I sow,
And with mine own hand wrought to make it grow;
    And this was all the Harvest that I reaped—
"I came like Water, and like Wind I go."

---

6. Sev'n Thousand Years: Ancient astronomers believed the world was seven thousand years old.

7. Sans: without. [French]

8. Doctor and Saint: philosopher and religious teacher.

9. About it: about life and death.

42

And if the Wine you drink, the Lip you press,
End in what All begins and ends in—Yes;
    Think that you are TODAY what YESTERDAY
You were—TOMORROW you shall not be less.

43

So when that Angel of the darker Drink
At last shall find you by the river brink,
    And offering his Cup, invite your Soul
Forth to your Lips to quaff—you shall not shrink.

63

Oh threats of Hell and Hopes of Paradise!
One thing at least is certain—*this* Life flies;
    One thing is certain and the rest is Lies—
The Flower that once has blown forever dies.

64

Strange, is it not? that of the myriads who
Before us passed the door of Darkness through,
    Not one returns to tell us of the Road,
Which to discover we must travel too.

65

The Revelations of Devout and Learned
Who rose before us, and as Prophets burned,
    Are all but Stories, which, awoke from Sleep,
They told their comrades, and to Sleep returned.

66

I sent my Soul through the Invisible,
Some letter of that Afterlife to spell;
    And by and by my Soul returned to me,
And answered, "I Myself am Heav'n and Hell"—

67

Heav'n but the Vision of fulfilled Desire,
And Hell the Shadow from a Soul on fire
    Cast on the Darkness into which Ourselves,
So late emerged from, shall so soon expire.

68

We are no other than a moving row
Of Magic Shadow-shapes that come and go
    Round with the Sun-illumined Lantern[10] held
In Midnight by the Master of the Show;

---

10. **Lantern:** the globe.

69

But helpless Pieces of the Game He plays
Upon this Checkerboard of Nights and Days;
    Hither and thither moves, and checks, and slays,
And one by one back in the Closet lays.

71

The Moving Finger writes, and, having writ,
Moves on; nor all your Piety nor Wit
    Shall lure it back to cancel half a line,
Nor all your Tears wash out a Word of it.

77

And this I know: whether the one True Light
Kindle to Love, or Wrath—consume me quite,
    One Flash of It within the Tavern caught
Better than in the Temple lost outright.

78

What! out of senseless Nothing to provoke
A conscious Something to resent the yoke
    Of unpermitted Pleasure, under pain
Of Everlasting Penalties, if broke!

79

What! from his helpless Creature be repaid
Pure Gold for what he lent him dross-allayed—
    Sue for a Debt he never did contract,
And cannot answer—Oh, the sorry trade!

80

O Thou, who didst with pitfall and with gin[11]
Beset the Road I was to wander in,
    Thou wilt not with Predestined Evil round
Enmesh, and then impute my Fall to Sin!

81

Oh Thou, who Man of Baser Earth didst make,
And ev'n with Paradise devise the Snake,
    For all the Sin wherewith the Face of Man
Is blackened—Man's forgiveness give—and take!

---

11. **gin**: a snare.

96

Yet, Ah, that Spring should vanish with the Rose!
That Youth's sweet-scented manuscript should close!
    The Nightingale that in the branches sang,
Ah whence, and whither flown again, who knows!

97

Would but the Desert of the Fountain yield
One glimpse—if dimly, yet indeed, revealed,
    To which the fainting Traveler might spring,
As springs the trampled herbage of the field!

98

Would but some wingèd Angel ere too late
Arrest the yet unfolded Roll of Fate,
    And make the stern Recorder otherwise
Enregister, or quite obliterate!

99

Ah, Love! could you and I with Him conspire
To grasp this sorry Scheme of Things entire,
    Would not we shatter it to bits—and then
Remold it nearer to the Heart's Desire!

DISCUSSION QUESTIONS

1. Fatalism is the belief that humans have no free will, that they are like puppets controlled by an outside force. Would you characterize this poem as fatalistic? Why or why not?

2. To what is the sun being compared in the first quatrain? What event is being described?

3. What is the "battered Caravanserai" in quatrain 17? Which other quatrains make use of journey metaphors?

4. According to Omar Khayyám, what effect do learning and religion have on one's life? (See quatrains 27, 28, and 65.)

5. In quatrain 13 what is meant by "take the Cash, and let the Credit go"? In which other quatrains can you find the same idea expressed?

SUGGESTION FOR WRITING

Quatrain 17 is filled with images from the medieval Middle East. Using the same rhyme scheme—*abaa*—rewrite this stanza with images drawn from modern American culture. Try to preserve the original idea expressed in the poem.

RUMI
(1207–1273)

Rumi, whose real name was Jalal al-Din, was raised in a scholarly and aristocratic family that was forced to flee from the invading Mongols. Leaving their home in Afghanistan, they eventually settled in Turkey. This pen name, Rumi, refers to this adopted home, a region the Medieval Arabs called Rum ("Rome") because it was part of the eastern Roman Empire.

Rumi taught theology at a college for a few years and then founded a mystical school called Maulana. Like other Islamic mystics, Rumi emphasized meditation, poverty, and retirement from society. He and his followers believed that a person's inner feelings and spiritual righteousness are more important than external acts such as prayers and fasting. They attempted to gain unity with God through a dance that culminates in a whirling frenzy.

Rumi's most famous work is the *Mathnavi* (Couplets), a collection of sermons and fables in verse that is often called "the Persian Koran." He also wrote numerous love poems. The mystical school of Maulana that Rumi founded still exists in Turkey. At its gatherings the participants sing the Mathnavi and express their ecstasy in a frenzied dance. ■

Translated from the Persian by Reynold A. Nicholson

POEMS

REMEMBERED MUSIC

'Tis said, the pipe and lute that charm our ears
Derive their melody from rolling spheres; [1]
But Faith, o'erpassing speculation's bound,
Can see what sweetens every jangled sound.

5   We, who are parts of Adam, heard with him
The song of angels and of seraphim. [2]
Our memory, though dull and sad, retains
Some echo still of those unearthly strains.

Oh, music is the meat of all who love,
10   Music uplifts the soul to realms above.
The ashes glow, the latent fires increase:
We listen and are fed with joy and peace.

---

1. rolling spheres: In Muslim philosophy it is believed that the celestial bodies create heavenly music as they turn.

2. seraphim: heavenly beings.

THE TRUTH WITHIN US

'Twas a fair orchard, full of trees and fruit
And vines and greenery. A Sufi[3] there
Sat with eyes closed, his head upon his knee,
Sunk deep in meditation mystical.
5 "Why," asked another, "dost thou not behold
These Signs of God the Merciful displayed
Around thee, which He bids us contemplate?"
"The signs," he answered, "I behold within;
Without is naught but symbols of the Signs."

10 What is all beauty in the world? The image,
Like quivering boughs reflected in a stream,
Of that eternal Orchard which abides
Unwithered in the hearts of Perfect Men.

THE EVIL IN OURSELVES

The Lion took the Hare with him: they ran together to the well
    and looked in.
The Lion saw his own image: from the water appeared the form of
    a lion with a plump hare beside him.
No sooner did he espy his enemy than he left the Hare and sprang
    into the well.
He fell into the pit which he had dug: his iniquity recoiled on his
    own head.
5 O Reader, how many an evil that you see in others is but your
    own nature reflected in them!
In them appears all that you are—your hypocrisy, iniquity, and
    insolence.
You do not see clearly the evil in yourself, else you would hate
    yourself with all your soul.
Like the Lion who sprang at his image in the water, you are only
    hurting yourself, O foolish man.
When you reach the bottom of the well of your own nature, then
    you will know that the wickedness is in you.

THE SOUL OF GOODNESS IN THINGS EVIL

Fools take false coins because they are like the true.
If in the world no genuine minted coin
Were current, how would forgers pass the false?

---

3. Sufi: a member of a Muslim mystical movement that believes communion with God can be
achieved by meditation and other practices.

<pre>
        Falsehood were nothing unless truth were there,
5   To make it specious. 'Tis the love of right
        Lures men to wrong. Let poison but be mixed
        With sugar, they will cram it into their mouths.
        Oh, cry not that all creeds are vain! Some scent
        Of truth they have, else they would not beguile.
10   Say not, "How utterly fantastical!"
        No fancy in the world is all untrue.
        Amidst the crowd of dervishes hides one,
        One true fakir.4 Search well and thou wilt find!
</pre>

THE PROGRESS OF MAN

<pre>
        First he appeared in the realm inanimate;
        Thence came into the world of plants and lived
        The plant life many a year, nor called to mind
        What he had been; then took the onward way
5   To animal existence, and once more
        Remembers naught of that life vegetive.
        Save when he feels himself moved with desire
        Towards it in the season of sweet flowers,
        As babes that seek the breast and know not why.

10   Again the wise Creator whom thou knowest
        Uplifted him from animality
        To Man's estate; and so from realm to realm
        Advancing, he became intelligent,
        Cunning and keen of wit, as he is now.
15   No memory of his past abides with him,
        And from his present soul he shall be changed.

        Though he is fallen asleep, God will not leave him
        In this forgetfulness. Awakened, he
        Will laugh to think what troublous dreams he had,
20   And wonder how his happy state of being
        He could forget and not perceive that all
        Those pains and sorrows were the effect of sleep
        And guile and vain illusion. So this world
        Seems lasting, though 'tis but the sleeper's dream;
25   Who, when the appointed Day shall dawn, escapes
        From dark imaginings that haunted him,
        And turns with laughter on his phantom griefs
        When he beholds his everlasting home.
</pre>

---

4. **fakir:** a holy person or miracle worker.

DISCUSSION QUESTIONS

1. "The Evil in Ourselves" is half fable and half explanation of the meaning. Do you think the fable would be better without the explanation, or does the explanation provide a satisfying conclusion?

2. What is the "remembered music" in the poem by that title?

3. In "The Truth Within Us" what does the Sufi mean when he says, "The signs [of God] I behold within; / Without is naught but symbols of the Signs."?

4. What idea is being presented in "The Soul of Goodness in Things Evil"? What three kinds of metaphors are used in the examples? It has been said that mystics like Rumi helped promote a spirit of tolerance. How might this poem be viewed as a plea for tolerance?

5. Trace the various stages of development of the human soul as they are outlined in "The Progress of Man." How did Rumi seem to view death?

SUGGESTIONS FOR WRITING

1. Throughout history humans have been variously viewed as basically good, basically evil, or simply blank pages for experience to write upon. How do you think Rumi viewed human nature? Give evidence from the poems in this section.

2. In "The Soul of Goodness in Things Evil" Rumi acknowledges that good and evil often seem to be inseparable. Using the same title, write a personal experience narrative in which you demonstrate how a bad experience also brought about something good.

HAFIZ

(1320–1391)

Born into a poor family in Shiraz (now in Iran), Hafiz[1] educated himself in both Arabic and Persian by attending the classes of famous scholars. He became a member of an order of Islamic mystics, taught religion, and occasionally served as a court poet. His birth name was Mohammed Shams al-Din, but he gained the respectful title Hafiz as a teacher of the Koran. (The name means "one who knows the Koran by heart.")

Hafiz's poems are often regarded as models of Persian poetry. He wrote over 500 poems. Some of his poems that express high ideals about such subjects as love, ethics, friendship, and loyalty; others satirize hypocritical religious leaders. Highly structured but expressing intense emotions, these elegant poems are sometimes compared to the sonnets of Shakespeare. Hafiz's love poetry can frequently be understood on two levels—as poems celebrating the pleasures of wine and love, or as poems describing union with God. ■

from THE DIVAN

Translated from the Persian by Gertrude Lowthian Bell

ODE 1

Wind from the east, oh Lapwing of the day,
I send thee to my Lady, though the way
Is far to Saba,[2] where I bid thee fly;
Lest in the dust thy tameless[3] wings should lie,
Broken with grief, I send thee to thy nest,
    Fidelity.

Or far or near there is no halting-place
Upon Love's road—absent, I see thy face,
And in thine ear my wind-blown greetings sound,
North winds and east waft them where they are bound,
Each morn and eve convoys of greeting fair
    I send to thee.

---

1. Hafiz (hä′ fəz)

2. Saba: an ancient kingdom in southwestern Arabia.

3. tameless: untamed; wild.

Unto mine eyes a stranger, thou that art
A comrade ever-present to my heart,
What whispered prayers and what full meed[4] of praise
　　I send to thee.

Lest Sorrow's army waste thy heart's domain,
I send my life to bring thee peace again,
Dear life thy ransom! From thy singers learn
How one that longs for thee may weep and burn;
Sonnets and broken words, sweet notes and songs
　　I send to thee.

Give me the cup! a voice rings in mine ears
Crying: "Bear patiently the bitter years!
For all thine ills, I send thee heavenly grace.
God the Creator mirrored in thy face
Thine eyes shall see, God's image in the glass
　　I send to thee.

"Hafiz, thy praise alone my comrades sing;
Hasten to us, thou that art sorrowing!
A robe of honor and a harnessed steed
　　I send to thee."

ODE 5

I cease not from desire till my desire
Is satisfied; or let my mouth attain
My love's red mouth, or let my soul expire,
Sighed from those lips that sought her lips in vain.
Others may find another love as fair;
Upon her threshold I have laid my head:
The dust shall cover me, still lying there,
When from my body life and love have fled.

My soul is on my lips ready to fly,
But grief beats in my heart and will not cease,
Because not once, not once before I die,
Will her sweet lips give all my longing peace.
My breath is narrowed down to one long sigh
For a red mouth that burns my thoughts like fire;
When will that mouth draw near and make reply
To one whose life is straitened[5] with desire?

---

4. **meed:** reward.

5. **straitened:** made narrow; confined.

When I am dead, open my grave and see
The cloud of smoke that rises round thy feet:
In my dead heart the fire still burns for thee;
Yea, the smoke rises from my winding-sheet!
Ah come, Beloved! for the meadows wait
Thy coming, and the thorn bears flowers instead
Of thorns, the cypress fruit, and desolate
Bare winter from before thy steps has fled.

Hoping within some garden ground to find
A red rose soft and sweet as thy soft cheek
Through every meadow blows the western wind,
Through every garden he is fain[6] to seek.
Reveal thy face! that the whole world may be
Bewildered by thy radiant loveliness;
The cry of man and woman comes to thee,
Open thy lips and comfort their distress!

Each curling lock of thy luxuriant hair
Breaks into barbed hooks to catch my heart,
My broken heart is wounded everywhere
With countless wounds from which the red drops start.
Yet when sad lovers meet and tell their sighs,
Not without praise shall Hafiz' name be said,
Not without tears, in those pale companies
Where joy has been forgot and hope has fled.

ODE 8

From Canaan Joseph shall return,[7] whose face
A little time was hidden: weep no more—
Oh, weep no more! in sorrow's dwelling-place
The roses yet shall spring from the bare floor!
And heart bowed down beneath a secret pain—
Oh stricken heart! joy shall return again,
Peace to the love-tossed brain—oh, weep no more!

Oh, weep no more! for once again Life's Spring
Shall throne her in the meadows green, and o'er
Her head the minstrel of the night shall fling
A canopy of rose leaves, score on score.
The secret of the world thou shalt not learn,
And yet behind the veil Love's fire may burn—
Weep'st thou? let hope return and weep no more!

---

6. fain: happy; pleased.

7. From Canaan . . . return: Joseph, a heroic figure in the Old Testament and the Koran, was born
in Canaan, sold into slavery in Egypt, and eventually became the Pharaoh's prime minister.

Today may pass, tomorrow pass, before
The turning wheel give me my heart's desire;
Heaven's self shall change, and turn not evermore
The universal wheel of Fate in ire.
Oh Pilgrim nearing Mecca's holy fane,[8]
The thorny maghilan[9] wounds thee in vain,
The desert blooms again—oh, weep no more!

What though the river of mortality
Round the unstable house of Life doth roar,
Weep not, oh heart, Noah shall pilot thee,
And guide thine ark to the desiréd shore!
The goal lies far, and perilous is thy road,
Yet every path leads to that same abode
Where thou shalt drop thy load—oh, weep no more!

Mine enemies have persecuted me,
My love has turned and fled from out my door—
God counts our tears and knows our misery;
Ah, weep not! He has heard thy weeping sore.
And chained in poverty and plunged in night,
Oh Hafiz, take thy Koran and recite
Litanies infinite, and weep no more!

-----

8. **Mecca's holy fane:** Mecca, one of the two capitals of Saudi Arabia, is the chief holy city of the Muslims and the birthplace of Mohammed. Fane is an archaic term for temple.

9. **maghilan:** a shrub growing on the outskirts of Mecca, whose presence signaled journey's end to the weary pilgrim.

DISCUSSION QUESTIONS

1. Do you think Ode 1 is strictly a love poem, or does it seem to be a symbolic poem describing a religious experience? Defend your answer.

2. Hafiz's love poems often contain examples of hyperbole (figures of speech involving great exaggeration). In Ode 5 find several examples of hyperbole.

3. Ode 8 is a series of variations on a theme. Each stanza presents a different situation, but the underlying idea is the same. What is the idea that connects these five stanzas?

4. Hafiz brings his own name into the final stanza of all three of these odes. What impression do you get of his general situation in life from these personal remarks?

SUGGESTIONS FOR WRITING

1. For one day keep a journal noting examples of hyperbole that occur in everyday conversation. (Example: "When I saw the chemistry test, I almost died.")

2. Imagine that you are the beloved of Hafiz in Ode 5. Respond to Hafiz's proclamation of love with a letter explaining your reaction to his images and to his description of his feelings. Are you flattered or annoyed by the ridiculous exaggerations? Feel free to be as humorous or serious as you wish in this letter.

TAWFIQ al-HAKIM

(1902–1987)

Generally recognized as the master of modern Arabic drama, Tawfiz al-Hakim was born into a wealthy family in Alexandria, Egypt. After studying law in Cairo and Paris, he worked for the Egyptian Ministry of Justice. Al-Hakim first won fame as a dramatist in 1933 for his play *The People of the Cave.* Shortly afterward, he resigned from his government post and dedicated himself completely to writing.

Al-Hakim's plays tend to be highly symbolic dramas of ideas and social themes, often written in defense of nonconformist styles of living and thinking. Some of his symbolic plays include *Solomon the Wise, Pygmalion, King Oedipus,* and *Shahrazad.* In addition to plays, al-Hakim wrote several novels dealing with the destructive impact of Western ideas on Arab culture, such as *Bird of the East* and *The Return of the Spirit.*

Before al-Hakim, prose plays in Arabic tended to be slapstick comedies that were not taken seriously. With the introduction of his plays, prose drama began to be regarded as genuine literature throughout the Arab world. ∎

THE RIVER OF MADNESS

(A symbolic play in one act, based on an Oriental legend)
Translated from the Arabic by Najib Ullah

CAST OF CHARACTERS

THE KING
THE VIZIR[1]
THE QUEEN
THE PHYSICIAN
THE GRAND PRIEST

>   THE KING. What you tell me is terrible!
>
>   THE VIZIR. Sire, this is the decree of fate.
>
>   THE KING (astonished). And also the Queen?
>
>   THE VIZIR (seriously). Unfortunately!
>
>   THE KING. Did she also drink the water of this river?
>
>   THE VIZIR. As all the other subjects of the kingdom did.

---

1. Vizir: a minister of state (often spelled vizier).

THE KING. Where was the Queen when you saw her?

THE VIZIR. She was strolling in the gardens of the palace.

THE KING. Have we not endured enough without this misfortune!

THE VIZIR. You warned her not to drink the water of this river, and ordered her to drink nothing but wine, but . . . destiny . . .

THE KING. Tell me, how did you discover that she drank the river's water?

THE VIZIR. Her face, her acts, all indicated this.

THE KING. Did she speak to you?

THE VIZIR. No. When I approached she went away in fear. And her escorts shared her emotion and were whispering with each other while glancing furtively at me.

THE KING (*talking to himself*). Yes, the vision I had predicted this.

THE VIZIR. O heaven, have pity on us!

THE KING. It seems that my eyes have already seen this.

(*A silence*)

THE VIZIR. When will heaven's malediction spare this river?

THE KING. Who knows?

THE VIZIR. Did not the vision give to his majesty some sign of future liberation?

THE KING (*trying to remember*). I do not remember.

THE VIZIR. Sire, try to remember.

THE KING (*again making an effort to remember*). I remember only what I have already told you. . . . The river was turned to the color of dawn. Suddenly a cloud of black snakes fell from the sky, vomiting into the clear water a torrent of poison. In one minute the water became as dark as the night. At the same time a voice told me: "Beware of drinking hereafter from the water of this river. . . ."

THE VIZIR. O gods!

THE KING. But yet, I saw that everyone drank.

THE VIZIR. Save two persons.

THE KING. I and you.

THE VIZIR. What good luck!

THE KING. I do not see here any good luck.

THE VIZIR (*conscious of his faux pas*). Forgive me, sire. In reality my grief is so great. Ah! I wish to be in the place of the Queen!

THE KING. I hate this sort of talk. I wish you could find her a remedy! I suffer to see one of the most brilliant intellects of the kingdom sinking in the shadows of madness.

THE VIZIR. Yes, she was the sun of this realm!

THE KING. You do not do anything but repeat what I say. Say that the Chief Physician of the court be summoned!

THE VIZIR. The Chief Physician?

THE KING. Yes, perhaps he would cure her.

THE VIZIR. Has his majesty forgotten that the Physician also . . .

THE KING. What?

THE VIZIR. He drank also.

THE KING. Oh, what a misfortune.

THE VIZIR. I saw him near the Queen; everything about him was uncertain. Each time that I encountered him he nodded in a very strange way.

THE KING. Is the Chief Physician mad?

THE VIZIR. Yes.

THE KING. He was the greatest practitioner of his time. What a shame that a man like him becomes mad.

THE VIZIR. And at the moment we are in utmost need of his knowledge.

THE KING. Then there is no one left in the kingdom other than one person to take us out of this dilemma.

THE VIZIR. Who is that, sire?

THE KING. The Grand Priest.

THE VIZIR. O heaven!

THE KING. What?

THE VIZIR. Sire, like all the others.

THE KING. What are you saying? Did he also drink?

THE VIZIR. Yes, like the others.

THE KING. What irreparable misfortune! The Grand Priest also mad. He, of all men the most wise, the most clear-minded, the best man of faith, the most pure and close to heaven!

THE VIZIR. It was predestined, sire. Have I not already said that destiny wanted it this way?

THE KING. Truly, this is a complete misfortune, which was not even known in the legends and stories of bygone times. Suddenly all the subjects of a kingdom affected by madness! A kingdom in which only the King and his vizir are in their right minds!

THE VIZIR (*raising his arms to heaven in supplication*). O! Heaven's pity on us!

THE KING. Hear me! This heaven which permitted us to be spared, will it refuse to fulfill our prayers? Let us go to the temple to prostrate ourselves and to pray for the recovery of the Queen and her subjects. This is our last refuge.

THE VIZIR. Yes, our ultimate and best refuge! O heaven!

(They go out. The queen enters through another door, accompanied by
THE CHIEF PHYSICIAN and THE GRAND PRIEST.)

THE QUEEN. It is a fearful misfortune!

THE PHYSICIAN and THE GRAND PRIEST (together). Yes, it is a catastrophe!

THE QUEEN (to THE PHYSICIAN). There is not any means to treat the minds of these two unfortunates?

THE PHYSICIAN. I suffer, madam, from my ignorance.

THE QUEEN. Do search.

THE PHYSICIAN. I did search very carefully; my science cannot do anything for their illness.

THE QUEEN. Then, should I lose hope for the recovery of my husband?

THE PHYSICIAN. Do not lose hope, madam. Heaven is full of miracles which go beyond the power of medicine.

THE QUEEN. When do the miracles happen?

THE PHYSICIAN. Who knows, madam?

THE QUEEN. Grand Priest, get a miracle quickly, at once . . . at once.

THE GRAND PRIEST. Get what?

THE QUEEN. One of heaven's miracles.

THE GRAND PRIEST. Who said, madam, that I have the power to get something from heaven?

THE QUEEN. Is not this your business?

THE GRAND PRIEST. Madam, heaven is not like these palm trees, whose fruits one picks at one's wish!

THE QUEEN. Then you cannot do anything? I love my husband. I want to save my man. Save my husband! Oh, save my husband!

THE PHYSICIAN. Patience, madam.

THE GRAND PRIEST. Do not stop the Queen's effusion! She has reason. She cries for an excellent husband, and the subjects, if they knew, would cry also for a just and good King.

THE QUEEN. Be careful that the people do not learn of this misfortune.

THE GRAND PRIEST. We are as mute as a tomb, madam, but I fear the consequences of such an event. We may do our best to keep the secret, but it will be revealed one day or another, and then, what an affair—that the people learn the King and his vizir—

THE QUEEN. Oh, stop it! It is horrible!

THE GRAND PRIEST. Verily, it is terrible.

THE QUEEN. What shall I do? Do not make it worse. Do something. If it continues, I will also lose my mind.

THE GRAND PRIEST. If I only knew what is passing through his head!

THE QUEEN. He speaks with dread of the river, which he claims to be poisoned.

THE GRAND PRIEST. Then what does he drink?

THE QUEEN. The wine, only wine.

THE PHYSICIAN. It is a matter of fact that he does not drink but wine. I believe that he already abused it, and his mind is disturbed by it.

THE QUEEN. If this were the only disease, its remedy would be easy: to take away his drinks.

THE PHYSICIAN. Then what would he drink?

THE QUEEN. The water of the river.

THE PHYSICIAN. Do you believe that he would permit it?

THE QUEEN. I would know how to convince him.

THE PHYSICIAN (turning to the sound of someone walking). It is the King who comes.

THE QUEEN (to THE PHYSICIAN and THE GRAND PRIEST). Leave us two alone.

> (*They go and* THE QUEEN *prepares herself to receive* THE KING. *The* KING *enters.*)

THE KING (seeing THE QUEEN, *he suddenly stops*). You . . . here?

THE QUEEN (staring at him curiously). Yes.

THE KING. Why do you look at me in this way?

THE QUEEN (she continues to stare, murmuring a prayer). Come to my help, O miracles!

THE KING (looking sadly at her). Ah! my heart tears itself into pieces. If you knew how I suffer.

THE QUEEN (staring). Do you suffer? Why?

THE KING. Why? Ah! Yes, you cannot understand. This fair head cannot understand now.

THE QUEEN. What makes you suffer?

THE KING (looking at her attentively). I suffer . . . but can I say it? Ah, I—it is more than I can bear. . . .

THE QUEEN (seeming astonished). So you would feel that—

THE KING. Is there reason to not feel, my friend? And do you ask me about it?

THE QUEEN (with astonishment). It is extraordinary!

THE KING. What a sadness!

THE QUEEN (looking at him for a while, then drawing him close). Come, darling, sit near me on this seat. Don't be so sad. The disease will disappear; the time has come.

THE KING. What are you talking about?

THE QUEEN. Yes, be sure that it will disappear.

THE KING (*looking at her in astonishment*). Do you feel that—

THE QUEEN. How not to feel it, my friend. It is a sore in my heart.

THE KING (*looking at her in wonder*). It is extraordinary!

THE QUEEN. Why do you look at me in this way?

THE KING (*with an imploring gesture*). O heavens!

THE QUEEN. You implore heaven? May heaven answer at last.

THE KING. What is this talk?

THE QUEEN (*joyfully*). We have found the remedy.

THE KING. Did you find the remedy? When?

THE QUEEN (*enthusiastically*). Today.

THE KING (*with interest*). Oh, what good fortune!

THE QUEEN. Yes, what good fortune! But you should hear me and follow my advice: you will cease hereafter to drink wine and you will not drink but the river's water.

THE KING (*looking at her, disillusioned*). The water of the river!

THE QUEEN (*forcefully*). Yes!

THE KING (*as if speaking to himself*). Woe is me! And I believed that heaven had kindly answered my prayers!

THE QUEEN (*persuasively*). Hear me and follow my advice.

THE KING (*with an air of disillusionment*). I see that evil is getting worse and worse. Could I predict that she would talk to me some day like this? O gods! However, she must be saved. She must be saved. I will lose my mind. (*He goes out quickly, and is heard calling.*) The Vizir! Call the Vizir!

THE QUEEN (*talking to herself*). The Physician is right. It is much more serious. (*She sighs and goes out.*)

THE VIZIR (*entering through the opposite door and looking upset*). Sire! Sire!

THE KING (*coming back in*). Vizir!

THE VIZIR. Do you know what the people say about us?

THE KING. What people?

THE VIZIR. The mad ones.

THE KING. What do they say?

THE VIZIR. They, those mad ones, claim that they are in their right minds, while the King and the Vizir are—

THE KING. Stop it! Who told you such nonsense?

THE VIZIR. Such is their conviction.

THE KING (*with a sad, ironic tone*). We the mad ones, and they the wise! . . . O! Heaven's pity! They cannot understand that they are mad.

THE VIZIR. You are right.

THE KING. It seems to me that the mad one does not realize his condition.

THE VIZIR. This is also what I think.

THE KING. Oh, what suffering! Just now the Queen was talking to me with an air of understanding. And more than that, she seemed to want to give me her advice and to pity my fate!

THE VIZIR. It is exactly the same with the persons who met me in the streets of the town or inside the palace.

THE KING. O heaven, have pity on them.

THE VIZIR (*with hesitation*). And on us.

THE KING. And on us?

THE VIZIR. Sire, I . . . I wanted to speak.

THE KING (*afraid*). What do you want to say?

THE VIZIR. That they are—

THE KING. Who are they?

THE VIZIR. The people, the mad ones; they accuse us of being mad. Already they murmur and conspire. Whatever may be the weakness of their minds, they are the majority, and thus they have logic on their side. More than that, they alone have the right to judge madness or wisdom. They are the ocean, while we, we are not more than two grains of sand. Do you want advice, sire?

THE KING. I know what you want to do.

THE VIZIR. Let us do like them. Let us drink the water of the river!

THE KING (*looking attentively at* THE VIZIR). O unfortunate! Did you also drink the water? I see in your eyes a gleam of madness.

THE VIZIR. No, sire, I did not drink.

THE KING. Speak frankly.

THE VIZIR (*forcefully*). I tell you in all frankness, I will drink. I have decided to be crazy like all the others. I do not know what to do with my reason.

THE KING. Then, do you want to extinguish with your own hands the flame of your spirit?

THE VIZIR. Oh, the flame of the spirit! What value can it have in a kingdom of the mad? Believe me, we are in danger of being overthrown by the people if we follow our own judgment. Already revolt shines in their eyes. It would not be too long before we would hear in the streets the people shouting: "The King and his Vizir are mad. Down with the madmen."

THE KING. Woe to you! Are you talking seriously?

THE VIZIR. Sire, you have just said that the mad ones do not realize their condition.

THE KING (*shouting*). But I am in my right mind, and these people are crazy!

THE VIZIR. They also claim the same thing.

THE KING. And you? Do you not think that I am in my right mind?

THE VIZIR. My opinion alone—of what use will it be? The word of a mad one in the favor of another has no weight!

THE KING. But you know very well that I did not drink the water of the river.

THE VIZIR. I know it.

THE KING. Therefore, I am not mad, because I did not drink, while the others are crazy because they did drink.

THE VIZIR. They say the contrary: They are not mad, because they drank the water, and you are mad because you did not!

THE KING. What stupidity!

THE VIZIR. This is what they say, and they are believed, while you cannot find a soul to hear what you say!

THE KING. Then is this the way to interpret the truth?

THE VIZIR. The truth? (*He covers his laugh.*)

THE KING. Do you laugh?

THE VIZIR. Now those words seem strange on our lips.

THE KING (*shivering*). Why?

THE VIZIR. Truth, reason, virtue, and all the words which are the exclusive property of those persons. They, alone, are their possessors.

THE KING. And I?

THE VIZIR. You, alone, you possess nothing.

(*A silence. The king meditates.*)

THE KING (*raising his head*). You are right. It is impossible to continue such a life.

THE VIZIR. Yes, sire, it is in your interest to live in perfect harmony with the Queen and your subjects. Do it, even if it requires you to offer your reason as a sacrifice!

THE KING (*reflecting*). Yes, this is in my interest. Madness guarantees my happy life with the Queen and among my subjects. What you said is right. And about wisdom—what does that wisdom offer me?

THE VIZIR. Nothing, sire! On the contrary, you may be banished by the others; you will be branded by your own subjects with folly. In one word, you will be considered mad.

THE KING. Therefore, it would be madness not to choose madness!

THE VIZIR. That is what I wanted to say.

THE KING. And it is wiser to prefer madness to any other thing?

THE VIZIR. I do not doubt this.

THE KING. Then, in that case, what difference exists between wisdom and madness?

THE VIZIR. Please wait. (*He reflects.*) I do not see any!

THE KING (*with insistence*). Let there be brought to me a cup of the river's water!

DISCUSSION QUESTIONS

1. In this play the king makes a monumental decision that can never be reversed. Do you think he was justified in drinking the river water? Do you think you would have done the same thing?

2 When the king and queen talk, they misunderstand each other completely. What is the cause of the misunderstanding?

3. The subtitle calls *The River of Madness* a "symbolic play." Explain the symbolism. (What ideas are represented by the king, the river, and the queen?)

4. An old proverb states: "Everyone is crazy except me and you, and sometimes I wonder about you." To what extent does *The River of Madness* reflect this view?

SUGGESTION FOR WRITING

The king and the vizir in this play both conclude that they will be in danger if they do not join the other people in their madness. Try to recall a period of history when exercising reason might put an individual in danger. Then imagine that you are planning to write a play about this time period based on *The River of Madness*. Write a letter to a publishing company summarizing your play and explaining its theme. Your purpose is to get the company interested in publishing the play.

Indian Literature

THE MAHABHARATA

India's two great epics, the *Ramayana* and the *Mahabharata,* were composed in Sanskrit, the classical language of ancient India, sometime between 500 and 300 B.C. While not specifically religious literature, these two works are regarded with great veneration by Hindus, occupying a pre-eminent place in Indian culture something like the position of Homer's *Iliad* and *Odyssey* within Greek culture. One of the longest works in world literature, the *Mahabharata* is a vast poem, composed of almost 100,000 Sanskrit verses—roughly seven times the length of the Homeric epics combined. The principal plot of the Sanskrit epic deals with a great civil war between two groups of royal cousins for control of a kingdom in northern India. However, this main plot is surrounded by a large number of loosely related narratives, such as the following story of Savitri. The two basic principles of Hindu ethics are *karma,* the idea that people's actions create their fate, and *dharma,* the duty of virtuous action. Both of these principles are seen at work in the story of Savitri's perfect love for her husband. ■

SAVITRI'S LOVE
Adapted by Romesh Dutt

There was a king in India named Aswapati, and his people loved him, for he helped all in need and served the shining gods with prayer and sacrifice.

But the king had no child in whom his name and line could live on, and his heart was very sad. So he fasted often, and he said hymns to the shining gods, hoping they would grant this one wish. After sixteen years his prayers were heard. In the red fire of the altar he saw a woman, fair of face and manner.

"Your devotions have pleased me," she said. "State your wish and it will be granted."

"My wish is to be blessed with a child who will live after I am gone," the king replied.

"The gods will grant you that wish," she said, and then she was gone and the king saw only the red flame.

A child was born—a girl with bright eyes, bright as the lotus lily—and she was the pride of her mother and father. Eventually she grew into a beautiful woman; so beautiful in fact that her father was sure other kings would come to seek her hand from near and far. But none came, for this lotus-eyed one was blessed with a soul too magnificent even for royalty, and her serious ways and mystic speech made men stand back in awe.

One day this maiden of grace—Savitri by name—knelt at the altar of Agni, god of the red flame. She asked the god's blessings and laid before it an offering of cakes and drink. Then she gathered a bunch of flowers to take to her father. Aswapati looked at her with tender eyes.

"My daughter, it is time you were married as is the fashion of all high-born ladies. We must lose no time as people might think it is my fault that no husband has been chosen for you. Since no one has come to seek your hand, I suggest you travel and select one for yourself."

So Savitri began her search. She traveled in a splendid train, accompanied by nobles and wise men. The royal procession passed through forests and moved along streets of great cities, and journeyed even through the small villages in the hills. Wherever Savitri went she gave alms to the poor, and greeted the mighty and the lowly, and the people all blessed her.

One day she finally returned. The king greeted her from the throne. At his side sat Narad, the wise man. "I have found my husband," the princess said. "He is the Prince Satyavan. Even though he does not live in a palace, still he is a noble of royal blood."

"What land does he rule?" the king asked.

"He has no kingdom, but lives in a cottage in the woods with his father and mother. Their lot is not a happy one. The old man is blind, and he and his queen have lived in the jungle since their son was an infant. Many years ago, the king's enemies drove him from his rightful throne and took away his lands. Ah, but my prince is as noble as his name; at his birth the Brahmans[1] called him Satyavan, or Truth Lover. He is manly and full of laughter, an excellent horseman, and he can paint pictures of horses that are a wonder to behold."

"What do you think?" the king asked the wise man, Narad.

"She has chosen badly," Narad answered. "The old king is indeed a just man, and the Prince Satyavan a noble youth. But I see a dark fate awaiting them, for it has been shown to me by the shining gods that the prince will die a year from this very day."

"Do you hear that, my daughter? I beg you to select another. It would be foolish to go ahead with your marriage since Yama, the god of death, will come in a year to claim your husband for his own."

"I can't choose another, dear father. My heart belongs to Satyavan alone. Whether he is taken from me or not, I will marry only him."

"You may do as you want, my child. But it is a strange wish you have shown. You ask to live in the wilds for twelve months, then to spend the rest of your years in mourning."

The next day the king and his daughter went into the jungle, accompanied by courtiers and priests, and carrying with them a great treasure. They found the blind old king seated on a grass mat beside a sal tree.

---

1. Brahmans: In Hinduism, the common religion of India, adherents are divided into four hereditary castes (classes), with members of one having no social connections or dealings with those of another. The Brahmans belong to the highest caste, which includes priests, scholars, and government officials.

At the blind king's request, Aswapati and his daughter sat down on the grass mat. The host offered his honored guests some water, for he was too poor to afford the customary wine. After cordialities, the two kings agreed upon the marriage, and not long afterwards the prince and princess were married. The lovely maiden thus became the queen of a small cottage nestled in the trees of a vast jungle. Once the wedding was concluded, her friends and father said their farewells amid many tears.

After her parents had gone, Savitri removed her sparkling jewels and her beautiful dress, and put on a plain robe fashioned from the bark of trees. This she bound around her with a cord of cheap yellow cloth. She would be a queen, not by her jewels or dress, but by serving the blind old king and his wife, and by her love and obedience to the prince of her choice.

So passed the happy year.

Now only four days remained before the Shadow of Death would glide into the forest kingdom. For three of these days Savitri fasted and went without sleep. Her heart was pained with the dread of that which had been preordained. But she told her story to no one, so neither the blind king nor the noble prince knew of the fate that lay ahead.

On the morning of that fatal day Satyavan arose in a joyful mood. He took his woodsman's ax and smiled at his princess. "I'm off to cut some wood," he announced. "I will be home again at the setting of the sun."

The prince's words broke Savitri's heart. She knew too well how the black-robed Yama would lay his thin hand upon her lover and so take him from her. "Let me go with you today," she said.

"No. The ground is too rugged for your dainty feet, and the way will be long, and the trip will be too exhausting. . . ."

"Please," she begged.

This plea Satyavan could not deny, and the prince and the princess set out for the depths of the jungle forest. They came to a distant place where there were many high trees for cutting and much fruit that could be gathered. The hour of noon had passed and dusk began to creep through the great forest. The sound of the ax echoed in the grove. Basket in hand, Savitri picked ripe berries from the shrubs. Again and again she would stop to look over at her husband.

Suddenly he cried out: "Oh, my wife!"

Savitri threw down her basket and rushed to his side.

"It's my head. A sharp pain is stabbing at my brain. Look, now my blood is hot. Oh, I must lie down."

Savitri helped him to a tree. Beneath the limbs she laid his head in her lap and fanned his face. His eyes had been closed for many moments when at last he fell silent. Then his pulse slowed and, finally, it was still.

The year had passed. The heartbroken Savitri looked up to see a huge shadow in the shape of a man. Its robe was black, its eyes shone like red lights, and it wore a strange crown on its head.

"Are you one of the gods?" she asked in a whisper.

"Princess, I am Yama, the god of Death. I have come this day for your husband, the prince."

At these words Yama raised his hands and threw a cord at the still form of Satyavan. The cord caught the life of the prince in its noose and drew it from his body. Then Yama turned towards his kingdom in the south.

The jungle became dark. And the power of Yama was strong. But the princess was brave. She got up and followed in the footsteps of Yama. After a short time the black god heard her; he turned.

"Go back. You have come too far. Go back and begin those sad rites which mourners make to show their sorrow for the dead."

"I follow my husband. It is my duty. The wise men say that to walk seven steps with another makes friendship. So let me walk more than seven steps with you. Besides the wise men tell that the way of righteousness is the way for all, and so it must be my way."

"Your loyalty and fidelity are great," Yama replied. "In return for these I will grant you one wish, any wish—except for the soul of the dead Satyavan."

"Then give me this. Let the eyes of my prince's father once again see the light of day, and let his strength be as the strength of the sun itself."

"It shall be done. Now turn back. You must return home. My way leads only to doom."

"Sad indeed will be the path home without my husband's guiding hand. There is no sweeter fruit on earth than the company of those we love."

The black god smiled, for Savitri's words were good and wise.

"I give you one more wish—except the soul of Satyavan."

"Then I ask that the kingdom of the old king be restored so that he may have his lands as well as his sight."

"It shall happen as you say. And now go back. The forest is wide and your home is far off."

"Yama, hear me once more. What is the goodness of a good man? Is it kindness to all things on earth, in the air or on the sea? It is indeed. So even if your enemy seeks help, grant him that help for by so doing you become good."

"Your words are the words of wisdom, princess. And for these last words I promise you still another wish. What will it be?"

"Oh, Yama, I only want to be the mother of noble children so that I can teach them to walk in the footsteps of their dear father, Satyavan. And for that—return my prince."

The god of death shook his cord. "Woman, your husband shall reign with you for many years, and you shall have sons to reign after you."

The dark shadow of Yama then floated off into the gloom of the jungle.

With quick feet Savitri ran. Breathless she flew. And when she reached the tree where the body of Satyavan lay she knelt. After putting his head on her lap, she waited and watched. At last the prince opened his eyes.

"I must have overslept. Strange, just as I was falling asleep I thought I saw something like a shadow. It reached out and grasped my life in some kind of magic noose. Then I was carried away into the darkness—"

"That was Yama, the god of death. But he is gone. Get up now, Satyavan. It is dark and we must go home."

"Ah, now I remember—a sharp pain was piercing my brain."

"We'll talk about it tomorrow. It's time to go."

"It's too dark. We'll never find the path."

"Look," she said. "There is a fire burning in the forest a long way off. Perhaps it's the work of the blazing mid-day sun. We will head towards it. You can use the burning wood to make a torch so that we can drive off the wild beasts as we walk. But if your pain is still present, we can remain here until you recover."

"The pain is gone, Savitri. I am strong again. You are right, father and mother will be worried by our absence."

As he spoke of his blind father, tears filled the prince's eyes. He jumped to his feet, brushing the dry leaves from his clothes.

"Get your basket of fruit."

"We'll get it tomorrow, Satyavan. We have enough to do to find our way in the darkness. Here, let me carry the ax."

Savitri carried the ax in her left hand and put her right arm about her husband. In this way they traveled through the jungle, harmed neither by bear nor tiger.

The sky had turned to gray by the time Savitri and Satyavan reached the cottage. As they approached, they heard voices, and a shout arose as the prince and princess broke through the clearing.

"My children," cried the king.

"Father," shouted Satyavan. "How are you able to see me?"

"I do not know how this miracle came about, but I do know that I can see you, my son. And you, dearest Savitri, now I can look upon my faithful daughter for the first time."

The old king embraced his son and daughter-in-law.

"Now tell me," he asked. "Where have you two been all night?"

After Satyavan explained their delay, Savitri told of the evil prophecy and of her encounter with Yama, the god of death. No sooner had she finished than a jumble of noises came from the forest and a crowd of people approached.

"Good news," they cried. "The tyrant who captured the old king's throne has been overthrown. Return to your kingdom, dear ruler. Even though you are blind, your loyal subjects stand by your side."

"But the shining gods have cleared my eyes," the old king announced. "Come, let us all return to the lands and people of my birth."

And that is the story of Savitri, of her meeting with the black god of death, and of her great love.

DISCUSSION QUESTIONS

1. Savitri is presented as the ideal of Indian womanhood. What special qualities make her a flawless wife? Do you think Savitri would be considered an ideal wife in our society today?

2. Although Savitri is beautiful, no men come to seek her hand in marriage. How do you explain this?

3. What characteristics does Prince Satyavan have that attract Savitri? Would you say that this is a case of opposites attracting or similarities attracting?

4. How would you describe Yama, the god of death who appears in this story? Does he behave the way you would expect a god of death to behave?

SUGGESTION FOR WRITING

Savitri is clearly an idealized portrait of a wife. Choose another role—such as friend, teacher, parent, or coach—and present a portrait of a character who plays this role perfectly. The character may be either fictional or actual.

BHATTA SOMADEVA

(11th century)

A Sanskrit writer living in Kashmir, Somadeva is famous for the *Kathasarit Sagara (Ocean of Story Streams)*, a collection of 350 stories and anecdotes composed between 1063 and 1081. It is said that Somadeva wrote these intriguing tales to amuse the grandmother of the Kashmiri king. Borrowed extensively from ancient Sanskrit folktales, these skillfully constructed narratives are written in a simple, fluent style that has helped to ensure their popularity for over 900 years. In addition to its literary value, the *Kathasarit Sagara* is also a rich source of information on the castes, religions, and social relations in India at this time. ■

THE CONFIDENCE MEN

Adapted by H. H. Wilson

Two confidence men named Madhava and Siva had lived in the city of Ratnapura[1] for some time and had fleeced every inhabitant in the place. They thought it high time, therefore, to change the scene of their operations. Now it came to them that a certain Brahman priest[2] named Sankara Swami was a weak, credulous old man, blessed with immense wealth and a beautiful daughter. Since the Brahman served on the staff of the King of Ujjayini, the two confidence men laid their plans, then set out for that city.

Madhava invested a sum of gold in the purchase of stately clothes and in the hire of a large, imposing caravan. He assumed the rank of a Rajput nobleman,[3] traveling with his train to a village a short distance from Ujjayini where he and his attendants set up camp. Siva, meanwhile, entered Ujjayini alone. Having located a deserted temple on the banks of the river Sipra, he took up residence there, posing as a holy man.

By the seeming severity of his penance, Siva soon attracted public attention. Each day at dawn he smeared his body with mud and plunged head first into the river, remaining there under water for many minutes. When the sun had risen well over the horizon, he returned to land to gaze

---

1. **Ratnapura:** a city in southern Ceylon.

2. **Brahman priest:** In Hinduism, the common religion in India, believers are divided into four hereditary castes (classes), with members of one caste having no social connections or dealings with those of another. The Brahmans belong to the highest caste, which includes priests, scholars, and government officials.

3. **Rajput nobleman:** a member of a warrior clan.

into the sun's bright rays as though lost in prayer and meditation. Towards evening he returned to the temple to offer flowers to the gods.

Sometimes Siva assumed the sacred positions of the cult of the Yogi[4] so that it appeared he was fully occupied with abstract devotion. But several times weekly he dressed in the skin of the black deer and, taking up his staff and hollow half of a coconut, journeyed to the city in quest of alms. He pretended to divide the rice so obtained into three parts: one part for the crows, one for the poor, and the last part he reserved for himself. Siva spent his nights alone in the temple, for he dared not visit the public houses where he might be recognized.

When Madhava learned that Siva had established himself in his fraudulent role, he judged it time to play his hand. Madhava entered the city and rented a spacious mansion not far from the residence of the wealthy Brahman. Pretending to pay homage at the temple of Sipra, he arranged an accidental encounter with Siva. Madhava promptly feigned extreme veneration for the holy man, informing all gathered there that Siva was a religious ascetic of singular sanctity whom he had previously encountered in his travels. That night Siva repaid the visit, and the two confidence men ate and drank, and made merry together, later agreeing on their next course of action.

The following morning Madhava sent a messenger bearing gifts to Sankara Swami. "A noble of Rajput rank," the messenger stated, "has only recently arrived from the Dakhin and he and his retainers would gladly take service with the King of Ujjayini. As you, Honored Priest, are favored by the good graces of the king, my lord presents these gifts and requests that you make the appeal on his behalf."

The old priest, being greedy and miserly by nature, was much impressed by the seeming value of the gifts and was quick to pledge his assistance. The priest's efforts resulted in the appointment of Madhava and his retainers to the king's court. Hoping to gain even richer rewards from the Rajput noble, the priest insisted that Madhava and his followers take up their residence in his own stately mansion.

The day Madhava appeared at Sankara Swami's home he requested permission to deposit his jewels in the old gentleman's private treasury. As Madhava spread the jewels on the table, Sankara Swami's eyes bulged like two huge balls. Before him lay all manner of beautiful and invaluable gems. As these gems had been fashioned with great skill Sankara Swami had not the slightest notion they were artificial and all but worthless. Thus the greedy priest agreed to have the counterfeit jewels placed in his vaults.

In the weeks that followed Madhava secretly abstained from food. He began to lose weight, and his color turned pale and sickly. Pretending to be dangerously ill, he asked Sankara Swami to seek out some pious holy man. "I fear death is at hand," wailed Madhava, "and it will be my final act to present all my possessions to some worthy ascetic."

---

4. Yogi: a practitioner of Yoga, a system of mental and physical disciplines.

The old man knew of many holy men, but none to be entrusted with such a treasure. Acting on earlier instructions, one of Madhava's attendants suggested they send for the holy man living in the temple on the banks of the Sipra. "He is held in high repute," the attendant counseled. "Even my own master speaks well of him."

Sankara Swami accepted the attendant's advice, but having plans of his own for the disposition of the jewels, he decided to see the ascetic before calling him to his mansion. So he went to the temple at Sipra where he bowed before the ascetic, saying:

"A Rajput of high rank is on the verge of death and wishes to present you with his entire estate which includes a valuable collection of jewelry."

"I forgive such a proposal, even though it comes from the lips of a priest," Siva replied with studied solemnity. "It is absurd to offer worldly treasures to an ascetic. Transitory, perishable goods are of no value to one who delights in penance and solitude. I seek divine knowledge, not wealth. Now go back, for I reject your offer."

Siva's apparent indifference only whetted Sankara's zeal, and the priest dwelt eloquently on the pleasures of a rich man's life as contrasted to the privation of an ascetic. He went on to tell of the lofty duties assumed by a landowner, suggesting that the ascetic had discharged his obligations to the gods, but had yet to attend to the betterment of humanity.

At length the old priest's arguments appeared to move the ascetic to a change of heart. Finally Siva sighed. "It is possible that I may be persuaded to resume my connection with society. Still I have no interest in gold or jewels. Now if I could only find a wife whose family is as pure and noble as my own . . ."

Seeing an opportunity for even greater profit, Sankara Swami instantly proposed that his own daughter become the holy man's wife. If Siva would relinquish the Rajput's wealth, signing it over to him, the priest not only would offer his daughter's hand in marriage, but would provide the holy man with a handsome dowry as well.

First affecting reluctance, Siva ultimately consented to wed the daughter of the priest. The matter of the disposition of the Rajput's property, he said, could be left entirely to his new father-in-law's discretion. Sankara Swami, concluding the ascetic was a fool and congratulating himself on his own cunning, lost no time in making the arrangements. He brought Siva to his house and married the holy man to his daughter.

Three days later the priest conducted Siva into the presence of the bedridden Madhava. The fake Rajput greeted the fake holy man with practiced reverence, even pleading with Siva to pray over his ashes after his death. Before the meeting ended Madhava presented Siva with his jewels. These the holy man turned over to his father-in-law, all the while professing utter ignorance as to their quality or value. After the holy man bestowed his benediction on the sick man, the two visitors left: Siva with his bride, Sankara Swami with his coveted box of jewelry.

Some days later Madhava pretended to regain his health, his sudden powers of recuperation being credited to the wondrous spell cast by the holy man's benediction. Although Sankara Swami was concerned over the Rajput's quick recovery, he had little time for reflection on this strange turn of events, for his newly-acquired son-in-law was now showing signs of great dissatisfaction with his lot. The holy man had now decided he wanted half of the Rajput's jewelry. In an effort to quiet Siva's clamors Sankara Swami suggested a settlement—he would not part with one jewel, but agreed instead on a considerable amount to be paid in gold and silver. On receiving the first of two payments, Siva took his beautiful bride, left Sankara's Swami's house, and moved into a spacious mansion in another section of the city.

By the time the second and final payment was due, Sankara Swami found he could not raise the full sum. In a state of great agitation he decided to pawn one of the Rajput's jewels. The jewelers examined the stone and, though they openly admired the skill with which it was made, each one pronounced it nothing more than crystal and colored glass set in brass, and of no real value. An apprehensive Sankara then brought out the remaining jewels. Like the first, each stone was judged counterfeit. Sankara Swami was struck as if by a thunderbolt, and it was some time before he knew where or who he was.

The priest's first thought after regaining his wits was to force Siva to return his money. But when he visited his son-in-law and proposed to trade the jewels for his first payment of gold and silver—all the while saying nothing of his discovery—the young man smiled and replied, "I have no objection to this offer, but unfortunately I have spent it all."

The terrified priest rushed to the court. After hearing Sankara Swami's tale the king commanded that Madhava and Siva be escorted to his chambers. Within the hour the two men were apprehended and brought to trial.

"I did not seek the bargain," Siva began in response to the charges made by Sankara. "Witnesses will testify that I professed all along my complete ignorance of the nature, quality and value of the Rajput's treasure. I do not understand how the old priest blames me merely because they have no value. Everyone knows I never laid eyes on the jewels, and all will vouch for the fact that I agreed to his proposals only at the insistence of my father-in-law himself."

In a like manner Madhava protested his innocence. "All these jewels," he pleaded, "were inherited from my dear departed father. Not once had I ever had the occasion to have them valued by one skilled in the art of appraisal. And as I gave them freely to the holy man, surely I could not have had any reason for passing off fake gems as genuine pieces. What had I to gain?" Affecting a final look of anguish, Madhava concluded, "It must be evident to Your Majesty that my sudden recovery from a strange and fatal disease is proof enough of my complete innocence."

The defense set up by the two confidence men was so plausible that they were immediately acquitted of fraudulent intent, while Sankara Swami was judged deserving of the consequences of his own greed. He was dismissed with ridicule from the court. In time Sankara Swami lost his official rank, not to mention his daughter and wealth.

On the other hand, Siva and Madhava found themselves praised for their honesty and virtue. The two confidence men reaped a twofold reward: both were introduced into the king's favorite circle and, of course, each enjoyed the wealth he so poorly deserved.

DISCUSSION QUESTIONS

1. With whom did your sympathies lie as you read this tale—the confidence men or their victim? Explain why.

2 One of the clever strategies underlying the hoax of Siva and Madhava is to make Sankara believe that he is the trickster rather than the one being tricked. How do the confidence men convey this impression?

3. How does the author prevent the reader from identifying too strongly with Sankara, the victim of the hoax? Why is it important to control the reader's response in this way?

SUGGESTION FOR WRITING

Imagine that your school wants to produce "The Confidence Men" as a play. The director has divided the action of the story into the five acts shown below and has invited you to write one of them. Select the act that interests you the most and begin by describing the setting. Then write a script for the dialogue that will take place. (If the act contains more than one scene, you will need to describe each new setting.)

Act I: Siva and Madhava review their situation and agree to try their luck with Sankara in the city of Ujjayini.

Act II: Siva establishes his reputation as a holy man.

Act III: Madhava worms himself into the good graces of Sankara.

Act IV: Sankara, believing that Madhava is about to die, strikes a deal with Siva.

Act V: Sankara discovers that the jewels are worthless and brings the two con-artists to court.

RABINDRANATH TAGORE
(1861–1941)

The greatest figure of modern Indian literature, Tagore was born into a cultured and wealthy family in Calcutta. After studying law in England for a brief time, he returned to India and began publishing poetry. Tagore's poetry is marked by a deeply religious imagery and a love of nature and homeland; his poetry collections include *Heart's Desire, The Golden Boat,* and *Armful of Leaves.* In 1913 Tagore became the first Asian writer to receive the Nobel Prize for literature. Two years later he was knighted by King George V of England. (In 1919, however, he renounced his knighthood following the British massacre of 400 Indian demonstrators in the city of Amritsar.)

Tagore lived during the British colonial era in India, and he was constantly aware of the conflict between Eastern and Western philosophies and cultures. He wrote fiction and articles that explored ways of harmonizing the rationality of the West with the spirituality of India. His activities, however, were not confined to writing. He founded an international university called Visva-Bharati, which offered courses that were a blend of Eastern and Western thinking. In addition, he conducted experiments in cooperative farming and lectured frequently in various countries. The following story reflects his enduring interest in conflicts between rational thought and spiritual orientations. ■

MY LORD, THE BABY

Translated from the Bengali by C. F. Andrews

Raicharan was twelve years old when he came as a servant to his master's house. He belonged to the same caste[1] as his master, and was given his master's little son to nurse. As time went on the boy left Raicharan's arms to go to school. From school he went on to college, and after college he entered the judicial service. Always, until he married, Raicharan was his sole attendant.

But, when a mistress came into the house, Raicharan found two masters instead of one. All his former influence passed to the new mistress. This was compensated for by a fresh arrival. Anukul had a son born to him, and Raicharan by his unsparing attentions soon got a complete hold over the child. He used to toss him up in his arms, call to him in absurd

---

1. **caste:** hereditary social class. Hindu society is divided into four castes, with members of one having no association with those of another. The four castes are, in order of rank: (1) *Brahmins,* priests, scholars, and government officials; (2) *Kshatriyas,* warriors and minor officials; (3) *Vaisyas,* merchants and artisans; (4) *Sudras,* unskilled workers. All people outside these groups were called "untouchables" and were considered outcasts. In 1955 the Indian government enacted a law making discrimination against untouchables a criminal offense.

baby language, put his face close to the baby's and draw it away again with a grin.

Presently the child was able to crawl and cross the doorway. When Raicharan went to catch him, he would scream with mischievous laughter and make for safety. Raicharan was amazed at the profound skill and exact judgment the baby showed when pursued. He would say to his mistress with a look of awe and mystery: "Your son will be a judge some day."

New wonders came in their turn. When the baby began to toddle, that was to Raicharan an epoch in human history. When he called his father Ba-ba and his mother Ma-ma and Raicharan Chan-na, then Raicharan's ecstasy knew no bounds. He went out to tell the news to all the world.

After a while Raicharan was asked to show his ingenuity in other ways. He had, for instance, to play the part of a horse, holding the reins between his teeth and prancing with his feet. He had also to wrestle with his little charge, and if he could not, by a wrestler's trick, fall on his back defeated at the end, a great outcry was certain.

About this time Anukul was transferred to a district on the banks of the Padma. On his way through Calcutta he bought his son a little go-cart. He bought him also a yellow satin waistcoat, a gold-laced cap, and some gold bracelets and anklets. Raicharan was wont to take these out, and put them on his little charge with ceremonial pride, whenever they went for a walk.

Then came the rainy season, and day after day the rain poured down in torrents. The hungry river, like an enormous serpent, swallowed down terraces, villages, cornfields, and covered with its flood the tall grasses and wild casuarinas[2] on the sandbanks. From time to time there was a deep thud, as the river-banks crumbled. The unceasing roar of the main current could be heard from far away. Masses of foam, carried swiftly past, proved to the eye the swiftness of the stream.

One afternoon the rain cleared. It was cloudy, but cool and bright. Raicharan's little despot did not want to stay in on such a fine afternoon. His lordship climbed into the go-cart. Raicharan, between the shafts, dragged him slowly along till he reached the rice-fields on the banks of the river. There was no one in the fields, and no boat on the stream. Across the water, on the farther side, the clouds were rifted in the west. The silent ceremonial of the setting sun was revealed in all its glowing splendor. In the midst of that stillness the child, all of a sudden, pointed with his finger in front of him and cried: "Chan-na! Pitty fow."

Close by on a mud-flat stood a large Kadamba tree in full flower. My lord, the baby, looked at it with greedy eyes, and Raicharan knew his meaning. Only a short time before he had made, out of these very flower balls, a small go-cart; and the child had been so entirely happy dragging it about with a string, that for the whole day Raicharan was not made to put on the reins at all. He was promoted from a horse into a groom.

---

2. **casuarina:** a type of tree or shrub.

But Raicharan had no wish that evening to go splashing knee-deep through the mud to reach the flowers. So he quickly pointed his finger in the opposite direction, calling out: "Oh, look, baby, look! Look at the bird." And with all sorts of curious noises he pushed the go-cart rapidly away from the tree.

But a child, destined to be a judge, cannot be put off so easily. And besides, there was at the time nothing to attract his eyes. And you cannot keep up for ever the pretense of an imaginary bird.

The little Master's mind was made up, and Raicharan was at his wits' end. "Very well, baby," he said at last, "you sit still in the cart, and I'll go and get you the pretty flower. Only mind you don't go near the water."

As he said this, he made his legs bare to the knee, and waded through the oozing mud toward the tree.

The moment Raicharan had gone, his little Master went off at racing speed to the forbidden water. The baby saw the river rushing by, splashing and gurgling as it went. It seemed as though the disobedient wavelets themselves were running away from some greater Raicharan with the laughter of a thousand children. At the sight of their mischief, the heart of the human child grew excited and restless. He got down stealthily from the go-cart and toddled off toward the river. On his way he picked up a small stick, and leant over the bank of the stream pretending to fish. The mischievous fairies of the river with their mysterious voices seemed inviting him into their play-house.

Raicharan had plucked a handful of flowers from the tree, and was carrying them back in the end of his cloth, with his face wreathed in smiles. But when he reached the go-cart, there was no one there. He looked on all sides and there was no one there. He looked back at the cart and there was no one there.

In that first terrible moment his blood froze within him. Before his eyes the whole universe swam round like a dark mist. From the depth of his broken heart he gave one piercing cry: "Master, Master, little Master." But no voice answered "Chan-na." No child laughed mischievously back; no scream of baby delight welcomed his return. Only the river ran on, with its splashing, gurgling noise as before—as though it knew nothing at all, and had no time to attend to such a tiny human event as the death of a child.

As the evening passed by Raicharan's mistress became very anxious. She sent men out on all sides to search. They went with lanterns in their hands, and reached at last the banks of the Padma. There they found Raicharan rushing up and down the fields, like a stormy wind, shouting the cry of despair: "Master, Master, little Master!"

When they got Raicharan home at last, he fell prostrate at his mistress's feet. They shook him, and questioned him, and asked him repeatedly where he had left the child; but all he could say was, that he knew nothing.

Though everyone held the opinion that the Padma had swallowed the child, there was a lurking doubt left in the mind. For a band of gypsies had been noticed outside the village that afternoon, and some suspicion rested on them. The mother went so far in her wild grief as to think it possible that Raicharan himself had stolen the child. She called him aside with piteous entreaty and said: "Raicharan, give me back my baby. Oh! give me back my child. Take from me any money you ask, but give me back my child!"

Anukul tried to reason his wife out of this wholly unjust suspicion: "Why on earth," he said, "should he commit such a crime as that?"

The mother only replied: "The baby had gold ornaments on his body. Who knows?"

It was impossible to reason with her after that.

Raicharan went back to his own village. Up to this time he had had no son, and there was no hope that any child would now be born to him. But it came about before the end of a year that his wife gave birth to a son and died.

An overwhelming resentment at first grew up in Raicharan's heart at the sight of this new baby. At the back of his mind was resentful suspicion that it had come as a usurper in place of the little Master. He also thought it would be a grave offense to be happy with a son of his own after what had happened to his master's little child. Indeed, if it had not been for a widowed sister, who mothered the new baby, it would not have lived long.

But a change gradually came over Raicharan's mind. A wonderful thing happened. This new baby in turn began to crawl about, and cross the doorway with mischief in its face. It also showed an amusing cleverness in making its escape to safety. Its voice, its sounds of laughter and tears, its gestures, were those of the little Master. On some days, when Raicharan listened to its crying, his heart suddenly began thumping wildly against his ribs, and it seemed to him that his former little Master was crying somewhere in the unknown land of death because he had lost his Chan-na.

Phailna (for that was the name Raicharan's sister gave to the new baby) soon began to talk. It learnt to say Ba-ba and Ma-ma with a baby accent. When Raicharan heard those familiar sounds the mystery suddenly became clear. The little Master could not cast off the spell of his Chan-na and therefore he had been reborn in his own house.

The arguments in favor of this were, to Raicharan, altogether beyond dispute:

(i.) The new baby was born soon after his little Master's death.

(ii.) His wife could never have accumulated such merit as to give birth to a son in middle age.

(iii.) The new baby walked with a toddle and called out Ba-ba and Ma-ma. There was no sign lacking which marked out the future judge.

Then suddenly Raicharan remembered that terrible accusation of the mother. "Ah," he said to himself with amazement, "the mother's heart was right. She knew I had stolen her child." When once he had come to this conclusion, he was filled with remorse for his past neglect. He now gave himself over, body and soul, to the new baby, and became its devoted attendant. He began to bring it up, as if it were the son of a rich man. He bought a go-cart, a yellow satin waistcoat, and a gold-embroidered cap. He melted down the ornaments of his dead wife, and made gold bangles and anklets. He refused to let the little child play with anyone of the neighborhood, and became himself its sole companion day and night. As the baby grew up to boyhood, he was so petted and spoilt and clad in such finery that the village children would call him "Your Lordship," and jeer at him; and older people regarded Raicharan as unaccountably crazy about the child.

At last the time came for the boy to go to school. Raicharan sold his small piece of land, and went to Calcutta. There he got employment with great difficulty as a servant, and sent Phailna to school. He spared no pains to give him the best education, the best clothes, the best food. Meanwhile he lived himself on a mere handful of rice, and would say in secret: "Ah! my little Master, my dear little Master, you loved me so much that you came back to my house. You shall never suffer from any neglect of mine."

Twelve years passed away in this manner. The boy was able to read and write well. He was bright and healthy and good-looking. He paid a great deal of attention to his personal appearance, and was specially careful in parting his hair. He was inclined to extravagance and finery, and spent money freely. He could never quite look on Raicharan as a father, because, though fatherly in affection, he had the manner of a servant. A further fault was this, that Raicharan kept secret from everyone that himself was the father of the child.

The students of the hostel, where Phailna was a boarder, were greatly amused by Raicharan's country manners, and I have to confess that behind his father's back Phailna joined in their fun. But, in the bottom of their hearts, all the students loved the innocent and tender-hearted old man, and Phailna was very fond of him also. But, as I have said before, he loved him with a kind of condescension.

Raicharan grew older and older, and his employer was continually finding fault with him for his incompetent work. He had been starving himself for the boy's sake. So he had grown physically weak, and no longer up to his work. He would forget things, and his mind became dull and stupid. But his employer expected a full servant's work out of him, and would not brook excuses. The money that Raicharan had brought with him from the sale of his land was exhausted. The boy was continually grumbling about his clothes, and asking for more money.

Raicharan made up his mind. He gave up the situation where he was working as a servant, and left some money with Phailna and said: "I have some business to do at home in my village, and shall be back soon."

He went off at once to Baraset where Anukul was magistrate. Anukul's wife was still broken down with grief. She had had no other child.

One day Anukul was resting after a long and weary day in court. His wife was buying, at an exorbitant price, an herb from a mendicant quack, which was said to insure the birth of a child. A voice of greeting was heard in the courtyard. Anukul went out to see who was there. It was Raicharan. Akukul's heart was softened when he saw his old servant. He asked him many questions, and offered to take him back into service. Raicharan smiled faintly, and said in reply: "I want to make obeisance to my mistress."

Anukul went with Raicharan into the house, where the mistress did not receive him as warmly as his old master. Raicharan took no notice of this, but folded his hands, and said: "It was not the Padma that stole your baby. It was I."

Anukul exclaimed: "Great God! Eh! What! Where is he?"

Raicharan replied: "He is with me. I will bring him the day after tomorrow."

It was Sunday. There was no magistrate's court sitting. Both husband and wife were looking expectantly along the road, waiting from early morning for Raicharan's appearance. At ten o'clock he came, leading Phailna by the hand.

Anukul's wife, without question, took the boy into her lap, and was wild with excitement, sometimes laughing, sometimes weeping, touching him, kissing his hair and his forehead, and gazing into his face with hungry, eager eyes. The boy was very good-looking and dressed like a gentleman's son. The heart of Anukul brimmed over with a sudden rush of affection.

Nevertheless the magistrate in him asked: "Have you any proofs?"

Raicharan said: "How could there be any proof of such a deed? God alone knows that I stole your boy, and no one else in the world."

When Anukul saw how eagerly his wife was clinging to the boy, he realized the futility of asking for proofs. It would be wiser to believe. And then—where could an old man like Raicharan get such a boy from? And why should his faithful servant deceive him for nothing?

"But," he added severely, "Raicharan, you must not stay here."

"Where shall I go, Master?" said Raicharan, in a choking voice, folding his hands; "I am old. Who will take an old man as a servant?"

The mistress said: "Let him stay. My child will be pleased. I forgive him."

But Anukul's magisterial conscience would not allow him. "No," he said, "he cannot be forgiven for what he has done."

Raicharan bowed to the ground, and clasped Anukul's feet. "Master," he cried, "let me stay. It was not I who did it. It was God."

Anukul's conscience was worse stricken than ever, when Raicharan tried to put the blame on God's shoulders. "No," he said, "I could not allow it. I cannot trust you any more. You have done an act of treachery."

Raicharan rose to his feet and said: "It was not I who did it."

"Who was it then?" asked Anukul.

Raicharan replied: "It was my fate."

But no educated man could take this for an excuse. Anukul remained obdurate.

When Phailna saw that he was the wealthy magistrate's son, and not Raicharan's, he was angry at first, thinking that he had been cheated all this time of his birthright. But seeing Raicharan in distress, he generously said to his father: "Father, forgive him. Even if you don't let him live with us, let him have a small monthly pension."

After hearing this, Raicharan did not utter another word. He looked for the last time on the face of his son; he made obeisance to his old master and mistress. Then he went out, and was mingled with the numberless people of the world.

At the end of the month Anukul sent him some money to his village. But the money came back. There was no one there of the name of Raicharan.

DISCUSSION QUESTIONS

1. How do you feel about Anukul's decision to send Raicharan away? Was it foolish, harsh, or justified under the circumstances?

2. Why does Raicharan think that his son Phailna is the reincarnated little master?

3. If Raicharan really believes that his son is the "little master," why does he wait twelve years before giving him back to Anukul?

4. In what ways does the young Phailna already show signs of developing into a judge? How does Raicharan feel about these budding judicial tendencies?

5. Tagore creates two sets of characters representing extreme positions. Raicharan typifies the traditional Hindu orientation, while Anukul typifies the cool professional rationality of the Western world. How does Tagore seem to feel about each of these orientations? Give evidence for your answer.

SUGGESTION FOR WRITING

The ending of this story involves an extreme case of misunderstanding, even though Anukul is a judge who is supposed to be able to unravel the truth. Imagine that Raicharan has been brought to court for kidnapping Anukul's son. You have been appointed to be his defense attorney. Write a script showing what questions you would ask Raicharan in front of the court and how he would likely respond. Finish your script with a short closing speech that will convince the court that your client is an honorable and innocent man.

DHUMKETU

(1892–1966)

Until the early twentieth century, almost all Indian literature, even plays and stories, was written in poetry. Dhumketu, whose real name was Gaurishankar Joshi, was one of the earliest prose fiction writers. His collection of short stories entitled *A Bunch of Sparks* was influential in arousing interest in prose fiction. Dhumketu lived in Gujarat, a region on the west coast of India, and wrote in the regional language of Gujarati. He published more than 45 works in a variety of forms that include novels, travel books, plays, biographical sketches, short stories, and an autobiography. ■

THE LETTER

Translated from the Gujarati by the author

In the gray sky of early dawn stars still glowed, as happy memories light up a life that is nearing its close. An old man was walking through the town, now and again drawing his tattered cloak tighter to shield his body from the cold and biting wind. From some houses standing apart came the sound of grinding mills and the sweet voices of women singing at their work, and these sounds helped him along his lonely way. Except for the occasional bark of a dog, the distant steps of a workman going early to work or the screech of a bird disturbed before its time, the whole town was wrapped in deathly silence. Most of its inhabitants were still in the arms of sleep, a sleep which grew more and more profound on account of the intense winter cold; for the cold used sleep to extend its sway over all things even as a false friend lulls his chosen victim with caressing smiles. The old man, shivering at times but fixed of purpose, plodded on till he came out of the town gate to a straight road. Along this he now went at a somewhat slower pace, supporting himself on his old staff.

On one side of the road was a row of trees, on the other the town's public garden. The night was darker now and the cold more intense, for the wind was blowing straight along the road and on it there only fell, like frozen snow, the faint light of the morning star. At the end of the garden stood a handsome building of the newest style, and light gleamed through the crevices of its closed doors and windows.

Beholding the wooden arch of this building, the old man was filled with the joy that the pilgrim feels when he first sees the goal of his journey. On the arch hung an old board with the newly painted letters: POST OFFICE. The old man went in quietly and squatted on the veranda. The voices of the two or three people busy at their routine work could be heard faintly through the wall.

"Police Superintendent," a voice inside called sharply. The old man started at the sound, but composed himself again to wait. But for the faith and love that warmed him he could not have borne the bitter cold.

Name after name rang out from within as the clerk read out the English addresses on the letters and flung them to the waiting postmen. From long practice he had acquired great speed in reading out the titles—Commissioner, Superintendent, Diwan Sahib,[1] Librarian—and in flinging out the letters.

In the midst of this procedure a jesting voice from inside called, "Coachman Ali!"

The old man got up, raised his eyes to Heaven in gratitude and, stepping forward, put his hand on the door.

"Godul Bhai!"

"Yes. Who's there?"

"You called out Coachman Ali's name, didn't you? Here I am. I have come for my letter."

"It is a madman, sir, who worries us by calling every day for letters that never come," said the clerk to the postmaster.

The old man went back slowly to the bench on which he had been accustomed to sit for five long years.

Ali had once been a clever *shikari*.[2] As his skill increased so did his love for the hunt, till at last it was as impossible for him to pass a day without it as it is for the opium eater to forego his daily portion. When Ali sighted the earth-brown partridge, almost invisible to other eyes, the poor bird, they said, was as good as in his bag. His sharp eyes would see the hare crouching in its form. When even the dogs failed to see the creature cunningly hidden in the yellow-brown scrub, Ali's eagle eyes would catch sight of its ears; and in another moment it was dead. Besides this, he would often go with his friends, the fishermen.

But when the evening of his life was drawing in, he left his old ways and suddenly took a new turn. His only child, Miriam, married and left him. She went off with a soldier to his regiment in the Punjab,[3] and for the last five years he had had no news of this daughter for whose sake alone he dragged on a cheerless existence. Now he understood the meaning of love and separation. He could no longer enjoy the sportsman's pleasure and laugh at the bewildered terror of the young partridges bereft of their parents.

Although the hunter's instinct was in his very blood and bones, such a loneliness had come into his life since the day Miriam had gone away that now, forgetting his sport, he would become lost in admiration of the green

---

1. **Diwan Sahib:** a high government official. Sahib is a term of respect used by Hindus and Moslems when addressing people of rank.

2. ***shikari:*** a hunter.

3. **Punjab:** formerly, a province in northwestern India, now divided between India and Pakistan.

corn fields. He reflected deeply and came to the conclusion that the whole universe is built up through love and that the grief of separation is inescapable. And seeing this, he sat down under a tree and wept bitterly. From that day he had risen each morning at four o'clock to walk to the post office. In his whole life he had never received a letter, but with a devout serenity born of hope and faith he continued and was always the first to arrive.

The post office, one of the most uninteresting buildings in the world, became his place of pilgrimage. He always occupied a particular seat in a particular corner of the building, and when people got to know his habit they laughed at him. The postmen began to make a game of him. Even though there was no letter for him, they would call out his name for the fun of seeing him jump and come to the door. But with boundless faith and infinite patience he came every day—and went away empty-handed.

While Ali waited, peons[4] would come for their firms' letters and he would hear them discussing their masters' scandals. These smart young peons in their spotless turbans and creaking shoes were always eager to express themselves. Meanwhile the door would be thrown open and the postmaster, a man with a head as sad and inexpressive as a pumpkin, would be seen sitting on his chair inside. There was no glimmer of animation in his features; and such men usually prove to be village schoolmasters, office clerks or postmasters.

One day he was there as usual and did not move from his seat when the door was opened.

"Police Commissioner!" the clerk called out, and a fellow stepped forward briskly for the letters.

"Superintendent!" Another peon came; and so the clerk, like a worshipper of Vishnu,[5] repeated his customary thousand names.

At last they had all gone. Ali too got up and, saluting the post office as though it housed some precious relic, went off, a pitiable figure, a century behind his time.

"That fellow," asked the postmaster, "is he mad?"

"Who, sir? Oh yes," answered the clerk. "No matter what sort of weather, he has been here every day for the last five years. But he doesn't get many letters."

"I can well understand that! Who does he think will have time to write to him every day?"

"But he's a bit touched, sir. In the old days he committed many sins; and maybe he shed blood within some sacred precincts and is paying for it now," the postman added in support to his statement.

"Madmen are strange people," the postmaster said.

"Yes. Once I saw a madman in Ahmedabad who did absolutely nothing but make little heaps of dust. Another had a habit of going every day to the river in order to pour water on a certain stone!"

---

4. **peon:** a messenger.

5. **Vishnu:** in Hinduism, the common religion of India, one of the three chief divinities.

"Oh, that's nothing," chimed in another. "I knew one madman who paced up and down all day long, another who never ceased declaiming poetry, and a third who would slap himself on the cheek and then begin to cry out because he was being beaten."

And everyone in the post office began talking of lunacy. All working-class people have a habit of taking periodic rests by joining in general discussion for a few minutes. After listening a little, the postmaster got up and said:

"It seems as though the mad live in a world of their own making. To them, perhaps, we too appear mad. The madman's world is rather like the poet's, I should think!"

He laughed as he spoke the last words, looking at one of the clerks who wrote indifferent verse. Then he went out and the office became still again.

For several days Ali had not come to the post office. There was no one with enough sympathy or understanding to guess the reason, but all were curious to know what had stopped the old man. At last he came again; but it was a struggle for him to breathe, and on his face were clear signs of his approaching end. That day he could not contain his impatience.

"Master Sahib," he begged the postmaster, "have you a letter from my Miriam?"

The postmaster was in a hurry to get out to the country.

"What a pest you are, brother!" he exclaimed.

"My name is Ali," answered Ali, absent-mindedly.

"I know! I know! But do you think we've got your Miriam's name registered?"

"Then please note it down, brother. It will be useful if a letter should come when I am not here." For how should the villager who had spent three quarters of his life hunting know that Miriam's name was not worth a *pice*[6] to anyone but her father?

The postmaster was beginning to lose his temper. "Have you no sense?" he cried. "Get away! Do you think we are going to eat your letter when it comes?" And he walked off hastily. Ali came out very slowly, turning after every few steps to gaze at the post office. His eyes were filling with tears of helplessness, for his patience was exhausted, even though he still had faith. Yet how could he still hope to hear from Miriam?

Ali heard one of the clerks coming up behind him and turned to him.

"Brother!" he said.

The clerk was surprised, but being a decent fellow he said, "Well?"

"Here, look at this!" and Ali produced an old tin box and emptied five golden guineas into the surprised clerk's hands. "Do not look so startled," he continued, "they will be useful to you, and they can never be so to me. But will you do one thing?"

"What?"

"What do you see up there?" said Ali, pointing to the sky.

"Heaven."

---

6. **pice:** formerly, a bronze coin of British India of very little value.

"Allah is there, and in His presence I am giving you this money. When it comes, you must forward my Miriam's letter to me."

"But where—where am I to send it?" asked the utterly bewildered clerk.

"To my grave."

"What?"

"Yes. It is true. Today is my last day: my very last, alas! And I have not seen Miriam, I have had no letter from her." Tears were in Ali's eyes as the clerk slowly left him and went on his way with the five golden guineas in his pocket.

Ali was never seen again and no one troubled to inquire after him.

One day, however, trouble came to the postmaster. His daughter lay ill in another town and he was anxiously waiting for news from her. The post was brought in and the letters piled on the table. Seeing an envelope of the color and shape he expected, the postmaster eagerly snatched it up. It was addressed to coachman Ali, and he dropped it as though it had given him an electric shock. The haughty temper of the official had quite left him in his sorrow and anxiety and had laid bare his human heart. He knew at once that this was the letter the old man had been waiting for: it must be from his daughter Miriam.

"Lakshmi Das!" called the postmaster, for such was the name of the clerk to whom Ali had given his money.

"Yes, sir?"

"This is for your old coachman Ali. Where is he now?"

"I will find out, sir."

The postmaster did not receive his own letter all that day.

He worried all night and, getting up at three, went to sit in the office. "When Ali comes at four o'clock," he mused, "I will give him the letter myself."

For now the postmaster understood all Ali's heart, and his very soul. After spending but a single night in suspense, anxiously waiting for news of his daughter, his heart was brimming with sympathy for the poor old man who had spent his nights for the last five years in the same suspense. At the stroke of five he heard a soft knock on the door: he felt sure it was Ali. He rose quickly from his chair, his suffering father's heart recognizing another, and flung the door wide open.

"Come in, brother Ali," he cried, handing the letter to the meek old man, bent double with age, who was standing outside. Ali was leaning on a stick and the tears were wet on his face as they had been when the clerk left him. But his features had been hard then and now they were softened by lines of kindliness. He lifted his eyes and in them was a light so unearthly that the postmaster shrank in fear and astonishment.

Lakshmi Das had heard the postmaster's words as he came towards the office from another quarter. "Who was that, sir? Old Ali?" he asked. But the postmaster took no notice of him. He was staring with wide-open eyes at the doorway from which Ali had disappeared. Where could he have gone? At last he turned to Lakshmi Das. "Yes, I was speaking to Ali," he said.

"Old Ali is dead, sir. But give me his letter."

"What! But when? Are you sure, Lakshmi Das?"

"Yes, it is so," broke in a postman who had just arrived. "Ali died three months ago."

The postmaster was bewildered. Miriam's letter was still lying near the door; Ali's image was still before his eyes. He listened to Lakshmi Das' recital of the last interview, but he could still not doubt the reality of the knock on the door and the tears in Ali's eyes. He was perplexed. Had he really seen Ali? Had his imagination deceived him? Or had it perhaps been Lakshmi Das?

The daily routine began. The clerk read out the addresses—Police Commissioner, Superintendent, Librarian—and flung the letters deftly.

But the postmaster now watched them as though each contained a warm, beating heart. He no longer thought of them in terms of envelopes and postcards. He saw the essential, human worth of a letter.

That evening you might have seen Lakshmi Das and the postmaster walking with slow steps to Ali's grave. They laid the letter on it and turned back.

"Lakshmi Das, were you indeed the first to come to the office this morning?"

"Yes, sir, I was the first."

"Then how . . . No, I don't understand . . ."

"What, sir?"

"Oh, never mind," the postmaster said shortly. At the office he parted from Lakshmi Das and went in. The newly-waked father's heart in him was reproaching him for having failed to understand Ali's anxiety. Tortured by doubt and remorse, he sat down in the glow of the charcoal *sigri*[7] to wait.

_____

7. *sigri:* a small heater made of earthenware or mud.

DISCUSSION QUESTIONS

1. Do you think the postmaster really saw Old Ali's ghost? If not, what did he see?

2. How does the first sentence of the story serve as a foreshadowing of Ali's situation?

3. What is the author's purpose in describing Ali's past fascination with hunting? How does this segment relate to the theme of the story?

SUGGESTION FOR WRITING

Imagine that you are one of the postal workers who see Old Ali every morning. You are disturbed by the situation and have decided to try to persuade Miriam to write to Ali. Compose a letter in which you politely explain the old man's behavior and try to convince her to write to her father.

ACHINTYA KUMAR SEN GUPTA

(20th century)

A fiction writer from Bengali, a region on the northeast coast of India whose capital is Calcutta, Sen Gupta has felt the influence of both Western realism and Indian spirituality. In his stories and novels he experiments with both traditions. The following story presents people and situations that are specifically Indian. ■

THE BAMBOO TRICK

Translated from the Bengali by the author

The annual Gajan Fair was being held in the maidan, or square, at Khorogachi.[1]

This year the fair wasn't much of a success, it hadn't drawn the usual crowds, and the variety of things offered for sale was poor: evil-smelling *papadams*[2] fried in rancid oil, popcorn and some hail-ridden green mangoes. The scarcity of paper had banished the kites and the fluttering paper toys. Clay toys were there—dogs and cats, horses and elephants—all in one color, with only a dot or a line in black to denote an eye or the end of a tail. Then split-cane and bamboo baskets, small and large. Earthenware pots and pans, cups and plates. But the piles of handwoven towels in gay checks and the glitter of multicolored glass bangles were missing.

Those who had come to the fair looked worn-out and lifeless, as if they had emerged more dead than alive from the bowels of some dark valley of fear. There was no gaiety either in their talk or in their walk. The clothes they wore were drab and shabby—on the verge of turning into rags.

The crowd was thickest under the pakur tree and all the noise and tumult of the fair had concentrated there.

As I went forward, I heard a child wailing, "I'll fall, I'll die!" Eyes blind with streaming tears he sobbed and wailed miserably. A little boy, six or

---

1. **Gajan Fair . . . Khorogachi:** In India fairs are named after deities or the nearest town. In this case Gajan, a town in southwestern Pakistan, is nearest the village of Khorogachi.

2. *papadams:* thin, crisp flatbread made from rice flour.

seven years old, with arms and legs like brittle sticks, a strip of rag tied tightly below his waist, he looked as helpless as a fledgling fallen from its nest.

"What is it? Why is he crying?"

A bamboo trick was about to be performed, they informed me.

I didn't understand at first. Were they going to beat up the boy with a bamboo and was that why he sobbed so ceaselessly?

No, the bamboo wasn't going to be used for beating him, they explained. It was to be used for a trick—a trick we were shortly to see.

I knew that orders of attachment[3] decreed by a court were sometimes executed by posting a notice on a bamboo pole near the property to be attached, with a beat of drums. But I was not aware of any other trick that could be performed with a piece of bamboo.

Someone asked, "Will the bamboo be planted in the ground?"

"Oh, no, this isn't an ordinary trick of that sort," someone in the know explained in a tone of authority. "No, the old man will set it on his own tummy and the boy will climb the bamboo pole and go right up to the top. Then the boy will balance himself on the other end and lie on it face downwards. The bamboo pole will then start spinning, and the boy with his hands and legs hanging free will spin on top. I've seen them perform many times before."

"Is that the old man?"

"Yes, that's Mantaj."

The old man's body was shriveled like a piece of twisted rope, a few gray hairs jutted out from his chin. His chest was arched, moundlike, his stomach a concave hollow, and the little flesh he had hung loose from his bones. His deep-set eyes glittered in the afternoon sunshine. It was his eyes alone that gave evidence of whatever courage and skill he had.

The audience fanned out in a circle. Mantaj went round with an empty old tin mug hoping to collect a few coppers.

Someone scolded him: "The show isn't on yet and here you're asking for money!"

But how was the show to commence? The performer who was to do the act of climbing the pole was busy creating a rumpus with his wailing—"I'll fall, I'll die!"

"What is all this wailing for? If you are so jittery about falling, why come to perform?"

But Mantaj took no notice of the boy's howling. He went round with his tin mug assuring everyone that the show would certainly take place.

"This isn't their first performance, is it? Then why is the boy crying?" I asked the man standing next to me.

"He didn't perform before, he is a novice."

"Then who did it?"

"His elder brother—"

---

3. **attachment:** legal seizure, as for a debt.

"No, no, this boy too has performed once or twice," someone else protested, "this boy climbed the bamboo when they gave a show during the Saraswati Puja,[4] in the schoolyard at Tentul. He isn't used to it yet, that day his performance consisted of just climbing up the bamboo. His elder brother is the real performer. But whatever you may say, I feel that the real credit for the trick goes to the man who spins the bamboo—Mantaj."

"Where's his brother?"

"I wish I knew!"

Not a solitary tinkle rang in Mantaj's mug. No one was prepared to part with a copper before the show commenced.

Having no other alternative, Mantaj went towards the boy. The boy screamed in fear as if he was facing a blank wall with a wild dog chasing him. "No, no, not I! I'll fall, I'll die—"

The father pulled the boy's hand roughly. He raised his hand to hit the boy.

"Pooh, see how frightened he is. Your father has shown this trick with many a grown-up young man on the bamboo, and now, you think he can't manage you—a stripling of a boy!"

A part of the audience now began to scold the boy on behalf of the father.

Mantaj smiled. Long experience lent a keen edge to his smile.

"Supposing you do slip and fall, won't your father be able to catch you in his arms? Come along, now."

The man who was beating the tom-tom plied his sticks harder.

But the boy refused to budge. The sound of his wailing rose above the din of the fair.

So there was to be no bamboo trick! One, then another, began to slip away.

In exasperation Mantaj craned his neck and looked over the circle of the crowd. A little later, another boy came forward walking on weak, unsteady feet, a half-eaten papadam clutched in his hand.

"That's the brother," some of the audience shouted.

A sickly looking ten-year-old boy with reedy arms and legs, a torn quilt wrapped round his body. All around his lips, on his cheeks and his chin were marks of cuts that had now become sores. A buzzing fly was worrying him as it settled again and again on the tip of his nose. His two big eyes held a blank meaningless look.

He went to his little brother and said, "Don't cry Akku, I'll climb the pole."

Akku quieted down and his tears dried up almost at once.

The crowd drew closer. The beat of the tom-tom became more frenzied.

---

4. **Saraswati Puja:** In Hinduism, the major religion in India, Saraswati Puja is a celebration dedicated to Saraswati (or Sarasvati), the goddess of learning and the arts.

Mantaj gathered and tightened the bit of cloth that hung between his waist and knees. He placed the bamboo on his stomach, in the hollow of his navel. He muttered something indistinctly. Perhaps he sent up a prayer to his god. Then he touched the bamboo to his forehead. He now drew it close to his mouth, whispered something to it, then stroked it with his hands.

Nobody had ever seen him behave thus—so lacking in poise, as he was now.

"Come on, Imtaj," he called out to his elder son.

In a moment Imtaj whipped off the torn quilt from his body.

It was as if something had hit me—I gasped in horror. The boy's chest and stomach were covered with sores which ran in long streaks. Scabs had formed on some, others were raw gaping wounds, some had festered and swelled with pus. That wretched fly had fetched a number of buzzing bluebottles to share his feast.

I felt a little relieved when the boy turned his back to me. His back was smooth, spotless.

"How did he get those sores? So many sores?" I asked.

Some of them knew, I learned. On the festival of spring, while performing at the house of the *zamindar*[5] at Champali, Imtaj had slipped. The old man had just recovered from a bout of malaria and couldn't keep the bamboo balanced on his stomach. Where Imtaj fell, the ground was covered with gravel and broken tiles, and it had badly cut and bruised his chest and stomach. The boy had been out of sorts ever since.

"Won't you wrap yourself with that rag?" asked Mantaj.

"No." The boy rubbed both hands with dust and jumped up on the bamboo pole which by then rested on his father's stomach. With the suppleness of long practice, he began climbing up swiftly. Mantaj stood motionless, still, the bamboo gripped in both hands and pressed into the pit of his stomach.

"Let him see, let Akkas see, how willingly his brother has come to perform despite his sores."

With his face turned upwards, Akkas or Akku stared at his brother. He had nothing to fear now. He could beat the tom-tom or go round with the mug if he so wished.

On reaching the top of the bamboo, Imtaj paused for a moment, then he gathered his cloth together to fix the pole-end against his stomach. His sores became visible again. The sight was unbearable. I turned to leave.

Somebody stopped me. He said, "When he lies stuck up on the pole like a frog, his arms and legs hanging loose, and starts spinning round and round in space, you won't see those sores any more."

"Does the father turn the bamboo with his hands?"

"He turns the bamboo with his hands a few times, then stuck on his navel, it spins on its own momentum. That's really the trick."

---

5. *zamindar:* an Indian landlord.

Someone else cut in: "To display acrobatics on a bamboo planted in the ground has become out of date now—what's so clever about that?"

The bamboo in the meantime had started spinning in Mantaj's hand. The boy must have become very light after his fall, he was spinning as fast as a paper cartwheel. His arms and legs were spread out and his hideous sores were no longer visible. One could hardly make out whether it was a human being or bat or flying fox that was whirling in space.

My gaze had been fixed skywards, now I turned my eyes to Mantaj when he suddenly placed the revolving pole in his navel and let go his hands. The father's belly, rather than his son's, was a sight worth seeing. The son's stomach was a mass of sores, but the father's stomach was a great big hollow. This pit was not something contrived for the moment to dig in the bamboo. I felt this deep pit must have been there for a long, long time. And who knows what fiery churnstick was churning away inside that pit?

I could hardly believe my eyes when I saw how far back the bamboo-end had pressed into his stomach. I had seen men with bellies flattened to their backs before this. But now I saw a man who seemed to have no belly at all—the bamboo seemed to press straight into his back from the front. His very entrails had shriveled and disappeared nobody knew where. At each turn the bamboo clattered against his backbone.

What I was apprehending every moment came about, but it was not Imtaj who slipped, it was Mantaj who reeled and crashed to the ground. At the last moment he had held out his hands to catch the falling boy. But however frail the boy was, his father's arms were not strong enough to support him.

"Nowadays the old man seems to be slipping again and again . . ." someone complained.

Mantaj squatted on his haunches with his head pressed into his hands, panting like a hard-run old horse. He was staring blankly at his empty mug.

No wonder he had taken round the mug before starting the performance. Had he obtained a few coppers, he could have eaten something—one or two *papadams,* or perhaps a few of the leathery batter-fried onion and *brinjal* slices selling nearby. A morsel of food could have made all the difference, it would perhaps have given some strength to his weary old arms. Long habit could train one to bear most things except perhaps to quench the pangs of hunger. The bamboo, the helpless arms, the son, the sores—one could face each in its turn with the courage that practice and experience endows—but hunger—it was unruly, ruthless.

The bamboo had slipped and fallen at a distance, and Imtaj still further away. The din of the crowd drowned his groans. Someone said, "He's finished." Said another: "His heart is still beating!"

There was a charity hospital nearby. Some people carried Imtaj there, doing their best to avoid contact with his sores. The accident had just happened, the hospital could hardly dare turn away the patient. Had Imtaj gone there to have his sores attended to, they would have driven him away because Mantaj couldn't always pay the one-*anna*[6] bite they demanded for medicine. If half-an-*anna* or one *anna* came his way, was Mantaj to spend it on medicine for sores that covered the stomach or to soothe the sores that burned inside!

Mantaj sat grim and silent, but the younger boy began wailing at the top of his voice. I thought he was crying because of his brother.

But no, it was the same lament, in a still more helpless tone: "It's my turn now! I'm sure to fall, I'll die—"

Without a word Mantaj got up, took Akku by the hand and walked towards the hospital.

"I'll fall, I'll die!" What unseen god was being beseeched by a child's piteous wails—for a misery which knew no remedy.

Mantaj remained silent. His stony face looked cruel in its chill detachment. This hard cold silence was the only reply he could give his son. What else could he do? He must eat.

---

6. *anna:* a former coin of Pakistan and India worth one-sixteenth of a rupee.

DISCUSSION QUESTIONS

1. Imagine that Mantaj has been accused of child abuse for his treatment of his two young sons. You have been asked to testify in court. Would you defend him or speak against him? Explain your reasoning.

2. How does the opening description of the fair prepare the reader for the story of Mantaj and his sons? How would you describe the mood of this story?

3. The narrator of this story is also one of the spectators at the Gajan fair. What function does he serve in the story? How are his reactions different from those of the other spectators watching the bamboo trick?

SUGGESTION FOR WRITING

The officials at the Gajan fair have asked you to create an advertising brochure for the event. They plan to pass out these brochures in the town of Gajan. Your task is to describe the attractions of the fair, including Mantaj and his bamboo trick, in a way that will draw crowds.

MULK RAJ ANAND

(20th century)

Born in Peshawar in northern India, Anand began writing at an early age to express his grief over the death of his young cousin. As a young man, he traveled to Europe to study philosophy but did not find the answers he was seeking. He returned to India and began a career as a professor of literature and writer of fiction. Anand came to believe that literature is preferable to systematic philosophies in fostering human understanding since it is a more direct form of communication.

Amand's fiction almost always focuses on the underprivileged members of Indian society and on the impact of colonialism and industrialization on their lives. His first novel, entitled *Untouchable,* dramatizes the life of a latrine cleaner. Later he wrote about the misery of a young orphan working at odd jobs in *The Coolie,* about the mistreatment of laborers on a British tea plantation in *Two Leaves and a Bud,* and about the plight of women in *The Old Woman and the Cow.* Amand describes his main literary interest as "rejects, outcasts, peasants, . . . and other eccentrics" who have been lost in the shuffle during the change from traditional Indian society to modern democracy. ∎

THE GOLD WATCH

There was something about the smile of Mr. Acton when he came over to Srijut Sudarshan Sharma's table which betokened disaster. But as the Sahib[1] had only said, "Mr. Sharma, I have brought something specially for you from London—you must come into my office on Monday and take it. . . ," the poor old dispatch clerk could not surmise the real meaning of the General Manager's remark. The fact that Mr. Acton should come over to his table at all, fawn upon him and say what he had said was, of course, most flattering, for very rarely did the head of the firm condescend to move down the corridor where the Indian staff of the distribution department of the great Marmalade Empire of Henry King & Co. worked.

But that smile on Mr. Acton's face! Specially as Mr. Acton was not known to smile too much, being a morose old Sahib, hard working, conscientious, and a slave driver, famous as a shrewd businessman, so devoted to the job of spreading the monopoly of King's Marmalade and sundry other products that his wife had left him after a three months' spell of marriage and never returned to India, though no one quite knew whether

---

1. **Sahib:** a term of respect used during the colonial era by Indians when addressing Europeans; it is also used when addressing people of rank.

she was separated or divorced from him or merely preferred to stay away. So the fact that Acton Sahib should smile was enough to give Srijut Sharma cause for thought. But then Srijut Sharma was, in spite of his nobility of soul and fundamental innocence, experienced enough in his study of the vague, detached faces of the white Sahibs by now and had clearly noticed the slight awkward curl of the upper lip, behind which the determined tobacco-stained long teeth showed for the briefest moment a snarl suppressed by the deliberation which Acton Sahib had brought to the whole operation of coming over and pronouncing those kind words. And what could be the reason for his having been singled out from among the twenty-five odd members of the distribution department? In the usual way, he, the dispatch clerk, only received an occasional greeting: "Hello, Sharma—how you getting on?" from the head of his own department, Mr. West Sahib, or a reprimand because some letters or packets had gone astray; otherwise, he himself being the incarnation of clockwork efficiency and well-versed in the routine of his job, there was no occasion for any break in the monotony of that anonymous, smooth-working Empire, so far at least as he was concerned.

To be sure, there was the continual gossip of the clerks and the accountants, the bickerings and jealousies of the people above him for grades and promotions and pay, but he, Sharma, had been employed twenty years ago as a special favor, was not even a matriculate,[2] but had picked up the work somehow and, though unwanted and constantly reprimanded by West Sahib in the first few years, had been retained in his job because of the general legend of saintliness which he had acquired . . . He had five more years of service to do, because then he would be fifty-five and the family-raising, *grhst* portion of his life in the fourfold scheme,[3] prescribed by religion, finished. He hoped to retire to his home town, Jullundhur, where his father still ran the confectioner's shop off the Mall Road.

"And what did Acton Sahib have to say to you, Mr. Sharma?" asked Miss Violet Dixon, the plain snub-nosed Anglo-Indian[4] typist in her singsong.

Since he was an old family man of fifty who had grayed prematurely, she considered her virginity safe enough with this "gentleman" and freely conversed with him, specially during the lunch hour.

"Han," he said, "he has brought something for me from England," Srijut Sharma answered.

"There are such pretty things in U.K.," she said. "My! I wish I could go there! . . . My sister is there, you know! Married! . . ."

---

2. **matriculate:** someone who has enrolled in a school of higher learning.

3. *grhst* . . . **fourfold scheme:** In Hinduism, the major religion of India, believers are divided into four hereditary castes (classes), with members of one having no social connections or dealings with those of another. The Brahmins, or Brahmans, belong to the highest caste, which includes priests, scholars, and government officials. The *grhst* is the second of four stages in the Brahmin scheme of life. In this stage the man assumes the responsibilities of a married householder.

4. **Anglo-Indian:** of mixed Indian and European parentage.

She had told Sharma all these things before. So he was not interested. Specially today, because all his thoughts were concentrated on the inner meaning of Mr. Acton's sudden visitation and the ambivalent smile.

"Well, half day today, I am off," said Violet and moved away with the peculiar snobbish agility of the Mem Sahib[5] she affected to be.

Srijut Sharma stared at her blankly, though taking her regular form into his subconscious with more than the old uncle's interest he had always pretended. It was only her snub nose, like that of Sarup-naka, the sister of the demon king, Ravana,[6] that stood in the way of her being married, he felt sure, for otherwise she had a tolerable figure. And his obsession about the meaning of Acton Sahib's words returned, from the pent-up curiosity, with greater force now that he realized the vastness of the space of time during which he would have to wait in suspense before knowing what the boss had brought for him and why.

He took up his faded sola topee,[7] which was, apart from the bush shirt and trousers, one of the few concessions to modernity which he had made throughout his life as a good Brahmin,[8] got up from his chair, beckoned Dugdu from the verandah on his way out and asked: "Has Acton Sahib gone you know?"

"Abhi-Sahib in lift,[9] going down," Dugdu said.

Srijut Sharma made quickly for the stairs and, throwing all caution about slipping on the polished marble steps to the winds, hurtled down. There were three floors below him and he began to sweat, both through fear of missing the Sahib and the heat of mid-April. As he got to the ground floor he saw Acton Sahib already going out of the door.

It was now or never.

Srijut Sharma rushed out. But he was conscious that quite a few employees of the firm would be coming out of the two lifts and he might be seen talking to the Sahib. And that was not done—outside the office. The Sahibs belonged to their private world where no intrusion was tolerated for they refused to listen to pleas for advancement through improper channels.

Mr. Acton's uniformed driver opened the door of the polished Buick and the Sahib sat down, spreading the shadow of grimness all around him.

Srijut Sharma hesitated, for the demeanor of the Goanese chauffeur was frightening.

By now the driver had smartly shut the back door of the car and was proceeding to his seat.

That was his only chance.

---

5. **Mem Sahib:** the feminine of Sahib. (See footnote 1.)

6. **Sarup-naka . . . Ravana:** characters in the Ramayana, one of the two great Indian epics.

7. **sola topee:** Indian sun helmet.

8. **Brahmin:** See footnote 2.

9. **lift:** the British term for elevator.

Taking off his hat, he rushed up to the window of the car and rudely thrust his face into the presence of Mr. Acton.

Luckily for him the Sahib did not brush him aside, but smiled a broader smile than that of a few minutes ago and said: "You want to know what I have brought for you—well, it is a gold watch with an inscription on it. See me Monday morning . . ." The Sahib's initiative in anticipating his question threw Srijut Sharma further off his balance. The sweat just poured down from his forehead, even as he mumbled, "Thank you, Sir, thank you . . ."

"Chalo,[10] driver!" the Sahib ordered.

And the chauffeur turned and looked hard at Srijut Sharma.

The dispatch clerk withdrew with a sheepish, abject smile on his face and stood, hat in left hand, the right hand raised to his forehead in the attitude of a nearly military salute.

The motor car moved off.

But Srijut Sharma stood still, as though he had been struck dumb. He was neither happy nor sad at this moment—only numbed by the shock of surprise. Why should he be singled out from the whole distribution department of Henry King & Co. for the privilege of the gift of a gold watch! . . . He had done nothing brave that he could remember. "A gold watch, with an inscription on it!" Oh, he knew now—the intuitive truth rose inside him—the Sahib wanted him to retire . . .

The revelation rose to the surface of his awareness from the deep obsessive fear which had possessed him for nearly half an hour, and his heart began to palpitate against his will, and the sweat sozzled[11] his body. He reeled a little, then adjusted himself and got onto the pavement, looking after the car which had already turned the corner into Nicol Road.

He turned and began to walk towards Victoria Terminus Station to take his train to Thana, thirty miles out, where he had resided for cheapness almost all the years he had been in Bombay. His steps were heavy, for he was reasonably sure now that he would get notice of retirement on Monday. He tried to think of some other possible reason why the Sahib may have decided to give him the gift of a gold watch with an inscription. There was no other explanation. His doom was sealed. What would he say to his wife? And his son had still not passed his Matric.[12] How would he support the family? The provident fund would not amount to very much, specially in these days of rising prices . . .

He felt a pull at his heart. He paused for breath and tried to calm himself. The old blood pressure! Or was it merely wind? . . . He must not get into a panic at any cost. He steadied his gait and walked along muttering to himself, "Shanti! Shanti! Shanti!"[13] as though the very incantation of the formula of peace would restore him to calm and equanimity.

---

10. **Chalo:** let's go.

11. **sozzled:** soaked.

12. **Matric:** an abbreviation for Matriculation, a British examination held at the end of high school.

13. **Shanti! Shanti! Shanti!:** peace [sanskrit].

During the weekend, Srijut Sharma was able to conceal his panic and confusion behind the façade of an exaggerated *bonhomie*[14] with the skill of an accomplished actor. On Saturday night he went with his wife and son to see Professor Ram's circus which was performing opposite the Portuguese Church. He spent a little longer on his prayers, but otherwise seemed normal enough on the surface. Only he ate very little of the gala meal of the rice kichri put before him by his wife and seemed lost in thought for a few moments at a time. And his illiterate but shrewd wife noticed that there was something on his mind.

"Thou has not eaten at all today," she said as he left the tasty papadum[15] and the mango pickle untouched. "Look at Hari! He has left nothing in his thali!"[16]

"Hoon," he answered abstractedly. And then, realizing that he might be found out for the worried, unhappy man he was, he tried to bluff her. "As a matter of fact, I was thinking of some happy news that the Sahib gave me yesterday: he said he had brought a gold watch as a gift for me from Vilayat . . ."

"Then, Papaji,[17] give me the silver watch you are using now," said Hari, his young son, impetuously. "I have no watch at all and am always late everywhere."

"Not so impatient, son!" counseled Hari's mother. "Let your father get the gold watch first and then . . . he will surely give you his silver watch!"

In the ordinary way, Srijut Sharma would have endorsed his wife's sentiments. But today he felt that, on the face of it, his son's demand was justified. How should Hari know that the silver watch, the gold watch and a gold ring would be all the jewelry he, the father, would have for security against hard days if the gold watch was, as he prognosticated, only a token being offered by the firm to sugarcoat the bitter pill they would ask him to swallow—retirement five years before the appointed time! He hesitated, then lifted his head, smiled at his son and said:

"Acha, Kaka, you can have my silver watch . . ."

"Can I have it really, Papaji, hurry!" the boy said, getting up to fetch it from his father's pocket. "Give it to me now, today!"

"Vay, son, you are so selfish!" his mother exclaimed. For, with the peculiar sensitiveness of the woman, she had surmised from the manner in which her husband had hung his head and then tried to smile as he lifted his face to his son that the father of Hari was upset inside him or at least not in his usual mood of accepting life evenly, accompanying this acceptance with the pious invocation, "Shanti! Shanti! Shanti!"

Hari brought the silver watch, adjusted it to his left ear to see if it ticked and, happy in the possession of it, capered a little caper.

---

14. **bonhomie:** a genial manner.

15. **papadum:** a lentil cake.

16. **thali:** a flat metal dish.

17. **Papaji:** Daddy. In India the suffix *ji* is added as a token of respect.

Srijut Sharma did not say anything, but pushing his thali away got up to wash his hands.

The next day it happened as Srijut Sharma had anticipated.

He went in to see Mr. Acton as soon as the Sahib came in, for the suspense of the weekend had mounted to a crescendo by Monday morning and he had been trembling with trepidation, pale and completely unsure of himself. The General Manager called him in immediately and the peon[18] Dugdu presented the little slip with the dispatch clerk's name on it.

"Please sit down," said Mr. Acton, lifting his gray-haired head from the papers before him. And then, pulling his keys from his trousers pocket by the gold chain to which they were adjusted, he opened a drawer and fetched out what Sharma thought was a beautiful red case.

"Mr. Sharma, you have been a loyal friend of this firm for many years . . . and . . . you know, your loyalty has been your greatest asset here . . . because . . . er . . . otherwise, we could have got someone with better qualifications to do your work! Now . . . we are thinking of increasing the efficiency of the business all around! And, well, we feel that you would also like, at your age, to retire to your native Punjab . . . So, as a token of our appreciation for your loyalty to Henry King & Co., we are presenting you this gold watch . . ." And he pushed the red case towards him.

"Sahib! . . ." Srijut Sharma began to speak, but though his mouth opened, he could not go on. "I am only fifty years old," he wanted to say, "and I still have five years to go." His facial muscles seemed to contract, his eyes were dimmed with the fumes of frustration and bitterness, his forehead was covered with sweat. At least they might have made a little ceremony of the presentation. He could not even utter the words, "Thank you, Sir."

"Of course, you will also have your provident fund and one month's leave with pay before you retire . . ."

Again Srijut Sharma tried to voice his inner protest in words which would convey his meaning without seeming to be disloyal, for he did not want to obliterate the one concession the Sahib had made to the whole record of his service with his firm. It was just likely that Mr. Acton might remind him of his failings as a dispatch clerk if he should as much as indicate that he was unamenable to the suggestion made by the Sahib on behalf of Henry King & Co.

"Look at the watch—it has an inscription on it which will please you," said Mr. Acton to get over the embarrassment created by the silence of the dispatch clerk.

These words hypnotized Sharma and, stretching his hands across the large table, he reached out heavily for the gift.

Mr. Acton noticed the unsureness of his hand and pushed it gently forward.

---

18. **peon:** a messenger.

Srijut Sharma picked up the red box, but, in his eagerness to follow the Sahib's behests, dropped it even as he had held it aloft and tried to open it.

The Sahib's face was livid as he picked up the box and hurriedly opened it. Then, lifting the watch from its socket, he wound it and applied it to his ear. It was ticking. He turned it round and showed the inscription to the dispatch clerk.

Srijut Sharma put both his hands out, more steadily this time, and took the gift in the manner in which a beggar receives alms. He brought the glistening object within the orbit of his eyes, but they were dimmed with tears and he could not read anything. He tried to smile, however, and then, with a great heave of his will which rocked his body from side to side, pronounced the words, "Thank you, Sir . . ."

Mr. Acton got up, took the gold watch from Srijut Sharma's hands and put it back in the socket of the red case. Then he stretched his right hand towards the dispatch clerk with a brisk shake-hand gesture and offered the case to him with his left hand.

Srijut Sharma instinctively took the Sahib's right hand gratefully in his two sweating hands and then opened the palms out to receive the case.

"Good luck, Sharma," Mr. Acton said. "Come and see me after your leave is over. And when your son matriculates let me know if I can do something for him . . ."

Dumb and with bent head, the fumes of his violent emotions rising above the mouth which could have expressed them, he withdrew in the abject manner of his ancestors going out of the presence of a feudal lord.

Mr. Acton saw the danger to the watch and went ahead to open the door so that the clerk could go out without knocking his head against the door or falling down.

As Srijut Sharma emerged from the General Manager's office, tears involuntarily flowed from his eyes and his lower lip fell in a pout that somehow controlled him from breaking down completely.

The eyes of the whole office staff were on him. In a moment, a few of the men clustered around his person. One of them took the case from his hands, opened it and read the inscription out loud: "In appreciation of the loyal service of Mr. Sharma to Henry King & Co. on his retirement."

The curiosity of his colleagues became a little less enthusiastic though the watch passed from hand to hand.

Unable to stand because of the waves of dizziness that swirled in his head, Srijut Sudarshan Sharma sat down on his chair with his head hidden in his hands and allowed the tears to roll down. One of his colleagues, Mr. Banaji, the accountant, patted his back understandingly. But the pity was too much for him.

"To be sure, Seth Makanji, the new partner, has a relation to fill Sharma's position," one said.

"No, no," another refuted him. "No one is required to kill himself with work in our big concern . . . We are given the Sunday off! And a fat pension years before it is due. The bosses are full of love for us! . . ."

"Damn fine gold watch, but it does not go!" said Shri Raman the typist.

Mr. Banaji took the watch from Srijut Raman and, putting it in the case, placed it before Srijut Sharma as he signed the others to move away.

As Srijut Sharma realized that his colleagues had drifted away, he lifted his morose head, took the case, as well as his hat, and began to walk away. Mr. Banaji saw him off to the door, his hand on Sharma's back. "Sahibji," the parsi[19] accountant said as the lift came up and the liftman took Sharma in.

On the way home he found that the gold watch only went when it was shaken. Obviously some delicate part had broken when he had dropped it on Mr. Acton's table. He would get it mended, but he must save all the cash he could get hold of and not go spending it on the luxury of having a watch repaired now. He shouldn't have been weak with his son and given him his old silver watch. But as there would be no office to attend, he would not need to look at the time very much, specially in Jullundhur where time just stood still and no one bothered about keeping appointments.

---

19. **parsi:** a member of a Zoroastrian religious sect in India, descended from a group of Persian refugees who fled from religious persecution by the Muslims in the 7th and 8th centuries. Zoroastrianism, founded about 600 B.C. by Zoroaster, includes belief in an afterlife and in the continuous struggle between the universal spirits of good and evil.

DISCUSSION QUESTIONS

1. Do you approve of Mr. Acton's method of telling Sharma about his forced retirement? If you were in charge, how would you have communicated this news to Sharma?

2. What do the scenes involving Sharma's wife and son show about the kind of man he is?

3. What seems to be the author's attitude toward the British presence in India? Give evidence to support your answer.

4. What does Sharma plan to do after his retirement? How do you know?

SUGGESTION FOR WRITING

Pretend that you are an employee at Henry King & Company. You have decided to circulate a petition asking Mr. Acton to give Sharma back his job. Begin with the words, "We, the undersigned, do respectfully request that Mr. Sharma's position at Henry King & Company be restored." Then present your reasons in a paragraph or two.

If you are artistically inclined, you might prefer to draw a cartoon showing Mr. Acton's dismissal of Sharma, which you will pin on the company bulletin board. This cartoon should communicate the employees' feeling that the dismissal was unjust.

Chinese Literature

HAN-SHAN

(7th or 8th century)

Beyond the fact that he was a Chinese poet and hermit, nothing definite is known about Han-shan, not even his real name. *Han-shan* means "cold mountain," a name that comes from the place in the T'ien-t'ai mountain range where he supposedly lived. The preface to a collection of his 300 poems, which were compiled by a government official named Lu Ch'iu-yin, has created a popular image of him as a Taoist who rejected all social conventions and lived at one with the natural world. Lu Ch'iu-yin claims that he had to copy the poems from trees, rocks, and walls where the poet had written them. It is entirely possible that the legends associated with Han-shan are nothing more than intriguing literary fictions. ■

from THE COLD MOUNTAIN POEMS

3

Translated by Red Pine

funny the road to Cold Mountain
no track of cart or horse
hard to mark which merging stream
or know which piled-up ridge
5   a jungle of plants weeps
a forest of pine sighs
and now where the trail is lost
form asks shadow where to

9

Translated by Gary Snyder

Rough and dark—the Cold Mountain trail,
Sharp cobbles—the icy creek bank.
Yammering, chirping—always birds
Bleak, alone, not even a lone hiker.
5   Whip, whip—the wind slaps my face
Whirled and tumbled—snow piles on my back.
Morning after morning I don't see the sun
Year after year, not a sign of spring.

18

Translated by Red Pine

I spur my horse past ruins
ruins move a traveler's heart
the old parapets high and low
the ancient graves large and small
5 the shuddering shadow of a tumbleweed
the steady sound of great trees
but what I lament are the common bones
all unnamed in the records of immortals

53

Translated by Red Pine

once I got to Cold Mountain
I stayed thirty years
finally looking up family and friends
most had entered the Springs
5 slowly fading like a sputtering candle
or far flowing like a passing stream
this morning facing a solitary shadow
suddenly two tears welled

82

Translated by Red Pine

spring water is pure in an emerald gorge
moonlight white on Cold Mountain
silence thought and spirit becomes clear
behold space and the world grows still

131

Translated by Red Pine

born thirty years ago
I've wandered a million miles
along rivers where green grass gathered
to the frontier where red dust swirled
5 concocted drugs sought immortality in vain
read books and chanted stories
and now retired to Cold Mountain
to lie in the stream and wash out my ears

205

Translated by Red Pine

my place is on Cold Mountain
perched on a cliff beyond the circuit of affliction
images leave no trace when they vanish
I roam the whole galaxy from here
5 lights and shadows flash across my mind
not one dharma[1] comes before me
since I found the magic pearl[2]
I can go anywhere everywhere it's perfect

218

Translated by Red Pine

the people who meet Cold Mountain
all think he's crazy
his looks don't stir men's eyes
a cloth robe wraps his body
5 they don't understand what I say
and I don't speak their language
I tell whoever I meet
come to Cold Mountain sometime

---

1. **dharma:** the religious and moral laws of Buddhism. These laws are incorporated into the teachings of the founder, Buddha.
2. **magic pearl:** a symbol of the Buddha nature (the seed of perfection) existing in all beings.

DISCUSSION QUESTIONS

1. Lu Ch'iu-yin, the man who collected the Cold Mountain poems, speculates that the poet was ecstatically happy with his hermit-like existence. Judging from the poems, would you say that Han-shan was completely content on Cold Mountain, or did he seem to have moments of regret?

2. In Poem 3, why is the road to Cold Mountain described as "funny"?

3. In Poem 131 what is the meaning of the last line: "to lie in the stream and wash out my ears"?

4. Poem 205 expresses some of the satisfactions of living on Cold Mountain. Explain what Han-shan means when he says, "I can roam the whole galaxy from here."

SUGGESTION FOR WRITING

Imagine that you are publishing a new edition of Han-shan's poems and have decided to write a preface for the book. Your first sentence will be the following: "Nothing is known about Han-shan, but from his poems we can infer a few things about the place he lived, why he lived there, and how other people in the area regarded him." Finish the preface, writing one paragraph for each of these three points.

LI PO

(c. 701–762)

Born in the Szechwan Province, Li Po entered into an apprenticeship with a religious hermit, followed by a period of reflective wandering. He had a reputation for being able to create brilliant verses on the spot, especially when he was drinking wine. For a short time he served as court poet, where he became a favorite of the Emperor. Either because of court politics, or simply because he was happier on his own, Li Po left the court and returned to his life of wandering. For most of his life he traveled the countryside, selling poems to dignitaries and wealthy citizens, enjoying nature, and drinking wine. According to legend, he drowned on a boating trip when, having had a little too much wine, he tried to embrace the moon's reflection in the water.

The Tang dynasty (618-907) was a golden age for Chinese culture. The poets of the 8th century are widely regarded as the best in Chinese history, and among them, Li Po is probably the most popular in the Western world. He wrote an immense number of poems, most of which are lost. About 2,000 poems have survived, which are famous for their rich imagery and musical quality. Brief and indirect like most Chinese poems, they celebrate the joys of nature, beauty, love, and wine. ■

POEMS

Translated by Kiang Kang-hu and Witter Bynner

A BITTER LOVE

How beautiful she looks, opening the pearly casement,
And how quiet she leans, and how troubled her brow is!
You may see the tears now, bright on her cheek,
But not the man she so bitterly loves.

A SIGH FROM A STAIRCASE OF JADE

Her jade-white staircase is cold with dew;
Her silk soles are wet, she lingered there so long . . .
Behind her closed casement, why is she still waiting,
Watching through its crystal pane the glow of the autumn moon?

ON HEARING CHÜN THE BUDDHIST MONK FROM SHU PLAY HIS LUTE

The monk from Shu with his green silk lute-case,
Walking west down O-mêi Mountain,[1]
Has brought me by one touch of the strings
The breath of pines in a thousand valleys.
5   I hear him in the cleansing brook,
I hear him in the icy bells;
And I feel no change though the mountain darkens
And cloudy autumn heaps the sky.

A SONG OF CH'ANG-KAN

My hair had hardly covered my forehead.
I was picking flowers, playing by my door,
When you, my lover, on a bamboo horse,
Came trotting in circles and throwing green plums.
5   We lived near together on a lane in Ch'ang-kan,[2]
Both of us young and happy-hearted.
. . . At fourteen I became your wife,
So bashful that I dared not smile,
And I lowered my head toward a dark corner
10   And would not turn to your thousand calls;
But at fifteen I straightened my brows and laughed,
Learning that no dust could ever seal our love,
That even unto death I would await you by my post
And would never lose heart in the tower of silent watching.
15   . . . Then when I was sixteen, you left on a long journey
Through the Gorges of Ch'ü-t'ang,[3] of rock and whirling water.
And then came the Fifth-month, more than I could bear,
And I tried to hear the monkeys in your lofty far-off sky.
Your footprints by our door, where I had watched you go,
20   Were hidden, every one of them, under green moss,
Hidden under moss too deep to sweep away.
And the first autumn wind added fallen leaves.
And now, in the Eighth-month, yellowing butterflies
Hover, two by two, in our west-garden grasses. . . .
25   And, because of all this, my heart is breaking
And I fear for my bright cheeks, lest they fade.
. . . Oh, at last, when you return through the three Pa districts,[4]

---

1. **O-mêi Mountain:** a mountain located in Szechwan, a province in southern China.

2. **Ch'ang-kan:** a port on the Yangtse near Nanking in southern China.

3. **Gorges of Ch'ü-t'ang:** famous series of gorges on the Yangtse River.

4. **three Pa districts:** the region in Szechwan province where the speaker's husband is trading.

Send me a message home ahead!
And I will come and meet you and will never mind the distance,
30   All the way to Chang-fêng Sha.[5]

PARTING AT A WINE-SHOP IN NAN-KING

A wind, bringing willow-cotton, sweetens the shop,
And a girl from Wu, pouring wine, urges me to share it
With my comrades of the city who are here to see me off;
And as each of them drains his cup, I say to him in parting,
5   Oh, go and ask this river running to the east
If it can travel farther than a friend's love!

------

5. **Chang-fêng Sha:** "Long Wind Sands," a river port a long way up the Yangtse from Ch'ang-kan.

DISCUSSION QUESTIONS

1. "A Bitter Love" and "A Sigh from a Staircase of Jade" both center on a forsaken woman. How is her pain revealed in each poem? Which of the two treatments do you prefer?

2. In the poem "On Hearing Chün the Buddhist Monk from Shu Play His Lute" what happens to the speaker of the poem when he hears the music of the lute?

3. In "A Song of Ch'ang-kan" the speaker never directly expresses her love for her husband. How is it revealed in the poem?

4. How does Li Po suggest the passage of time in "A Song of Ch'ang-kan"?

5. "Parting at a Wine-Shop in Nan-king" might be described as a bittersweet poem, since the speaker feels a mixture of pleasant and unpleasant sensations. Explain the two kinds of feelings that are blended in this poem.

SUGGESTION FOR WRITING

Pretend that you are the husband who received the message expressed in "A Song of Ch'ang-kan." You would like your wife to know that you are on your way home. Write her a letter communicating your plans and your feelings.

TU FU

(712–770)

Regarded by most Chinese scholars as the greatest poet of China, Tu Fu was raised in a poor but scholarly family. Although he was a bright student, he failed the examination that would have brought him a permanent government job. He was consequently forced to travel most of his life, accepting one position after another as a civil servant. He admired the wandering poet Li Po but discovered that he could not adopt Li Po's carefree lifestyle. Tu Fu suffered considerable financial hardship after the rebellions and civil wars that beset the Tang Dynasty in 755, and he traveled in poverty until his death.

Most of Tu Fu's early poems were written in simple praise of the natural world, but his later poems tended to include elements of satire and expressions of personal suffering. As his life grew more difficult, his poems focused more and more on social protest, with special emphasis on heavy taxation, war, and forced military service. ■

POEMS

Translated by Kiang Kang-hu and Witter Bynner

ON MEETING LI KUÊI-NIEN DOWN THE RIVER

I met you[1] often when you were visiting princes
And when you were playing in noblemen's halls.
. . . Spring passes. . . . Far down the river now,
I find you alone under falling petals.

REMEMBERING MY BROTHERS ON A MOONLIGHT NIGHT

A wanderer hears drums portending battle.
By the first call of autumn from a wild goose at the border,
He knows that the dews tonight will be frost.
. . . How much brighter the moonlight is at home!
5   O my brothers, lost and scattered,
What is life to me without you?
Yet if missives in time of peace go wrong—
What can I hope for during war!

---

1. you: Li Kuêi-nien, a musician and favorite performer of Emperor Hsuan-tsung.

A NIGHT ABROAD

A light wind is rippling at the grassy shore. . . .
Through the night, to my motionless tall mast,
The stars lean down from open space,
And the moon comes running up the river.

5   . . . If only my art might bring me fame
And free my sick old age from office!—
Flitting, flitting, what am I like
But a sand-snipe in the wide, wide world!

ON THE GATE-TOWER AT YO-CHOU

I had always heard of Lake Tung-t'ing—
And now at last I have climbed to this tower.
With Wu country to the east of me and Ch'u[2] to the south,
I can see heaven and earth endlessly floating.

5   . . . But no word has reached me from kin or friends.
I am old and sick and alone with my boat.
North of this wall there are wars and mountains—
And here by the rail how can I help crying?

A HEARTY WELCOME

TO VICE-PREFECT TS'UÊI

North of me, south of me, spring is in flood,
Day after day I have seen only gulls . . .
My path is full of petals—I have swept it for no others.
My thatch gate has been closed—but opens now for you.

5   It's a long way to the market, I can offer you little—
Yet here in my cottage there is old wine for our cups.
Shall we summon my elderly neighbor to join us,
Call him through the fence, and pour the jar dry?

TO MY RETIRED FRIEND WÊI

It is almost as hard for friends to meet
As for the morning and evening stars.
Tonight then is a rare event,
Joining, in the candlelight,

5   Two men who were young not long ago
But now are turning gray at the temples.

---

2. **Wu . . . Ch'u:** formerly, two powerful states in China.

. . . To find that half our friends are dead
Shocks us, burns our hearts with grief.
We little guessed it would be twenty years
10   Before I could visit you again.
When I went away, you were still unmarried;
But now these boys and girls in a row
Are very kind to their father's old friend.
They ask me where I have been on my journey;
15   And then, when we have talked awhile,
They bring and show me wines and dishes,
Spring chives cut in the night-rain
And brown rice cooked freshly a special way.
. . . My host proclaims it a festival,
20   He urges me to drink ten cups—
But what ten cups could make me as drunk
As I always am with your love in my heart?
. . . Tomorrow the mountains will separate us;
After tomorrow—who can say?

NIGHT IN THE WATCH-TOWER

While winter daylight shortens in the elemental scale
And snow and frost whiten the cold-circling night,
Stark sounds the fifth-watch with a challenge of drum and bugle.
5   . . . The stars and the River of Heaven pulse over the three mountains;
I hear women in the distance, wailing after the battle;
I see barbarian fishermen and woodcutters in the dawn.
. . . Sleeping-Dragon, Plunging-Horse, are no generals now, they are dust—
Hush for a moment, O tumult of the world.

A DRAWING OF A HORSE BY GENERAL TS'AO
AT SECRETARY WÊI FÊNG'S HOUSE

Throughout this dynasty no one had painted horses
Like the master-spirit, Prince Chiang-tu—
And then to General Ts'ao through his thirty years of fame
The world's gaze turned, for royal steeds.
5   He painted the late Emperor's luminous white horse.
For ten days the thunder flew over Dragon Lake,
And a pink-agate plate was sent him from the palace—
The talk of the court-ladies, the marvel of all eyes.
The General danced, receiving it in his honored home. . . .
10   After this rare gift, followed rapidly fine silks
From many of the nobles, requesting that his art

Lend a new luster to their screens.
. . . First came the curly-maned horse of Emperor T'ai-tsung,[3]
Then, for the Kuos, a lion-spotted horse . . .
15 But now in this painting I see two horses,
A sobering sight for whosoever knew them.
They are war-horses. Either could face ten thousand.
They make the white silk stretch away into a vast desert.
And the seven others with them are almost as noble. . . .
20 Mist and snow are moving across a cold sky,
And hoofs are cleaving snow-drifts under great trees—
With here a group of officers and there a group of servants.
See how these nine horses all vie with one another—
The high clear glance, the deep firm breath.
25 . . . Who understands distinction? Who really cares for art?
You, Wêi Fêng, have followed Ts'ao; Chih Tun preceded him.
. . . I remember when the late Emperor came toward his Summer
Palace,
The procession, in green-feathered rows, swept from the eastern
sky—
Thirty thousand horses, prancing, galloping,
30 Fashioned, every one of them, like the horses in this picture. . . .
But now the Imperial Ghost receives secret jade from the River-
God,[4]
For the Emperor hunts crocodiles no longer by the streams.
Where you see his Great Gold Tomb, you may hear among the
pines
A bird grieving in the wind that the Emperor's horses are gone.

A SONG OF WAR-CHARIOTS

The war-chariots rattle,
The war-horses whinny.
Each man of you has a bow and a quiver at his belt.
Father, mother, son, wife, stare at you going,
5 Till dust shall have buried the bridge beyond Ch'ang-an.[5]
They run with you, crying, they tug at your sleeves,
And the sound of their sorrow goes up to the clouds;
And every time a bystander asks you a question,
You can only say to him that you have to go.

---

3. **Emperor T'ai-tsung** (tī´ tsùng): one of China's outstanding emperors (597–649), who defeated
her enemies and instituted domestic reforms.

4. **Imperial Ghost . . . River-God:** Since early times, the Chinese have considered jade as a sacred
stone. According to mythology, it was given by the gods to their lords as a symbol of recognition.

5. **Ch'ang-an:** a city in the province of Shensi, in southern China.

10   . . . We remember others at fifteen sent north to guard the river
And at forty sent west to cultivate the camp-farms.
The mayor wound their turbans for them when they started out.
With their turbaned hair white now, they are still at the border,
At the border where the blood of men spills like the sea—

15   And still the heart of Emperor Wu is beating for war.
      . . . Do you know that, east of China's mountains, in two hundred districts
And in thousands of villages, nothing grows but weeds,
And though strong women have bent to the plowing,
East and west the furrows all are broken down?

20   . . . Men of China are able to face the stiffest battle,
But their officers drive them like chickens and dogs.
Whatever is asked of them,
Dare they complain?
For example, this winter

25   Held west of the gate,
Challenged for taxes,
How could they pay?
      . . . We have learned that to have a son is bad luck—
It is very much better to have a daughter

30   Who can marry and live in the house of a neighbor,
While under the sod we bury our boys.
      . . . Go to the Blue Sea, look along the shore
At all the old white bones forsaken—
New ghosts are wailing there now with the old,

35   Loudest in the dark sky of a stormy day.

DISCUSSION QUESTIONS

1. What would you say is the theme or message of the poem entitled "On Meeting Li Kuêi-nien down the River"?

2. In "Remembering My Brothers on a Moonlight Night" how do the season and time of day reinforce the poet's message? What does the speaker mean when he says, "How much brighter the moonlight is at home!"?

3. In "A Night Abroad" and "On the Gate-Tower at Yo-chou" what attitude toward his travels does Tu Fu express? How is the setting in "A Night Abroad" appropriate to the comparison in the last two lines?

4. "A Hearty Welcome" and "To My Retired Friend Wêi" express the pleasures of hospitality, but both poems are weighed down by a tone of sadness as well. What is the cause of the sadness in each poem?

5. What are the reflections of the speaker in "Night in the Watch-Tower"? The last line of the poem is not in the original Chinese version. Why do you think the translator added it? Do you prefer the poem with or without the last line?

6. Tu Fu obviously feels tremendous admiration for the artist in "A Drawing of a Horse by General Ts'ao at Secretary Wêi Fêng's House," but the drawing inspires other thoughts as well. What other reflections are expressed in the poem?

7. In "A Song of War-Chariots" how does the poet indicate that the war has been going on a long time? Why does he conclude that "to have a son is bad luck"?

8. Li Po once remarked that Tu Fu had grown extremely thin and joked that he "must have been suffering from poetry again." In fact, Tu Fu's poetry does express quite a bit of misery and suffering. Judging from the poems you have read, do you think Tu Fu's experiences and subjects are genuinely sad, or does he just like to wallow in pain, as Li Po humorously implies?

SUGGESTION FOR WRITING

Almost all of the poems shown in this section are based on Tu Fu's personal experiences. Imagine that you are Tu Fu and that you keep a journal of your experiences so that you can write poems later. Writing one journal entry for each poem, describe the experience and the thoughts that might have occurred to you as you encountered each situation.

PO CHÜ-I

(772–846)

Born in the province of Hunan to a family of minor officials, Po Chü-i passed the civil service examination and served in various government jobs throughout his life, including Minister of Justice. One of his early positions was as a tax collector, a job that exposed him to the sad plight of poor people. He was deeply concerned about the social problems of his time and wrote poems, both humorous and serious, protesting heavy taxation, court extravagance, the military draft, and general oppression. Believing that literature should be understood by everyone, he wrote his poems in a simple, natural style.

Po Chü-i was an immensely popular and productive writer. He wrote approximately 3,500 poems, most of which have survived. Their survival is due partly to the fact that Po Chü-i himself collected and arranged them. He classified his poetry into four categories: (1) poems with a social purpose, (2) poems of leisure and contentment, (3) poems of sorrow, and (4) miscellaneous poems. Although he wrote poetry on a wide variety of subjects, he claimed that the poems in the first category, those that seek to redress social wrongs, are by far the most important. Po Chü-i referred to them as "compositions written for the purpose of saving the world." ■

POEMS

Translated by Arthur Waley

LAO-TZU

"Those who speak know nothing;
Those who know are silent."
These words, as I am told,
Were spoken by Lao-tzu.[1]
5   If we are to believe that Lao-tzu
    Was himself one who knew,
How comes it that he wrote a book
    Of five thousand words?

---

1. Lao-tzu (lou tsə): Chinese philosopher (c. 604? B.C.), the reputed founder of Taoism, one of the principal Chinese religious philosophies. It teaches that people can acquire happiness by leading a life of simplicity and renouncing material desires.

THE RED COCKATOO

Sent as a present from Annam[2]—
A red cockatoo.
Colored like the peach-tree blossom,
Speaking with the speech of men.
5   And they did to it what is always done
To the learned and eloquent.
They took a cage with stout bars
And shut it up inside.

GOLDEN BELLS

    When I was almost forty
I had a daughter whose name was Golden Bells.
Now it is just a year since she was born;
She is learning to sit and cannot yet talk.
5   Ashamed,—to find that I have not a sage's heart:
I cannot resist vulgar thoughts and feelings.
Henceforward I am tied to things outside myself:
My only reward,—the pleasure I am getting now.
If I am spared the grief of her dying young,
10   Then I shall have the trouble of getting her married.
My plan for retiring and going back to the hills
Must now be postponed for fifteen years!

REMEMBERING GOLDEN BELLS

Ruined and ill,—a man of two score;
    Pretty and guileless,—a girl of three.
Not a boy,—but still better than nothing: [3]
To soothe one's feeling,—from time to time a kiss!
5   There came a day,—they suddenly took her from me;
Her soul's shadow wandered I know not where.
And when I remember how just at the time she died
She lisped strange sounds, beginning to learn to talk,
Then I know that the ties of flesh and blood
10   Only bind us to a load of grief and sorrow.
At last, by thinking of the time before she was born,
By thought and reason I drove the pain away.
Since my heart forgot her, many days have passed
And three times winter has changed to spring.
15   This morning, for a little, the old grief came back,
Because, in the road, I met her foster-nurse.

---

2. Annam: a region in Southeast Asia, now part of Vietnam.

3. Not a boy . . . nothing: In China women were traditionally considered inferior to men.

CHU-CH'ĒN VILLAGE

In Hsü-chou, in the District of Ku-feng
There lies a village whose name is Chu-ch'ēn—
A hundred miles away from the county-town,
Amid fields of hemp and green of mulberry-trees.
5   Click, click goes the sound of the spinning-wheel;
Mules and oxen pack the village-streets.
The girls go drawing the water from the brook;
The men go gathering firewood on the hill.
So far from the town Government affairs are few;
10   So deep in the hills, man's ways are simple.
Though they have wealth, they do not traffic with it;
Though they reach the age,[4] they do not enter the Army.
Each family keeps to its village trade;
Gray-headed, they have never left the gates.

15   Alive, they are the people of Ch'ēn Village;
Dead, they become the dust of Ch'ēn Village.
Out in the fields old men and young
Gaze gladly, each in the other's face.
In the whole village there are only two clans;
20   Age after age Chus have married Ch'ēns.
Near or distant, they have kinsmen in every house;
Young or old, they have friends wherever they go.
On white wine and roasted fowl they fare
At joyful meetings more than "once a week."
25   While they are alive, they have no distant partings;
To choose a wife they go to a neighbor's house.
When they are dead,—no distant burial;
Round the village graves lie thick.
They are not troubled either about life or death;
30   They have no anguish either of body or soul.
And so it happens that they live to a ripe age
And great-great-grandsons are often seen.

I was born in the Realms of Etiquette;
In early years, unprotected and poor.
35   Alone, I learnt to distinguish between Evil and Good;
Untutored, I toiled at bitter tasks.
The World's Law honors Learning and Fame;
Scholars prize marriages and Caps.
With these fetters I gyved my own hands;
40   Truly I became a much-deceived man.
At ten years old I learnt to read books;
At fifteen, I knew how to write prose.
At twenty I was made a Bachelor of Arts;

---

4. the age: the age for being drafted into military service.

At thirty I became a Censor at the Court.
45 Above, the duty I owe to Prince and parents;
Below, the ties that bind me to wife and child.
The support of my family, the service of my country—
For these tasks my nature is not apt.
I reckon the time that I first left my home;
50 From then till now,—fifteen Springs!
My lonely boat has thrice sailed to Ch'u;
Four times through Ch'in my lean horse has passed.
I have walked in the morning with hunger in my face;
I have lain at night with a soul that could not rest.
55 East and West I have wandered without pause,
Hither and thither like a cloud astray in the sky.
In the civil-war my old home was destroyed;
Of my flesh and blood many are scattered and lost.
  North of the River, and South of the River—
60 In both lands are the friends of all my life;
Life-friends whom I never see at all,—
Whose deaths I hear of only after the lapse of years.
Sad at morning, I lie on my bed till dusk;
Weeping at night, I sit and wait for dawn.
65 The fire of sorrow has burnt my heart's core;
The frost of trouble has seized my hair's roots.
In such anguish has my whole life passed;
Long I have envied the people of Ch'ēn Village.

DISCUSSION QUESTIONS

1. Who are the targets of satire in "Lao-tzu" and "The Red Cockatoo"? Which attack do you consider more serious, and why?

2. In the poems "Golden Bells" and "Remembering Golden Bells" what kind of a parent does Po Chü-i seem to be? How does he try to banish the pain he feels after his daughter's death?

3. What is the poet's attitude toward the place he describes in "Chu-ch'ēn Village"? What does the village seem to represent to him?

4. How is the life of the poet different from the life of the villagers in Chu-ch'ēn Village?

SUGGESTION FOR WRITING

The Welcoming Committee of Chu-ch'ēn Village has appointed you to create materials for the new residents of the community. Design and write a pamphlet that will present the features of Chu-ch'ēn and the special benefits of living there. Divide your pamphlet into categories with separate headings.

LU HSÜN

(1881–1936)

A pioneer in modern fiction writing, Lu Hsün was raised in an impoverished but educated family. He received a good education and then attended medical school, but he eventually abandoned his plans to become a doctor. Moving to Beijing, he dedicated himself to teaching school and serving in the Ministry of Education. While he was teaching, Lu Hsün began writing fiction and became a founding member of several leftist organizations, including League of Left-Wing Writers, China Freedom League, and League for the Defense of Civil Rights. In 1918 he published a short story entitled "A Madman's Diary," which appeared in a progressive magazine of the time. This story,

probably the first Chinese story written in the Western tradition, was enormously successful, and his literary career was launched.

Lu Hsün's stories are clear and compact tales that tend to dramatize the rejected members of traditional Chinese society and the indifference of their fellow humans. He sought to modernize literature by replacing the formal, classical style of prose with the language of the common people. He avoided traditional omniscient narration and replaced it with a single narrator through whose eyes the story is filtered. Lu Hsün's best-known stories are collected in two volumes, *A Call to Arms* (1923) and *Hesitation* (1926). ■

THE WIDOW

Translated by Wang Chi-chen

The year-end according to the old calendar is, after all, more like what a year-end should be, for the holiday spirit is not only reflected in the life of the people, but seems to pervade the atmosphere itself. Frequent flashes light up the heavy, gray evening clouds, followed by the crisp report of firecrackers set off in honor of the kitchen god.[1] Those fired in the immediate neighborhood explode, of course, with a louder noise, and before the deafening sound has ceased ringing in one's ears, the air is filled with the acrid aroma of sulphuric smoke. On such an evening I returned for a visit to my native village, Luchen. As we no longer had a house there, I stayed with His Honor Lu the Fourth. He was my kin—my Uncle Four, as he was one generation above me—and a very moral and righteous old graduate. He had not changed much since my previous visit; he had grown a little older, but he did not yet have a beard. After we had exchanged greetings, he remarked that I was stouter, and immediately

---

1. **kitchen god:** in Chinese mythology a household god who annually reported the behavior of every member of the family to heaven.

thereafter launched into a tirade against the reform movement. I knew, however, that his tirade was not directed against me but against the ancient reformers of the nineties, such as K'ang Yu-wei. In any case we could not be said to understand each other, and I was left alone in the study shortly afterwards.

I got up very late the next day. After the midday meal I went out to call on friends and relatives. On the third day I did the same thing. None of them had changed much, they were merely a little older. All were busy with the preparations for the Invocation of Blessings, the most solemn and elaborate ceremony of the year, at which they offered the most generous sacrifices to the God of Blessings and prayed for good luck for the coming year. Chickens and ducks were killed and pork was bought at the butcher's. Carefully washed by women (whose hands and arms—some adorned with silver bracelets—became red from long immersions in the water), and then boiled and studded with chopsticks, they were offered with candles and incense in the early hour of the fifth watch. Only the male members of the family participated in the ceremony, which was always concluded with firecrackers. Every year it was like this in families that could afford it, and so it was this year.

The overcast sky grew darker and darker, and in the afternoon it began to snow. The dancing snowflakes, as large as plum flowers, the smoke from burning incense and from the chimneys, and the bustle of the people all gave Luchen a festive air. When I returned to Uncle Four's study, the rooftops were white, making the room lighter than usual at that hour. I could make out very clearly the large shou (longevity) character on a scroll hung on the wall, a rubbing based on what was supposed to be the actual handwriting of the Taoist immortal Ch'en T'uan. One of the side scrolls had come off and lay loosely rolled up on the long table against the wall; the one still hanging on the wall expressed the sentiment "Peace comes with understanding." I strolled over to the desk by the window and looked over the books. There were only a few odd volumes of the K'ang Hsi Dictionary and an annotated edition of the *Analects*.[2]

I decided that I must leave the next day, whatever happened. What had depressed me most was a meeting with Sister Hsiang-lin the day before. I encountered her in the afternoon as I was returning home along the riverbank after visiting some friends in the eastern part of the village, and by the direction of her vacant stare I knew that she was heading for me. Of the people that I had seen at Luchen on this visit no one had changed as much as she. Her gray hair of five years ago had turned entirely white; she was not at all like a woman of only forty. Her face was intolerably drawn and thin; it had lost its sad and sorrowful aspect and was now as expressionless as if carved of wood. Only an occasional movement of her eyes indicated that she was still a living creature. She held in one hand a bamboo basket containing a chipped and empty bowl; with the other hand,

---

2. *Analects:* a collection of the teachings and maxims of Confucius (551?–478 B.C.), Chinese philosopher and moral teacher.

she supported herself with a bamboo stick, a little split at the lower end. She had evidently become a beggar.

I stopped, expecting her to ask for money.

"Have you come back?" she asked.

"Yes."

"I am very glad. You are a scholar, and you have been to the outside world and learned of many things. I want to ask you about something." Her lusterless eyes suddenly lighted up as she advanced a few steps towards me, lowered her voice, and said in a very earnest and confidential manner, "It is this: is there another life after this one?"

I was taken aback by the unexpectedness of the question; the wild look in her eyes, which were fixed on mine, gave me a creepy sensation on my back and made me feel more uncomfortable than I used to at school when an examination was sprung upon us, with the teacher watching vigilantly by our side. I had never concerned myself with the afterlife. How was I to answer her now? Most people here believe in the survival of the soul, I thought rapidly as I considered an answer, but this woman seemed to have her doubts. Perhaps it was a matter of hope with her, the hope that there was an afterlife and that the afterlife would be a better one than this. Why should I add to the unhappiness of this miserable woman? For her sake I had better say that there was another life after this one.

"Maybe there is . . . I think," I said haltingly and without conviction.

"Then there would also be a hell?"

"Oh! Hell?" I was again taken unawares and so I temporized, "Hell?— It would seem logical . . . though it may not necessarily exist . . . but who cares about such things?"

"Then we will meet members of our family after death?"

"Er, er, do we meet them?" I then realized that I was still a very ignorant man and that no amount of temporizing and cogitation would enable me to stand the test of three questions. I became less and less sure of myself and wished to recant all that I had said. "That . . . but really, I cannot say. I cannot really say whether souls survive or not."

Before she could ask any more questions, I fled back to Uncle Four's house very much agitated in spirit. I told myself that my answer to her questions might lead to something unfortunate and that I should be held responsible for what might happen. She probably felt lonely and unhappy at a time when others were celebrating; but was that all, or had she formed a definite plan of action? Then I laughed at myself for taking such a trivial incident so seriously, for pondering upon it and analyzing it. The psychologists would undoubtedly call such a morbid interest or fear pathological. Besides, had I not explicitly said "I cannot really say," thus annulling all my answers and relieving myself of all responsibility?

"I cannot really say" is a very useful sentence. Inexperienced youths are often rash enough to give answers to the difficult problems of life and prescribe remedies for others, and thus lay themselves open to blame when things go wrong. If, however, they qualify their statements by concluding them with "I cannot really say," they will assure themselves of a safe and happy life. I then realized the indispensability of this sentence, indispensable even when one is talking with a beggarwoman.

But my uneasiness persisted; I kept recalling the meeting with a presentiment of evil. On this dark, heavy, snowy afternoon in that dreary study my uneasiness became stronger. I felt I had better go away and spend a day at the county seat. I recalled Fu-hsing-lou's excellent shark's fin cooked in clear broth at only a dollar a plate, and wondered if the price had gone up. Although my friends of former days had scattered hither and yon, I must not fail to feast upon this delicacy, even if I had to eat by myself. Whatever happens, I must leave this place tomorrow, I repeated to myself.

Because I have often seen things happen which I had hoped would not happen, which I had told myself might not necessarily happen, but which had a way of happening just the same, I was very much afraid that it would be so on this occasion. And surely something did happen, for towards evening I overheard a discussion going on in the inner courtyard. Presently it stopped, and after a silence I distinguished the voice of Uncle Four.

"Of course a thing like that would choose of all times a time like this."

I was first puzzled and then felt uncomfortable, for the remark sounded as if it might have something to do with me. I looked out the door but did not see anyone that I could ask. Not until the hired man came in to replenish my tea toward suppertime did I have an opportunity to make inquiries.

"With whom was His Honor Four angry a little while ago?" I asked.

"Who else but Sister Hsiang-lin?" he answered very simply.

"Sister Hsiang-lin? What did she do?" I hurriedly pursued.

"She died."

"Died?" My heart sank and I almost jumped. My face must have changed color. But the man did not raise his head and so did not notice it. I calmed myself and continued:

"When did she die?"

"When? Last night or early this morning. I can't really say."

"What did she die of?"

"What did she die of? Why, what else would it be if not poverty?" the man answered in a matter of course way and went out without ever raising his head to look at me.

My terror was transient, for I realized that, since that which was to come to pass had come to pass, there was no longer need for me to worry about my responsibility. Gradually I regained my composure; a sense of regret and disquiet only occasionally intruded. Supper was served, with Uncle Four keeping me company. I wanted to find out more about Sister Hsianglin, but I knew that though he had read that "Ghosts and spirits are only the manifestations of the two cardinal principles of nature," he was still subject to many taboos; that such topics as sickness and death should be carefully avoided at a time when New Year blessings were about to be asked; and that if I must satisfy my curiosity, I should resort to some well-considered euphemism. As I unfortunately knew no such euphemisms, I withheld the question I was several times on the point of asking. From the look of displeasure on his face I began to imagine it quite possible that he considered me a "thing like that" for coming to bother him at such a time; thereupon I hastened to set him at ease and told him that I was going to leave Luchen the following day. He did not show much warmth in urging me to stay. Thus we dragged through supper.

Winter days are short at best, and, with snow falling, night soon enveloped the village. Everyone was busy by the lamplight, but outdoors it was quiet and still. Falling upon a thick mattress of snow, the flakes seemed to swish-swish, making one feel all the more lonely and depressed. Sitting alone under the yellow light of the vegetable-oil lamp, I thought of the fate of the poor, forlorn woman who had been cast into the garbage dump like a discarded toy. Hitherto she had continued to remind people of her miserable existence in the garbage dump, much to the surprise and wonder of those who have reason to find life worth living. Now she had at last been swept away clean by the Unpredictable. Whether souls continue to exist or not I do not know, but I did know that at least one who had no reason to find life worth living was at last no longer living and that those who looked upon her as an eyesore no longer had to look at her. It was a good thing, whether looked at from her point of view or from that of others. As I listened to the swish-swishing of the snowflakes outside and pondered along this line of thought I began to take comfort and to feel better.

And I began to put together the fragments that I had heard about her until her story became a fairly coherent whole.

Sister Hsiang-lin was not a native of Luchen. One year in the early part of winter they needed a new maid at Uncle Four's and the middlewoman, old Mrs. Wei, had brought her. She wore a black skirt, a blue, lined coat and light blue vest, and her hair was tied with white strings as a sign of mourning. She was about twenty-six years old, of a dark yellow complexion, with a faint suggestion of color in her cheeks. Old Mrs. Wei called her Sister Hsiang-lin, said that she was a neighbor of her mother's and that as her husband had recently died she had come out to seek employment. Uncle Four frowned and Aunt Four guessed the cause; he did not like the idea of widows. But the woman had regular features and large, strong hands and feet. She was quiet and docile and it appeared that she would make an industrious and faithful servant. Aunt Four kept her in spite of Uncle Four's frown. During the trial period she worked all day as though unhappy without employment. She was strong and could do everything that a man could do. On the third day they decided to keep her, at a monthly wage of 500 *cash*.[3]

---

3. *cash:* The Chinese traditional currency, known as cash to foreigners, consisted of copper coins. After Europeans trade began, Mexican silver dollars were used for major transactions. One dollar was worth a thousand cash.

Everyone called her Sister Hsiang-lin; no one asked her surname, but since the middlewoman was from Weichiashan and said that she was a neighbor of her mother's, her name was probably Wei. She was not talkative and spoke only in answer to questions, and that rather briefly. Not until after some ten days did it gradually become known that she had at home a stern mother-in-law, a brother-in-law about ten years old and able to go out to gather fuel, and that her husband who had died in the spring was ten years younger than she and also made his living by cutting firewood. This was all that was known about her.

The days went by quickly and she showed no signs of losing her initial industry; she never complained about her fare or spared her strength. People all talked about the woman help in the house of His Honor Lu who was more capable and industrious than a man. At the year-end she did all the cleaning, sweeping, and killed the chickens and ducks and cooked them; it was actually not necessary to hire temporary help. She seemed happy too; her face grew fuller and traces of smiles appeared around the corners of her mouth.

But shortly after the New Year she returned one day, pale and agitated, from washing rice at the river; she said she had seen a man who looked like an elder cousin-in-law loitering in the distance on the opposite bank, and she feared he was watching her. Aunt Four questioned her but could get no more out of her. When he heard of this incident, Uncle Four knitted his brows and said, "I do not like it. I am afraid that she ran away from home."

As a matter of fact, she had come away without her mother-in-law's permission, and it was not long before this supposition proved to be true.

About ten days later, when the incident had been almost forgotten, old Mrs. Wei suddenly appeared with a woman about thirty years old, whom she introduced as Sister Hsiang-lin's mother-in-law. Though dressed like a woman from the hill villages, she was self-composed and capable of speech. She apologized for her intrusion and said that she had come to take her daughter-in-law home to help with the spring chores, as only she and her young son were at home.

"What else can we do since her mother-in-law wants her back?" Uncle Four said.

Therefore, her wages, which amounted to 1,750 cash and of which she had not spent a penny, were handed over to the mother-in-law. The woman took Sister Hsiang-lin's clothes, expressed her thanks, and went away.

Sister Hsiang-lin was not present during this transaction and it did not occur to Aunt and Uncle Four to summon her. It was not until toward noon when she began to feel hungry that Aunt Four suddenly remembered that Sister Hsiang-lin had gone out to wash rice and wondered what had happened to her.

"Aiya! Where is the rice?" she exclaimed. "Did not Sister Hsiang-lin go out to wash the rice?"

She began searching for the washing basket, first in the kitchen, then in the courtyard, then in the bedroom, but there was no trace of it. Uncle Four looked outside the gate but did not see it either, and it was not until he went to the river that he saw the basket resting peacefully on the bank, a head of green vegetable beside it.

Then he learned from eyewitnesses what had happened. A covered boat had been moored in the river all morning, but no one paid any attention to it at the time. When Sister Hsiang-lin came out to wash rice, two men that looked like people from the hills jumped out, seized her as she bent over her task and dragged her into the boat. Sister Hsiang-lin uttered a few cries but was soon silent, probably because she was gagged. Then two women embarked, one a stranger and the other old Mrs. Wei. Some thought that they did see Sister Hsiang-lin lying bound on the bottom of the boat.

"The rascals! But . . . ," Uncle Four said.

That day Aunt Four cooked the midday dinner herself, while her son Niu-erh tended the fire.

Old Mrs. Wei returned after the midday dinner.

"What do you mean by your outrageous behavior? And you have the audacity to come back to see us!" Aunt Four said vehemently over the dishwashing. "You brought her here yourself, and then you conspire with them to kidnap her, causing such a scandal. What will people say? Do you want to make a laughingstock of us?"

"Aiya, aiya! I was duped, really, and I have come back to explain. She came to me and asked me to find a place for her. How was I to know that her mother-in-law knew nothing of it? I beg your forgiveness. It was all my fault, old and weak woman that I am. I should have been more careful. Fortunately, your house has been noted for its generosity and I know you would not return measure for measure with people like us. I shall most certainly find you a good maid to atone for myself."

Thus the episode was closed and shortly afterwards forgotten.

Only Aunt Four, who had difficulty in finding a satisfactory servant, sometimes mentioned Sister Hsiang-lin, whose successors either were lazy or complained of their food, or both. "I wonder what has become of her," Aunt Four would say, hoping that she might come back again. By the beginning of the following year she gave up this hope.

Toward the end of the first month, however, old Mrs. Wei came to offer her New Year's greetings. She was slightly intoxicated with wine and said at she had been late in coming because she had visited her mother at Weichiashan for a few days. The conversation naturally turned to Sister Hsiang-lin.

"That one. She has entered her lucky years," old Mrs. Wei said with pleasure. "When her mother-in-law came to get her, she was already promised to Huo Lao-lui of Huochiatsun and so a few days after her return she was put into a wedding-sedan and carried away."

"Aiya! what a mother-in-law!" Aunt Four said, surprised.

"Aiya! you talk exactly like a lady of a great family. Among us poor people in the hills this is nothing. She has a younger brother-in-law who had to get married. If they did not marry her off where were they to get the money for his wedding? Her mother-in-law was a capable and clever one. She knew how to go about things. She married her off into the hills. In the village, she would not have gotten much for Sister Hsiang-lin, but because there are not many who will marry into the hills, she got 80,000 cash. Now her second son is married. She spent only 50,000 and had a clear profit of over 10,000 after expenses. See what a good stroke of business that was?"

"But how could Sister Hsiang-lin ever consent to such a thing?"

"What is there to consent or not to consent? Any bride will make a scene; but all one has to do is bind her up, stuff her into the sedan, carry her to the groom's house, put the bridal hat on her, assist her through the ceremony, put her into the bridal chamber, shut the door—and leave the rest to the groom. But Sister Hsiang-lin was different and unusually difficult. People said it was probably because she had worked in the house of a scholar that she acted differently from the common people. Tai-tai,[4] we have seen all sorts of them, these 'again' women; we have seen the kind that weep and cry, the kind that attempt suicide, and the kind that spoil the wedding ceremony by upsetting and breaking things. But Sister Hsiang-lin was worse than any of these. I was told that she bellowed and cursed all the way, so that she had lost her voice when she reached the Huo village. Dragging her out of the sedan, three men were not enough to hold her through the ceremony. Once they loosed their hold on her for a moment, and—Amitofo—she dashed her head against the corner of the wedding table, and gave herself a big gash. The blood flowed so freely that two handfuls of incense ash and a bandage could not stop it. She continued to curse after she had been dragged into the wedding chamber and shut in with her man. Aiya-ya, I never . . ." she shook her head, lowered her eyes and was silent for a moment.

"And later?" Aunt Four asked.

"It was said that she did not get up all the next day," she answered, raising her eyes.

"And after that?"

"Well, she got up eventually and by the end of the year she gave birth to a boy. Someone happened to visit the Huo village while I was at my mother's and said on his return that he had seen the mother and the child and that they were both healthy and plump. There is no mother-in-law above her and her man is strong and a willing worker. They have their own house. Ai-ai, she has entered her lucky years."

After that Aunt Four no longer mentioned Sister Hsiang-lin.

But in the fall of one year—it must have been two years after the news of Sister Hsiang-lin's good luck was brought by Mrs. Wei—she reappeared in the courtyard of Uncle Four's house. She put on the table a round basket in the form of a water chestnut and outside under the eaves

4. **Tai-tai:** mistress. [Chinese]

she left her bundle of bedding. She wore, as on her first visit, white hair-strings, black skirt, blue, lined coat, light blue vest, and her skin was dark yellow as before, but without any trace of color in her cheeks. Instead, traces of tears could be observed around her eyes, which were not as alive as before. Old Mrs. Wei again accompanied her and made this recital to Aunt Four:

"This is truly what is called 'Heaven has unpredictable storms.' Her man was a strong and sturdy one. Who would ever have thought that he would die of influenza? He had gotten well, but he ate a bowl of cold rice and it came back again. Fortunately she had her son and she was capable, could cut firewood, pick tea, or raise silkworms. She was managing all right. Who would ever have thought that her child would be carried off by a wolf? Spring was nearing its end and yet a wolf appeared in the village. Who would have thought of such a thing? Now she is alone. Her elder brother-in-law took possession of her house and put her out. She is now at the end of her road and has no other way except to appeal to her old mistress. Now she has no entanglements and as tai-tai happens to be in need of a new maid I have brought her. I think as she is familiar with things here she would be much better than a strange hand."

"I was a fool, really," Sister Hsiang-lin raised her lusterless eyes and said. "I knew that the wild beasts came down to the village to seek food when they couldn't find anything in the hills during the snow season, but I did not know they would come down in the spring. I got up early and opened the door. I gave a basket of beans to our Ah Mao and told him to sit on the gate sill and peel them. He was an obedient child and did everything I told him. He went out and I went behind the house to cut wood and wash rice. After putting the rice in the pot, I wanted to put the beans over it to steam. I called Ah Mao but he did not answer. I went out and looked. I saw beans spilled all over the ground but could not see our Ah Mao. He never went out to play at the neighbors' but I went and looked for him. I did not find him. I was frightened and asked people to go out and search for him. In the afternoon they found one of his shoes in the bramble. They all said there was no hope, that the wolf must have got him. They went into the bush and sure enough they found him lying in the grass, all his insides gone, his hand still holding on tightly to the handle of the basket . . ." She broke off sobbing.

Aunt Four hesitated at first, but her eyes reddened after hearing the story. Then she told Sister Hsiang-lin to take the basket and bundle to the maid's room. Old Mrs. Wei sighed with relief, and Sister Hsiang-lin seemed to feel better than when she arrived. As she was familiar with the house, she went and set her things in order without being directed, and thenceforward she again became a maidservant at Luchen.

And everybody called her Sister Hsiang-lin as before.

But this time her fortune had changed considerably. Two or three days later her employers realized that her hands were not as clever and efficient as formerly, her memory failed, her deathlike face never showed the shadow of a smile. Aunt Four could not conceal her displeasure. Uncle

Four had frowned as usual when she came, but made no protest as he knew how difficult it was to find a satisfactory servant; he only cautioned Aunt Four, saying that though such people were a pitiable lot, yet she was after all a bane against morality, and that it was all right for her to help in ordinary tasks but she must not touch anything in connection with the ancestral sacrifices. These Aunt Four must prepare herself, else they would be unclean and the ancestors would not touch them.

Preparation of the ancestral sacrifices was the most important event in Uncle Four's house and Sister Hsiang-lin used to be busiest at such a time. Now she had nothing to do. When the table was placed in the center of the hall with a curtain in front of it, she started to arrange the wine cups and chopsticks as she used to do.

"Sister Hsiang-lin, please leave those things alone. I will arrange them," Aunt Four hastened to say.

She drew back her hands in embarrassment and then went to get the candlesticks.

"Sister Hsiang-lin, leave that alone. I'll get it," Aunt Four again said hastily. After hovering around for a little while, Sister Hsiang-lin withdrew in bewilderment. The only thing she was permitted to do that day was to tend the fire in the kitchen.

People in the village still called her Sister Hsiang-lin, but the tone of their voices was different; they still talked with her, but they were scornful of her. She did not seem to notice the change; she only stared vacantly and recited the story that she could not forget, night or day—

"I was a fool, really . . ." Her tears would flow and her voice grow tremulous.

It was a very effective story; men would stop smiling and walk away in confusion; women not only seemed to forgive her and to banish the look of scorn on their faces, but shed tears with her. Some older women, not having heard her own recital, would come to her and listen to her until her voice broke, when they would let fall the tears that had been gradually accumulating in their eyes, heave some sighs and go away satisfied. She was their chief topic of conversation.

Sister Hsiang-lin continued to repeat her story and often attracted three or five listeners. But the story soon became familiar to everyone, and after a while even the kindest and most patient of old ladies ceased to shed any tears. Still later almost everyone in the village could recite her story, and was bored by it.

"I was really a fool, really," she would begin.

"Yes, you knew that wild beasts came down to the village to seek food only when they cannot find anything in the hills," people would thus stop her and walk away.

She would stand gaping and staring for a while and then walk away, a little embarrassed. Still, she tried to bring up the story of Ah Mao by some ruse—a basket, beans, or some other children. For instance, if she saw a child two or three years old, she would say, "Ai-ai, if our Ah Mao were alive he would be as big as that . . ."

The children were afraid of her and of the look in her eyes, and they would tug at their mothers' coats and urge them to go away. And thus Sister Hsiang-lin would be left alone to wander off by herself. Soon people caught on to her new trick; they would forestall her when there were children around by saying, "Sister Hsiang-lin, if your Ah Mao were alive, would he not be as big as that?"

She might not have realized that her sorrow, after having been carefully chewed and relished for so long, had now become insipid dregs, only fit to spit out; but she was able to sense the indifference and the sarcasm in the question and to realize that there was no need of her answering it.

The New Year festivities last a long time in Luchen and begin to occupy people after the twentieth of the last month of the year. At Uncle Four's house they had to hire a temporary man helper, but the work was too much for him and another woman was hired. But she, Liu-ma, was a devout vegetarian and would not kill the chickens and ducks; she only washed dishes. Sister Hsiang-lin had nothing to do but tend the fire. She sat and watched Liu-ma wash the dishes. A light snow was falling outside.

"Ai-ai, I was really a fool," Sister Hsiang-lin soliloquized after looking at the sky, sighing.

"Sister Hsiang-lin, there you go again," Liu-ma looked at her impatiently. "Let me ask you, did you not get your scar when you dashed your head against the table that time?"

"Mmm," she answered evasively.

"Let me ask you, why did you finally give in?"

"I?"

"Yes, you. I think you must have been willing. Otherwise . . ."

"Ah-ah, but you do not know how strong he was."

"I do not believe it. I do not believe that a strong woman like you could not resist him. You must have finally become willing though you now blame it on his strength."

"Ah-ah you . . . you should have tried to resist him yourself," she said with a smile.

Liu-ma laughed, her wrinkled face shriveling up like a peach stone; her tiny dry eyes shifted from the scar on Sister Hsiang-lin's forehead to the latter's eyes, discomforting her and causing her to gather up her smile and turn her eyes to look at the snowflakes.

"Sister Hsiang-lin, you have miscalculated badly," Liu-ma said mysteriously. "You should have resisted to the end, or dashed your head until you were dead. That would have been the thing to do. But now? You lived with your second man only two years and got for it a monstrous evil name. Just think, when you get to the lower world, those two ghost husbands will fight over you. Whom would they give you to? The Great King Yenlo[5] could only have you sawed in two and divided between them . . ."

Sister Hsiang-lin was terrified: this was something that she had not heard about in the hills.

---

5. **King Yenlo:** in Chinese mythology lord of the fifth hell (there are eighteen) and infernal judge.

"I think you should atone for your crime while there is still time. Donate a doorsill to the T'u-ti temple as your effigy, so that you might be trampled upon by a thousand men's feet and straddled over by ten thousand men's legs as atonement for your great sin. Then you may escape the tortures in store for you."

Sister Hsiang-lin did not say anything then, but she must have been deeply affected. The next day she got up with black rings around her eyes. After breakfast she went to the T'u-ti temple on the western edge of the village to donate the doorsill. At first the keeper would not accept the gift, but her tears and entreaties finally prevailed and he accepted the offer at the price of 12,000 cash.

She had not spoken with anyone for a long time, for she had become an avoided object because of the tiresome story about her Ah Mao; nevertheless, after her conversation with Liu-ma—which seemed to have been broadcast immediately—people began to take a new interest in her and would try to coax her to talk. As to the subject, it was naturally a new one, centering upon the scar on her forehead.

"Sister Hsiang-lin, let me ask you, why did you finally give in?" one would say.

"Ai, too bad you broke your head for nothing," another would echo, looking at her scar.

From their faces and voices she gathered that they were making fun of her; she only stared vacantly and said nothing, later she did not even turn her head. She tightened her mouth and went about her duties—sweeping, washing vegetables and rice, running errands, bearing the scar of her shame. In about a year, she got all the wages that Aunt Four had kept for her, changed them into twelve Mexican dollars, asked for leave to go to the western edge of the village. She soon returned and told Aunt Four that she had donated her doorsill at the T'u-ti temple. She appeared to be in better spirits than she had been for a long time and her eyes showed signs of life.

She worked unusually hard at the ancestral sacrifices at the winter solstice. After watching Aunt Four fill the dishes with the sacrificial things and Ah Niu place the table in the center of the hall, she went confidently to get the wine cups and chopsticks. "Don't you bother, Sister Hsiang-lin!" Aunt Four said in a panicky voice.

She withdrew her hands as if from a hot iron, her face black and pale like burnt coal. She did not try to get the candlesticks. She only stood as if lost, and did not go away until Uncle Four came in to light the incense sticks and dismissed her. This time the change in her was extraordinary. Not only were her eyes sunken the next day, but her wits seemed to have left her entirely. She became terribly afraid, not only of the night and dark corners, but also of people, including her own employers. She would sneak about, trembling like a mouse that had ventured out of its hole in daylight; or she would sit abstractedly like a wooden idol. In less than half a year, her hair became gray, her memory grew worse and worse, until she sometimes forgot to go out to wash rice in the river.

"What is the matter with Sister Hsiang-lin? We should not have kept her in the first place," Aunt Four would say sometimes, in her hearing, as a warning to her.

But she continued in the same condition, and showed no signs of recovering her wits. They began to think of sending her away, to tell her to go back to old Mrs. Wei. When I was still living at Luchen they used to talk of sending her away, but they only talked about it; from what I saw on this visit, it was evident that they did finally carry out their threat. But whether she became a beggar immediately after leaving Uncle Four's house, or whether she first went to old Mrs. Wei and then became a beggar, I could not say.

I was awakened by loud explosions of firecrackers close by. As I blinked at the yellow lamp flame about the size of a bean I heard the crackling of a string of firecrackers—the New Year's ceremony was on at Uncle Four's and I knew that it must be about the fifth watch. With half-shut eyes I heard dreamily the continued crackling in the distance; it seemed to form a thick cloud of festive sounds in the sky, mingling with the snowflakes and enveloping the entire village. In the arms of this festive sound, I felt carefree and comfortable, and the fears and melancholy I had felt all the previous day and the first part of the night were swept away by this atmosphere of joy and blessedness. I fancied that the gods and sages of heaven above and earth below, drunk and satiated with incense and sacrifices of wine and meat, were reeling unsteadily in the sky, ready to confer unlimited blessings upon the inhabitants of Luchen.

DISCUSSION QUESTIONS

1. The narrator of the story says that his uncle is "very moral and righteous." Do you agree with his assessment of Uncle Four? Explain your reasoning.

2. Who is the narrator of the story? What kind of a person is he? How does he differ from the other villagers?

3. What is the purpose of the rather long introduction before the story of Sister Hsiang-lin begins?

4. Why is Sister Hsiang-lin eager to know about the afterlife? What motivates the narrator to answer her questions as he does? Do you think his answers contribute to her death?

5. The story begins and ends with the New Year celebrations. Why do you think the story was placed in this particular time setting?

SUGGESTION FOR WRITING

Imagine that you are a journalist who has observed the recent events in the Chinese village of Luchen and knows all the details of Sister Hsiang-lin's story. You have been asked to write an article on the position of women in this part of China. Using plenty of concrete details, present your observations on this subject.

MAO TUN
(1896–1981)

One of China's greatest realistic novelists, Mao Tun, whose real name was Shen Te-hung, was born into a family of scholars and attended Beijing University. He began his career as a proofreader and editor in Shanghai and eventually took control of a literary magazine. At that point he began promoting a new kind of fiction that aimed at impersonal, objective narration. His first important work of fiction was entitled *The Eclipse,* a trilogy of novels that depicted revolutionary intellectuals. In 1930 Mao Tun helped found the League of Left-Wing Writers, an organization that encouraged literature featuring realistic portrayals of working-class people. Shortly afterward he wrote his most famous novel, *Shanghai in Twilight,* which presented different classes of Chinese society and showed them coming into conflict.

Mao Tun continued his literary activities until the establishment of the Chinese Communist Party in 1949, when he devoted himself full time to politics. He served on various committees and became Minister of Culture for several years. He even served as secretary to Chairman Mao Tse-tung, the leader of the Communist Party. His last significant novel, *Corruption,* depicts wartime terror in Chungking. ■

SPRING SILKWORMS
Translated by Wang Chi-chen

Tung Pao sat on a rock along the bank of the canal with his back to the sun, his long-stemmed pipe leaning against his side. The sun was already strong, though the period of Clear Bright[1] had just set in, and felt as warm as a brazier of fire. It made him hotter than ever to see the Shaohing trackers pulling hard at their lines, large drops of sweat falling from their brows in spite of their open cotton shirts. Tung Pao was still wearing his winter coat; he had not foreseen the sudden warm spell and had not thought of redeeming his lighter garment from the pawnshop.

"Even the weather is not what it used to be!" muttered Tung Pao, spitting into the canal.

There were not many passing boats, and the occasional ripples and eddies that broke the mirrorlike surface of the greenish water and blurred the placid reflections of the mud banks and neat rows of mulberry trees never lasted long. Presently one could make out the trees again, swaying

---

1. Clear Bright: the spring season.

from side to side at first like drunken men and then becoming motionless and clear and distinct as before, their fistlike buds already giving forth tiny, tender leaves. The fields were still cracked and dry, but the mulberry trees had already come into their own. There seemed to be no end to the rows along the banks and there was another extensive grove back of Tung Pao. They seemed to thrive on the sunlit warmth, their tender leaves growing visibly each second.

Not far from where Tung Pao sat there was a gray white building, used by the cocoon buyers during the season but now quite deserted. There were rumors that the buyers would not come at all this year because the Shanghai factories had been made idle by the war, but Tung Pao would not believe this. He had lived sixty years and had yet to see the time when mulberry leaves would be allowed to wither on the trees or be used for fodder, unless of course if the eggs should not hatch, as has sometimes happened according to the unpredictable whims of Heaven.

"How warm it is for this time of the year!" Tung Pao thought again, hopefully, because it was just after a warm spring like this almost two score years ago that there occurred one of the best silk crops ever known. He remembered it well: it was also the year of his marriage. His family fortune was then on the upward swing. His father worked like a faithful old ox, knew and did everything; his grandfather, who had been a Taiping captive[2] in his time, was still vigorous in spite of his great age. At that time too, the house of Chen had not yet begun its decline, for though the old squire had already died, the young squire had not yet taken to opium smoking. Tung Pao had a vague feeling that the fortunes of the Chens and that of his own family were somehow intertwined, though one was about the richest family in town while his was only well-to-do as peasants went.

Both his grandfather and the old squire had been captives of the Taiping rebels and had both escaped before the rebellion was suppressed. Local legend had it that the old squire had made off with a considerable amount of Taiping gold and that it was this gold which enabled him to go into the silk business and amass a huge fortune. During that time Tung Pao's family flourished too. Year after year the silk crops had been good and in ten years his family had been able to acquire twenty mou[3] of rice land and more than ten mou of mulberry trees. They were the most prosperous family in the village, just as the Chens were the richest in the town.

But gradually both families had declined. Tung Pao no longer had any rice land left and was more than three hundred dollars in debt besides. As for the Chen family, it was long ago "finished." It was said that the reason for their rapid decline was that the ghosts of the Taiping rebels had sued in the courts of the nether world and had been warranted by King Yenlo[4]

---

2. **Taiping captive:** a prisoner of the Taiping rebels. The Taiping Rebellion (1851–1864) was the most important of the revolts in the 1800s against the Manchu dynasty (1644–1912).

3. **mou:** a Chinese land measure, approximately one sixth of an acre.

4. **King Yenlo:** in Chinese mythology lord of the fifth hell (there are eighteen) and infernal judge.

to collect. Tung Pao was inclined to think that there was something to this notion, otherwise why should the young squire suddenly acquire the opium habit? He could not, however, figure out why the fortunes of his own family should have declined at the same time. He was certain that his grandfather did not make away with any Taiping gold. It was true that his grandfather had to kill a Taiping sentinel in making his escape, but had not his family atoned for this by holding services for the dead rebel as long as he could remember? He did not know much about his grandfather, but he knew his father as an honest and hardworking man and could not think of anything he himself had done that should merit the misfortunes that had befallen him. His older son Ah Ssu and his wife were both industrious and thrifty, and his younger son Ah Dou was not a bad sort, though he was flighty at times as all young people were inclined to be.

Tung Pao sadly lifted his brown, wrinkled face and surveyed the scene before him. The canal, the boats, and the mulberry groves on both sides of the canal—everything was much the same as it was two score years ago. But the world had changed: often they lived on nothing but pumpkins, and he was more than three hundred dollars in debt.

Several blasts from a steam whistle suddenly came from around a bend in the canal. Soon a tug swept majestically into view with a string of three boats in tow. The smaller crafts on the canal scurried out of the way of the puffing monster, but soon they were engulfed in the wide wake of the tug and its train and seesawed up and down as the air became filled with the sound of the engine and the odor of oil. Tung Pao watched the tug with hatred in his eyes as it disappeared around the next bend. He had always entertained a deep enmity against such foreign deviltry as steamboats and the like. He had never seen a foreigner himself, but his father told him that the old squire had seen some, that they had red hair and green eyes and walked with straight knees. The old squire had no use for foreigners either and used to say that it was they that had made off with all the money and made everyone poor. Tung Pao had no doubt that the old squire was right. He knew from his own experience that since foreign yarn and cloth and kerosene appeared in town and the steamer in the river, he got less and less for the things that he produced with his own labor and had to pay more and more for the things that he had to buy. It was thus that he became poorer and poorer until now he had none of his rice land that his father had left him and was in debt besides. He did not hate the foreigners without reason! Even among the villagers he was remarkable for the vehemence of his anti-foreign sentiments.

Five years back someone told him that there had been another change in government and that it was the aim of the new government to rescue the people from foreign oppression. Tung Pao did not believe it, for he had noticed on his trips to town that the youngsters who shouted "Down with the foreigners" all wore foreign clothes. He had a suspicion that these youths were secretly in league with the foreigners and only pretended to be their enemies in order to fool honest people like himself. He was even more convinced that he was right when the slogan "Down with the foreigners" was dropped and things became dearer and dearer and the taxes heavier and heavier. Tung Pao was sure that the foreigners had a hand in these things.

The last straw for Tung Pao was that cocoons hatched from foreign eggs should actually sell for ten dollars more a picul.[5] He had always been on friendly terms with his daughter-in-law, but they quarreled on this score. She had wanted to use foreign eggs the year before. His younger son Ah Dou sided with her, and her husband was of the same mind though he did not say much about it. Unable to withstand their pressure, Tung Pao had to compromise at last and allow them to use one sheet of foreign eggs out of three that they decided to hatch this year.

"The world is becoming worse and worse," he said to himself. "After a few years even the mulberry leaves will have to be foreign! I am sick of it all!"

The weather continued warm and the fingerlike tender leaves were now the size of small hands. The trees around the village itself seemed to be even better. As the trees grew so did the hope in the hearts of the peasants. The entire village was mobilized in preparation for the silkworms. The utensils used in the rearing were taken out from the fuel sheds to be washed and repaired, and the women and children engaged in these tasks lined the brook that passed through the village.

None of the women and children were very healthy looking. From the beginning of spring they had to cut down on their meager food, and their garments were all old and worn. They looked little better than beggars. They were not, however, dispirited; they were sustained by their great endurance and their great hope. In their simple minds they felt sure that so long as nothing happened to their silkworms everything would come out all right. When they thought how in a month's time the glossy green leaves would turn into snow white cocoons and how the cocoons would turn into jingling silver dollars, their hearts were filled with laughter though their stomachs gurgled with hunger.

Among the women was Tung Pao's daughter-in-law Ssu-da-niang with her twelve-year-old boy Hsiao Pao. They had finished washing the feeding trays and the hatching baskets and were wiping their brows with the flap of their coats.

"Ssu-sao, are you using foreign eggs this year?" one of the women asked Ssu-da-niang.

"Don't ask me!" Ssu-da-niang answered with passion, as if ready for a quarrel. "Pa is the one that decides. Hsiao Pao's pa did what he could to persuade the old man, but in the end we are hatching only one sheet of foreign eggs. The doddering old fool hates everything foreign as if it were his sworn foe, yet he doesn't seem to mind at all when it comes to 'foreign money.'"[6]

---

5. **picul:** a Chinese unit of weight, from about 133 to about 143 pounds.

6. **'foreign money':** the Mexican silver dollar, introduced into China by European traders.

The gibe provoked a gale of laughter.

A man walked across the husking field on the other side of the brook. As he stepped on the log bridge, Ssu-da-niang called to him:

"Brother Dou, come and help me take these things home. These trays are as heavy as dead dogs when they are wet."

Ah Dou lifted the pile of trays and carried them on his head and walked off swinging his hands like oars. He was a good-natured young man and was always willing to lend a hand to the women when they had anything heavy to be moved or to be rescued from the brook. The trays looked like an oversize bamboo hat on him. There was another gale of laughter when he wriggled his waist in the manner of city women.

"Ah Dou! Come back here and carry something home for me too," said Lotus, wife of Li Keng-sheng, Tung Pao's immediate neighbor, laughing with the rest.

"Call me something nicer if you want me to carry your things for you," answered Ah Dou without stopping.

"Then let me call you godson!" Lotus said with a loud laugh. She was unlike the rest of the women because of her unusually white complexion, but her face was very flat and her eyes were mere slits. She had been a slave girl in some family in town and was already notorious for her habit of flirting with the menfolk though she had been married to the taciturn Li Keng-sheng only half a year.

"The shameless thing!" someone muttered on the other side of the brook. Thereupon Lotus's pig-like eyes popped open as she shouted:

"Whom are you speaking of? Come out and say it in the open if you dare!"

"It is none of your business! She who is without shame knows best whom I'm speaking of, for 'Even the man who lies dead knows who's kicked his coffin with his toes.' Why should you care?"

They splashed water at each other. Some of the women joined the exchange of words, while the children laughed and hooted. Ssu-da-niang, not wishing to be involved, picked up the remaining baskets and went home with Hsiao Pao. Ah Dou had set down the trays on the porch and was watching the fun.

Tung Pao came out of the room with the tray stands that he had to repair. His face darkened when he caught Ah Dou standing there idle, watching the women. He never approved of Ah Dou's exchanging banter with the women of the village, particularly with Lotus, whom he regarded as an evil thing that brought bad luck to anyone who had anything to do with her.

"Are you enjoying the scenery, Ah Dou?" he shouted at his son. "Ah Ssu is making cocoon trees in the back; go and help him!" He did not take his disapproving eyes off his son until the latter had gone. Then he set to work examining the worm holes on the stands and repaired them wherever necessary. He had done a great deal of carpentering in his time, but his fingers were now stiff with age. After a while he had to rest his aching fingers and as he did so he looked up at the three sheets of eggs hanging from a bamboo pole in the room.

Ssu-da-niang sat under the eaves pasting paper over the hatching baskets. To save a few coppers they had used old newspapers the year before. The silkworms had not been healthy, and Tung Pao had said that it was because it was sacrilegious to use paper with characters on it. In order to buy regular paper for the purpose this year they had all gone without a meal.

"Ssu-da-niang, the twenty-loads of leaves we bought has used up all the thirty dollars that we borrowed through your father. What are we going to do after our rice is gone? What we have will last only two more days." Tung Pao raised his head from his work, breathing hard as he spoke to his daughter-in-law. The money was borrowed at 2½ percent monthly interest. This was considered low, and it was only because Ssu-da-niang's father was an old tenant of the creditor that they had been able to get such a favorable rate.

"It was not such a good idea to put all the money in leaves," complained Ssu-da-niang, setting out the baskets to dry. "We may not be able to use all of them as was the case last year."

"What are you talking about! You would bring ill luck on us before we even got started. Do you expect it to be like last year always? We can only gather a little over ten loads from our own trees. How can that be enough for three sheets of eggs?"

"Yes, yes, you are always right. All I know is that you can cook rice only when there is some to cook and when there isn't you have to go hungry!"

Ssu-da-niang answered with some passion, for she had not yet forgiven her father-in-law for their arguments over the relative merit of foreign and domestic eggs. Tung Pao's face darkened and he said no more.

As the hatching days approached, the entire village of about thirty families became tense with hope and anxiety, forgetting it seemed, even their gnawing hunger. They borrowed and sought credit wherever they could and ate whatever they could get, often nothing but pumpkins and potatoes. None of them had more than a handful of rice stored away. The harvest had been good the year before but what with the landlord, creditors, regular taxes, and special assessments, they had long ago exhausted their store. Their only hope now lay in the silkworms; all their loans were secured by the promise that they would be paid after the "harvest."

As the period of Germinating Rains drew near, the "cloth" in every family began to take on a green hue. This became the only topic of conversation wherever women met.

"Lotus says they will be warming the cloth tomorrow. I don't see how it can be so soon."

"Huang Tao-shih went to the fortune teller. The character he drew indicated that leaves will reach four dollars per picul this year!"

Ssu-da-niang was worried because she could not detect any green on their own three sheets of eggs. Ah Ssu could not find any either when he took the sheets to the light and examined them carefully. Fortunately their anxiety did not last long, for spots of green began to show the following day. Ssu-da-niang immediately put the precious things against her breast to warm, sitting quietly as if feeding an infant. At night she slept with them, hardly daring to stir though the tiny eggs against her flesh made her itch. She was as happy, and as fearful, as before the birth of her first child!

The room for the silkworms had been made ready some days before. On the second day of "warming" Tung Pao smeared a head of garlic with mud and put it in a corner of the room. It was believed that the more leaves there were on the garlic on the day that silkworms were hatched, the better would be the harvest. The entire village was now engaged in this warming of the cloths. There were few signs of women along the brooks or on the husking grounds. An undeclared state of emergency seemed to exist: even the best of friends and the most intimate of neighbors refrained from visiting one another, for it was no joking matter to disturb the shy and sensitive goddess who protected the silkworms. They talked briefly in whispers when they met outside. It was a sacred season.

The atmosphere was even tenser when the "black ladies" began to emerge from the eggs. This generally happened perilously close to the day that ushered in the period of Germinating Rains and it was imperative to time the hatching so that it would not be necessary to gather them on that particular day. In Tung Pao's house, the first grubs appeared just before the tabooed day, but they were able to avoid disaster by transferring the cloths from the warm breast of Ssu-da-niang to the silkworms' room. Tung Pao stole a glance at the garlic and his heart almost stopped beating, for only one or two cloves had sprouted. He did not dare to take another look but only prayed for the best.

The day for harvesting the "black ladies" finally came. Ssu-da-niang was restless and excited, continually watching the rising steam from the pot, for the right moment to start operations was when the steam rose straight up in the air. Tung Pao lit the incense and candles and reverently set them before the kitchen god.[7] Ah Ssu and Ah Dou went out to the fields to gather wild flowers, while Hsiao Pao cut up lampwick grass into fine shreds for the mixture used in gathering the newly hatched worms. Toward noon everything was ready for the big moment. When the pot began to boil vigorously and steam to rise straight up into the air, Ssu-da-niang jumped up, stuck in her hair a paper flower dedicated to the silkworms and a pair of goose feathers and went into the room, accompanied by Tung Pao with a steelyard beam and her husband with the prepared mixture of wild flowers and lampwick grass. Ssu-da-niang separated the two layers of cloth and sprinkled the mixture on them. Then taking the beam from Tung Pao she laid the cloths across it, took a goose feather and began to brush the "black ladies" off gently into the papered baskets. The same procedure was followed with the second sheet, but the last, which contained the foreign eggs was brushed off into separate baskets. When

---

7. kitchen god: in Chinese mythology a household god who annually reported to heaven the behavior of every member of the family.

all was done, Ssu-da-niang took the paper flower and the feathers and stuck them on the edge of one of the baskets.

It was a solemn ceremony, one that had been observed for hundreds and hundreds of years. It was as solemn an occasion as the sacrifice before a military campaign, for it was to inaugurate a month of relentless struggle against bad weather and ill luck during which there would be no rest day or night. The "black ladies" looked healthy as they crawled about in the small baskets; their color was as it should be. Tung Pao and Ssu-da-niang both breathed sighs of relief, though the former's face clouded whenever he stole a glance at the head of garlic, for the sprouts had not grown noticeably. Could it be that it was going to be like last year again?

Fortunately the prognostications of the garlic did not prove very accurate this time. Though it was rainy during the first and second molting and the weather colder than around Clear Bright, the "precious things" were all very healthy. It was the same with the "precious things" all over the village. An atmosphere of happiness prevailed, even the brook seemed to gurgle with laughter. The only exception was the household of Lotus, for their worms weighed only twenty pounds at the third "sleep,"[8] and just before the fourth Lotus's husband was seen in the act of emptying three baskets into the brooks. This circumstance made the villagers redouble their vigilance against the contamination of the unfortunate woman. They would not even pass by her house and went out of their way to avoid her and her taciturn husband. They did not want to catch a single glance of her or exchange a single word with her for fear that they might catch her family's misfortune. Tung Pao warned Ah Dou not to be seen with Lotus. "I'll lay a charge against you before the magistrate if I catch you talking to that woman," he shouted at his son loud enough for Lotus to hear. Ah Dou said nothing; he alone did not take much stock in these superstitions. Besides, he was too busy to talk to anyone.

Tung Pao's silkworms weighed three hundred pounds after the "great sleep." For two days and two nights no one, not even Hsiao Pao, had a chance to close his eyes. The worms were in rare condition; in Tung Pao's memory only twice had he known anything equal to it—once when he was married and the other time when Ah Ssu was born. They consumed seven loads of leaves the first day, and it did not take much calculation to know how much more leaf would be needed before the worms were ready to climb up the "mountain."

"The squire has nothing to lend," Tung Pao said to Ah Ssu. "We'll have to ask your father-in-law to try his employers again."

"We still have about ten loads on our own trees, enough for another day," Ah Ssu said, hardly able to keep his eyes open.

"What nonsense," Tung Pao said impatiently. "They have started

---

8. the third "sleep": The feeding period of the silkworm is interrupted by four 24-hour intervals of sleep.

eating only two days ago. They'll be eating for another three days without counting tomorrow. We need another thirty loads, thirty loads."

The price of leaves had gone up to four dollars a load as predicted by the fortune teller, which meant that it would cost one hundred and twenty dollars to buy enough leaves to see them through. There was nothing to do but borrow the required amount on the only remaining mulberry land that they had. Tung Pao took some comfort in the thought that he would harvest at least five hundred pounds of cocoons and that at fifty dollars a hundred pounds he would get more than enough to pay his debts.

When the first consignment of leaves arrived, the "precious things" had already been without food for more than half an hour and it was heartbreaking to see them raise their heads and swing them hither and yon in search of leaves. A crunching sound filled the room as soon as the leaves were spread on the beds, so loud that those in the room had difficulty in hearing one another. Almost in no time the leaves had disappeared and the beds were again white with the voracious worms. It took the whole family to keep the beds covered with leaves. But this was the last five minutes of the battle; in two more days the "precious things" would be ready to "climb up the mountain" and perform their appointed task.

One night Ah Dou was alone on watch in the room, so that Tung Pao and Ah Ssu could have a little rest. It was a moonlit night and there was a small fire in the room for the silkworms. Around the second watch he spread a new layer of leaves on the beds and then squatted by the fire to wait for the next round. His eyes grew heavy and he gradually dozed off. He was awakened by what he thought was a noise at the door, but he was too sleepy to investigate and dozed off again, though subconsciously he detected an unusual rustling sound amidst the familiar crunching of leaves. Suddenly he awoke with a jerk of his drooping head just in time to catch the swishing of the reed screen against the door and a glimpse of someone gliding away. Ah Dou jumped up and ran out. Through the open gate he could see the intruder walking rapidly toward the brook. Ah Dou flew after him and in another moment he had flung him to the ground.

"Ah Dou, kill me if you want to but don't tell anyone!"

It was Lotus's voice, and it made Ah Dou shudder. Her piggish eyes were fixed on his but he could not detect any trace of fear in them.

"What have you stolen?" Ah Dou asked.

"Your precious things!"

"Where have you put them?"

"I have thrown them into the brook!"

Ah Dou's face grew harsh as he realized her wicked intention.

"How wicked you are! What have we done to you?"

"What have you done? Plenty! It was not my fault that our precious things did not live. Since I did you no harm and your precious things have flourished, why should you look upon me like the star of evil and avoid me like the plague? You have all treated me as if I were not a human being at all!"

Lotus had got up as she spoke, her face distorted with hatred. Ah Dou looked at her for a moment and then said:

"I am not going to hurt you; you can go now!"

Ah Dou went back to the room, no longer sleepy in the least. Nothing untoward happened during the rest of the night. The "precious things" were as healthy and strong as ever and kept on devouring leaves as if possessed. At dawn Tung Pao and Ssu-da-niang came to relieve Ah Dou. They picked up the silkworms that had gradually turned from white to pink and held them against the light to see if they had become translucent. Their hearts overflowed with happiness. When Ssu-da-niang went to the brook to draw water, however, Liu Pao, one of their neighbors, approached her and said to her in a low voice:

"Last night between the Second and Third Watch I saw that woman come out of your house, followed by Ah Dou. They stood close together and talked a long time. Ssu-da-niang, how can you let such things go on in your house?"

Ssu-da-niang rushed home and told her husband and then Tung Pao what had happened. Ah Dou, when summoned, denied everything and said that Liu Pao must have been dreaming. Tung Pao took some consolation in the fact that so far there had been no sign of the curse on the silkworms themselves, but there was Liu Pao's unshakable evidence and she could not have made up the whole story. He only hoped that the unlucky woman did not actually step into the room but had only met Ah Dou outside.

Tung Pao became full of misgivings about the future. He knew well that it was possible for everything to go well all along the way only to have the worms die on the trees. But he did not dare to think of that possibility, for just to think of it was enough to bring ill luck.

The silkworms had at last mounted the trees but the anxieties of the growers were by no means over, for there was as yet no assurance that their labor and investment would be rewarded. They did not, however, let these doubts stop them from their work. Fires were placed under the "mountains" in order to force the silkworms to climb up. The whole family squatted around the trees and listened to the rustling of the straws as the silkworms crawled among them, each trying to find a corner to spin its chamber of silk. They would smile broadly or their hearts would sink according to whether they could hear the reassuring sound or not. If they happened to look up and catch a drop of water from above, they did not mind at all, for that meant that there was at least one silkworm ready to get to work at that moment.

Three days later the fires were withdrawn. No longer able to endure the suspense, Ssu-da-niang drew aside one corner of the surrounding reed screens and took a peep. Her heart leaped with joy, for the entire "mountain" was covered with a snowy mass of cocoons! She had never seen a crop like this in all her life! Joy and laughter filled the household. Their anxieties were over at last. The "precious things" were fair and had not devoured leaves at four dollars a load without doing something to show for it; and they themselves had not gone with practically no food or sleep for nothing; Heaven had rewarded them.

The same sound of joy and laughter rose everywhere in the village. The Goddess of Silkworms[9] had been good to them. Everyone of the twenty or thirty families would gather at least a seventy or eighty percent capacity crop. As for Tung Pao's family they expected a hundred-and-twenty or even a hundred-and-thirty percent crop.

Women and children were again seen on the husking fields and along the brook. They were thinner than a month ago, their eyes more sunken and their voices more hoarse, but they were in high spirits. They talked about their struggles and dreamed of piles of bright silver dollars; some of them looked forward to redeeming their summer garments from the pawnshop, while others watered at the mouth in anticipation of the head of fish that they might treat themselves to at the Dragon Boat Festival.

The actual harvesting of the cocoons followed the next day, attended by visits from friends and relatives bringing presents and their good wishes. Chang Tsai-fa, Ssu-da-niang's father, came to congratulate Tung Pao and brought with him cakes, fruits and salted fish. Hsiao Pao was as happy as a pup frolicking in the snow.

"Tung Pao, are you going to sell your cocoons or reel them yourself?" Chang asked, as the two sat under a willow tree along the brook.

"I'll sell them, of course."

"But the factories are not buying this year," Chang said, standing up and pointing in the direction of the buildings used by the buyers.

Tung Pao would not believe him but when he went to see for himself he found that the buyers' buildings were indeed still closed. For the moment Tung Pao was panic-stricken, but when he went home and saw the basket upon basket of fine, firm cocoons that he had harvested he forgot his worries. He could not believe it that such fine cocoons would find no market.

Gradually, however, the atmosphere of the village changed from one of joy and laughter to one of despair, as news began to arrive that none of the factories in the region were going to open for the season. Instead of the scouts for the cocoon buyers who in other years used to march up and down the village during this season, the village was now crowded with creditors and tax collectors. And none of them would accept cocoons in payment.

Curses and sighs of despair echoed through the entire village. It never occurred to the villagers even in their dreams that the extraordinarily fine crop of cocoons would increase their difficulties. But it did not help to complain and say that the world had changed. The cocoons would not keep and it was necessary to reel them at home if they could not sell them to the factories. Already some of the families had got out their long neglected spinning wheels.

"We'll reel the silk ourselves," Tung Pao said to his daughter-in-law.

---

9. **The Goddess of Silkworms:** Si Ling Chi, an empress who was deified for discovering the usefulness of silkworms.

"We had always done that anyway until the foreigners started this factory business."

"But we have over five hundred pounds of cocoons! How many spinning wheels do you plan to use?"

Ssu-da-niang was right. It was impossible for them to reel all the cocoons themselves and they could not afford to hire help. Ah Ssu agreed with his wife and bitterly reproached his father, saying:

"If you had only listened to us and hatched only one sheet of eggs, we would have had enough leaves from our own land."

Tung Pao had nothing to say to this.

Presently a ray of hope came to them. Huang Tao-shih, one of Tung Pao's cronies, learned from somewhere that the factories at Wusih were buying cocoons as usual. After a family conference it was decided that they would borrow a boat and undertake the journey of around three hundred li[10] in order to dispose of their crop.

Five days later they returned with one basket of cocoons still unsold. The Wusih factory was unusually severe in their selection and paid only thirty dollars a hundred pounds of cocoons from foreign eggs and twelve dollars for the native variety. Though Tung Pao's cocoons were of the finest quality, they rejected almost a hundred pounds of the lot.

Tung Pao got one hundred and eleven dollars in all and had only an even hundred left after expenses of the journey, not enough to pay off the debts they contracted in order to buy leaves. Tung Pao was so mortified that he fell sick on the way and had to be carried home.

Ssu-da-niang borrowed a spinning wheel from Liu Pao's house and set to work reeling the rejected cocoons. It took her six days to finish the work. As they were again without rice, she sent Ah Ssu to the town to sell the silk. There was no market for it at all and even the pawnshop would not loan anything against it. After a great deal of begging and wheedling, he was allowed to use it to redeem the picul of rice that they had pawned before Clear Bright.

And so it happened that everyone in Tung Pao's village got deeper into debt because of their spring silkworm crop. Because Tung Pao had hatched three sheets of eggs and reaped an exceptional harvest, he lost as a consequence a piece of land that produced fifteen loads of mulberry leaves and thirty dollars besides, to say nothing of a whole month of short rations and loss of sleep!

---

10. li: a Chinese unit of distance, approximately one third of a mile.

DISCUSSION QUESTIONS

1. How would you characterize the peasants in this story who raise the silkworms?

2. How do the first two paragraphs of the story establish Tung Pao's age and income level without any direct statements?

3. What does the secondary plot, concerning Lotus and Ah Dou, contribute to this story?

4. The author of "Spring Silkworms" devotes a great deal of space to describing the actual process of raising silkworms. What might be his purpose in doing so?

SUGGESTION FOR WRITING

Imagine that you are a talk show host and that Tung Pao has agreed to appear on your show to discuss the job of raising silkworms. What questions would you ask him? How would you expect him to answer? Write a script for the show, providing both the questions and the answers.

LAO SHÊ

(1899–1966)

Lao Shê[1] was born in Beijing with the name Shu Shê-yü. He worked as a teacher and principal in an elementary school and then traveled to England, where he taught Mandarin Chinese for six years. When he returned home, he began writing satirical fiction and action-packed stories that were widely admired throughout China. Lao Shê was particularly interested in writing tales about extraordinary happenings, which were later published under the title *Collection of Hastily Exacted Stories.*

In 1934 a sharp change in the tone of his fiction occurred. He began writing novels that depicted the strong impact of social factors and the relative helplessness of individuals. The most famous of these novels is *Hsiang-tzu the Camel.* After the onset of the Chinese-Japanese War in the 1940s, Lao Shê became active in public life. He served on various cultural committees and, from that time on, wrote mostly political propaganda. ■

THE LAST TRAIN

Edited and translated by Yuan Chia-hua and Robert Payne

The train started a long while ago, and now the wheels rumbled mournfully along the rails, the passengers sighed and counted the hours: seven o'clock, eight, nine, ten—by ten o'clock the train would arrive, and they would be home around midnight. It might not be too late, for the children might already be put to bed. It was New Year's Day, and they were all in a hurry to get home. They looked at the cans, the fruit and the toys heaped up on the shelves, and already they could hear the children crying "Papa, papa!" and thinking of all this, they lost themselves in their thoughts; but there were others who were well aware that they would not be home before daybreak. They studied their fellow passengers, and to their consternation they discovered that there was not a single soul with whom they could claim the faintest acquaintance. When they reached home it would already be the New Year! And there were others who cursed the train, because it was moving only at a snail's pace, and though they remained physically in the carriage, smoking, sipping tea, yawning, pressing their noses to the windowglass and seeing there only an unfathomable abyss of darkness outside, they were really not in the carriage at all—they had been home and returned a hundred times since the train left the station. And now they lowered their heads and yawned to conceal the tears in their eyes.

---

1. Lao Shê (lou shə)

There were not many passengers in the second-class carriage. There was fat Mr. Chang and thin Mr. Chiao, and they sat in the same compartment opposite one another. Whenever they got up, they spread their blankets over their seats to show that intruders would not be welcomed. When the train started they found to their surprise that there were very few passengers indeed, and somehow this led them more than ever to feel grieved at the thought that they were traveling in a train on Christmas New Year Day.[2] There were other similarities between the two passengers: they were both holding free passes, and both of them had been unable to obtain the pass until the previous day, and they therefore agreed that a man who could give free passes at his will had a perfect right to annoy bona fide travelers by keeping them to the last moment. They were both indignant at this treatment, for in the good old days friends were made of sterner stuff, and so they shook their heads and put the blame on these so-called friends who had prevented them from reaching their homes before the New Year's Day.

Old Mr. Chang removed his fox-fur coat and tucked his legs under his body, but he discovered that the seat was too narrow for sitting comfortably in this posture. Meanwhile, the temperature of the carriage rose and beads of perspiration began to roll down his brow. "Boy, towels!" he shouted, and then to Mr. Chiao he said: "I wonder why they turn so much heat on nowadays." He gasped. "It wouldn't be so hot if we were traveling on an airplane."

Old Mr. Chiao had taken off his coat a long while ago, and now he was wearing a robe lined with white sheep's fur, and over that a sleeveless jacket of shining black satin. He showed no sign of feeling faint. He said: "One can get a free pass on an airplane, too. It isn't difficult." And he drawled off with a faint smile.

"It's better not to risk traveling by air," Old Mr. Chang said, trying hard to keep his crossed legs under him, but succeeding only with great difficulty. "Boy, towels!"

The "boy" was over forty, and his neck was as thin as a stick, so thin that one imagined that it was quite easy to pluck off his head and plant it back again. You could see him hurrying backwards and forwards along the passageway, his hands full of steaming towels. He was always eager to serve, but really—the way the management made you work on such a sacred day—it was really inconceivable. When he reached the compartment in front, he found Little Tsui and vented his injured feelings on him. "Listen to this! I was on duty on the twenty-seventh and twenty-eighth, and I counted on having today free. Well, at the last moment Mr. Liu comes to me and says, 'Look here, you'll have to have a run on New Year's Day'—that's what he says. There are sixty boys working on this line, and they have to pick on me. I don't care a damn about New Year's Day, but it's lousy all the same!" And saying this, he craned his neck in the

---

2. **Christmas New Year Day**: the New Year of the Gregorian calendar, as opposed to the one of the Chinese.

direction of fat Mr. Chang, but he remained exactly where he was, and untwining the twisted towels, he offered one of them to Little Tsui. "Have one," he said, and went on with his complaint. "I told Mr. Liu that I didn't care about New Year's Day, but he must understand that it was my turn to be off duty that evening. I said I had been working the whole year and ought to have a day off." He gulped something down his throat, and his Adam's apple floated up like the bubbles in water when a bottle is suddenly turned upside down. He was so choked that he could not speak for a few moments. "I'm fed up with it all—everything's all wrong nowadays."

From the pale yellow face of Little Tsui something like a smile flowered out. He wanted to incline his head a little to demonstrate his sympathy, but for some reason he found himself unable to do this. He had his own difficulties. Everyone on the railway knew him—even the stationmasters and the mechanics. They were all his friends. His pale yellow face was equivalent to a second-class ticket: the Ministry of Transport itself would not dare to dispute its validity. And everyone knew that he always traveled with one or two hundred ounces of opium in his luggage, and everyone admitted that he was entitled to do this. At the same time Little Tsui was careful never to intimidate anybody, nor to be partial in the distribution of his favors, for fear of arousing people's jealousy, and he understood their sorrows perfectly well and wished to show his sympathy. Because he offended no one, he was afraid of no one; and this, the supreme wisdom of life, could be read on his ticket—or rather, on his face.

"We're all so busy," he complained, hoping in some way that a recital of his troubles would benefit the "boy." And he went on to say that he had had to take this trip entirely against his will, he would have much preferred to remain comfortably at home, but on the very next day he would have to meet a blood-sucking girl who would take all his money away. He smiled, showing darkened teeth, and puffing out his cheeks he spat on the floor.

What he had said began to tell on the "boy," who seemed to be forgetting his own sorrows and nodding appreciatively. The towels in his hand had grown cold and he returned to his cabin to resoak them in water. When he emerged, he passed Little Tsui without saying a word and without looking at him, closing his eyes languidly as though to show that he had not forgotten the injuries done to him in spite of Little Tsui's consolations. Taking advantage of the rocking movement of the train, he swung his body towards a certain Mr. K'ou. "Like a towel, sir? It's trying to travel at this time of the year." He would have liked to vent his feelings on a new audience, but since he did not know Mr. K'ou very well, he went about it in as circuitous a manner as possible.

Mr. K'ou was dressed with considerable éclat. He wore a dark serge overcoat with a beaver collar, with a brand new black satin, melon-shaped hat. He had removed neither his coat nor his hat, and he sat there as rigid as a chairman on a platform waiting solemnly for the moment when he would address a huge audience. He took the towel, stretching out his arm at full length, and taking care not to fold his elbow he described a semicircle with the towel until it reached his face. Then he rubbed his face fastidiously and ostentatiously. When his face emerged from the whirling cloud of the towel it dazzled and lent to his person a renewed splendor and dignity. He nodded to the "boy," without explaining why he was traveling on New Year's Day.

"It's a bad thing—being a waiter," the "boy" said, reluctant to let Mr. K'ou go as easily as that. He knew that it would be inadvisable to repeat what he had said to Little Tsui. It would be necessary to talk with measured deliberation in order to seem both reverent and intimate. "People ought to rest on New Year's Day," he continued, "but there is no rest for us. We can do nothing." And taking back the used towel: "Another one, sir?"

Mr. K'ou shook his head. It was now clear that he was almost touched by the "boy's" misfortunes, but would rather not enter into any conversation. Everyone on the line knew that he was a friend of the manager, and it was his privilege to enjoy a free ride in a second-class carriage any time he pleased. He had only to show his identity, and he could do this by not entering into desultory conversations with a waiter.

And meanwhile the waiter was at a loss to understand why Mr. K'ou had been shaking his head; but he could do nothing, for he knew perfectly well that the man was a friend of the manager. The carriage began to rock again, and the movement of the carriage hurled him into the passageway. Steadying himself, he untwisted a towel and holding it delicately by two corners he offered it to Mr. Chang. "Would you like one, sir?" and the man reached out for it, his thick palm touching the central part of it, which was the hottest. He pressed it to his face, rubbing hard as though he were cleaning a mirror. Then he handed another one to Mr. Chiao, who showed no enthusiasm, but took the towel and with it proceeded to clean his nostrils and fingernails delicately. When he returned it to the waiter, it was all greasy and black.

"The inspectors will soon be coming now," he began, believing that no policy could be worse than that which introduced a conversation with a recital of his own troubles. He decided upon a flank attack. "When they have gone, you will want to have a rest, and if any of you gentlemen would like a cushion, just let me know." And he went on a little later: "There are not many passengers on board, and you'll all be able to have a nap. It's a pity you gentlemen are spending a day like this on a train, but as for us waiters—" He sighed. He realized that he had been talking too much. He should have discovered in which way the wind was blowing. And he handed Mr. Chang another towel. Mr. Chang found that his toilet was taking up too much of his time, but remembered that he had not wiped his hair, which had only recently been cut. Although it was just as hard, or even harder, to rub his scalp, he determined that he would go through with the ordeal, and when he had finished he sighed with relief. However, Mr. Chiao declined a second offer, and gently picked his teeth with his now-clean fingernails.

"What's wrong with the heating system?" Mr. Chang asked, as he tossed back the towel.

"I wouldn't advise you to open the window," the waiter answered. "Nine to ten you'll catch cold. The railway is under a rotten management." The chance lay wide open for him, and he entered quickly. "They make you work all the year round, and don't even let you rest on New Year's Day. Well, all talking is vain."

And so it was, for the train had drawn into a small wayside station.

From the third-class carriages a few passengers stepped down with their bags and baskets, and hurried towards the exit. Some of them stopped and hesitated, as though they were wondering whether they had left anything on the train. Those who remained in the train pressed their noses on the windowpane and looked out, their faces wearing an expression of envy and anxiety. No one in the second-class left the train, but half a dozen soldiers came into the compartment. Their boots thundered on the floor, their leather belts flashed in the light and their luggage consisted of four large cases of fireworks wrapped in scarlet paper and decorated with characters cut out of gold paper. The boxes were so large that for a long time they were undecided what to do with them. Meanwhile, boots crackled, men bustled about, their voices grew louder, and the question where to place the pile of fireworks remained for a long time unsettled. Finally, a man who resembled a battalion commander said that they should be put on the floor. The platoon commander repeated the order, and then all the men bent double and executed the order; afterwards they rose stiffly and clicked their heels. The battalion commander returned the salute and ordered them to dismiss. Boots thundered. A cloud of gray caps, gray uniforms and gray leggings. A moment later someone said: "Hurry!" and they obediently disappeared. A whistle sounded from the train, rather muffled. Lights and shadows flitted about, and the wheels began to rumble and the train to roll out of the station.

The waiter walked from one end of the carriage to the other, looking as though there was something on his mind. He stole a glance at the two soldiers and then at the heap of fireworks which lay so uncompromisingly on the floor, barring his way; but he dare not say anything. He went into a desultory conversation with Little Tsui, harping on the old theme, repeating what he had said a moment before, but adding a more detailed and to him more satisfactory account of his misfortunes. Little Tsui began to talk about his girl friends.

But the waiter was still perturbed by the presence of the fireworks. He left Little Tsui, and resumed his furtive strolling among the compartments. The battalion commander was lying down, tired out, his pistol on the little table at the side of the carriage. The platoon commander had not yet dared to imitate him, but he had removed his cap and was now violently scratching his scalp. The waiter took care not to awaken the senior officer, but he smiled voluminously at the junior. "What was I going to say?" he said in a half-apologetic tone of voice, hesitantly. "Oh yes, I was going to suggest that it might be a better idea to put the crackers up on the shelf."

"Why?" the officer answered, mouth awry with head scratching.

"You know, I was afraid people might step on them," the waiter replied, his head shrinking tortoise-fashion into his shoulders.

"No one would dare to touch them! Why should they touch them?" the officer answered, his little beady eyes askew.

"That's quite all right!" The waiter was all smiles, and his face became smaller as though under the weight of an enormous invisible rock. "It doesn't matter at all. May I know where you are traveling to?"

"If I have any more trouble from you, what about fighting it out?" the officer suddenly shouted. He had been worn thin by the ill-humor of his senior officer, and he was perfectly prepared to fight.

But the waiter was in no need of a fight, and he abruptly disappeared. As he passed Mr. Chang, he said: "The inspectors will be here soon, sir."

Mr. Chang and Mr. Chiao were developing a cordial friendship. The ticket inspection began. There were two inspectors followed by three other men. The first wore a cap with gold braid, was white-skinned, stern, his nose in the air. The second also wore a cap with gold braid, but he was dwarfish, dark, and his face was full of smiles and somehow possessed the power of reconciling all those who were put out by the sternness of the first. As they went through the third-class carriages they pulled long faces, but when they went into the second-class the dwarf inspector was wreathed with smiles, and when they reached the first-class carriages they would both be smiling broadly. The third man was a giant from Tientsin, with a pistol and many rounds of ammunition in his belt. The fourth was a giant from Shantung, and he too carried a belt and a pistol, but he also wore a long sword. And the fifth was the waiter, whose head troubled him—for it was always popping upward and he found the greatest difficulty in maintaining it in its proper position.

The group came to a pause opposite Little Tsui. They all knew him, his pale yellow face and dark teeth, which immediately formed into a smile as between familiar acquaintances. It was an awkward moment.

The first inspector gazed blankly into the distance as though absorbed in meditation; he kept on tapping his ticket-punch gently against his thigh. The second nodded recognition to Little Tsui. The Tientsin giant smiled at him, and immediately afterwards turned off the smile exactly as though he had pressed a switch. The Shantung giant touched the peak of his cap with his hand, and his eloquent eyes seemed to be saying: "I've got a long story to tell you, but wait until all this nonsense is finished." The waiter felt that the inspection had lasted long enough, and as the group moved on he said: "Please sit down. There aren't many passengers—it will be all over in a moment, and then I'll come back to you." Little Tsui found himself alone, a shadow flitting across his brow. At last he sat down.

The waiter caught them up a little later, but he did not join in their procession. He slipped up to Mr. K'ou. "Mr. K'ou, sir," he said, but the procession leader was slightly irritated by his interference, and giving his hand to Mr. K'ou he said: "How is the manager these days? You know it's late in the year to start on a long journey." Mr. K'ou, his respectability unimpaired and even increased by this encounter, smiled weakly, murmured inaudibly, bowed and smiled again. The two guards stood bolt upright, quite still, feeling that they were outsiders in whatever game was now being employed. Their low positions in life denied them the privilege of entering into the conversation, but they contrived to maintain their dignity by puffing out their chests and standing at attention.

Meanwhile the waiter was taking this opportunity to inform Mr. Chang and Mr. Chiao to get their tickets ready. They gave him their tickets. He was awestruck when he realized that the tickets were free passes, and his reverence for the two gentlemen became even greater than before. He returned Mr. Chang's pass at once, but he ventured to detain Mr. Chiao's for a moment because it was clearly indicated on the pass that the holder was a woman, and there was indisputable evidence that Mr. Chiao was a man. The two inspectors drew apart and began to whisper into each other's ear. A moment later they nodded to one another, and it was clear that they had reached a common understanding that on New Year's Day a man might pass for a woman. The waiter returned Mr. Chiao's ticket with both hands, apologetically.

The battalion commander was now snoring. As soon as he noticed the arrival of the inspectors, the platoon commander put his legs up on the seat and showed every sign of an unwillingness to be disturbed. The inspectors' attention was immediately arrested by the pile of fireworks which littered the passageway. The Shantung giant nodded in admiration, overcome by the length and the solidity of the fireworks. And they passed through the compartment, and it was not until the first inspector reached the door that he turned to the waiter and said: "You'd better tell them to put the fireworks on the shelves," and in order to save the waiter from further embarrassment the second inspector added quickly: "Better still if you did it for them." The waiter nodded his thin neck like a pendulum without saying anything, but all the while he was asking himself: "You haven't the courage to tell them—that's what it is—so what can I do except nod my head?—and besides, there is a great difference between nodding and doing." The truth dawned on his mind. The fireworks must not be moved.

When he returned to Little Tsui, he was surprised to find the little fellow sunk in misery and knew at once that he was in need of a cup of water. Without saying anything he brought along the kettle. Little Tsui took something from his pocket—the waiter did not see it, but dimly suspected that it was opium—and pressed it into his left palm with the ball of his thumb, grinning, his face so pale that it resembled paper. He was almost perspiring and something like a faint vapor was rising from his face, which was glazed like an onion in a hothouse. Then he covered his mouth with his cupped hand, and the fingers began to wave in gentle undulations. He closed his eyes, took a sip from the cup and puffed out his cheeks. Afterwards his eyes opened, and an indubitable smile floated over his pale yellow face.

"It's more important than food," Little Tsui said wonderingly.

"Oh yes, far more important," the waiter nodded.

Go-home-go-home-go-home-go-home. The wheels roared in chorus. But they were very slow. The star-strewn sky undulated. Hills, trees, villages, graves, flashed past in clusters. The train dashed on and on in the darkness. Smoke, soot and sparks shot up furiously, and then disappeared. The train ran on, flying breathlessly, one patch of darkness following on another. A stretch of snow and a string of low mounds glowed and darkened and were gone. Go-home-go-home-go-home. The lights were ablaze, the temperature steaming, all the passengers were weary to death, and not one was inclined to sleep. Go-home-go-home-go-home. The farewell rites to the Old Year, the libations to the gods, the offerings to the Ancestors, the writing on the spring scrolls, the firecrackers, the dumplings, the sweetmeats, the dinners and the wine—all these became suddenly very real to them, filling their eyes and their ears, their palates and their nostrils. A smile would light upon their lips and instantly disappear, dying away at the recollection that they were still physically in the train. Go-home-go-home-go-home-go-home. Darkness, darkness, darkness. The starry sky undulated. Patches of snowy ground rose and fell. No human sounds, no traffic, nothing visible. Darkness endlessly receding, an interminable road tightly hugging the brightly lit train which struggled furiously to tear itself away from the menace of the surrounding darkness. And yet the darkness never forsook the train. Go-home-go-home-go-home . . .

Mr. Chang took down from the shelf two bottles of distilled wine, and said to Mr. Chiao: "We're just like old friends now. How about a drop of this? We might as well enjoy New Year's Day—no reason why we shouldn't enjoy ourselves." He handed over a cup of the wine. "Real Yinkow wine. Twenty years old. You can't get it on the market. Bottoms up."

Mr. Chiao was too polite to refuse. He asked himself what he should offer Mr. Chang in return, and all the time he kept his eyes fixed on the cup, and his hands were fidgeting. He reached up to the shelf, took down a large parcel, gently unwrapped it and revealed a number of smaller parcels. He pinched them one by one, and finally removed the three parcels which he felt sure contained dried lichees,[3] preserved dates and spiced bean-curd. He then unwrapped them and offered them to Mr. Chang. "We're like old friends. Don't stand on any ceremony."

Mr. Chang picked a lichee, which burst under the pressure of his fingers. The sound amused him. It was an appropriate sound, reminiscent of New Year's Day. He watched Mr. Chiao sipping the wine and, waiting till his friend had swallowed it all, he asked: "Well, how do you like the stuff?"

"Marvelous!" Mr. Chiao wetted his lips. "Marvelous! Nothing like it anywhere."

---

3. lichee: a sweet, white Asian fruit.

They filled up one another's cups, and slowly and imperceptibly their faces turned crimson. Their tongues were unloosened. They talked of their families, their jobs, their friends, the difficulty of earning money, free passes. Their cups clinked, their hearts clinked, their eyes moistened, they were permeated with warmth. It was time for one of them to be generous. Mr. Chiao unwrapped another parcel which contained preserved oranges. Mr. Chang looked at the two remaining bottles and said: "Well, we'll have to finish them. One each. Mustn't leave a drop. We're old friends now. Come on. Bottoms up!"

"I'm not very good at drinking."

"Nonsense. Twenty years old. Mellow. Won't make you drunk. It's God's will that we should become friends. Drink up!"

Mr. Chiao was profoundly honored. Mr. Chang looked at his bottle—there was not very much left now. He untied his collar. Beads of perspiration stood out on his brow; his eyes were bloodshot and his tongue was stiff. Though still talkative, his talk was reduced to mere babbling; he had not yet completely lost his self-control, he could still put a curb on the curious inner urge which nearly led him to curse in front of his new-found friend, and the resultant of these forces took the form, not of a quarrel, or incivility, but rather of exultation and gaiety. Mr. Chiao, on the other hand, had been able to stomach only half of the bottle assigned to him, but his face was already turning deathly pale. He produced a packet of cigarettes and threw one at Mr. Chang. Both lit their cigarettes. Cigarette in mouth, Mr. Chang reclined along the seat, his legs dangling nonchalantly. He itched to sing, but his throat was scorched and hoarse, and he breathed heavily through his nose like an angry bull. Mr. Chiao also leaned back, cigarette in hand, his eyes fixed on the legs of the seat opposite him, his heart beating wildly. He hiccupped. His face was pale, and he felt a faint itching all over his body.

Go-home-go-home-go-home-go-home. In Mr. Chang's ears the wheels sounded as though they were going at breakneck speed. His heart beat fast, and suddenly everything began buzzing. His head turned round and round in the air, buzzing like a fly. All objects were dancing and glowing in red circles. When the buzzing ceased, his heart once more began to beat at its accustomed ritual, and he opened his eyes slightly, partially regaining his strength. He pretended that nothing had happened, and groping for the matchbox he relit his extinguished cigarette. Then he threw the match away. Suddenly on the table a greenish flame flared up, smelling of alcohol, spinning among the cups and bottles, fluttering, rising, spreading out. Mr. Chiao was startled out of his dreams as the cigarette which he held in his hand suddenly caught fire. He threw it away. He beat the table with both hands to extinguish the fire, and in doing this he knocked down the cups and bottles. Iridescent tongues licked the unopened parcels. Mr. Chang's face was hidden in flames. Mr. Chiao thought of running away. The flames on the table soared up, and the parcels on the shelf above seemed to reach down to catch the rising columns of flames. Flame linked with flame. Mr. Chiao himself was ablaze. The fire reached his eyebrows, charring them, snapping at his hair, which sizzled, lighting up the alcohol on his lips and turning him into a fire-breathing monster.

Suddenly: pop, pop, pop . . . It sounded like machine-gun fire. The platoon commander had hardly opened his eyes when a cracker exploded on his nose and sent sparks and blood flying in fine sprays. He rose, and began frantically running. There were explosions everywhere, under his feet, all round his body. The noise was deafening as though they had stepped on a land mine. The battalion commander was swallowed up in the fire before he could open his eyes. He was trying to open his eyes when the right eye received a direct hit from one of the exploding crackers.

Mr. K'ou started up. He cast a quick glance at his luggage on the shelf. Some of the parcels were already burning, and the fire was closing in from all sides—from above, from below, and even from a long way away. Flames licked at him, and an idea flashed through his mind. He picked up one of his shoes from the floor and smote at the windowpane. He wanted to jump out of the window. The glass was broken, a gale rushed in, the fire turned wild. His collar of beaver skin, the four bedrolls, the five boxes, his clothes—they were all swallowed up in the flames. The train ran on, the wind was roaring, the firecrackers kept going off. Mr. K'ou ran like a wild animal.

Little Tsui was a seasoned traveler. He had heard the sounds, but he was too lazy to open his eyes. The fire finally reached his feet and spread along his body. He felt hot, and sat up. He saw nothing but smoke and fire. The crackers continued to explode, the opium which he carried on his body began to melt and burn. The delicious smell assailed his nostrils. He felt a scorching heat. His legs could not move. The fire spread over his chest. His huddled body was wrapped in flames, a gigantic bubbling ball of opium paste, until it was reduced to the shape of a cocoon.

So Little Tsui stirred no more. Mr. Chang was dead-drunk, and he lay there like a log. Mr. Chiao, Mr. K'ou and the platoon commander were running about in all directions, stark staring mad. The battalion commander knelt on the bench and wailed. The fire had already penetrated every corner of the carriage; the smell of sulfur was suffocating. The crackers were no longer exploding—they had all been burnt. The noise died away, but the smoke grew thicker. And at last those who were running about no longer ran about, and those who were wailing no longer wailed. The fire began to devour the furniture. The train kept darting forward, the wind kept roaring. Red tongues of flame struggled within the dense clouds of smoke, hoping for an outlet. The smoke turned milky, and the flames began to thrash at the windows. The whole carriage was transparent with light, and tongues of fire streamed away like streamers, a thousand torches burning brightly in the wind.

The train slowed down as it drew near a small station, but it did not stop. The trackman turned the lever and said to himself: "Fire!" The signalman flashed his green lamp and said to himself: "Fire!" The guards stood at attention and said to themselves: "Fire!" The stationmaster was late in arriving, and when he arrived the train had already left, but he saw dimly in his half-drunken stupor that there was a train on fire, and preferred to believe that it was an hallucination. The signalman blew out his lamp, the trackman shifted the lever back by which the rails resumed their normal position; the guards returned with their rifles to their recreation quarters, and each of them retained in his mind a picture of the fire, and yet not one of them was inclined to admit that he had seen it. Gradually the idea of the fire died away in their minds, and they were concerned only about how they could enjoy the festival. They lit firecrackers, drank, played mahjong. Everything was right with the world.

As the train left the station, it gained speed. The wind howled, and the fire crackled. Brilliant rockets shot out in sprays. The night was dark and the train was a chain of lanterns pouring out licking flames. Of the second-class carriage, only a charred skeleton remained. The flames, having nothing to feed on, moved backwards and forwards, and finally entered the third-class carriage. Smoke came first, sending out a pungent, and slightly sweet smell of charred flesh and furniture. Fire followed. "Fire! Fire! Fire!" Everyone was shouting in fearful panic. They lost their heads. They broke the windows in an attempt to leap out, and then hesitated. Some began to run, and then they would fall against one another and fall down. Some sat transfixed to their seats, unable even to cry. Turbulence. Panic. Every effort proved vain. They howled, folded their arms round their heads, beat off the flames with their clothes, ran, jumped out of the carriage. . . .

The fire had discovered a new colony, with rich resources and a great population. It was mad with joy. It licked out with one of its tongues, pawed with another, hid a third in the smoke, and suddenly thrust a fourth through the window. A fifth wandered without any fixed goal. It was the sixth which joined all the others together. Hundreds of flames began dancing in the most fantastic patterns. They rolled themselves up into balls, shot out like meteors, gathered in red-and-green pools of fire. They glowed, dwindled, crept in the wake of the smoke, and then disappeared. Then they burst out of the smoke in torrents. They squeaked and gibbered as they burned human flesh and broiled human hair. The crowd howled, the wind roared, the fire crackled. The whole car was on fire. The smoke was heavy. It was a lovely cremation.

The train arrived at the next station, where it was due to stop. It stopped. Signalmen, ticket-inspectors, guards, the stationmaster and the assistant stationmaster, the clerks and the hangers-on all looked at the burning carriages in amazement, and could do nothing, because there were no fire engines and no implements for putting out fires. The second-class carriage, and the two adjacent third-class carriages in front and behind were silent and still. From them a plume of blue smoke curled up—languidly and leisurely.

It was reported later that fifty-two corpses were found on the train, and the bodies of eleven more, who had jumped off and killed themselves, were found along the line.

After the Lantern Festival—that is, fifteen days after the New Year—an inspector arrived. For the first three days he attended official receptions, and had little time to spare for the investigation. The next three days were spent in looking after some personal affairs which could no longer be laid aside. Then the investigation began.

The guard knew nothing. The first inspector knew nothing. The second inspector knew nothing. Neither the Tientsin giant, nor the Shantung giant, nor the waiter, knew anything about the cause of the fire. Reports from the various stations on the number of tickets sold tallied closely with the number of tickets collected, taking into account the sixty-three tickets which were missing. These corresponded exactly with the number of casualties and so must have been burnt. No station reported the sale of second-class tickets; it followed that the second class must have been empty, and therefore the fire could not have started in the second-class carriage.

Finally, the waiter was re-examined. He declared that he knew nothing about the fire, which must have started when he was in the dining-car. The tribunal decided that he was irrevocably wrong, and should be punished for having left his post of duty. And he was duly discharged from the service.

The inspector submitted his report with a detailed account of the tragedy written in the most admirable style.

"I don't care at all," the waiter said to his wife. "They put you on duty on New Year's Day, and then, when everything goes wrong, they think we will be starved if we leave their wretched railway."

"What nonsense!" his wife answered. "I'm not worried about that. What I am worried about is the cabbage that got burnt."

DISCUSSION QUESTIONS

1. In this story the author tends to create characters by giving them a single trait or topic of conversation. How does he characterize the waiter ("the boy"), Mr. Chiao, Little Tsui, and Mr. Chang? In general, would you say that the characters are pictured as sympathetic or unattractive?

2. The fire in this story is presented in such a way that it seems to have thoughts and emotions of its own. Reread the paragraph that begins, "The fire had discovered a new colony . . ." and describe the "feelings" of the fire.

3. Do you think the investigation of the fire was handled competently? Why or why not?

4. What is the purpose of the short conversation between the waiter and his wife at the end of the story? How does this conversation reinforce the theme of the story?

SUGGESTION FOR WRITING

Imagine that you are a television newscaster who has been assigned to report on the mysterious train fire that occurred on New Year's Day. You have seen the remains of the train, talked to some people who were at the station, and received the inspector's report. There are, of course, no living witnesses who can tell you how the fire started. Write the news report that you will deliver on television.

Japanese Literature

THE HYAKU MONOGATARI

(18th century)

The *Hyaku Monogatari* (Hundred Tales) was written during an era of peace in Japanese history. The growing literacy among the people, the emergence of new writers who were not court nobles, and the development of mass printing helped to bring literature to a much wider public. Many of the works in this collection were based on older, traditional tales.

The story that follows was influenced by an actual historical event of the 1100s, the fall of the mighty and highly cultivated house of Heiké (hā kā). This royal house's enemies, the Genji, killed the emperor and forced the Heiké to flee their home. For a while they lived a hunted existence on the waters and tiny islands of western Japan, doing their best to protect the emperor's infant son. In 1185, however, their fate was decided in the battle of Dan-no-ura, when the emperor's widow, Nii-no-Ama, plunged into the sea with the royal child in her arms rather than face capture and humiliation.

In Japan the influence of this story is, in many respects, comparable to the influence of the Trojan War on the literature of Greece and Rome. The story of the house of Heiké was sung by minstrels for several centuries after the event, and it inspired hundreds of later literary works. It evolved as something close to a national epic, with stirring accounts of battle, loyalty, and courage, as well as pathos and tragedy. The main character in the story below, Hōichi, is one of the minstrels who narrated and sang this well-known tale. ■

HŌICHI THE EARLESS

Translated by Lafcadio Hearn

Some centuries ago there lived at Akamagaséki a blind man named Hōichi,[1] who was famed for his skill in recitation and in playing upon the *biwa*.[2] From childhood he had been trained to recite and to play; and while yet a lad he had surpassed his teachers. As a professional *biwa hoshi*[3] he became famous chiefly by his recitations of the history of the Heiké and the Genji; and it is said that when he sang the song of the battle of Dan-no-ura "even the goblins [*kijin*] could not refrain from tears."

---

1. **Hōichi:** (hō ē chē).

2. *biwa:* a lute.

3. *biwa hoshi:* a lute-playing minstrel.

At the outset of his career, Hōichi was very poor; but he found a good friend to help him. The priest of the Amidaji[4] was fond of poetry and music; and he often invited Hōichi to the temple to play and recite. Afterwards, being much impressed by the wonderful skill of the lad, the priest proposed that Hōichi should make the temple his home; and this offer was gratefully accepted. Hōichi was given a room in the temple building; and, in return for food and lodging, he was required only to gratify the priest with a musical performance on certain evenings, when otherwise disengaged.

One summer night the priest was called away, to perform a Buddhist service at the house of a dead parishioner; and he went there with his acolyte,[5] leaving Hōichi alone in the temple. It was a hot night; and the blind man sought to cool himself on the verandah before his sleeping room. The verandah overlooked a small garden in the rear of the Amidaji. There Hōichi waited for the priest's return, and tried to relieve his solitude by practicing upon his biwa. Midnight passed; and the priest did not appear. But the atmosphere was still too warm for comfort within doors; and Hōichi remained outside. At last he heard steps approaching from the back gate. Somebody crossed the garden, advanced to the verandah, and halted directly in front of him—but it was not the priest. A deep voice called the blind man's name—abruptly and unceremoniously, in the manner of samurai[6] summoning an inferior:

"Hōichi!"

Hōichi was too much startled, for the moment, to respond; and the voice called again, in a tone of harsh command.

"Hōichi!"

"Hai!" answered the blind man, frightened by the menace in the voice. "I am blind!—I cannot know who calls!"

"There is nothing to fear," the stranger exclaimed, speaking more gently. "I am stopping near this temple, and have been sent to you with a message. My present lord, a person of exceedingly high rank, is now staying in Akamagaséki, with many noble attendants. He wished to view the scene of the battle of Dan-no-ura; and today he visited that place. Having heard of your skill in reciting the story of the battle, he now desires to hear your performance: so you will take your biwa and come with me at once to the house where the august assembly is waiting."

In those times, the order of a samurai was not to be lightly disobeyed. Hʻoichi donned his sandals, took his biwa, and went away with the stranger, who guided him deftly, but obliged him to walk very fast. The hand that guided was iron; and the clank of the warrior's stride proved him fully armed—probably some palace guard on duty. Hoichi's first alarm was over: he began to imagine himself in good luck;

---

4. Amidaji: a Buddhist temple near Akamagaséki, the site of the battle. It was built to pacify the spirits of the Heiké dead who, it was believed, haunted the sea and beaches of Dan-no-ura.

5. acolyte: a priest's attendant.

6. samurai: a member of a hereditary military class in feudal Japan.

for, remembering the retainer's assurance about a "person of exceedingly high rank," he thought that the lord who wished to hear the recitation could not be less than a lord of the first class. Presently the samurai halted; and Hoichi became aware that they had arrived at a large gateway; and he wondered, for he could not remember any large gate in that part of the town, except the main gate of the Amidaji. "Kaimon!"[7] the samurai called, and there was a sound of unbarring; and the twain[8] passed on. They traversed a space of garden, and halted again before some entrance; and the retainer cried in a loud voice, "Within there! I have brought Hoichi." Then came sounds of feet hurrying, and screens sliding, and rain-doors opening, and voices of women in converse. By the language of the women Hoichi knew them to be domestics in some noble household; but he could not imagine to what place he had been conducted. Little time was allowed him for conjecture. After he had been helped to mount several stone steps, upon the last of which he was told to leave his sandals, a woman's hand guided him along interminable reaches of polished planking, and round pillared angles too many to remember, and over amazing widths of matted floor, into the middle of some vast apartment. There he thought that many great people were assembled: the sound of the rustling of silk was like the sound of leaves in a forest. He heard also a great humming of voices, talking in undertones; and the speech was the speech of courts.

Hōichi was told to put himself at ease, and he found a kneeling-cushion ready for him. After having taken his place upon it, and tuned his instrument, the voice of a woman—whom he divined to be the *Rojo,* or matron in charge of the female service—addressed him, saying,

"It is now required that the history of the Heiké be recited, to the accompaniment of the *biwa.*"

Now the entire recital would have required a time of many nights: therefore Hōichi ventured a question:

"As the whole of the story is not soon told, what portion is it augustly desired that I now recite?"

The woman's voice made answer:

"Recite the story of the battle at Dan-no-ura, for the pathos is most deep."

Then Hōichi lifted up his voice, and chanted the chant of the fight on the bitter sea, wonderfully making his *biwa* to sound like the straining of oars and the rushing of ships, the whirr and the hissing of arrows, the shouting and trampling of men, the crashing of steel upon helmets, the plunging of slain in the flood. And to left and right of him, in the pauses of his playing, he could hear voices murmuring praise: "How marvelous an artist!" "Never in our own province was playing heard like this!" "Not in all the empire is there another singer like Hōichi!" Then fresh courage came to him, and he played and sang yet better than before; and a hush of wonder deepened about him. But when at last he came to tell the fate

---

7. **"Kaimon!":** a polite term used to request admission from a guard on duty.

8. **twain:** a pair; two.

of the fair and helpless, the piteous perishing of the women and children, and the death-leap of Nii-no-Ama, with the imperial infant in her arms, then all the listeners uttered together one long, long shuddering cry of anguish; and thereafter they wept and wailed so loudly and so wildly that the blind man was frightened by the violence of the grief that he had caused. For some time the sobbing and the wailing continued. But gradually the sounds of lamentation died away; and again, in the great stillness that followed, Hōichi heard the voice of the woman whom he supposed to be the *Rojo*.

She said:

"Although we had been assured that you were a very skillful player upon the *biwa*, and without an equal in recitation, we did not know that anyone could be so skillful as you have proved yourself tonight. Our lord has been pleased to say that he intends to bestow upon you a fitting reward. But he desires that you shall perform before him once every night for the next six nights—after which time he will probably make his august return journey. Tomorrow night, therefore, you are to come here at the same hour. The retainer who tonight conducted you will be sent for you. . . . There is another matter about which I have been ordered to inform you. It is required that you shall speak to no one of your visits here, during the time of our lord's sojourn at Akamagaséki. As he is traveling incognito,[9] he commands that no mention of these things be made. . . . You are now free to go back to your temple."

After Hōichi had duly expressed his thanks, a woman's hand conducted him to the entrance of the house, where the same retainer, who had guided him before, was waiting to take him home. The retainer led him to the verandah at the rear of the temple, and there bade him farewell.

It was almost dawn when Hōichi returned; but his absence from the temple had not been observed, as the priest, coming back at a very late hour, had supposed him asleep. During the day Hōichi was able to take some rest; and he said nothing about his strange adventure. In the middle of the following night the samurai again came for him, and led him to the august assembly, where he gave another recitation with the same success that had attended his previous performance. But during this second visit his absence from the temple was accidentally discovered; and after his return in the morning he was summoned to the presence of the priest who said to him, in a tone of kindly reproach:

"We have been very anxious about you, friend Hōichi. To go out, blind and alone, at so late an hour, is dangerous. Why did you go without telling us? I could have ordered a servant to accompany you. And where have you been?"

Hōichi answered, evasively,

"Pardon me, kind friend! I had to attend to some private business; and I could not arrange the matter at any other hour."

---

9. **incognito:** in disguise.

The priest was surprised, rather than pained, by Hōichi's reticence: he felt it to be unnatural, and suspected something wrong. He feared that the blind lad had been bewitched or deluded by some evil spirits. He did not ask any more questions; but he privately instructed the men servants of the temple to keep watch upon Hōichi's movements, and to follow him in case that he should again leave the temple after dark.

On the very next night, Hōichi was seen to leave the temple; and the servants immediately lighted their lanterns, and followed after him. But it was a rainy night, and very dark; and before the temple-folks could get to the roadway, Hōichi had disappeared. Evidently he had walked very fast, a strange thing, considering his blindness; for the road was in a bad condition. The men hurried through the streets, making inquiries at every house which Hōichi was accustomed to visit; but nobody could give them any news of him. At last, as they were returning to the temple by way of the shore, they were startled by the sound of a *biwa*, furiously played, in the cemetery of the Amidaji. Except for some ghostly fires—such as usually flitted there on dark nights—all was blackness in that direction. But the men at once hastened to the cemetery; and there, by the help of their lanterns, they discovered Hōichi, sitting alone in the rain before the memorial tomb of Antoku Tennō,[10] making his *biwa* resound, and loudly chanting the chant of the battle of Dan-no-ura. And behind him, and about him, and everywhere above the tombs, the fires of the dead were burning, like candles. Never before had so great a host of *Oni-bi*[11] appeared in the sight of mortal man. . . .

"Hōichi San![12] Hōichi San!" the servants cried, "you are bewitched! . . . Hōichi San!"

But the blind man did not seem to hear. Strenuously he made his biwa to rattle and ring and clang; more and more wildly he chanted the chant of the battle of Dan-no-ura. They caught hold of him; they shouted into his ear:

"Hōichi San! Hōichi San!—come home with us at once!"

Reprovingly he spoke to them:

"To interrupt me in such a manner, before this august assembly, will not be tolerated."

Whereat, in spite of the weirdness of the thing, the servants could not help laughing. Sure that he had been bewitched, they now seized him, and pulled him up on his feet, and by main force hurried him back to the temple, where he was immediately relieved of his wet clothes, by order of the priest, and reclad, and made to eat and drink. Then the priest insisted upon a full explanation of his friend's astonishing behavior.

---

10. **Antoku Tennō:** the infant emperor of the Heiké who drowned at the battle of Dan-no-ura.

11. *Oni-bi:* demon fires, so-called by the fishermen who claimed that the sea and beaches of Dan-no-ura were covered by ghostly fires.

12. **San:** a Japanese term of respect used in addressing a male or female.

Hōichi long hesitated to speak. But at last, finding that his conduct had really alarmed and angered the good priest, he decided to abandon his reserve; and he related everything that had happened from the time of the first visit of the samurai.

The priest said:

"Hōichi, my poor friend, you are now in great danger! How unfortunate that you did not tell me all this before! Your wonderful skill in music has indeed brought you into strange trouble. By this time you must be aware that you have not been visiting any house whatever, but have been passing your nights in the cemetery, among the tombs of the Heiké; and it was before the memorial tomb of Antoku Tenno that our people tonight found you, sitting in the rain. All that you have been imagining was illusion—except the calling of the dead. By once obeying them, you have put yourself in their power. If you obey them again, after what has already occurred, they will tear you in pieces. But they would have destroyed you, sooner or later, in any event. . . . Now I shall not be able to remain with you tonight: I am called away to perform another service. But, before I go, it will be necessary to protect your body by writing holy texts upon it."

Before sundown the priest and his acolyte stripped Hōichi: then, with their writing-brushes, they traced upon his breast and back, head and face and neck, limbs and hands and feet—even upon the soles of his feet, and upon all parts of his body—the text of the holy sûtra[13] called Hannya-Shin-Kyo. When this had been done, the priest instructed Hōichi, saying:

"Tonight, as soon as I go away, you must seat yourself on the verandah, and wait. You will be called. But, whatever may happen, do not answer, and do not move. Say nothing, and sit still—as if meditating. If you stir, or make any noise, you will be torn asunder. Do not get frightened; and do not think of calling for help—because no help could save you. If you do exactly as I tell you, the danger will pass, and you will have nothing more to fear."

After dark the priest and the acolyte went away; and Hoichi seated himself on the verandah, according to the instructions given him. He laid his biwa on the planking beside him, and, assuming the attitude of meditation, remained quite still, taking care not to cough, or to breathe audibly. For hours he stayed thus.

Then, from the roadway, he heard the steps coming. They passed the gate, crossed the garden, approached the verandah, stopped—directly in front of him.

"Hōichi!" the deep voice called. But the blind man held his breath, and sat motionless.

"Hōichi!" grimly called the voice a second time. Then a third time—savagely:

---

13. **holy sûtra:** in Buddhism the sûtras are treatises, often in verse, based on the religious and philosophical discourses of the Buddha.

"Hōichi!"

Hōichi remained as still as a stone, and the voice grumbled:

"No answer!—that won't do! . . . Must see where that fellow is."

There was a noise of heavy feet mounting upon the verandah. The feet approached deliberately, halted beside him. Then, for long minutes, during which Hōichi felt his whole body shake to the beating of his heart, there was dead silence.

At last the gruff voice muttered close to him:

"Here is the *biwa*; but of the *biwa* player I see—only two ears! . . . So that explains why he did not answer: he had no mouth to answer with—there is nothing left of him but his ears. . . . Now to my lord those ears I will take—in proof that the august commands have been obeyed, so far as was possible."

At that instant Hōichi felt his ears gripped by fingers of iron, and torn off! Great as the pain was, he gave no cry. The heavy footfalls receded along the verandah, descended into the garden, passed out to the roadway, ceased. From either side of his head, the blind man felt a thick warm trickling; but he dared not lift his hands.

Before sunrise the priest came back. He hastened at once to the verandah in the rear, stepped and slipped upon something clammy, and uttered a cry of horror; for he saw, by the light of his lantern, that the clamminess was blood. But he perceived Hōichi sitting there, in the attitude of meditation—with the blood still oozing from his wounds.

"My poor Hōichi!" cried the startled priest, "what is this? . . . You have been hurt?"

At the sound of his friend's voice, the blind man felt safe. He burst out sobbing, and tearfully told his adventure of the night.

"Poor, poor Hōichi!" the priest exclaimed, "all my fault! my very grievous fault! . . . Everywhere upon your body the holy texts had been written—except upon your ears! I trusted my acolyte to do that part of the work; and it was very, very wrong of me not to have made sure that he had done it! . . . Well, the matter cannot now be helped; we can only try to heal your hurts as soon as possible. . . . Cheer up, friend!—the danger is now well over. You will never again be troubled by those visitors."

With the aid of a good doctor, Hōichi soon recovered from his injuries. The story of his strange adventure spread far and wide, and soon made him famous. Many noble persons went to Akamagaséki to hear him recite; and large presents of money were given to him, so that he became a wealthy man. . . . But from the time of his adventure, he was known only by the appellation of *Mimi-nashi-Hōichi*: "Hōichi-the-Earless."

DISCUSSION QUESTIONS

1. What was your first impression of the supernatural beings that Hōichi entertained? (Did they seem benevolent or threatening?) Was this impression later confirmed or modified?

2. How does the first paragraph foreshadow the main episode of the story?

3. What hints are given that Hōichi might be dealing with supernatural forces?

4. Which part of Hōichi's recital do the spirits in the cemetery find especially moving? Why?

5. What long-term benefits does Hōichi receive from his strange experience?

SUGGESTION FOR WRITING

Imagine that you heard Hōichi's performance in the cemetery and have decided to write a review of it for the *Amidaji Times,* a local newspaper. Evaluate the performance, explaining its special strengths.

SEAMI
(1363–1443)

The greatest playwright of the Noh theater, Seami (also spelled Zeami) Motokiyo was, in a sense, the Shakespeare of Japan. He began acting at the age of seven, attracted the attention of the shogun (the military governor who ruled Japan at that time in the name of the emperor), and launched a brilliant career that was to lead to the writing of some 240 plays. Together with his father, he opened an acting school and shaped the Noh drama out of popular theatrical traditions of the time. In 1422, Seami retired from the world to become a Zen monk, leaving the leadership of the acting school to his son. Noh, which is characterized by its tragic tone, stylized gestures, poetic language, heavy reliance on a chorus, and the use of masked performers, has endured to this day as the oldest living drama in the world. ■

THE DAMASK DRUM
Translated by Arthur Waley

PERSONS

A COURTIER
AN OLD GARDNER
THE PRINCESS

COURTIER. I am a courtier at the Palace of Kinomaru in the country of Chikuzen. You must know that in this place there is a famous pond called the Laurel Pond, where the royal ones often take their walks; so it happened that one day the old man who sweeps the garden here caught sight of the Princess. And from that time he has loved her with a love that gives his heart no rest.

Someone told her of this, and she said, "Love's equal realm knows no divisions," and in her pity she said, "By that pond there stands a laurel tree, and on its branches there hangs a drum. Let him beat the drum, and if the sound is heard in the Palace, he shall see my face again."

I must tell him of this.

Listen, old Gardener! The worshipful lady has heard of your love and sends you this message: "Go and beat the drum that hangs on the tree by the pond, and if the sound is heard in the Palace, you shall see my face again." Go quickly now and beat the drum!

GARDNER. With trembling I receive her words. I will go and beat the drum.

COURTIER. Look, here is the drum she spoke of. Make haste and beat it!

(He leaves the GARDNER *standing by the tree and seats himself at the foot of the "Waki's pillar.[1])*

GARDNER. They talk of the moon-tree, the laurel that grows in the Garden of the Moon. . . . But for me there is but one true tree, this laurel by the lake. Oh, may the drum that hangs on its branches give forth a mighty note, a music to bind up my bursting heart.
Listen! the evening bell to help me chimes;
But then it tolls in
A heavy tale of day linked on to day,

CHORUS *(speaking for the* GARDNER*)*. And hope stretched out from dusk to dusk
But now, a watchman of the hours, I beat
The longed-for stroke.

GARDNER. I was old, I shunned the daylight,
I was gaunt as an aged crane;
And upon all that misery
Suddenly a sorrow was heaped,
The new sorrow of love.
The days had left their marks,
Coming and coming, like waves that beat on a sandy shore . . .

CHORUS. Oh, with a thunder of white waves
The echo of the drum shall roll.

GARDNER. The afterworld draws near me,
Yet even now I wake not
From this autumn of love that closes
In sadness the sequence of my years.

CHORUS. And slow as the autumn dew
Tears gather in my eyes, to fall
Scattered like dewdrops from a shaken flower
On my coarse-woven dress.
See here the marks, imprint of tangled love,
That all the world will read.

GARDNER. I said "I will forget,"

CHORUS. And got worse torment so
Than by remembrance. But all in this world

---

1. Waki's pillar: a support on stage used in Noh plays.

Is as the horse of the aged man of the land of Sai; [2]
And as a white colt flashes
Past a gap in the hedge, even so our days pass.
And though the time be come,
Yet can none know the road that he at last must tread,
Goal of his dewdrop life.
All this I knew; yet knowing,
Was blind with folly.

GARDNER. "Wake, wake," he cries,—

CHORUS. The watchman of the hours,—
"Wake from the sleep of dawn!"
And batters on the drum.
For if its sound be heard, soon shall he see
Her face, the damask[3] of her dress . . .
Aye, damask! He does not know
That on a damask drum he beats,
Beats with all the strength of his hands, his aged hands,
But hears no sound.
"Am I grown deaf?" he cries, and listens, listens:
Rain on the windows, lapping of waves on the pool—
Both these he hears, and silent only
The drum, strange damask drum.
Oh, will it never sound?
I thought to beat the sorrow from my heart,
Wake music in a damask drum; an echo of love
From the voiceless fabric of pride!

GARDNER. Longed for as the moon that hides
In the obstinate clouds of a rainy night
Is the sound of the watchman's drum,
To roll the darkness from my heart.

CHORUS. I beat the drum. The days pass and the hours.
It was yesterday, and it is today.

GARDNER. But she for whom I wait.

CHORUS. Comes not even in dream. At dawn and dusk

GARDNER. No drum sounds.

CHORUS. She has not come. Is it not sung that those
Whom love has joined

---

2. **the horse . . . Sai:** According to a Japanese tale, a man's horse bolted and consequently was
saved from being seized by the government during a revolutionary period. After the revolution,
the man found his horse. The moral is that what appears to be bad luck is sometimes good luck
and vice versa.

3. **damask:** a rich, lustrous fabric with a woven design that shows on both sides of the cloth. The
robes of Japanese royalty were often made of damask.

Not even the God of Thunder can divide?
Of lovers, I alone
Am guideless, comfortless.
Then weary of himself and calling her to witness of his woe,
"Why should I endure," he cried,
"Such life at this?" and in the waters of the pond
He cast himself and died.

(GARDNER *leaves the stage.*)
(*Enter the* PRINCESS.)

COURTIER. I would speak with you, madam.
 The drum made no sound, and the aged Gardener in despair
 has flung himself into the pond by the laurel tree, and died.
 The soul of such a one may cling to you and do you injury. Go
 out and look upon him.

PRINCESS (*speaking wildly, already possessed by the* GARDNER's *angry ghost,*
 which speaks through her). Listen, people, listen!
 In the noise of the beating waves
 I hear the rolling of a drum.
 Oh, joyful sound, oh joyful!
 The music of a drum.

COURTIER. Strange, strange!
 This lady speaks as one
 By fantasy possessed.
 What is amiss, what ails her?

PRINCESS . Truly, by fantasy I am possessed.
 Can a damask drum give sound?
 When I bade him beat what could not ring,
 Then tottered first my wits.

COURTIER. She spoke, and on the face of the evening pool
 A wave stirred.

PRINCESS. And out of the wave

COURTIER. A voice spoke.

(*The voice of the* GARDNER *is heard; as he gradually advances along*
 the hashigakari[4] *it is seen that he wears a "demon mask," leans on*
 a staff, and carries the "demon mallet" at his girdle.)

GARDNER'S GHOST. I was driftwood in the pool, but the waves of
 bitterness

CHORUS. Have washed me back to the shore.

GHOST. Anger clings to my heart,
 Clings even now when neither wrath or weeping
 Are aught but folly.

---

4. **hashigakari:** the runway on a Noh stage

CHORUS. One thought consumes me,
> The anger of lust denied
> Covers me like darkness.
> I am become a demon dwelling
> In the hell of my dark thoughts,
> Storm cloud of my desires.

GHOST. "Though the waters parch in the fields
> Though the brooks run dry,
> Never shall the place be shown
> Of the spring that feeds my heart."
> So I had resolved. Oh, why so cruelly
> Set they me to win
> voice from a voiceless drum,
> Spending my heart in vain?
> And I spent my heart on the glimpse of a moon that slipped
> Through the boughs of an autumn tree.

CHORUS. This damask drum that hangs on the laurel tree

GHOST. Will it sound, will it sound?

> (*He seizes the* PRINCESS *and drags her towards the drum.*)

> Try! Strike it!

CHORUS. "Strike!" he cries;
> "The quick beat, the battle-charge!
> Loud, loud! Strike, strike," he rails,
> And brandishing his demon stick
> Gives her no rest.
> "Oh woe!" the lady weeps,
> "No sound, no sound. Oh misery!" she wails.
> And he, at the mallet stroke, "Repent, repent!"
> Such torments in the world of night
> Abōrasetsu, chief of demons, wields,
> Who on the Wheel of Fire
> Sears sinful flesh and shatters bones to dust.
> Not less her torture now!
> "Oh, agony!" she cries, "What have I done,
> By what dire seed this harvest sown?"

ghost. Clear stands the cause before you.

CHORUS. Clear stands the cause before my eyes;
> I know it now.
> By the pool's white waters, upon the laurel's bough
> The drum was hung.
> He did not know his hour, but struck and struck
> Till all the will had ebbed from his heart's core;
> Then leapt into the lake and died.
> And while his body rocked
> Like driftwood on the waves,

His soul, an angry ghost,
Possessed the lady's wits, haunted her heart with woe,
The mallet lashed, as these waves lash the shore,
Lash on the ice of the eastern shore.
The wind passes; the rain falls
On the Red Lotus, the Lesser and the Greater.[5]
The hair stands up on my head.
"The fish that leaps the falls
To a fell snake is turned,"[6]
I have learned to know them;
Such, such are the demons of the World of Night.
"O hateful lady, hateful!" he cried, and sank again
Into the whirlpool of desire.

---

5. **the rain . . . Greater:** In Buddhism the Red Lotus is an emblem of paradise, whereas the Lesser and the Greater are the names of two cold hells. Accordingly the rain falls on both the virtuous and the evil.

6. **"The fish . . . turned":** According to a legend, the fish which successfully cleared a certain waterfall became a dragon. Thus, the Gardener's efforts to reach the Princess have turned him into an evil spirit.

DISCUSSION QUESTIONS

1. The princess in *The Damask Drum* decides to discourage the old gardener by humiliating him. What do you think is the best way to discourage unwanted attention? Can it be done without cruelty?

2. How is this Noh play different from most of the American or European dramas you have seen or read?

3. It has been said that Seami's plays often create a sense of eternity by emphasizing (a) the quick passing of time and (b) the insignificance of human life. Select several phrases or statements from the play that demonstrate these themes.

4. Seami is known for his skillful use of figurative language. Discuss the meaning of the following figures of speech:

   • The damask drum is called "the voiceless fabric of pride."

   • The ghost of the gardener says, "I spent my heart on the glimpse of a moon that slipped / Through the boughs of an autumn tree."

   • As the princess is being tormented by the ghost, she cries, "By what dire seed this harvest sown?"

5. In what way does "the punishment fit the crime" in this play?

SUGGESTIONS FOR WRITING

1. Write a paragraph describing either the pain of rejection or the annoyance of being pursued by an unwanted suitor. Use figurative language to describe your feelings. Try to use related images. The sample below, for instance, draws all its images from the sea:

> I needed him as much as a fish needs water, but he needed me about as much as a fish needs a pair of shoes. When I realized how things stood, I felt like a fish left gasping on the seashore.

2. Write a short one-act play about a disappointing experience that a high school student might have. Try to introduce some of the characteristics of Noh drama, such as its contemplative mood and a character who functions as the chorus. Use plenty of figurative language to express the disappointment of the main character. Resolve the situation by showing some kind of justice done.

HAIKU

One of the shortest of all poetic forms, the haiku is a traditional Japanese verse form consisting of 17 syllables arranged in three lines (5-7-5). Its extreme brevity tends to make it a poem of suggestion and unexpected associations. Traditionally the haiku is a poem of quiet dignity that focuses on the natural world, the fleeting moment, and the interdependence of all things. In recent years, however, the haiku has been used to express a wide range of attitudes about almost any subject, including highly emotional subjects presented with shocking imagery.

By far the most influential writer of haiku was Matsuo Bashō, who developed the form as we know it today. He dedicated himself to poetry as a way of life, traveling constantly in search of artistic impressions and occasionally withdrawing from society to reflect. Stressing objectivity in poetry and stern discipline in living, he gathered a group of disciples and established a literary school. His haiku are noted for their restrained elegance, inventiveness, desolate beauty, and sense of eternity. The joining of two seemingly unrelated phenomena is a feature of his haiku that has been widely imitated.

More than half a century later Taniguchi Buson built on the work of Bashō, creating haiku that are colorful, imaginative, and sensuous. Equally famous as a landscape painter and a poet, he was a dedicated craftsman whose poems, which are ornate and rich in detail, reflect his interest in painting.

Among the general Japanese reading public, Kobayashi Issa (who uses the simple pen name "Issa") is probably the best loved of the haiku poets. The main charm of his poetry stems from his intense personality and his ability to lay bare his emotions in simple, unadorned language. A number of unhappy incidents in his life, including cruel treatment from a stepmother and the death of his wife and children, brought distrust and alienation into his life. By expressing his doubts and his loneliness in highly personal haiku, he expresses the doubts and loneliness of many people.

Translating Japanese haiku is an extremely difficult task since the strict form of these poems cannot be reproduced in English without drastically changing the meaning. For this reason, many English translators have tried to capture the overall effect of the poems rather than attempt to imitate their structure. ∎

MATSUO BASHŌ (1644–1694)

Translated by Harold G. Henderson

PERSISTENCE

Did it yell
till it became *all* voice?
   Cicada-shell!

CLOUDS

Clouds come from time to time—
    and bring to men a chance to rest
        from looking at the moon.

IN A WIDE WASTELAND

On the moor: from things
    detached completely—
        how the skylark sings!

THE POOR MAN'S SON

Poverty's child—
    he starts to grind the rice,
        and gazes at the moon.

THE SUN PATH

The sun's way:
    hollyhocks turn toward it
        through all the rain of May.

SUMMER VOICES

So soon to die,
    and no sign of it showing—
        locust-cry.

LIGHTNING AT NIGHT

A lightning gleam:
    into darkness travels
        a night heron's scream.

TANIGUCHI BUSON (1715–1783)

Translated by Harold G. Henderson

THE SOUND

Here . . . there . . .
    the sound of waterfalls is heard—
        young leaves, everywhere.

SYMPHONY IN WHITE

Blossoms on the pear—
    and a woman in the moonlight
        reads a letter there.

SPRING BREEZE

These morning airs—
    one can see them stirring
        caterpillar hairs!

SUMMER GARMENTS

Upon the golden screens
    gauze clothes are painted—whose?
        The autumn winds . . .

ISSA (1762–1826)

Translated by Harold G. Henderson

CONTENTMENT IN POVERTY

A one-foot waterfall—
    it too makes noises,
        and the night is cool.

THE GREAT BUDDHA AT NARA

Out from the hollow
    of Great Buddha's nose—
        comes a swallow!

CONSCIENCE

Somehow it seems wrong:
    to take one's noonday nap and hear
        a rice-planting song.

A WISH

My grumbling wife—
    if only she were here!
        This moon tonight . . .

DISCUSSION QUESTIONS

1. Why do you think the Japanese haiku has become such a popular form of poetry?

2. What are the most common subjects of these traditional haiku?

3. Explain the witty hyperbole (exaggeration) in the haiku entitled "Persistence."

4 Unable to reproduce the Japanese 17-syllable pattern in the English translation, the translator of these haiku has imposed structure in another way. What technique has he used to give the poems a structured pattern?

5. It has been said that the haiku often expresses hidden hopes in small things. Which of the haiku in this collection fit this description?

SUGGESTION FOR WRITING

Choose an academic subject or a school-related activity that is part of your life right now. Write two haiku that capture the essence of this subject or your feelings about it. Follow the syllabic requirements for the haiku (5-7-5).

SHIGA NAOYA

(1883-1971)

A fiction writer known for his meticulous style, Shiga was the son of a wealthy businessman. He studied literature at Tokyo University and then joined with several college friends in founding a monthly literary magazine called *The White Birch*. This magazine helped influence literary development in Japan for over a decade.

Shiga's short stories are characterized by a simple, rhythmical style and a very spare plot structure. They usually focus on the inner experience of a single character, who tends to be the only character with a name. These stories are highly regarded in Japan but are difficult to translate because of their subtle style. Shiga's most important work is a psychological novel entitled *A Dark Night's Journey*, which took him 25 years to complete. In 1949 he was awarded the Order of Cultural Merit for his literary achievements. ■

SEIBEI'S GOURDS

Translated by Ivan Morris

This is the story of a young boy called Seibei, and of his gourds.[1] Later on Seibei gave up gourds, but he soon found something to take their place: he started painting pictures. It was not long before Seibei was as absorbed in his paintings as he once had been in his gourds.

· · · · ·

Seibei's parents knew that he often went out to buy himself gourds. He got them for a few sen[2] and soon had a sizable collection. When he came home, he would first bore a neat hole in the top of the gourd and extract the seeds. Next he applied tea leaves to get rid of the unpleasant gourd smell. He then fetched the saké[3] which he had saved up from the dregs in his father's cup and carefully polished the surface.

Seibei was passionately interested in gourds. One day as he was strolling along the beach, absorbed in his favorite subject, he was startled by an unusual sight: he caught a glimpse of the bald, elongated head of an old man hurrying out of one of the huts by the beach. "What a splendid gourd!" thought Seibei. The old man disappeared from sight, wagging

---

1. **gourds:** In Japan the cultivation and collection of gourds, the hard-shelled fruit of certain vines, is a popular pastime. The dried shells are used as bottles.

2. **sen:** a Japanese coin of little value.

3. **saké:** a Japanese alcoholic beverage made from rice.

his bald pink pate. Only then did Seibei realize his mistake and he stood there laughing loudly to himself. He laughed all the way home.

Whenever he passed a grocery, a curio shop, a confectioner's, or in fact any place that sold gourds, he stood for minutes on end, his eyes glued to the window, appraising the precious fruit.

Seibei was twelve years old and still at primary school. After class, instead of playing with the other children, he usually wandered about the town looking for gourds. Then in the evening he would sit cross-legged in the corner of the living room working on his newly acquired fruit. When he had finished treating it, he poured in a little sake, inserted a cork stopper which he had fashioned himself, wrapped it in a towel, put this in a tin especially kept for the purpose and finally placed the whole thing on the charcoal foot warmer. Then he went to bed.

As soon as he woke the next morning, he would open the tin and examine the gourd. The skin would be thoroughly damp from the overnight treatment. Seibei would gaze adoringly at his treasure before tying a string round the middle and hanging it in the sun to dry. Then he set out for school.

Seibei lived in a harbor town. Although it was officially a city, one could walk from one end to the other in a matter of twenty minutes. Seibei was always wandering about the streets and had soon come to know every place that sold gourds and to recognize almost every gourd on the market.

He did not care much about the old, gnarled, peculiarly formed gourds usually favored by collectors. The type that appealed to Seibei was even and symmetrical.

"That youngster of yours only seems to like the ordinary looking ones," said a friend of his father's who had come to call. He pointed at the boy, who was sitting in the corner busily polishing a plain, round gourd.

"Fancy a lad spending his time playing around like that with gourds!" said his father, giving Seibei a disgusted look.

"See here, Seibei my lad," said the friend, "there's no use just collecting lots of those things. It's not the quantity that counts, you know. What you want to do is to find one or two really unusual ones."

"I prefer this kind," said Seibei and let the matter drop.

Seibei's father and his friend started talking about gourds.

"Remember that Bakin gourd they had at the agricultural show last spring?" said his father. "It was a real beauty, wasn't it?"

"Yes, I remember. That big, long one. . . ."

As Seibei listened to their conversation, he was laughing inwardly. The Bakin gourd had made quite a stir at the time, but when he had gone to see it (having no idea, of course, who the great poet Bakin might be) he had found it rather a stupid-looking object and had walked out of the show.

"I didn't think so much of it," interrupted Seibei. "It's just a clumsy great thing."

His father opened his eyes wide in surprise and anger.

"What's that?" he shouted. "When you don't know what you're talking about, you'd better shut up!"

Seibei did not say another word.

One day when he was walking along an unfamiliar back street he came upon an old woman with a fruit stall. She was selling dried persimmons and oranges; on the shutters of the house behind the stall she had hung a large cluster of gourds.

"Can I have a look?" said Seibei and immediately ran behind the stall and began examining the gourds. Suddenly he caught sight of one which was about five inches long and at first sight looked quite commonplace. Something about it made Seibei's heart beat faster.

"How much is this one?" he asked, panting out the words.

"Well," said the old woman, "since you're just a lad, I'll let you have it for ten sen."

"In that case," said Seibei urgently, "please hold it for me, won't you? I'll be right back with the money."

He dashed home and in no time at all was back at the stall. He bought the gourd and took it home.

From that time on, he was never separated from his new gourd. He even took it along to school and used to polish it under his desk during class time. It was not long before he was caught at this by one of the teachers, who was particularly incensed because it happened to take place in an ethics class.

This teacher came from another part of Japan and found it most offensive that children should indulge in such effeminate pastimes as collecting gourds.[4] He was forever expounding the classical code of the samurai,[4] and when Kumoemon, the famous Naniwabushi performer,[5] came on tour and recited brave deeds of ancient times, he would attend every single performance, though normally he would not deign to set foot in the disreputable amusement area. He never minded having his students sing Naniwabushi ballads, however raucously. Now, when he found Seibei silently polishing his gourd, his voice trembled with fury.

"You're an idiot!" he shouted. "There's absolutely no future for a boy like you." Then and there he confiscated the gourd on which Seibei had spent so many long hours of work. Seibei stared straight ahead and did not cry.

When he got home, Seibei's face was pale. Without a word, he put his feet on the warmer and sat looking blankly at the wall.

After a while the teacher arrived. As Seibei's father was not yet home from the carpenter's shop where he worked, the teacher directed his attack at Seibei's mother.

"This sort of thing is the responsibility of the family," he said in a stern

---

4. **samurai:** a member of a hereditary military class in feudal Japan.

5. **Naniwabushi performer:** a ballad singer who performs in a small theater and accompanies himself on a samisen (a guitar-like instrument).

voice. "It is the duty of you parents to see that such things don't happen." In an agony of embarrassment, Seibei's mother muttered some apology.

Meanwhile, Seibei was trying to make himself as inconspicuous as possible in the corner. Terrified, he glanced up at his vindictive teacher and at the wall directly behind where a whole row of fully prepared gourds was hanging. What would happen if the teacher caught sight of them?

Trembling inside, he awaited the worst, but at length the man exhausted his rhetoric and stamped angrily out of the house. Seibei heaved a sigh of relief.

Seibei's mother was sobbing softly. In a querulous whine she began to scold him, and in the midst of this, Seibei's father returned from his shop. As soon as he heard what had happened, he grabbed his son by the collar and gave him a sound beating. "You're no good!" he bawled at him. "You'll never get anywhere in the world the way you're carrying on. I've a good mind to throw you out into the street where you belong!" The gourds on the wall caught his attention. Without a word, he fetched his hammer and systematically smashed them to pieces one after another. Seibei turned pale but said nothing.

The next day the teacher gave Seibei's confiscated gourd to an old porter who worked in the school. "Here, take this," he said, as if handing over some unclean object. The porter took the gourd home with him and hung it on the wall of his small, sooty room.

About two months later the porter, finding himself even more hard pressed for money than usual, decided to take the gourd to a local curio shop to see if he could get a few coppers for it. The curio dealer examined the gourd carefully; then, assuming an uninterested tone, he handed it back to the porter saying: "I might give you five yen[6] for it."

The porter was astounded, but being quite an astute old man, he replied coolly: "I certainly wouldn't part with it for that." The dealer immediately raised his offer to ten yen, but the porter was still adamant.

In the end the curio dealer had to pay fifty yen for the gourd. The porter left the shop, delighted at his luck. It wasn't often that the teachers gave one a free gift equivalent to a year's wages! He was so clever as not to mention the matter to anyone, and neither Seibei nor the teacher ever heard what had happened to the gourd. Yes, the porter was clever, but he was not clever enough: little did he imagine that this same gourd would be passed on by the curio dealer to a wealthy collector in the district for six hundred yen.

· · · · ·

Seibei is now engrossed in his pictures. He no longer feels any bitterness either toward the teacher, or toward his father who smashed all his precious gourds to pieces.

Yet gradually his father has begun to scold him for painting pictures.

---

6. **yen:** Japanese monetary unit.

DISCUSSION QUESTIONS

1. What words would you use to describe Seibei? Were you able to sympathize with his rather unusual interest in gourds?

2. What is the purpose of the short scene at the beginning of the story in which Seibei mistakes a man's bald head for a gourd?

3. What kind of gourds does Seibei like? What does this say about his artistic taste?

4. Explain the unintended irony in the words of Seibei's father, who shouts, "When you don't know what you're talking about, you'd better shut up!"

5. What does "Seibei's Gourds" seem to imply about the place of an artist in society?

SUGGESTION FOR WRITING

Think of an interest, preference, or pastime that you have that is not understood or respected by some of your acquaintances. First write a letter or E-mail message from your acquaintances' point of view, explaining why this seems like a strange pastime. Then write a response from your own point of view, explaining the value of this pastime.

TANIZAKI JUNICHIRO

(1886–1965)

Born in Tokyo, where his family owned a printing press, Tanizaki studied Japanese literature at Tokyo Imperial University. Shortly afterward he helped found a literary magazine and began to write stories for it. At this point in his development his stories were strongly influenced by such western writers as Edgar Allan Poe and Oscar Wilde.

Tanizaki remained in the heart of Tokyo until the earthquake of 1923, when he moved to Kyoto, the ancient capital of Japan. The historic and cultured atmosphere of this city inspired him to a new appreciation of Japan's past, and he soon stopped using Western models. From that time forward, his fiction changed completely. His novels began to dramatize the conflict between modern ideas and traditional Japanese values. His well-known novel *Some Prefer Nettles,* for example, focuses on a marriage that must confront changing cultural values. *The Makioka Sisters* is a long novel about four sisters who must deal with the encroachment of modern life on their gentle, traditional values. In 1949 Tanizaki received the Imperial Prize in Literature for *The Makioka Sisters.* ∎

THE THIEF

Translated by Howard Hibbett

It was years ago, at the school where I was preparing for Tokyo Imperial University.

My dormitory roommates and I used to spend a lot of time at what we called "candlelight study" (there was very little studying to it), and one night, long after lights-out, the four of us were doing just that, huddled around a candle talking on and on.

I recall that we were having one of our confused, heated arguments about love—a problem of great concern to us in those days. Then, by a natural course of development, the conversation turned to the subject of crime: we found ourselves talking about such things as swindling, theft, and murder.

"Of all crimes, the one we're most likely to commit is murder." It was Higuchi, the son of a well-known professor, who declared this. "But I don't believe I'd ever steal—I just couldn't do it. I think I could be friends with any other kind of person, but a thief seems to belong to a different species." A shadow of distaste darkened his handsome features. Somehow that frown emphasized his good looks.

"I hear there's been a rash of stealing in the dormitory lately." This time it was Hirata who spoke. "Isn't that so?" he asked, turning to Nakamura, our other roommate.

"Yes, and they say it's one of the students."

"How do they know?" I asked.

"Well, I haven't heard all the details—" Nakamura dropped his voice to a confidential whisper. "But it's happened so often it must be an inside job."

"Not only that," Higuchi put in, "one of the fellows in the north wing was just going into his room the other day when somebody pushed the door open from the inside, caught him with a hard slap in the face, and ran away down the hall. He chased after him, but by the time he got to the bottom of the stairs the other one was out of sight. Back in his room, he found his trunk and bookshelves in a mess, which proves it was the thief."

"Did he see his face?"

"No, it all happened too fast, but he says he looked like one of us, the way he was dressed. Apparently he ran down the hall with his coat pulled up over his head—the one thing sure is that his coat had a wisteria crest."

"A wisteria crest?" said Hirata. "You can't prove anything by that." Maybe it was only my imagination, but I thought he flashed a suspicious look at me. At the same moment I felt that I instinctively made a wry face, since my own family crest is a wisteria design. It was only by chance that I wasn't wearing my crested coat that night.

"If he's one of us it won't be easy to catch him. Nobody wants to believe there's a thief among us." I was trying to get over my embarrassment because of that moment of weakness.

"No, they'll get him in a couple of days," Higuchi said emphatically. His eyes were sparkling. "This is a secret, but they say he usually steals things in the dressing room of the bathhouse, and for two or three days now the proctors have been keeping watch. They hide overhead and look down through a little hole."

"Oh? Who told you that?" Nakamura asked.

"One of the proctors. But don't go around talking about it."

"If *you* know so much, the thief probably knows it too!" said Hirata, looking disgusted.

Here I must explain that Hirata and I were not on very good terms. In fact, by that time we barely tolerated each other. I say "we," but it was Hirata who had taken a strong dislike to me. According to a friend of mine, he once remarked scornfully that I wasn't what everyone seemed to think I was, that he'd had a chance to see through me. And again: "I'm sick of him. He'll never be a friend of mine. It's only out of pity that I have anything to do with him."

He only said such things behind my back; I never heard them from him directly, though it was obvious that he loathed me. But it wasn't in my nature to demand an explanation. "If there's something wrong with me he ought to say so," I told myself. "If he doesn't have the kindness to tell me what it is, or if he thinks I'm not worth bothering with, then I won't think of him as a friend either." I felt a little lonely when I thought of his contempt for me, but I didn't really worry about it.

Hirata had an admirable physique and was the very type of masculinity that our school prides itself on, while I was skinny and pale and high-strung. There was something basically incompatible about us: I had to resign myself to the fact that we lived in separate worlds. Furthermore, Hirata was a judo expert of high rank, and displayed his muscles as if to say: "Watch out, or I'll give you a thrashing!" Perhaps it seemed cowardly of me to take such a meek attitude toward him, and no doubt I was afraid of his physical strength; but fortunately I was quite indifferent to matters of trivial pride or prestige. "I don't care how contemptuous the other fellow is; as long as I can go on believing in myself I don't need to feel bitter toward him." That was how I made up my mind, and so I was able to match Hirata's arrogance with my own cool magnanimity. I even told one of the other boys: "I can't help it if Hirata doesn't understand me, but I appreciate his good points anyway." And I actually believed it. I never considered myself a coward. I was even rather conceited, thinking I must be a person of noble character to be able to praise Hirata from the bottom of my heart.

"A wisteria crest?" That night, when Hirata cast his sudden glance at me, the malicious look in his eyes set my nerves on edge. What could that look possibly mean? Did he know that my family crest was wisteria? Or did I take it that way simply because of my own private feelings? If Hirata suspected *me*, how was I to handle the situation? Perhaps I should laugh good-naturedly and say: "Then I'm under suspicion too, because I have the same crest." If the others laughed along with me, I'd be all right. But suppose one of them, say Hirata, only began looking grimmer and grimmer—what then? When I visualized that scene I couldn't very well speak out impulsively.

It sounds foolish to worry about such a thing, but during that brief silence all sorts of thoughts raced through my mind. "In this kind of situation what difference is there, really, between an innocent man and an actual criminal?" By then I felt that I was experiencing a criminal's anxiety and isolation. Until a moment ago I had been one of their friends, one of the elite of our famous school. But now, if only in my own mind, I was an outcast. It was absurd, but I suffered from my inability to confide in them. I was uneasy about Hirata's slightest mood—Hirata who was supposed to be my equal.

"A thief seems to belong to a different species." Higuchi had probably said this casually enough, but now his words echoed ominously in my mind.

"A thief belongs to a different species. . . ." A thief! What a detestable name to be called! I suppose what makes a thief different from other men is not so much his criminal act itself as his effort to hide it at all costs, the strain of trying to put it out of his mind, the dark fears that he can never confess. And now I was becoming enshrouded by that darkness. I was trying not to believe that I was under suspicion; I was worrying about fears that I could not admit to my closest friend. Of course it must have been because Higuchi trusted me that he told us what he'd heard from the proctor. "Don't go around talking about it," he had said, and I was glad. But why should I feel glad? I thought. After all, Higuchi has never suspected me. Somehow I began to wonder about his motive for telling us.

It also struck me that if even the most virtuous person has criminal tendencies, maybe I wasn't the only one who imagined the possibility of being a thief. Maybe the others were experiencing a little of the same discomfort, the same elation. If so, then Higuchi, who had been singled out by the proctor to share his secret, must have felt very proud. Among the four of us it was he who was most trusted, he who was thought least likely to belong to that "other species." And if he won that trust because he came from a wealthy family and was the son of a famous professor, then I could hardly avoid envying him. Just as his social status improved his moral character, so my own background—I was acutely conscious of being a scholarship student, the son of a poor farmer—debased mine. For me to feel a kind of awe in his presence had nothing to do with whether or not I was a thief. We did belong to different species. I felt that the more he trusted me, with his frank, open attitude, the more the gulf between us deepened. The more friendly we tried to be, joking with each other in apparent intimacy, gossiping and laughing together, the more the distance between us increased. There was nothing I could do about it.

For a long time afterward I worried about whether or not I ought to wear that coat of mine with the "wisteria crest." Perhaps if I wore it around nonchalantly no one would pay any attention. But suppose they looked at me as much as to say: "Ah, he's wearing it!" Some would suspect me, or try to suppress their doubts of me, or feel sorry for me because I was under suspicion. If I became embarrassed and uneasy not only with Hirata and Higuchi but with all the students, and if I then felt obliged to put my coat away, that would seem even more sinister. What I dreaded was not the bare fact of being suspect, but all the unpleasant emotions that would be stirred up in others. If I were to cause doubt in other people's minds I would create a barrier between myself and those who had always been my friends. Even theft itself was not as ugly as the suspicions that would be aroused by it. No one would want to think of me as a thief: as long as it hadn't been proved, they'd want to go on associating with me as freely as ever, forcing themselves to trust me. Otherwise, what would friendship mean? Thief or not, I might be guilty of a worse sin than stealing from a friend: the sin of spoiling a friendship. Sowing seeds of doubt about myself was criminal. It *was* worse than stealing. If I were a prudent, clever thief—no, I mustn't put it that way—if I were a thief with the least bit of conscience and consideration for other people, I'd try to keep my friendships untarnished, try to be open with my friends, treat them with a sincerity and warmth that I need never be ashamed of, while carrying out my thefts in secrecy. Perhaps I'd be what people call "a brazen thief," but if you look at it from the thief's point of view, it's the most honest attitude to take. "It's true that I steal, but it's equally true that I value my friends," such a man would say. "That is typical of a thief, that's why he belongs to a different species." Anyhow, when I started thinking that way, I couldn't help becoming more and more aware of the distance between me and my friends. Before I knew it I felt like a full-fledged thief.

One day I mustered up my courage and wore the crested coat out on the school grounds. I happened to meet Nakamura, and we began walking along together.

"By the way," I remarked, "I hear they haven't caught the thief yet."

"That's right," Nakamura answered, looking away.

"Why not? Couldn't they trap him at the bathhouse?"

"He didn't show up there again, but you still hear about lots of things being stolen in other places. They say the proctors called Higuchi in the other day and gave him the devil for letting their plan leak out.

"Higuchi?" I felt the color drain from my face.

"Yes. . . ." He sighed painfully, and a tear rolled down his cheek. "You've got to forgive me! I've kept it from you till now, but I think you ought to know the truth. You won't like this, but you're the one the proctors suspect. I hate to talk about it—I've never suspected you for a minute. I believe in you. And because I believe in you, I just had to tell you. I hope you won't hold it against me."

"Thanks for telling me. I'm grateful to you." I was almost in tears myself, but at the same time I thought: "It's come at last!" As much as I dreaded it, I'd been expecting this day to arrive.

"Let's drop the subject," said Nakamura, to comfort me. "I feel better now that I've told you."

"But we can't put it out of our minds just because we hate to talk about it. I appreciate your kindness, but I'm not the only one who's been humiliated—I've brought shame on you too, as my friend. The mere fact that I'm under suspicion makes me unworthy of friendship. Any way you look at it, my reputation is ruined. Isn't that so? I imagine you'll turn your back on me too."

"I swear I never will—and I don't think you've brought any shame on me." Nakamura seemed alarmed by my reproachful tone. "Neither does Higuchi. They say he did his best to defend you in front of the proctors. He told them he'd doubt himself before he doubted you."

"But they still suspect me, don't they? There's no use trying to spare my feelings. Tell me everything you know. I'd rather have it that way."

Then Nakamura hesitantly explained: "Well, it seems the proctors get all kinds of tips. Ever since Higuchi talked too much that night there haven't been any more thefts at the bathhouse, and that's why they suspect you."

"But I wasn't the only one who heard him!"—I didn't say this, but the thought occurred to me immediately. It made me feel even more lonely and wretched.

"But how did they know Higuchi told us? There were only the four of us that night, so if nobody else knew it, and if you and Higuchi trust me—"

"You'll have to draw your own conclusions," Nakamura said, with an imploring look. "You know who it is. He's misjudged you, but I don't want to criticize him."

A sudden chill came over me. I felt as if Hirata's eyes were glaring into mine.

"Did you talk to him about me?"

"Yes. . . . But I hope you realize that it isn't easy, since I'm his friend as well as yours. In fact, Higuchi and I had a long argument with him last night, and he says he's leaving the dormitory. So I have to lose one friend on account of another."

I took Nakamura's hand and gripped it hard. "I'm grateful for friends like you and Higuchi," I said, tears streaming from my eyes. Nakamura cried too. For the first time in my life I felt that I was really experiencing the warmth of human compassion. This was what I had been searching for while I was tormented by my sense of helpless isolation. No matter how vicious a thief I might be, I could never steal anything from Nakamura.

After a while I said: "To tell you the truth, I'm not worth the trouble I'm causing you. I can't stand by in silence and see you two lose such a good friend because of someone like me. Even though he doesn't trust me, I still respect him. He's a far better man than I am. I recognize his value as well as anyone. So why don't I move out instead, if it's come to that? Please—let me go, and you three can keep on living together. Even if I'm alone I'll feel better about it."

"But there's no reason for you to leave," said Nakamura, his voice charged with emotion. "I recognize his good points too, but you're the one that's being persecuted. I won't side with him when it's so unfair. If *you* leave, *we* ought to leave too. You know how stubborn he is—once he's made up his mind to go he's not apt to change it. Why not let him do as he pleases? We might as well wait for him to come to his senses and apologize. That shouldn't take very long anyway."

"But he'll never come back to apologize. He'll go on hating me forever "

Nakamura seemed to assume that I felt resentful toward Hirata. "Oh, I don't think so," he said quickly. "He'll stick to his word—that's both his strength and his weakness—but once he knows he's wrong he'll come and apologize, and make a clean breast of it. That's one of the likable things about him."

"It would be fine if he did . . . ," I said thoughtfully. "He may come back to you, but I don't believe he'll ever make friends with me again. . . . But you're right, he's really likable. I only wish he liked me too."

Nakamura put his hand on my shoulder as if to protect his poor friend, as we plodded listlessly along on the grass. It was evening and a light mist hung over the school grounds: we seemed to be on an island surrounded by endless gray seas. Now and then a few students walking the other way would glance at me and go on. They already know, I thought; they're ostracizing me. I felt an overwhelming loneliness.

That night Hirata seemed to have changed his mind; he showed no intention of moving. But he refused to speak to us—even to Higuchi and

Nakamura. Yet for me to leave at this stage was impossible, I decided. Not only would I be disregarding the kindness of my friends, I would be making myself seem all the more guilty. I ought to wait a little longer.

"Don't worry," my two friends were forever telling me. "As soon as they catch him the whole business will clear up." But even after another week had gone by, the criminal was still at large and the thefts were as frequent as ever. At last even Nakamura and Higuchi lost some money and a few books.

"Well, you two finally got it, didn't you? But I have a feeling the rest of us won't be touched." I remember Hirata's taunting look as he made this sarcastic remark.

After supper Nakamura and Higuchi usually went to the library, and Hirata and I were left to confront each other. I found this so uncomfortable that I began spending my evenings away from the dormitory too, either going to the library or taking long walks. One night around nine-thirty I came back from a walk and looked into our study. Oddly enough, Hirata wasn't there, nor did the others seem to be back yet. I went to look in our bedroom, but it was empty too. Then I went back to the study and over to Hirata's desk. Quietly I opened his drawer and ferreted out the registered letter that had come to him from his home a few days ago. Inside the letter were three ten-yen[1] money orders, one of which I leisurely removed and put in my pocket. I pushed the drawer shut again and sauntered out into the hall. Then I went down to the yard, cut across the tennis court, and headed for the dark weedy hollow where I always buried the things I stole. But at that moment someone yelled: "Thief!" and flew at me from behind, knocking me down with a blow to my head. It was Hirata.

"Come on, let's have it! Let's see what you stuck in your pocket!"

"All right, all right, you don't have to shout like that," I answered calmly, smiling at him. "I admit I stole your money order. If you ask for it I'll give it back to you, and if you tell me to come with you I'll go anywhere you say. So we understand each other, don't we? What more do you want?"

Hirata seemed to hesitate, but soon began furiously raining blows on my face. Somehow the pain was not wholly unpleasant. I felt suddenly relieved of the staggering burden I had been carrying.

"There's no use beating me up like this, when I fell right into your trap for you. I made that mistake because you were so sure of yourself—I thought: 'Why the devil can't I steal from *him*?' But now you've found me out, so that's all there is to it. Later on we'll laugh about it together."

I tried to shake Hirata's hand good-naturedly, but he grabbed me by the collar and dragged me off toward our room. That was the only time Hirata seemed contemptible in my eyes.

"Hey, you fellows, I've caught the thief! You can't say I was taken in by

---

1. **yen:** a Japanese monetary unit, worth about one quarter of a U.S. cent.

him!" Hirata swaggered into our room and shoved me down in front of Nakamura and Higuchi, who were back from the library. Hearing the commotion, the other boys in the dormitory came swarming around our doorway.

"Hirata's right!" I told my two friends, picking myself up from the floor. "I'm the thief." I tried to speak in my normal tone, as casually as ever, but I realized that my face had gone pale.

"I suppose you hate me," I said to them. "Or else you're ashamed of me. . . . You're both honest, but you're certainly gullible. Haven't I been telling you the truth over and over again? I even said: 'I'm not the person you think I am. Hirata's the man to trust. He'll never be taken in.' But you didn't understand. I told you: 'Even if you become friendly with Hirata again, he'll never make friends with *me!* I went as far as to say: 'I know better than anyone what a fine fellow Hirata is!' Isn't that so? I've never lied to you, have I? You may ask why I didn't come out and tell you the whole truth. You probably think I was deceiving you after all. But try looking at it from my position. I'm sorry, but stealing is one thing I can't control. Still, I didn't like to deceive you, so I told you the truth in a roundabout way. I couldn't be any more honest than that—it's your fault for not taking my hints. Maybe you think I'm just being perverse, but I've never been more serious. You'll probably ask why I don't quit stealing, if I'm so anxious to be honest. But that's not a fair question. You see, I was born a thief. I tried to be as sincere as I could with you under the circumstances. There was nothing else I could do. Even then my conscience bothered me—didn't I ask you to let me move out, instead of Hirata? I wasn't trying to fool you, I really wanted to do it for your sake. It's true that I stole from you, but it's also true that I'm your friend. I appeal to your friendship: I want you to understand that even a thief has feelings."

Nakamura and Higuchi stood there in silence, blinking with astonishment.

"Well, I can see you think I've got a lot of nerve. You just don't understand me. I guess it can't be helped, since you're of a different species." I smiled to conceal my bitterness, and added: "But since I'm your friend I'll warn you that this isn't the last time a thing like this will happen. So be on your guard! You two made friends with a thief because of your gullibility. You're likely to run into trouble when you go out in the world. Maybe you get better grades in school, but Hirata is a better man. You can't fool Hirata!"

When I singled him out for praise, Hirata made a wry face and looked away. At that moment he seemed strangely ill at ease.

Many years have passed since then. I became a professional thief and have often behind bars; yet I cannot forget those memories—especially my memories of Hirata. Whenever I am about to commit a crime I see his face before me. I see him swaggering about as haughtily as ever, sneering at me: "Just as I suspected!" Yes, he was a man of character with great promise. But the world is mysterious. My prediction that the naïve

Higuchi would "run into trouble" was wrong: partly through his father's influence, he has had a brilliant career—traveling abroad, earning a doctoral degree, and today holding a high position in the Ministry of Railways. Meanwhile nobody knows what has become of Hirata. It's no wonder we think life is unpredictable.

I assure my reader that this account is true. I have not written a single dishonest word here. And, as I hoped Nakamura and Higuchi would, I hope you will believe that delicate moral scruples can exist in the heart of a thief like me.

But perhaps you won't believe me either. Unless of course (if I may be pardoned for suggesting it) you happen to belong to my own species.

DISCUSSION QUESTIONS

1. Did you suspect the narrator of being the thief before it was revealed? If so, what made you suspicious?

2. What is known about the narrator, other than that he is a thief?

3. The narrator claims that he did his best to warn his friends "in a round about way" and that he even tried to protect them by offering to move out. Do you think he was trying to warn and protect them, or did he have another motive?

4. How would this story have been different if it had been told from the point of view of one of the other boys?

SUGGESTION FOR WRITING

The personality and character of the narrator are the center of interest in this story, but his three friends also emerge as individuals. Select one of these three minor characters and describe his personality. Support your description with details and quotations from the story.

AKUTAGAWA RYŪNOSUKÉ
(1892–1927)

A short story writer known for his grotesque tales, Akutagawa studied English at Tokyo Imperial University. He worked as a newspaper editor and soon established himself as a unique fiction writer with his early story "Rashoman," which was later made into one of the classics of the Japanese cinema. His stories eventually caught the attention of the famous novelist Natsume Soseki, who encouraged the young writer.

Widely read in Chinese, Japanese, and European literature, Akutagawa often based his stories on older tales but retold them in the light of modern psychology. Many of the stories have an intense, feverish quality that is well suited to their strange, often macabre, themes. Akutagawa was a stylistic perfectionist who experimented repeatedly with various ways of presenting the short story. He produced 150 stories that are characterized by a polished and original style, masterful description, subtle irony, and penetrating psychological insights. At the age of 35 Akutagawa committed suicide. ■

HELL SCREEN
Translated by W. H. H. Norman

1

I doubt whether there will ever be another man like the Lord of Horikawa. Certainly there has been no one like him till now. Some say that a Guardian King appeared to her ladyship his mother in a dream before he was born; at least it is true that from the day he was born he was a most extraordinary person. Nothing he did was commonplace; he was constantly startling people. You have only to glance at a plan of Horikawa to perceive its grandeur. No ordinary person would ever have dreamt of the boldness and daring with which it was conceived.

But it certainly was not his lordship's intention merely to glorify himself; he was generous, he did not forget the lower classes; he wanted the whole country to enjoy itself when he did.

There is the story about the famous Kawara Palace at Higashi Sanjo. It was said that the ghost of Toru, Minister of the Left, appeared there night after night until his lordship exorcised it by rebuking it. Such was his prestige in the capital that everyone, man, woman, and child, regarded him, with good reason, as a god incarnate. Once, as he was returning in his carriage from the Feast of the Plum Blossoms, his ox got loose and injured an old man who happened to be passing. But the latter, they say, put his hands together in reverence and was actually grateful that he had been knocked over by an ox of his lordship.

Thus, there are the makings of many good stories in the life of his lordship. At a certain banquet he made a presentation of thirty white horses; another time he gave a favorite boy to be the human pillar of Nagara Bridge. There would be no end if I started to tell them all. Numerous as these anecdotes are, I doubt if there are any that match in horror the story of the making of the Hell Screen, one of the most valuable treasures in the house. His lordship is not easily upset, but that time he seemed to be startled. How much more terrified, then, were we who served him; we feared for our very souls. As for me, I had served him for twenty years, but when I witnessed that dreadful spectacle I felt that such a thing could never have happened before. But in order to tell this story, I must first tell about Yoshihide, who painted the Hell Screen.

2

Yoshihide is, I expect, remembered by many even today. In his time he was a famous painter surpassed by no contemporary. He would be about fifty then, I imagine. He was cross-grained, and not much to look at: short of stature, a bag of skin and bones, and his youthful red lips made him seem even more evil, as though he were some sort of animal. Some said it was because he put his reddened paint brush to his lips, but I doubt this. Others, more unkind, said that his appearance and movements suggested a monkey. And that reminds me of this story. Yoshihide's only daughter, Yuzuki, a charming girl of fifteen, quite unlike her father, was at that time a maid in Horikawa. Probably owing to the fact that her mother had died while she was still very small, Yuzuki was sympathetic and intelligent beyond her years, and greatly petted by her ladyship and her attendants in consequence.

About that time it happened that someone presented a tame monkey from Tamba. The mischievous young lord called it Yoshihide. The monkey was a comical-looking beast, anyway; with this name, nobody in the mansion could resist laughing at him. But they did more than that. If he climbed the pine tree in the garden, or soiled the mats, whatever he did they teased him, shouting, "Yoshihide, Yoshihide."

One day Yuzuki was passing along one of the long halls with a note in a twig of red winter-plum blossom when the monkey appeared from behind a sliding door, fleeing as fast as he could. Apparently he had dislocated a leg, for he limped, unable, it seemed, to climb a post with his usual agility. After him came the young lord, waving a switch, shouting, "Stop thief! Orange thief!" Yuzuki hesitated a moment, but it gave the fleeing monkey a chance to climb to her skirt, crying most piteously. Suddenly she felt she could not restrain her pity. With one hand she still held the plum branch, with the other, the sleeve of her mauve kimono sweeping in a half-circle, she picked the monkey up gently. Then bending before the young lord, she said sweetly, "I crave your pardon. He is only an animal. Be kind enough to pardon him, my lord."

But he had come running with his temper up; he frowned and stamped his foot two or three times. "Why do you protect him? He has stolen some oranges."

"But he is only an animal." She repeated it; then after a little, smiling sadly, "And since you call him Yoshihide, it is as if my father were being punished. I couldn't bear to see it," she said boldly. This defeated the young lord.

"Well, if you're pleading for your father's skin, I'll pardon him," he said reluctantly, "against my better judgment." Dropping the switch, he turned and went back through the sliding door through which he had come.

3

Yuzuki and the monkey were devoted to each other from that day. She hung a golden bell that she had received from the Princess by a bright red cord around the monkey's neck, and the monkey would hardly let her out of his sight. Once, for instance, when she caught cold and took to her bed, the monkey, apparently much depressed, sat immovable by her pillow, gnawing his nails.

Another strange thing was that from that time the monkey was not teased as badly as before. On the contrary, they began to pet him and even the young lord would occasionally toss him a persimmon or a chestnut. Once he got quite angry when he caught a samurai[1] kicking the monkey. As for his lordship, they say that when he heard his son was protecting the monkey from abuse, he had Yuzuki appear before him with the monkey in her arms. On that occasion he must have heard why she had made a pet of the monkey.

"You're a filial girl. I'll reward you for it," he said, and gave her a crimson ceremonial kimono. Whereupon the monkey with the greatest deference mimicked her acceptance of the kimono. That greatly tickled his lordship. Thus the girl who befriended the monkey became a favorite of his lordship, because he admired her filial piety—not, as rumor had it, because he was too fond of her. There may have been some grounds for this rumor, but of that I shall tell later. It should be enough to say that the Lord of Horikawa was not the sort of person to fall in love with an artist's daughter, no matter how beautiful she was.

Thus honored, Yoshihide's daughter withdrew from his presence. Since she was wise and good, the other maids were not jealous of her. Rather she and her monkey became more popular than ever, particularly, they say, with the Princess, from whom she was hardly ever separated. She invariably accompanied her in her pleasure carriage.

---

1. **samurai:** a member of a hereditary military class in feudal Japan.

However, we must leave the daughter awhile and turn to the father. Though the monkey was soon being petted by everybody, they all disliked the great Yoshihide. This was not limited to the mansion folk only. The Abbot of Yokogawa hated him, and if Yoshihide were mentioned would change color as though he had encountered a devil. (That was after Yoshihide had drawn a caricature of the Abbot, according to the gossip of the domestics, which, after all, may have been nothing more than gossip.) Anyhow, the man was unpopular with anyone you met. If there were some who did not speak badly of him, they were but two or three fellow-artists, or people who knew his pictures, but not the man.

Yoshihide was not only very repellent in appearance: people disliked him more because of his habits. No one was to blame for his unpopularity except himself.

4

He was stingy, he was bad-tempered, he was shameless, he was lazy, he was greedy, but worst of all, he was arrogant and contemptuous, certain that he was the greatest artist in the country.

If he had been proud only of his work it would not have been so bad, but he despised everything, even the customs and amenities of society.

It was in character, therefore, that when he was making a picture of the Goddess of Beauty he should paint the face of a common harlot, and that for Fudō[2] he should paint a villainous ex-convict. The models he chose were shocking. When he was taken to task for it, he said coolly, "It would be strange if the gods and buddhas I have given life with my brush should punish me."

His apprentices were appalled when they thought of the dreadful fate in store for him, and many left his studio. It was pride—he imagined himself to be the greatest man in Japan.

In short, though exceptionally gifted, he behaved much above his station. Among artists who were not on good terms with him, many maintained that he was a charlatan, because his brushwork and coloring were so unusual. Look at the door paintings of the famous artists of the past! You can almost smell the perfume of the plum blossom on a moonlit night; you can almost hear some courtier on a screen playing his flute. That is how they gained their reputation for surpassing beauty. Yoshihide's pictures were reputed to be always weird or unpleasant. For instance, he painted the "Five Aspects of Life and Death" on Ryugai Temple gate, and they say if you pass the gate at night you can hear the sighing and sobbing of the divinities he depicted there. Others say you can smell rotting corpses. Or when, at the command of his lordship, he painted the portraits of some of his household women, within three years everyone of them sickened as though her spirit had left her, and died.

---

2. **Fudō:** in Japanese Buddhism a god of righteousness and subduer of demons.

Those who spoke ill of Yoshihide regarded this as certain proof that his pictures were done by means of the black art.

Yoshihide delighted in his reputation for perversity. Once, when his lordship said to him jokingly, "You seem to like the ugly," Yoshihide's unnaturally red lips curled in an evil laugh. "I do. Daubers usually cannot understand the beauty of ugly things," he said contemptuously.

But Yoshihide, the unspeakably unscrupulous Yoshihide, had one tender human trait.

5

And that was his affection for his only child, whom he loved passionately. As I said before, Yuzuki was gentle, and deeply devoted to her father, but his love for her was not inferior to her devotion to him. Does it not seem incredible that the man who never gave a donation to a temple could have provided such kimono and hairpins for his daughter with reckless disregard of cost?

But Yoshihide's affection for Yuzuki was nothing more than the emotion. He gave no thought, for instance, to finding her a good husband. Yet he certainly would have hired roughs to assassinate anyone who made improper advances to her. Therefore, when she became a maid at Horikawa, at the command of his lordship, Yoshihide took it very badly; and even when she appeared before the daimyo,[3] he sulked for awhile. The rumor that, attracted by her beauty, his lordship had tasted her delights in spite of her father, was largely the guess of those who noted Yoshihide's displeasure.

Of course, even if the rumor were false it was clear that the intensity of his affection made Yoshihide long to have his daughter come down from among his lordship's women. When Yoshihide was commanded to paint Monju, the God of Wisdom, he took as his model his lordship's favorite page, and the Lord of Horikawa, highly pleased—for it was a beautiful thing—said graciously, "I will give you whatever you wish as a reward. Now what would you like?" Yoshihide acknowledged the tribute; but what do you think was the bold request that he made? That his daughter should leave his lordship's service! It would be presumptuous to ask that one's daughter be taken in; who but Yoshihide would have asked for his daughter's release, no matter how much he loved her! At this even the genial daimyo seemed ruffled, and he silently watched Yoshihide's face for a long moment.

"No," he spat out, and stood up suddenly. This happened again on four or five different occasions, and as I recall it now, with each repetition, the eye with which his lordship regarded Yoshihide grew colder. Possibly it was on account of this that Yuzuki was concerned for her father's safety, for often, biting her sleeves, she sobbed when she was in her room.

---

3. **the daimyo:** the feudal lord (Horikawa).

Without doubt it was this that made the rumors that his lordship had fallen in love with Yoshihide's daughter become widely current. One of them had it that the very existence of the Hell Screen was owing to the fact that she would not comply with his wishes, but of course this could not have been true.

We believe his lordship did not dismiss her simply because he pitied her. He felt sorry for her situation, and rather than leave her with her hardened father he wanted her in the mansion where there would be no inconvenience for her. It was nothing but kindness on his part. It was quite obvious that the girl received his favors, but it would have been an exaggeration to say that she was his mistress. No, that would have been a completely unfounded lie.

Be that as it may, owing to his request about his daughter, Yoshihide came to be disliked by his lordship. Then suddenly the Lord of Horikawa summoned Yoshihide, whatever may have been his reason, and bade him paint a screen of the circles of hell.

6

When I say screen of the circles of hell, the scenes of those frightful paintings seem to come floating before my very eyes. Other painters have done Hell Screens, but from the first sketch Yoshihide's was different. In one corner of the first leaf he painted the Ten Kings[4] and their households in small scale, the rest was an awful whirlpool of fire around the Forest of Swords which likewise seemed ready to burst into flames. In fact, except for the robes of the hellish officials, which were dotted yellows and blues, all was a flame color, and in the center leapt and danced pitch-black smoke and sparks like flying charcoal.

The brushwork of this alone was enough to astonish one, but the treatment of the sinners rolling over and over in the avenging fire was unlike that of any ordinary picture of hell. From the highest noble to the lowest beggar every conceivable sort of person was to be seen there. Courtiers in formal attire, alluring young maidens of the court in palace robes, priests droning over their prayer beads, scholars on high wooden clogs, little girls in white shifts, diviners flourishing their papered wands—I won't name them all. There they all were, enveloped in flame and smoke, tormented by bull- and horse-headed jailers: blown and scattered in all directions like fallen leaves in a gale, they fled hither and yon. There were female fortune-tellers, their hair caught in forks, their limbs trussed tighter than spiders' legs. Young princes hung inverted like bats, their breasts pierced with javelins. They were beaten with iron whips, they were crushed with mighty weights of adamant, they were pecked by weird birds, they were devoured by poisonous dragons. I don't know how many sinners were depicted, nor can I list all their torments.

---

4. **Ten Kings:** in Japanese mythology the judges of the underworld.

But I must mention one dreadful scene that stood out from the rest. Grazing the tops of the sword trees, that were as sharp as an animal's fangs—there were several souls on them, spitted two or three deep—came falling through space an ox-carriage. Its blinds were blown open by the winds of hell and in it an emperor's favorite, gorgeously attired, her long black hair fluttering in the flames, bent her white neck and writhed in agony. Nothing made the fiery torments of hell more realistic than the appearance of that woman in her burning carriage. The horror of the whole picture was concentrated in this one scene. So inspired an accomplishment was it that those who looked at her thought they heard dreadful cries in their ears.

Ah, it was for this, it was for this picture that that dreadful event occurred! Without it how could even Yoshihide have expressed so vividly the agonies of hell? It was to finish this screen that Yoshihide met a destiny so cruel that he took his own life. For this hell he pictured was the hell that he, the greatest painter in the country, was one day to fall into. . . .

I may be telling the strange story of the Hell Screen too hastily; I may have told the wrong end of the story first. Let me return to Yoshihide, bidden by his lordship to paint a picture of hell.

7

For five or six months Yoshihide was so busy working on the screen that he was not seen at the mansion at all. Was it not remarkable that with all his affection, when he became absorbed in his painting, he did not even want to see his daughter? The apprentice to whom I have already referred said that when Yoshihide was engaged on a piece of work it was as though he had been bewitched by a fox.[5] According to the stories that circulated at that time Yoshihide had achieved fame with the assistance of the black art because of a vow he had made to some great god of fortune. And the proof of it was that if you went to his studio and peered at him unbeknownst you could see the ghostly foxes swarming all around him. Thus it was that when once he had taken up his brushes everything was forgotten till he had finished the picture. Day and night he would shut himself up in one room, scarcely seeing the light of day. And when he painted the Hell Screen this absorption was complete.

The shutters were kept down during the day and he mixed his secret colors by the light of a tripod lamp. He had his apprentices dress in all sorts of finery, and painted each with great care. It did not take the Hell Screen to make him behave like that: he demanded it for every picture he painted. At the time he was painting the "Five Aspects of Life and Death" at Ryugaiji, he chanced to see a corpse lying beside the road. Any ordinary person would have averted his face, but Yoshihide stepped out of the

---

5. fox: In Japanese folklore the fox is believed to be able to bewitch people and assume human form.

crowd, squatted down, and at his leisure painted the half-decayed face and limbs exactly as they looked.

How can I convey his violent concentration? Some of you will still fail to grasp it. Since I cannot tell it in detail, I shall relate it broadly.

The apprentice, then, was one day mixing paints. Suddenly Yoshihide appeared. "I'd like to take a short nap," he said. "But I've been bothered a lot by bad dreams recently."

Since this was not extraordinary the apprentice answered briefly but politely, "Indeed, sir," without lifting his hand from his work. Whereupon the artist said, with a loneliness and diffidence that were strange to him, "I mean I would like to have you sit by my pillow while I rest." The apprentice thought it unusual that he should be troubled so badly by dreams, but the request was a simple one and he assented readily. Yoshihide, still anxious, asked him to come back in at once. "And if another apprentice comes, don't let him enter the room while I am sleeping," he said hesitantly. By "room" he meant the room where he was painting the screen. In that room the doors were shut fast as if it were night, and a light was usually left burning. The screen stood around the sides of the room; only the charcoal sketch of the design was completed. Yoshihide put his elbow on the pillow like a man completely exhausted and quietly fell asleep. But before an hour was out an indescribably unpleasant voice began to sound in the apprentice's ears.

8

At first it was nothing more than a voice, but presently there were clear words, as of a drowning man moaning in the water. "What . . . you are calling me? Where? Where to . . . to hell? To the hell of fire . . . Who is it? Who is your honor? Who is your honor? If I knew who . . ."

Unconsciously the apprentice stopped mixing the colors; feeling that he was intruding on privacy he looked at the artist's face. That wrinkled face was pale; great drops of sweat stood out on it, the lips were dry, and the mouth with its scanty teeth was wide open, as though it gasped for air. And that thing that moved so dizzily as if on a thread, was that his tongue!

"If I knew who . . . Oh, it is your honor, is it? I thought it was. What! You have come to meet me. So I am to come. I am to go to hell! My daughter awaits me in hell!"

At that moment a strange, hazy shadow seemed to descend over the face of the screen, so uncanny did the apprentice feel. Immediately, of course, he shook the master with all his might, but Yoshihide, still in the clutch of the nightmare, continued his monologue, unable, apparently, to wake out of it. Thereupon the apprentice boldly took the water that stood at hand for his brushes and poured it over Yoshihide's face.

"It is waiting: get in this carriage. Get in this carriage and go down to hell." As he said these words Yoshihide's voice changed, he sounded like a man being strangled, and at length he opened his eyes. Terrified, he leapt up like one pierced with needles: the weird things of his dream must still have been with him. His expression was dreadful, his mouth gaped, he stared into space. Presently he seemed to have recovered himself. "It's all right now. You may leave," he said curtly.

As the apprentice would have been badly scolded had he disobeyed, he promptly left the room. When he saw the good light of day, he sighed with relief like one awakening from a bad dream.

But this was not the worst. A month later another apprentice was called into the back room. As usual Yoshihide was gnawing his brushes in the dim light of the oil lamp. Suddenly he turned to the apprentice. "I want you to strip again."

Since he had been asked to do this several times before, the apprentice obeyed immediately. But when that unspeakable man saw him stark naked before him, his face became strangely distorted. "I want to see a man bound with a chain. I want you to do as I tell you for a little while," he said coldly and unsympathetically. The apprentice was a sturdy fellow who had formerly thought that swinging a sword was better than handling a brush, but this request astonished him. As he often said afterwards, "I began to wonder if the master hadn't gone crazy and wasn't going to kill me." Yoshihide, however, growing impatient with the other's hesitation, produced from somewhere a light iron chain a-rattle in his hand; and without giving him the opportunity of obeying or refusing, sprang on the apprentice, sat on his back, twisted up his arms and bound him around and around. The pain was almost intolerable, for he pulled the end of the chain brutally, so that the apprentice fell loudly sideways and lay there extended.

9

He said that he lay there like a wine jar rolled over on its side. Because his hands and feet were cruelly bent and twisted he could move only his head. He was fat, and with his circulation impeded, the blood gathered not only in his trunk and face but everywhere under his skin. This, however, did not trouble Yoshihide at all; he walked all around him, "a wine jar," making sketch after sketch. I do not need to elaborate on the apprentice's sufferings.

Had nothing occurred, doubtless the torture would have been protracted longer. Fortunately—or maybe unfortunately—something like black oil, a thin streak, came flowing sinuously from behind a jar in the corner of the room. At first it moved slowly like a sticky substance, but then it slid more smoothly until, as he watched it, it moved gleaming up to his nose. He drew in his breath involuntarily. "A snake! A snake!" he screamed. It seemed that all the blood in his body would freeze at once, nor was it surprising. A little more and the snake would actually have touched with its cold tongue his head into which the chains were biting. Even the unscrupulous Yoshihide must have been startled at this. He dropped his brush, bent down like a flash, deftly caught the snake by its tail and lifted it up, head downward. The snake raised its head, coiled itself in circles, twisted its body, but could not reach Yoshihide's hand.

"You have made me botch a stroke." Complaining offensively, Yoshihide dropped the snake into the jar in the corner of the room and reluctantly loosed the chain that bound the apprentice. All he did was to loose him; not a word of thanks did the long-suffering fellow get. Obviously Yoshihide was vexed that he had botched a stroke instead of letting his apprentice be bitten by the snake. Afterwards they heard that he kept the snake there as a model.

This story should give you some idea of Yoshihide's madness, his sinister absorption. However, I should like to describe one more dreadful experience that almost cost a young apprentice his life. He was thirteen or fourteen at the time, a girlish, fair-complexioned lad. One night he was suddenly called to his master's room. In the lamplight he saw Yoshihide feeding a strange bird, about the size of an ordinary cat, with a bloody piece of meat which he held in his hand. It had large, round, amber-colored eyes and feather-like ears that stuck out on either side of its head. It was extraordinarily like a cat.

10

Yoshihide always disliked anyone sticking his nose into what he was doing. As was the case with the snake, his apprentices never knew what he had in his room. Therefore sometimes silver bowls, sometimes a skull, or one-stemmed lacquer stands—various odd things, models for what he was painting—would be set out on his table. But nobody knew where he kept these things. The rumor that some great god of fortune lent him divine help certainly arose from these circumstances.

Then the apprentice, seeing the strange bird on the table and imagining it to be something needed for the Hell Screen, bowed to the artist and said respectfully, "What do you wish, sir?" Yoshihide, as if he had not heard him, licked his red lips and jerked his chin towards the bird. "Isn't it tame!"

While he was saying this the apprentice was staring with an uncanny feeling at that catlike bird with ears. Yoshihide answered with his sneer, "What! Never seen a bird like this? That's the trouble with people who live in the capital. It's a horned owl. A hunter gave it to me two or three days ago. But I'll warrant there aren't many as tame as this."

As he said this he slowly raised his hand and stroked the back of the bird, which had just finished eating the meat, the wrong way. The owl let out a short piercing screech, flew up from the table, extended its claws, and pounced at the face of the apprentice. Panic-stricken, the latter raised his sleeve to shield his face. Had he not done so he undoubtedly would have been badly slashed.

As he cried out he shook his sleeve to drive off the owl, but it screeched and, taking advantage of his weakness, attacked again. Forgetting the master's presence, the lad fled distracted up and down the narrow room; standing, he tried to ward it off, sitting, to drive it away. The sinister bird wheeled high and low after its prey, darting at his eyes, watching for an opening.

The noisy threshing of its wings seemed to evoke something uncanny like the smell of dead leaves, or the spray of a waterfall. It was dreadful, revolting. The apprentice had the feeling that the dim oil lamp was the vague light of the moon, and the room a valley shut in the ill-omened air of some remote mountain.

But the apprentice's horror was due not so much to the attack of the horned owl. What made his hair stand on end was the sight of the artist Yoshihide.

The latter watched the commotion coolly, unrolled his paper deliberately, and began to paint the fantastic picture of a girlish boy being mangled by a horrible bird. When the apprentice saw this out of the corner of his eye, he was overwhelmed with an inexpressible horror, for he thought that he really was going to be killed for the artist.

11

You could not say that this was impossible to believe. Yoshihide had called the apprentice deliberately that night in order to set the owl after him and paint him trying to escape. Therefore the apprentice, when he saw what the master was up to, involuntarily hid his head in his sleeves, began screaming he knew not what, and huddled down in the corner of the room by the sliding door. Then Yoshihide shouted as though he were a little flustered and got to his feet, but immediately the beating of the owl's wings became louder and there was the startling noise of things being torn or knocked down. Though he was badly shaken, the apprentice involuntarily lifted his head to see. The room had become as black as night, and out of it came Yoshihide's voice harshly calling for his apprentices.

Presently one of them answered from a distance, and in a minute came running in with a light. By its sooty illumination he saw the tripod lamp overturned and the owl fluttering painfully with one wing on mats that were swimming in oil. Yoshihide was in a half-sitting position beyond the table. He seemed aghast and was muttering words unintelligible to mortals. This is no exaggeration. A snake as black as the pit was coiling itself rapidly around the owl, encircling its neck and one wing. Apparently in crouching down the apprentice had knocked over the jar, the snake had crawled out, and the owl had made a feeble attempt to pounce on it. It was this which had caused the clatter and commotion. The two apprentices exchanged glances and simply stood dumbfounded, eyeing that remarkable spectacle. Then without a word they bowed to Yoshihide and withdrew. Nobody discovered what happened to the owl and the snake.

This sort of thing was matched by many other incidents. I forgot to say that it was in the early autumn that Yoshihide received orders to paint the screen. From then until the end of the winter his apprentices were in a constant state of terror because of his weird behavior. But towards the end of the winter something about the picture seemed to trouble Yoshihide; he became even more saturnine than usual and spoke more harshly. The sketch of the screen, eight-tenths completed, did not progress. In fact, there did not seem to be any chance that the outlines would ever be painted in and finished.

Nobody knew what it was that hindered the work on the screen and nobody tried to find out. Hitherto the apprentices had been fascinated by everything that happened. They had felt that they were caged with a wolf or a tiger, but from this time they contrived to keep away from their master as much as possible.

12

Accordingly, there is not much that is worth telling about this period. But if one had to say something, it would be that the stubborn old man was, for some strange reason, easily moved to tears, and was often found weeping, they say, when he thought no one was by. One day, for instance, an apprentice went into the garden on an errand. Yoshihide was standing absently in the corridor, gazing at the sky with its promise of spring, his eyes full of tears. The apprentice felt embarrassed and withdrew stealthily without saying a word. Was it not remarkable that the arrogant man who had used a decaying corpse as model for the "Five Aspects of Life and Death" should weep so childishly?

While Yoshihide painted the screen in a frenzy incomprehensible to the sane, it began to be noticed that his daughter was very despondent and often appeared to be holding back tears. When this happens to a girl with a pale modest face, her eyelashes become heavy, shadows appear around her eyes, and her face grows still sadder. At first they said that she was suffering from a love affair, or blamed her father, but soon it got around that the Lord of Horikawa wanted to have his way with her. Then suddenly all talk about the girl ceased as if everybody had forgotten her.

It was about that time that late one night I happened to be passing along a corridor. Suddenly the monkey Yoshihide sprang out from somewhere and began pulling the hem of my skirt insistently. As I remember it, the night was warm, there was a pale moon shining, and the plum blossoms were already fragrant. The monkey bared his white teeth, wrinkled the tip of his nose, and shrieked wildly in the moonlight as though he were demented. I felt upset and very angry that my new skirts should be pulled about. Kicking the monkey loose, I was about to walk on when I recalled that a samurai had earned the young lord's displeasure by chastising the monkey. Besides his behavior did seem most unusual. So at last I walked a dozen yards in the direction he was pulling me.

There the corridor turned, showing the water of the pond, pale white in the night light, beyond a pine tree with gently bending branches. At that point what sounded like people quarreling fell on my ears, weird and startling, from a room nearby. Except for this everything around was sunk in silence. In the half-light that was neither haze nor moonlight I heard no other voices. There was nothing but the sound of the fish jumping in the pond. With that din in my ears, I stopped instinctively. My first thought was "Some ruffians," and I approached the sliding door quietly, holding my breath, ready to show them my mettle.

13

But the monkey must have thought me too hesitant. He ran around me two or three times, impatiently, crying out as though he were being strangled, then leapt straight up from the floor to my shoulder. I jerked back my head so as not to be clawed, but he clung to my sleeve to keep from falling to the floor. Staggering back two or three steps, I banged heavily into the sliding door. After that there was no cause for hesitation. I opened the door immediately and was about to advance into the inner part of the room where the moonlight did not fall. But just then something passed before my eyes—what was this?—a girl came running out from the back of the room as though released from a spring. She barely missed running into me, passed me, and half fell outside the room, where she knelt gasping, looking up at my face, and shuddering as though she still saw some horror.

Do I need to say she was Yuzuki? That night she appeared vivid, she seemed to be a different person. Her big eyes shone, her cheeks flamed red. Her disordered kimono and skirt gave her a fascination she did not ordinarily possess. Was this really that shrinking daughter of Yoshihide's? I leaned against the sliding door and stared at her beautiful figure in the moonlight. Then, indicating the direction where the alarmed footsteps had died away, "What was it?" I asked with my eyes.

But she only bit her lips, shook her head, and said nothing. She seemed unusually mortified. Then I bent over her, put my mouth to her ear, and asked, "Who was it?" in a whisper. But the girl still shook her head; tears filled her eyes and hung on her long lashes; she bit her lips harder than ever.

I have always been a stupid person and unless something is absolutely plain I cannot grasp it. I did not know what to say and stood motionless for a moment, as though listening to the beating of her heart. But this was because I felt I ought not to question her too closely.

I don't know how long it lasted. At length I closed the door I had left open and, looking back at the girl, who seemed to have recovered from her agitation, said as gently as possible, "You had better go back to your room." Then, troubled with the uncomfortable feeling that I had seen something I should not have, embarrassed though no one was near, I quietly returned to where I had come from. But before I had gone ten steps, something again plucked the hem of my skirt, timidly this time. Astonished, I stopped and turned around. What do you think it was? The monkey Yoshihide, his gold bell jingling, his hands together like a human, was bowing most politely to me, again and again.

14

About two weeks later Yoshihide came to the mansion and asked for an immediate audience with the Lord of Horikawa. He belonged to the lower classes but he had always been in favor, and his lordship, ordinarily difficult of access, granted Yoshihide an audience at once. The latter prostrated himself before the daimyo deferentially and presently began to speak in his hoarse voice.

"Some time ago, my lord, you ordered a Hell Screen. Day and night have I labored, taking great pains, and now the result can be seen: the design has almost been completed."

"Congratulations. I am content." But in his lordship's voice there was a strange lack of conviction, of interest.

"No, congratulations are not in order." With his eyes firmly lowered Yoshihide answered almost as if he were becoming angry. "It is nearly finished, but there is just one part I cannot paint—now."

"What! You cannot paint part of it!"

"No, my lord. I cannot paint anything for which a model is lacking. Even if I try, the pictures lack conviction. And isn't that the same as being unable to paint it?"

When he heard this a sneering sort of smile passed over his lordship's face. "Then in order to paint this Hell Screen, you must see hell, eh?"

"Yes, my lord. Some years ago in a great fire I saw flames close up that resembled the raging fires of hell. The flames in my painting are what I then saw. Your lordship is acquainted with that picture, I believe."

"What about criminals? You haven't seen jailers, have you?" He spoke as though he had not heard Yoshihide, his words following the artist's without pause.

"I have seen men bound in iron chains. I have copied in detail men attacked by strange birds. So I cannot say I have not seen the sufferings of criminals under torture. As for jailers—" Yoshihide smiled repulsively, "I have seen them before me many times in my dreams. Cows' heads, horses' heads, three-faced six-armed demons, clapping hands that make no noise, voiceless mouths agape—they all come to torment me. I am not exaggerating when I say that I see them every day and every night. What I wish to paint and cannot are not things like that."

His lordship must have been thoroughly astonished. For a long moment he stared at Yoshihide irritably; then he arched his eyebrows sharply. "What is it you cannot paint?"

15

"In the middle of the screen I want to paint a carriage falling down through the sky," said Yoshihide, and for the first time he looked sharply at his lordship's face. When Yoshihide spoke of pictures I have heard that he looked insane. He certainly seemed insane when he said this. "In the carriage an exquisite court lady, her hair disordered in the raging fire, writhes in agony. Her face is contorted with smoke, her eyebrows are drawn; she looks up at the roof of the carriage. As she plucks at the bamboo blinds she tries to ward off the sparks that shower down. And strange birds of prey, ten or twenty, fly around the carriage with shrill cries. Ah, that beauty in the carriage. I cannot possibly paint her."

"Well, what else?"

For some reason his lordship took strange pleasure in urging Yoshihide on. But the artist's red lips moved feverishly, and when he spoke it was like a man in a dream. "No," he repeated, "I cannot paint it." Then suddenly he almost snarled, "Burn a carriage for me. If only you could . . ."

His lordship's face darkened, then he burst out laughing with startling abruptness. "I'll do entirely as you wish," he said, almost choking with the violence of his laughter. "And all discussion as to whether it is possible or not is beside the point."

When I heard this I felt a strange thrill of horror. Maybe it was a premonition. His lordship, as though infected with Yoshihide's madness, changed, foam gathered white on his lips, and like lightning the terror flashed in the corners of his eyes. He stopped abruptly, and then a great laugh burst from his throat. "I'll fire a carriage for you. And there'll be an exquisite beauty in the robes of a fine lady in it. Attacked by flames and black smoke the woman will die in agony. The man who thought of painting that must be the greatest artist in Japan. I'll praise him. Oh, I'll praise him!"

When he heard his lordship's words, Yoshihide became pale and moved his lips as though he were gasping. But soon his body relaxed, and placing both hands on the mats, he bowed politely. "How kind a destiny," he said, so low that he could scarcely be heard. Probably this was because the daimyo's words had brought the frightfulness of his plan vividly before his eyes. That was the only time in my life that I pitied Yoshihide.

16

Two or three days after this his lordship told Yoshihide that he was ready to fulfill his promise. Of course the carriage was not to be burned at Horikawa, but rather at a country house outside the capital, which the common people called Yukige. Though it had formerly been the residence of his lordship's younger sister, no one had occupied Yukige for many years. It had a large garden that had been allowed to run wild. People attributed its neglect to many causes: for instance, they said that on moonless nights the daimyo's dead sister, wearing a strange scarlet skirt, still walked along the corridors without touching the floor. The mansion was desolate enough by day, but at night, with the splashing sounds of the invisible brook and the monstrous shapes of the night herons flying through the starlight, it was entirely eerie.

As it happened, that night was moonless and pitch black. The light of the oil lamps shone on his lordship, clad in pale yellow robes and a dark purple skirt embroidered with crests, sitting on the veranda on a plaited straw cushion with a white silk embroidered hem. I need not add that before and behind, to the left and to the right of him, five or six attendants stood respectfully. The choice of one was significant—he was a powerful samurai who had eaten human flesh to stay his hunger at the Battle of Michinoku, and since then, they say, he has been able to tear apart the horns of a live deer. His long sword sticking out behind like a gull's tail, he stood, a forbidding figure, beneath the veranda. The flickering light of the lamps, now bright, now dark, shone on the scene. So dreadful a horror was on us that we scarcely knew whether we dreamed or waked.

They had drawn the carriage into the garden. There it stood, its heavy roof weighing down the darkness. There were no oxen harnessed to it, and the end of its black tongue rested on a stand. When we saw its gold metalwork glittering like stars, we felt chilly in spite of the spring night. The carriage was heavily closed with blue blinds edged with embroidery, so that we could not know what was inside. Around it stood attendants with torches in their hands, worrying over the smoke that drifted towards the veranda and waiting significantly.

Yoshihide knelt facing the veranda, a little distance off. He seemed smaller and shabbier than usual, the starry sky seemed to oppress him. The man who squatted behind him was doubtless an apprentice. The two of them were at some distance from me and below the veranda so that I could not be sure of the color of their clothes.

17

It must have been near midnight. The darkness that enveloped the brook seemed to watch our very breathing. In it was only the faint stir of the night wind that carried the sooty smell of the pine torches to us. For some time his lordship watched the scene in silence, motionless. Presently he moved forward a little and called sharply, "Yoshihide."

The latter must have made some sort of reply, though what I heard sounded more like a groan.

"Yoshihide, tonight in accordance with your request I am going to burn this carriage for you."

His lordship glanced sidelong at those around him and seemed to exchange a meaningful smile with one or two, though I may have only imagined it. Yoshihide raised his head fearfully and looked up at the veranda, but said nothing and did not move from where he squatted.

"Look. That is the carriage I have always used. You recognize it, don't you? I am going to burn it and show you blazing hell itself."

Again his lordship paused and winked at his attendants. Suddenly his tone became unpleasant. "In that carriage, by my command, is a female malefactor. Therefore, when it is fired her flesh will be roasted, her bones burnt, she will die in extreme agony. Never again will you find such a model for the completion of your screen. Do not flinch from looking at snow-white skin inflamed with fire. Look well at her black hair dancing up in sparks."

His lordship ceased speaking for the third time. I don't know what thoughts were in his mind, but his shoulders shook with silent laughter.

"Posterity will never see anything like it. I'll watch it from here. Come, come, lift up the blinds and show Yoshihide the woman inside."

At the daimyo's word one of the attendants, holding high his pine torch in one hand, walked up to the carriage without more ado, stretched out his free hand, and raised the blind. The flickering torch burned with a sharp crackling noise. It brightly lit up the narrow interior of the carriage, showing a woman on its couch, cruelly bound with chains. Who was she? Ah, it could not be! She was clad in a gorgeously embroidered cherry-patterned mantle; her black hair, alluringly loosened, hung straight down; the golden hairpins set at different angles gleamed beautifully, but there was a gag over her mouth tied behind her neck. The small slight body, the modest profile—the attire only was different—it was Yuzuki. I nearly cried aloud.

At that moment the samurai opposite me got to his feet hastily and put his hand on his sword. It must have been Yoshihide that he glared at. Startled I glanced at the artist. He seemed half-stunned by what he now saw.

Suddenly he leapt up, stretched out both his arms before him, and forgetting everything else, began to run toward the carriage. Unfortunately, as I have already said, he was at some distance in the shadow, and I could not see the expression on his face. But that was momentary, for now I saw that it was absolutely colorless. His whole form cleaving the darkness appeared vividly before our eyes in the half-light—he was held in space, it seemed, by some invisible power that lifted him from the ground. Then, at his lordship's command, "Set fire," the carriage with its passenger, bathed in the light of the torches that were tossed on to it, burst into flames.

18

As we watched, the flames enveloped the carriage. The purple tassels that hung from the roof corners swung as though in a wind, while from below them the smoke swirled white against the blackness of the night. So frightful was it that the bamboo blinds, the hangings, the metal ornaments in the roof, seemed to be flying in the leaping shower of sparks. The tongues of flame that licked up from beneath the blinds, those serried flames that shot up into the sky, seemed to be celestial flames of the sun fallen to the earth. I had almost shouted before, but now I felt completely overwhelmed and dumbfounded; mouth agape, I could do nothing but watch the dreadful spectacle. But the father—Yoshihide. . . .

I still remember the expression on his face. He had started involuntarily toward the carriage, but when the fire blazed up he stopped, arms outstretched, and with piercing eyes watched the smoke and fire that enveloped the carriage as though he would be drawn into it. The blaze lit his wrinkled face so clearly that even the hairs of his head could be seen distinctly: in the depths of his wide staring eyes, in his drawn distorted lips, in his twitching cheeks, the grief, dread, and bewilderment that passed through his soul were clearly inscribed. A robber, guilty of unspeakable crimes and about to be beheaded, or dragged before the court of the Ten Kings, could hardly have looked more agonized. Even that gigantic samurai changed color and looked fearfully at the Lord of Horikawa.

But the latter, without taking his eyes off the carriage, merely bit his lips or laughed unpleasantly from time to time. As for the carriage and its passenger, that girl—I am not brave enough to tell you all that I saw. Her white face, choking in the smoke, looked upward; her long loosened hair fluttered in the smoke, her cherry-patterned mantle—how beautiful it all was! What a terrible spectacle! But when the night wind dropped and the smoke was drawn away to the other side, where gold dust seemed to be scattered above the red flames, when the girl gnawed her gag, writhing so that it seemed the chains must burst, I, and even the gigantic samurai, wondered whether we were not spectators of the torments of hell itself, and our flesh crept.

Then once more we thought the night wind stirred in the treetops of the garden. As that sound passed over the sky, something black that neither touched ground nor flew through the sky, dancing like a ball, leaped from the roof of the house into the blazing carriage. Into the crumbling blinds, cinnabar-stained, he fell, and putting his arms around the straining girl, he cried shrill and long into the smoke, a cry that sounded like tearing silk. He repeated it two or three times, then we forgot ourselves and shouted out together. Against the transparent curtain of flames, clinging to the girl's shoulder, was Yoshihide, Yoshihide the monkey, that had been left tied at the mansion.

19

But we saw him only for a moment. Like gold leaf on a brown screen the sparks climbed into the sky. The monkey and Yuzuki were hidden in black smoke while the carriage blazed away with a dreadful noise in the garden. It was a pillar of fire—those awful flames stabbed the very sky.

In front of that pillar Yoshihide stood rooted. Then, wonderful to say, over the wrinkled face of this Yoshihide, who had seemed to suffer on a previous occasion the tortures of hell, over his face the light of an inexpressible ecstasy passed, and forgetful even of his lordship's presence he folded his arms and stood watching. It was almost as if he did not see his daughter dying in agony. Rather he seemed to delight in the beautiful color of the flames and the form of a woman in torment.

What was most remarkable was not that he was joyfully watching the death of his daughter. It was rather that in him seemed to be a sternness not human, like the wrath of a kingly lion seen in a dream. Surprised by the fire, flocks of night birds that cried and clamored seemed thicker—though it may have been my imagination—around Yoshihide's cap. Maybe those soulless birds seemed to see a weird glory like a halo around that man's head.

If the birds were attracted, how much more were we, the servants, filled with a strange feeling of worship as we watched Yoshihide. We quaked within, we held our breath, we watched him like a Buddha unveiled. The roaring of the fire that filled the air, and Yoshihide, his soul taken captive by it, standing there motionless—what awe we felt, what intense pleasure at this spectacle. Only his lordship sat on the veranda as though he were a different sort of being. He grew pale, foam gathered on his lips, he clutched his purple-skirted knee with both hands, he panted like some thirsty animal. . . .

20

It got around that his lordship had burnt a carriage at Yukige that night—though of course nobody said anything—and a great variety of opinions were expressed. The first and most prevalent rumor was that he had burnt Yoshihide's daughter to death in resentment over thwarted love. But there was no doubt that it was the daimyo's purpose to punish the perversity of the artist, who was painting the Hell Screen, even if he had to kill someone to do so. In fact, his lordship himself told me this.

Then there was much talk about the stony-heartedness of Yoshihide, who saw his daughter die in flames before his eyes and yet wanted to paint the screen. Some called him a beast of prey in human form, rendered incapable of human love by a picture. The Abbot of Yokogawa often said, "A man's genius may be very great, great his art, but only an understanding of the Five Virtues[6] will save him from hell."

However, about a month later the Hell Screen was completed. Yoshihide immediately took it to the mansion and showed it with great deference to the Lord of Horikawa. The Abbot happened to be visiting his lordship at the time, and when he looked at it he must have been properly startled by the storm of fire that rages across the firmament on one of the leaves. He pulled a wry face, stared hard at Yoshihide, but said, "Well done," in spite of himself. I still remember the forced laugh with which his lordship greeted this.

From that time on, there was none that spoke badly of Yoshihide, at least in the mansion. And anyone who saw the screen, even if he had hated the artist before, was struck solemn, because he felt that he was experiencing hell's most exquisite tortures.

But by that time Yoshihide was no longer among the living. The night after the screen was finished he hanged himself from a beam in his studio. With his only daughter preceding him he felt, no doubt, that he could not bear to live on in idleness. His remains still lie within the ruins of his house. The rains and winds of many decades have bleached the little stone that marked his grave, and the moss has covered it in oblivion.

---

6. the Five Virtues: The ethical teachings formulated by the Chinese sage Confucius (551–478 B.C.) are based on five cardinal virtues: Humanity, Justice, Propriety, Wisdom, and Fidelity.

DISCUSSION QUESTIONS

1. How would you describe the narrator of "Hell Screen"? Do you agree with his self-description: "I have always been a stupid person and unless something is absolutely plain I cannot grasp it"? Why do you think Akutagawa created a narrator like this?

2. Why are the stories of the two apprentices to Yoshihide included (one almost bitten by a snake, the other attacked by an owl)?

3. How do you account for the fact that Yoshihide stood "joyfully watching the death of his daughter"?

4. Explain the role of the monkey in this story. What purpose does he serve?

5. At the end of Section 6 of the story, the narrator tells us that the hell screen eventually caused Yoshihide to take his own life. Then he says, "I may have told the wrong end of the story first." Why did the author give us a glimpse of the ending at this point?

6. What would you say is the main theme or message of this story?

SUGGESTION FOR WRITING

Analyze Akutagawa's likely attitude toward one of the following: (1) artists (2) members of royalty (3) animals. Your observations should be based on how these individuals are depicted in "Hell Screen." Support your observations with specific examples.

IBUSÉ MASUJI

(1898–1993)

A novelist noted for his satiric portraits, Ibusé was born in Hiroshima and attended Waseda University. As a university student, he first studied painting and poetry but later dedicated himself to fiction, which became his life's work. Most of his fictional works are highly symbolic or allegorical, though he has also written a few historical novels.

Ibusé's greatest popularity came after World War II, when his sharp satire and fresh sense of humor gained him widespread recognition. *No Consultations Today,* a novel that depicts a town by showing the patients who visit a doctor's office, and *A Far-Worshiping Commander,* an anti-military novel, were especially admired. In 1966 Ibusé was awarded the Japanese Order of Culture for his novel *Black Rain,* which demonstrates the long-lasting social effects of the American bombing of Hiroshima. The following story is an allegory of modern Japan shortly after its defeat in World War II. ■

THE CHARCOAL BUS

Translated by Ivan Morris

On a recent trip to the country, I rode once again on the Binan-line bus. I hadn't been on this bus for some time—not since the war,[1] in fact. However, I remembered it well.

During the war, all the country buses were pretty decrepit, but the bus on the Binan route was in a class of its own. It rarely got through a run without a series of mishaps: first there would be a puncture, then the engine would break down, and when this had finally been repaired the gear box would give trouble. Almost all the windows were broken; some of the openings were covered with cellophane, others with wooden boards.

Now, five years after the war, the bus still ran on charcoal, though the body had been painted over and most of the windows repaired. The driver was a young fellow whom I recognized from the war days, when he had been the conductor. Apparently he had changed places with the mustachioed man who had previously occupied the driver's seat. I wondered whether this had any particular significance.

"Haven't the driver and the conductor switched round?" I said to a woman in the seat next to mine. "Surely this conductor used to be the driver. Has he had an accident or something so that he can't drive any longer?"

---

1. the war: World War II.

"No," put in the woman's companion, "he became unpopular during the war and had to be demoted. He was too strict with the passengers, you see. As soon as the war was over, people began to write the company complaining about his behavior and saying he should be purged. . . . Well, this is where we get off."

The couple nodded to me and left the bus. An old man in a peasant's smock, who had been listening to the conversation, took the woman's place beside me.

"That's all very well," he said as soon as he had sat down, "but the conductor will soon be back where he was before, mark my words. Of course, he was so unpopular after the war that they couldn't help purging him; they lowered his salary and made him a conductor. But nowadays the purgees are all coming back into favor. It's people like him who are going to get ahead now." The old man nodded his head and murmured, as if to himself: "Yes, that's how things are moving these days."

I glanced at the conductor. How well I remembered that little mustache! He was standing now at the back of the bus looking out the window. We crossed a bridge over a dried-up river; beyond the rice fields I could see the slopes of a barren-looking mountain. As we passed a Shinto shrine[2] by the side of the road, the conductor removed his cap and wiped the perspiration from his forehead. As he did so, he bowed his head slightly, and I wondered whether this was intended as a mark of respect for the shrine. Such reverence had been unfashionable for some time after the war but was now gradually coming back into favor. The conductor's gesture seemed deliberately ambiguous.

My memories of the man were far from favorable. During his long term of duty as driver for the Binan-line bus, he had never missed an opportunity to hector the young man who was then conductor. The burden of his abuse was usually the alleged misdemeanors of the passengers, and among his favorite points of attack were rucksacks.

"No rucksacks inside the bus!" he used to roar at the conductor. "Kindly tell that passenger to remove his rucksack. You know perfectly well they aren't allowed. What are you waiting for anyhow? Make him get off!"

There was indeed a rule that each piece of luggage, including rucksacks, had to be checked, paid for, and piled on top of the bus. Occasionally the police would stop the bus at a crossroads and examine the luggage for black-market articles, such as rice or firewood, the discovery of which meant confiscation and a fine. Under the circumstances we preferred to take our baggage with us and push it under the seats, but such attempts were almost invariably frustrated by the mustachioed driver. He, on the other hand, did not scruple to transport large quantities of carrots, peas, and other contraband in the tool box next to his seat.

---

2. **Shinto shrine:** a shrine of Shintoism, the native religion of Japan, primarily a form of nature and ancestor worship.

Not only did I and the other regular passengers regard the driver as a disagreeable bully, but we also despised him for his inefficiency in handling the bus. The constant delays and breakdowns used to leave him quite unperturbed. As soon as the engine failed, he would announce in a stentorian[3] tone: "All passengers out! Start pushing!" When we had pushed for fifty or sixty yards, the engine usually started and he would order us aboard.

Toward the end of the war, however, these periodic breakdowns became more serious and the last time I had taken the bus (shortly before the destruction of Hiroshima) I had helped push it almost four miles. I had gone fishing in a mountain stream and after spending the night at an inn, had gone early next morning to the Otaki Bridge bus stop. About forty people were already waiting. The time for departure came but there was no sign of the bus. A few people gave up at once and left; others vented their annoyance by reviling the driver, a luxury that they certainly would not have permitted themselves had he been within earshot. Only about half of us remained when the bus finally arrived, over two hours late.

I gave the conductor my return ticket and luggage check, passed him my rucksack, and stepped aboard. There were seats for all of us. When the conductor had finished stoking the burner with charcoal, the driver pressed the starting button. Nothing happened. He pressed it again several times, but still the engine would not fire. This, of course, was a fairly normal occurrence and, without waiting to be told, we all got out of the bus—all, that is, except for a young couple who remained unconcernedly in their seats. They were obviously not familiar with the Binan-line bus.

With one accord we started to push. As the burner, which stuck out in the back, was extremely hot, we split into groups on each side. One enterprising passenger found a long board and used it to push the burner. The conductor also jumped down and began pushing. The road here was at a slight incline and the bus moved along without too much effort on our part. The driver sat calmly in his seat, hands on the steering wheel.

We had pushed the bus three or four hundred yards without the engine once firing, when suddenly we heard a hysterical voice from inside the bus. It was the driver, who evidently had just noticed the young couple.

"Hey, you two back there!" he roared. "What do you think you're doing? Can't you see that everyone else is pushing? Get out and lend a hand! Don't just sit there!"

A man's voice answered calmly: "Would you mind not shouting at me? I may not be much of a traveler, but I always thought that buses ran on their engines."

"I see," said the driver. "So that's your attitude! You're too good to push like everyone else, eh? Well, let me tell you something: I don't care if you're honeymooners or not, if you don't get out this minute and start pushing, you'll damned well wish you had!"

---

3. stentorian: very loud.

"If you want to continue this conversation," answered the man, "you'd better address me politely."

There was a pause. A little later, as the road passed through a quiet grove, the driver's voice again broke the silence.

"Hey, you two back there! Don't be so damned stubborn. How can you go on sitting there in comfort when all the others are sweating away on the road? We're beginning to go uphill now. Get out and help!"

"Why don't you pay attention to the engine?" said the young man loudly. "You're the one that's stubborn! You're so interested in making us get out and push that you aren't even trying to start the engine. Concentrate on your job like other drivers! You're a disgrace to the public-transport system!"

"Shut up!" said the driver. Then in a milder tone he added: "See here, young man, we're going up Sampun Hill now. You don't want to let the others do all the work, do you? Look at them back there sweating away!"

Sampun Hill was a steep cutting; both sides of the road were clay cliffs. It took all our strength to move the bus. From the top of the cutting the road went steeply downward, and if the engine didn't fire there, it was hard to see when it would. We all stopped at the summit and watched the bus gathering speed as it ran downhill. It passed a large irrigation tank on one side of the road and disappeared behind a clump of trees. We pricked up our ears for the sound of the engine, while the conductor ran down the hill after the bus.

A man in an open-neck shirt, a peaked cap, and a pair of khaki plus-fours[4] stained with paint came up to me. "Can you hear if it's started?" he said.

"I believe it's started," replied a girl in slacks who was standing next to me. "I think I can hear the engine. . . . But maybe it's just my imagination."

"I can't hear a thing," said the man in plus-fours. "How many more miles is it to town?"

"About four and a half," said the girl. "But in just over two miles we come to Three Corners Crossing, where we can catch a decent bus."

"And I'm taking that bus for the rest of the way," declared the man in plus-fours. "I'm fed up with this charcoal contraption!"

Just then the conductor appeared at the bottom of the hill. He stood there waving his arms and shaking his head, before disappearing again in a clump of trees.

"We've never had to push this far before," said the girl in slacks as we started disconsolately down the hill. "That couple has annoyed the driver. He's taking it out on the rest of us."

"Yes, I bet he'll have us pushing the bus all the way to the end of the line," said the man in plus-fours angrily. "There's only one thing for us to do—look exhausted. We must make him think we're on our last legs; then

---

4. **plus-fours:** baggy trousers gathered by a band below the knees.

maybe he'll change his mind." He pulled his shirt out of his trousers to give himself a disheveled appearance.

Finally we caught sight of the bus parked by a farmhouse near the trees. The driver was standing beside it with arms folded, while the conductor was busily turning the handle to stoke the burner. I could see a girl in a green dress drawing water from a well.

"Isn't that the girl who was in the bus?" I suggested.

"That's right," said a horse-faced man in an old army uniform with a mourning band.[5] "I've got a feeling something's gone wrong. Look, the girl's carrying a bucket into the bus. Hey, what's got into you?" he called out to the driver. "What are you doing, just standing there looking up at the sky? Have you decided to give up driving or what?"

"That's right," said the driver, fingering his mustache. "I've resigned."

"What do you mean, you've resigned?" said the horse-faced man.

"That stubborn fool in there wouldn't get out and push when I told him. So I had to give him a good beating. But first I resigned, because employees aren't allowed to hit the passengers. Once I'd resigned, I was a private citizen and could give him the beating he deserved."

"Look here," said the horse-faced man, "you've gone too far this time. And who do you think is going to drive if you don't?"

The driver shrugged his shoulders. He glanced disdainfully at the passengers assembled beside the bus. "I can't drive any more," he repeated stubbornly. "I tell you I've resigned."

At this point a tall old man stalked out of the farmhouse.

"I've had about enough of this!" he shouted to the driver. "I've seen everything that's gone on. I saw you attacking that peaceful couple. What do you mean by behaving like that in front of my house?"

"I'm a private citizen," said the driver. "I've got a perfect right to strike anyone I want to."

"Don't talk like a fool," said the old farmer. "And kindly get your bus away from my house. I'll help push the damned thing in place of the honeymoon couple if that's what's bothering you. My old woman can give a hand too. You get in and steer!"

We all followed the old couple to the back of the bus, and as I passed one of the windows, I glanced inside. The young man was lying back pale in his seat. He had some tissue paper stuffed in his nostrils and one of his eyes was red and swollen. The girl in the green dress had apparently just finished swabbing his face; she took the bucket to the back of the bus and handed it to one of the passengers, who returned it to the well.

The driver stood with his arms folded and refused to get into his seat. The old couple began pushing the bus with all their might. It would not budge.

"Hey, all you others," shouted the old man, "give us a hand!"

---

5. **mourning band:** strip of black cloth worn on the upper arm as a sign of grief for a person's death.

"Right you are," said the horse-faced man and ran to the back of the bus. "Come on, all of you," he shouted, "push away! Yo-heave-ho!"

We all pushed. The bus began to move. The driver opened his eyes wide in amazement. "Hey, wait a minute!" he shouted. "Don't be crazy! Wait till I get hold of the wheel."

He ran after the bus, jumped on to the driver's platform, and grasped the steering wheel before even sitting down. We all pushed now with redoubled vigor, spurred on by the feeling that we had taken matters into our own hands, at least temporarily. The road was fairly straight and the bus ran along at a steady speed.

"Hey, driver," shouted the horse-faced man, "can't you get the engine started? Are you sure you aren't doing it on purpose?"

"Don't be so suspicious," answered the driver. "It's not my fault it won't start. The engine's worn out. The battery isn't charging right either. But of course you people wouldn't know about such things."

"That's right," said a man who was wearing a light yellow shirt and a surplice[6] inscribed with a Buddhist prayer. "We laymen are only good for pushing. 'Push and don't ask questions!' That seems to be the motto of this bus company."

"Yes, it's going a little too far," said the horse-faced man. "We've got to push whether we want to or not, and no one even bothers to tell us what's wrong with the damned bus. I'm exhausted!"

The driver turned round with a cigarette in his mouth.

"Hey there, you two," he shouted to the honeymoon couple, "did you hear what that passenger said just now? He's exhausted. They're all exhausted because of your damned selfishness! Aren't you ashamed of yourselves? Listen to the voice of the people back there! Get out this minute and push—both of you!"

"Are you still worrying about us, you poor fool?" said the young man. "I've told you already—leave us alone and concentrate on the engine or the battery or whatever it is. First you charge us high fares and then you try to make us do a lot of useless pushing. I'll have something to say about all this when we arrive, I warn you!"

"What's that, you bastard?" roared the conductor. "Do you want another beating?"

"You tell me to listen to the voice of the people," answered the young man calmly. "Well, by protesting like this, I'm trying to make it penetrate your ears too."

"So you still think you're pretty smart, do you?" cried the driver, shaking with fury. "You still think you're better than everyone else? All right, I'll show you! You've asked for it!" He got to his feet.

"Sit down, sit down!" shouted the horse-faced man, who had now become our spokesman. "Don't let go of the steering wheel!" Then turning to us, he said: "Come on, push harder! Don't let the driver leave the steering wheel. Push away!"

---

6. surplice: loose-fitting white garment worn by a priest.

We pushed harder than ever and the bus moved rapidly along the straight, narrow road. On the left was a low stone wall beyond which was a steep drop to the paddy fields;[7] on the right was a shallow river. The driver could ill afford to let the bus swerve in either direction. In the distance I noticed a car approaching.

"Stop a minute!" cried the driver. "I've got to give that fool another beating."

"Oh no, you don't!" said the horse-faced man. "Come on, everyone, push away! Let's really get this old crate moving!"

We pushed—in fact we almost hurled ourselves at the back of the bus. In our excitement we had forgotten that the driver could stop the bus whenever he wanted simply by applying the brakes. We were all out of breath by now, but this did not deter us.

"Hey, what's wrong with you all?" shouted the driver. "Why do you stand up for that insolent bastard anyway? It's his fault you're all worn out."

"Don't worry about us!" said the horse-faced man. "Just keep steering! If you let go of that wheel, you'll really have something to worry about."

"That's right," added the man with the surplice. "You'll be with your ancestors before you know it."

Just then a large van approached from the opposite direction. The bus jerked to a sudden stop which almost knocked us off balance; it was a moment before I realized that the driver had applied the brakes. We exchanged disappointed, frustrated looks.

"Well, at least we've arrived at the crossroads," remarked the horse-faced man. "We've pushed it four miles already. Quite an achievement, I must say! But I've had enough. I'm taking the proper bus from here on."

He gave his luggage check to the conductor, loaded his rucksack on his back, and started walking toward Three Corners Crossing. I also decided to take the other bus; so did the man in plus-fours, the girl in slacks, and a few others. The rest said they would continue pushing—some because they were convinced the bus was about to start, others to prevent the driver from attacking the honeymoon couple, still others because they did not want to lose their fares. The refractory couple decided to remain in the bus. The man in plus-fours went to fetch his luggage and joined us at the crossroads. "They're sitting in there having lunch," he reported. "They've taken out a tin of dried beef."

"What about the driver?"

"It looks as if he's going to leave them in peace to enjoy their meal. They've got a bottle of whisky too."

I looked back at the charcoal bus. The driver had opened the hood and was tinkering at the engine with a wrench more for form's sake than anything, I imagined. The conductor put some charcoal in the burner and began turning the blower furiously. He seemed to have unbounded confidence in the engine. I noticed that the old farmer and his wife were trudging back toward their home.

---

7. **paddy fields:** rice fields.

DISCUSSION QUESTIONS

1. On the basis of the story, how would you describe the situation in wartime Japan?

2. Why do you think the characters in this story are all unnamed?

3. What is the allegorical significance of the fact that, after the war, the bus has been painted and the windows repaired but it still has to run on charcoal?

4. What is implied by such remarks as "the purgees are all coming back into favor" and "reverence had been unfashionable for some time after the war but was now gradually coming back into favor"?

SUGGESTIONS FOR WRITING

1. Do some research on Japan during World War II and in the years shortly afterward. Then write an essay explaining the specific allegorical details in "The Charcoal Bus." (Who might the bus driver and conductor represent? What do you think the young married couple represent? What about the old farm couple?)

2. Write a short allegory of your own that demonstrates a mishandled situation. Your main allegorical symbol should not be a bus or any other vehicle.

Acknowledgments

vii From "Kwan Chu" in *The Book of Songs* translated by Arthur Waley. © 1937 by Arthur Waley. Reprinted by permission of Grove / Atlantic, Inc.

xi Excerpt from *The Rubáiyát of Omar Khayyám*, translated by Justin Huntly McCarthy. Copyright © 1932 by Platinum Press, Inc. Reprinted by permission.

xi Excerpt from *The Rubáiyát of Omar Khayyám,* trans. Robert Graves and Omar Ali Shah. Reprinted by permission of A. P. Watt, Ltd. on behalf of The Trustees of the Robert Graves Copyright Trust and Omar Ali Shah.

xi No. 98 (p. 71, 4 lines) and No. 234 (p. 104, 4 lines) from *The Rubáiyát of Omar Khayyám* translated by Peter Avery and John Heath-Stubbs (Allen Lane, 1979) copyright © Peter Avery and John Heath-Stubbs, 1979. Reproduced by permission of Penguin Books, Ltd.

3 "The Adventures of Gilgamesh," from *The Oldest Stories in the World* by Theodor H. Gaster, translated by Theodor H. Gaster, Translation copyright 1952, renewed © 1980 by Theodor H. Gaster. Used by permission of Viking Penguin, a division of Penguin Putnam, Inc.

32 "Summer Is Dying" by Hayyim Nahman Bialik, from *An Anthology of Modern Hebrew Poetry,* edited by Abraham Birman. © 1968 by Abraham Birman. Reprinted by permission of HarperCollins Publishers, Inc.

33 "On My Return" by Hayyim Nahman Bialik, from *An Anthology of Modern Hebrew Poetry,* edited by Abraham Birman. © 1968 by Abraham Birman. Reprinted by permission of HarperCollins Publishers, Inc.

35 From "The Clock Overhead" by Ka-tzetnik, in *An Anthology of Modern Hebrew Poetry,* edited by Abraham Birman. © 1968 by Abraham Birman. Reprinted by permission of HarperCollins Publishers, Inc.

45 "The Name," from *Israeli Stories* by Joel Blocker, editor. Copyright © 1962 by Schocken Books, Inc. Reprinted by permission of Schocken Books, distributed by Pantheon Books, a division of Random House, Inc.

59 "The Overthrowing" from *The Meaning of the Glorious Koran.* Trans. Mohammed Marmaduke Pickthall.

60 "The Cleaving" from *The Meaning of the Glorious Koran.* Trans. Mohammed Marmaduke Pickthall.

61 "The Unity" from *The Meaning of the Glorious Koran.* Trans. Mohammed Marmaduke Pickthall.

62 "Flies and Mosquitoes" from *The Book of Animals* by Al-Jahiz translated by Reynold A. Nicholson.

71 "Remembered Music," "The Truth Within Us," "The Evil in Ourselves," "The Soul of Goodness in Things Evil," and "The Progress of Man" from *Rumi: Poet and Mystic* by Rumi. Trans. Reynold A. Nicholson. Reprinted by permission of Oneworld Publications, Oxford, England.

75 "Ode 1," "Ode 5," "Ode 8" from *The Divan of Hafiz* by Hafiz. Trans. Gertrude Lowthian Bell.

80 "The River of Madness" by Tawfiq al-Hakim, is reprinted with the permission of Simon & Schuster from *Islamic Literature, An Introductory History with Selections* by Najib Ullah. Copyright © 1963 by Najib Ullah and copyright renewed 1991 by William Naj.

97 "The Confidence Men" by Bhatta Somadeva, from *Fifty Great Oriental Stories,* ed. Gene Z. Hanrahan. New York: Bantam, 1965.

102 "My Lord, the Baby" by Rabindranath Tagore is reprinted with the permission of Simon & Schuster from *The Hungry Stones and Other Stories* by Rabindranath Tagore, translated by C. F. Andrews. Copyright © 1916 by Macmillan Publishing Company, renewed 1944 by Rabindranath Tagore.

109 "The Letter" by Dhumketu Guarishankar Joshi, from *Ten Tales for Indian Students,* translated by Dhumketu Guarishankar Joshi.

115 "The Bamboo Trick" by Achintya Kumar Sen Gupta, from *Green and Gold.* Ed. Humayan Kabir. Trans. by the author. Copyright © 1958 by Government of West Bengal, India. Reprinted by permission of New Directions Publishing Corp.

121 "The Gold Watch" by Mulk Raj Anand from *Modern Stories from Many Lands.* Ed. Decker and Angoff. First published in The Literary Review.

131 Poems from *The Collected Songs of Cold Mountain: Revised and Expanded* © 1999 by Cold Mountain, translated by Red Pine (Bill Porter). Published by Mercury House, San Francisco, CA and reprinted by permission.

131 "Rough and dark—the Cold Mountain Trail" from *Riprap and Cold Mountain Poems* by Gary Snyder. Copyright © 1990 by Gary Snyder. Reprinted by

permission of North Point Press, a division of Farrar, Straus & Giroux, Inc."

135 "A Bitter Love," "A Sigh from a Staircase of Jade," "On Hearing Chün the Buddhist Monk from Shu Play His Lute," "A Song of Ch'ang-kan," and "Parting at a Wine Shop in Nan-king" by Li Po, from *The Jade Mountain* by Witter Bynner, trans. Copyright 1929 and renewed 1957 by Alfred A. Knopf, Inc. Reprinted by permission of the publisher.

138 "On Meeting Li Kuei-nien Down the River," "Remembering My Brothers on a Moonlight Night," "A Night Abroad," "On the Gate-Tower at Yo-chou," "A Hearty Welcome," "To My Retired Friend Wêi," "Night in the Watch-Tower," "A Drawing of a Horse by General Ts'ao at Secretary Wêi Fêng's House," and "A Song of War-Chariots" by Tu Fu, from *The Jade Mountain* by Witter Bynner, trans. Copyright 1929 and renewed 1957 by Alfred A. Knopf, Inc. Reprinted by permission of the publisher.

144 "Golden Bells," "Remembering Golden Bells," "Chu-ch'ēn Village," "The Philosophers (Lao-tzu)," and "The Red Cockatoo" by Po Chü-i, from *Translations from the Chinese* by Arthur Waley, translated by Arthur Waley. Copyright 1947 and renewed 1969 by Alfred A. Knopf, Inc. Reprinted by permission of the publisher and John Robinson for the Arthur Waley Estate.

175 "The Last Train" from *Contemporary Chinese Short Stories,* translated by Yuan Chia-hua and Robert Payne. London and New York: N. Carrington, 1947.

199 "The Damask Drum (Aya No Tsuzumi)" by Seami, translated by Arthur Waley, from *The No Plays of Japan.* New York: Grove Press.

206 From *An Introduction to Haiku* by Harold G. Henderson. Copyright © 1958 by Harold G. Henderson. Used by permission of Doubleday, a division of Bantam Doubleday Dell Publishing Group, Inc.

210 "Seibei's Gourds" by Shiga Naoya, translated by Ivan Morris in *Paper Door.* Boston and Tokyo: Charles E. Tuttle & Co., Inc. Reprinted by permission.

215 "The Thief" from *Seven Japanese Tales* by Junichiro Tanizaki, Howard Hibbett, trans. Copyright © 1963 by Alfred A. Knopf, Inc. Reprinted by permission of the publisher.

224 "Hell Screen" by Akutagawa Ryūnosuké, translated by W. H. H. Norman, from *Modern Japanese Literature* edited by Donald Keene. Copyright © 1956 by Grove Press, Inc. Used by permission of Grove / Atlantic, Inc.

244 "The Charcoal Bus" by Ibusé Masuji, translated by Ivan Morris, from *Modern Japanese Short Stories.* Boston and Tokyo: Charles E. Tuttle & Co., Inc. Reprinted by permission.

Pronunciation Key

a	bat	ėr	her	oi	soil	ch	change		a	in along
ā	cage	i	hit	ou	scout	ng	song		e	in shaken
ä	star	ī	nice	u	up	sh	shell	ə	i	in stencil
â	dare	o	cot	ù	put	th	think		o	in lemon
au	law	ō	old	ü	tube	TH	there		u	in circus
e	bet	ô	for			zh	pleasure			
ē	me									

Index of Authors, Titles, and Translators

LITERATURE OF

Asia

Teacher's Manual

TRADITIONS IN WORLD LITERATURE

National Textbook Company
a division of NTC/CONTEMPORARY PUBLISHING GROUP
Lincolnwood, Illinois USA

Contents

CHINESE LITERATURE

JAPANESE LITERATURE

THE EPIC OF GILGAMESH

SUMMARY

After introducing Gilgamesh as the powerful King of Erech, the narrative relates the story of how Enkidu, a wild man of the fields, enters the city and fights with him, eventually overpowering him. Enkidu then offers his friendship to Gilgamesh, and together the two men embark on a series of heroic adventures. They destroy the monster Humbaba, who lives in the cedar forests, and then kill the ferocious heavenly bull sent by the goddess Ishtar. In revenge Ishtar places a curse on Enkidu, who sickens and dies.

Gilgamesh, overcome with grief and frightened by the prospect of his own death, begins a journey in search of immortality. After a number of hardships, he finds the man he is seeking, Utnapishtim, who is the only survivor of the great flood and the only person ever to gain immortality. To his disappointment, Gilgamesh learns that Utnapishtim was granted everlasting life as a special gift from the gods and that there is no secret knowledge that will lead to immortality. Knowing that his long search has been in vain, Gilgamesh prepares to leave. As he is departing, Utnapishtim offers some consolation by telling him about a plant that grows on the ocean bottom that can restore youth. Gilgamesh is successful in finding the plant but later, while he is bathing, a snake eats it. Deeply distressed but resigned to his fate as a mortal being, Gilgamesh returns to his kingdom.

GUIDELINES FOR DISCUSSION QUESTIONS

1. **Unlike most legendary heroes, Gilgamesh fails in his quest. Why, then, do you think Gilgamesh emerged as a great epic hero among the ancient Babylonians?**

   Responses could vary widely since the question calls for speculation on the part of students. Some students may attribute the popularity of the Gilgamesh legend to the many successful exploits of the hero prior to his ultimate failure. Others may point to the universal nature of Gilgamesh's quest, which represents the hope of virtually every human being on earth, as the basis of the story's appeal. In a sense, Gilgamesh becomes more likable as he becomes more vulnerable, and his futile search for immortality makes him sympathetic as well as heroic. Readers can identify with his fear and grief even more, perhaps, than with his brave deeds.

2. What impression of Gilgamesh do you get from the first paragraph? How does Gilgamesh change in the course of the epic? How do you account for this change?

In the first paragraph Gilgamesh emerges as a tyrannical ruler who seeks only his own pleasure. He is described as part god and part human, but he seems to see himself as all god, omnipotent and invincible. His friendship with Enkidu, however, gradually humanizes him and makes him a more caring person. Enkidu's death heightens his awareness of his own helplessness and mortality and deepens his compassion for other mortals. It is significant that Gilgamesh does not immediately eat the special plant that will restore his youth but saves it to give to his people. The mighty king we met at the beginning of the epic would not have thought of sharing this precious gift with his subjects. By the end of the epic, he has come to see himself as a human among other humans, powerless in the face of death.

3. What is the purpose of the episode in which Gilgamesh sleeps for six days and seven nights? Why does he deny that he was ever asleep?

Sleep may be viewed as a milder form of death, and Gilgamesh's inability to ward off sleep is an indication of his inability to ward off death. He denies that he was asleep because he wants to show himself strong and worthy of immortality.

4. What view of the gods is presented in this epic? Do they tend to be wise and just, like the God of the Bible or the Koran, or irresponsible troublemakers, like the Greek and Roman gods, or something else entirely? Support your answer.

The gods in Gilgamesh are, for the most part, depicted as arbitrary, irresponsible, and vindictive. Ishtar's revenge on Gilgamesh for rejecting her offer of love is the most obvious example. The description of the gods in council arguing over which of the two heroes to kill certainly does not paint an attractive picture of these deities. (Although this description is part of Enkidu's dream, it is clear in this epic that dreams are accurate portrayals of reality.) It is interesting that the gods intend to punish Gilgamesh and Enkidu for the slaying of Humbaba and the heavenly bull, even though two of the gods encouraged them to fight Humbaba and actually came to their aid during the battle. The gods are definitely not depicted as agents of justice in this epic.

5. When the *Epic of Gilgamesh* was first discovered, people were amazed at the parallels between this epic and parts of the Bible. If you are familiar with the book of Genesis in the Bible, point out some of the similarities.

The most obvious parallel between Gilgamesh and the book of Genesis is the story of the great flood. Both accounts are strikingly similar in details concerning the ark, the rescued animals, the releasing of the dove, and the eventual landing on a mountain. Other parallels include the garden of delights and the biblical Garden of Eden, the use of dreams to foretell the future, and the serpent that deprives humanity of eternal life.

6. Ancient works of literature often make use of repetition. In the *Epic of Gilgamesh* the statement "that which you seek you will never find" is repeated at three different times. Who are the three speakers? What does this repetition accomplish?

The three speakers are the sun-god, Siduri the alewife, and Utnapishtim. (The scorpion-men say essentially the same thing, though they do not use exactly the same words.) Like the refrain of a song, the words receive special emphasis by being repeated several times. When Gilgamesh himself uses these words at the end of his quest ("that which he had sought he would never find"), the impact is more powerful because the phrase has been gathering strength through repetition.

GUIDELINES FOR ASSESSING STUDENT WRITING

Toward the beginning of the *Epic of Gilgamesh* the main character is said to be "rampaging like a bull." This simile is the first of numerous figures of speech in the epic. Make a chart showing as many similes and metaphors as you can find. Classify them as either animals, clothing and household items, or weapons. Then choose one figure of speech that strikes you as particularly apt and explain what makes it effective.

This exercise can be done in small groups or even as a whole-class activity. There are numerous ways to organize and present the chart. Below are most of the figures of speech in Gilgamesh, classified into the three categories:

Images of Animals
   rampaging like a bull
   preened like a jaybird
   like a lion, perfect in strength
   like a charger, glorious in battle
   like a spider caught in a spot where it cannot move
   like a lioness robbed of her whelps
   the butterfly . . . lives but a day [implied comparison to humans]

Images of Clothing and Household Items
   you are but a drafty door
   you are . . . a palace tottering to its ruin
   you are . . . a turban which fails to cover the head
   you are . . . pitch that defiles the hand
   you are . . . a bottle that leaks
   you are . . . a shoe that pinches
   you were . . . my robe

Images of Weapons
   you ensnare [your lovers] into pits sevenfold
   you were the ax at my side
   you were . . . the bow in my hand
   you were . . . the dirk in my belt
   you were . . . my shield

THE BIBLE

King James Version

SUMMARY

The story of Samson opens with a visit from an angel, who tells Samson's parents of his forthcoming birth. They are told that he will deliver the Israelites from their Philistine overlords and that they are not to cut his hair. The next excerpt describes Samson's wedding to a Philistine woman and gives an account of a riddle he poses to the thirty Philistine men who attend him before the ceremony. They are promised new sheets and garments if they can solve the riddle. The men prevail upon the bride to find out the answer for them, and she does so. Angry at the betrayal, Samson sets fire to their grain fields, after which he is captured and bound. He easily breaks the bonds, however, and, picking up the jawbone of an ass, kills a thousand Philistines.

Later, Samson falls in love with another Philistine woman named Delilah. When the Philistines learn of the affair, they urge Delilah to find out the secret of Samson's tremendous strength. After three false answers, Samson finally gives in to her pleas and reveals that his strength lies in his hair. While he sleeps, she has a servant cut his locks, allowing the Philistines to capture him. They put out his eyes and imprison him.

Eventually Samson's hair grows back, and he recovers his strength. Unaware of this, the Philistines command that he be brought to their festival in the temple so that they can make fun of him. When he discovers that he is standing between two pillars, Samson grabs one in each arm and brings the building down upon them all, killing himself and all the Philistines.

The Psalms printed here include four songs of thanksgiving extolling the wonders of God's creation (Psalms 8, 19, 95, and 98), the famous Psalm 23 with its extended shepherd metaphor, and a song of love (Psalm 45). Ecclesiastes 3 is the well-known chapter that sets forth the philosophy that there is a time appointed for everything, though the meaning of life and humanity's ultimate destiny remain a mystery.

GUIDELINES TO DISCUSSION QUESTIONS

1. On a scale of 1 (low) to 10 (high) how would you rate Samson's success as a leader and deliverer of his people? Defend your answer.

Evaluations of Samson's success are likely to vary considerably. Students who give him a relatively low rating might mention some of his foolish escapades, such as the silly lion-and-honey riddle and the absurd way he makes off with the city gates of Gaza. He is petulant and unnecessarily destructive, as evidenced by his burning of the Philistine fields just because his wife was not available to him after he, in effect, gave her away. He is, of course, foolishly susceptible to the pleading of Delilah, even when her earlier behavior makes it perfectly clear that she intends to destroy him. One might also question the wisdom of having affairs with Philistine women.

Students who give Samson a high rating could mention the indisputable fact that, through all his bumbling, he does manage to conquer a large number of Philistines and to fulfill the prophecy that he will "begin to deliver Israel from the hand of the Philistines." Some of his questionable deeds, such as his dalliances with Philistine woman, are described as part of God's plan. God's selection of Samson to be judge over the Hebrews seems to be a rather strange choice, but perhaps this is just a case where God "works in mysterious ways." Certainly Samson's final heroic act is one of tremendous dignity and triumph, and it is accomplished at a terrible personal cost.

2. Why does the writer of the Samson story spend so much time on events that occurred before Samson's birth?

A whole chapter of the Samson story is devoted to the special circumstances surrounding his birth. An angel of the lord appears to his parents and announces that they will have a son who will triumph over the Philistines. The fact that Samson is chosen to be a deliverer before he is even born, along with the miraculous birth from a barren woman, prepares the reader to expect great things from Samson.

3. How does Samson's experience with his wife foreshadow his experience with Delilah?

Samson is betrayed in almost exactly the same fashion twice. His wife coaxes information from him by weeping and accusing him of not loving her. Similarly, Delilah eventually conquers Samson by saying, "How canst thou say , I love thee, when thine heart is not with me?" It is interesting that Samson can stand up to his enemies even when they number in the thousands, but he cannot stand up to a wheedling woman.

4. Psalm 8 asks the question, "What is man that thou art mindful of him?" and then provides an answer, describing man's place in a hierarchy of beings. Starting with God, describe this hierarchy in descending order of importance. Why does the psalmist wonder why God is "mindful" of man?

The hierarchy begins with God and moves down the scale to the angels, human beings, beasts, birds, and fish. Human beings seem insignificant next to the heavens, the moon, and the stars, and the poet rejoices that God is aware of them at all.

5. Psalm 19 and Psalm 98 are both celebrations of God's creation, and both poems present personifications of the creation. What are these personifications, and what is their intended effect on the reader?

Psalm 19 presents the creation as something that speaks knowledgeably in a human voice, using words such as "declare," "uttereth speech," and "sheweth knowledge." Psalm 98 presents the creation as something that rejoices by making music. There seems to be a great musical outburst at the end of the psalm where everything acknowledges God with a "joyful noise" (the sea, the hills, the floods). In both cases the earth is personified by being given a voice so that it can offer up praise.

6. What images in Psalm 23 suggest protection and trust? How are the images in the second half of the psalm different from those in the first half?

The shepherd image, of course, has strong protective overtones, and the peaceful pastoral images of "green pastures" and "still waters" suggest a sheltering, soothing setting. In the second half of the poem God has become a gracious host rather than a guiding shepherd, and the images become indoor household images. Since this shift follows the reference to "the shadow of death," the psalmist is probably referring to an afterlife in "the house of the Lord."

7. How would you describe the tone and world view expressed in Ecclesiastes 3?

The book of Ecclesiastes is sometimes described as pessimistic, dark, or even cynical, but these are perhaps overstatements. The tone is definitely somber, but it is not defeatist. The repeated statement that "all is vanity" refers to the long view of human existence. Humans cannot penetrate the mysteries of life or change the timings of such processes as birth and death, sowing and reaping, war and peace. In the long run it does not matter if someone is wise or foolish, industrious or lazy, human or animal, since they all come to the same end. However, the chapter closes with the short view of human existence, which is more upbeat. Within one's allotted and unpredictable life span, it is still possible for a person to "enjoy the good of all his labor" and to "rejoice in his own works." That is the writer's final recommendation.

GUIDELINES FOR ASSESSING STUDENT WRITING

1. Samson, who is described by one scholar as a "simpleminded, muscle-bound boy," has fascinated readers over the years because

he is an interesting combination of strengths and weaknesses. Do you agree that he is "simpleminded," that stupidity is one of his problems? Write an essay defending your point of view.

There is ample evidence for concluding that Samson is not terribly bright. The prime clue, of course, is Delilah's success in duping him. On three previous occasions it was revealed that Delilah had Philistines in hiding who were waiting for an opportunity to subdue Samson as soon as they learned the secret of his strength. The fact that Samson, knowing this, is still swayed by her pleas is nothing short of amazing. Some students, however, may attribute Samson's behavior not to stupidity but to his touching faith in God. Certainly he has reason to believe that God will take care of him, since it was predetermined that he would someday deliver Israel. Samson's first thought as he is being captured is, in fact, surprise that God would abandon him: "And he wist not that the Lord was departed from him."

2. The book of Psalms and the book of Ecclesiastes are filled with concrete images that are preserved in the King James translation. Some translators, however, have chosen to dispense with these images in favor of direct statements. In Chapter 11 of Ecclesiastes, for example, the King James translators write, "He that observeth the wind shall not sow, and he that regardeth the clouds shall not reap." In the Living Bible translation the passage reads, "If you wait for perfect conditions, you will never get anything done."
    Write a new version of Psalm 23 in which you use no metaphors but rely entirely on direct statements. Then write a brief commentary explaining what is gained and what is lost when the poem is expressed in abstract statements.

A conversion of Psalm 23 into a "direct statement" that is free of all imagery would result in a short, rather bare "poem" like the following:

> The Lord takes care of me
> And I am not afraid of anything.
> Even if I should die, I would have no fear.
> I know that the Lord will honor me and treat me justly,
> And our relationship will endure forever.

The advantage to this style of expression, of course, is that it is perfectly clear. There are no ambiguities or questions of interpretation. On the other hand, students should see that eliminating the concrete images destroys the "feel" of the poem, the direct appeal to our senses that makes it seem like a first-hand experience.

HAYYIM NAHMAN BIALIK

Poems

SUMMARY

"Summer Is Dying" and "On My Return" are both poems that present a disgruntled view of a change that has just taken place. In the first poem it is a change of season. In gorgeous images the poet describes the passing away of the lush summer, and in bleak images he indicates the coming of winter. In the second poem the transition is one of place rather than time. The reader does not know where the poet has been, but his return is clearly an unpleasant one. The passive scene he describes is one of degeneration and stagnation. The man and woman in the poem, as well as the napping cat and the spiders in the corner, are so inert that they seem to be virtually rotting away.

GUIDELINES FOR DISCUSSION QUESTIONS

1. **How would you describe the mood of these two poems? What particular phrases or images contribute to the mood of each poem?**

   Students might describe the mood of these two poems as "sad," "melancholy," "unpleasant," or any other descriptors suggesting that the poet is distressed over the change. In "On My Return," there is also a note of protest since the unpleasant scene is not an inevitable event like the passing of the seasons but one that is under human control. Some of the words and images that contribute to the mood of "Summer Is Dying" are *twilight, deserted, last and lingering, casting an eye and a sigh,* and *heart is orphaned.* Some of the significant words and images in "On My Return" are *wizened, shriveled, fumbling, choked with flies, rot,* and *stink.* Students may point out other expressions that contribute to the mood.

2. **In "Summer Is Dying" how do the images used in the first stanza differ from those in the last stanza? What is the effect of this difference?**

In the first stanza of "Summer Is Dying," the images are rich, luxuriant, and suggestive of wealth and leisure ("fine gold," "purple bed"). In the final stanza they are bare, paltry, and suggestive of poverty ("orphaned," "patch up your coats"). The effect of this difference is to create a picture of summer as a bounteous, giving season, while winter emerges as a season of struggle and deprivation.

3. In line 9, what does Bialik mean when he says, "The heart is orphaned"? How does this relate to the changing of the season?

The expression "heart is orphaned" indicates that the speaker suddenly feels cut off and deserted. The summer season is depicted as nurturing and sustaining, rather like a parent figure. When the season dies, human beings are, in a sense, orphaned.

4. In "On My Return" the poet paints an unpleasant picture of the scene of his return. What do you think he is criticizing? What do the animal images (cat, mouse, spiders, flies) contribute to the impact of this poem?

By creating the static and degenerative scene in "On My Return" Bialik would seem to be directing criticism toward passivity and compliance. The people have become "dry," "shriveled," and "wizened" from inactivity. Even the animals have reached a stage of stagnation that is clearly unnatural. A cat, for example, would be expected to dream about chasing a mouse, not making "a treaty with a mouse." The spider is passively letting the dead bodies of flies collect in webs without making use of them. It is clear that no one in the scene is engaged in any kind of active pursuit.

5. In the last line what does Bialik mean by the expression "join your club"? How do the final lines drive home the point of the poem?

The expression "join your club" is probably a reference, not to an official club, but to a defeatist inclination to give up, let go, or drift along. The poem may have political implications and may suggest that the Jews in the emerging state of Israel are not exerting themselves to the fullest. Whatever the case, the images of rotting and stinking in the last two lines drive home the point that inactivity will eventually cause one to stagnate and rot away.

GUIDELINES FOR ASSESSING STUDENT WRITING

Both of these poems deal with a transition, a change in time or place. Select a transition in your life that you feel strongly about. Write a poem or a paragraph dramatizing the contrast between the old time or place and the new one and your feelings about them. You might want to consider a change from one school to another, from one town to another, from one class to another, from one age to another, or from one time of year to another.

Whatever format students choose for this assignment, their main task is to create a series of sharp contrasts. The poem or paragraph should present a vivid set of images that successfully communicates the difference between the two times or places. Since this is an exercise in self-expression as well as description, the student's attitude toward these two entities should also be apparent.

KA-TZETNIK 135633

from STAR ETERNAL

SUMMARY

These selections are prose poems that vividly recreate Ka-tzetnik's experiences in the death camps at Auschwitz. The author describes the naked marches into the bathhouses, where terrified prisoners wait to be gassed but sometimes receive actual showers. He also describes the remnants (shoes, hair) of various family members and grimly speculates on how these items are being put to use by the Germans. The passage ends with some scornful remarks about the monetary "reparations" being considered by the German government.

GUIDELINES FOR DISCUSSION QUESTIONS

1. **With remarks such as "I still can't figure how many German marks a burnt Mother comes to," Ka-tzetnik ridicules the idea of "reparation" to the Jews. What, if anything, do you think the German government should do for the Jews who were victims of Nazi persecutions?**

   Responses to this difficult question will no doubt vary widely. Some students may discuss monetary compensation, while others may suggest various types of memorials. Students may also suggest intangible reparations, such as formal apologies or educational programs to prevent bigotry and persecution in the future. Help students to see the difficulty in trying to make reparations for something that can never be "repaired."

2. **In the section called "Face to Face" Ka-tzetnik uses the word** *spark* **to signify several different things. Explain how the meaning of the word changes in this section.**

   The word *spark* is first used to refer to the sparks of fire coming from the chimneys of the crematoriums. Later it is used to refer to the spiritual spark of life that burns within every individual no matter how hopeless the situation (the "single spark you still carry within you"). As each prisoner dies, the spiritual spark is transformed into a literal spark of fire, which will shoot from the chimney and "mingle with the stars." The author is proposing that the human spark of life, which rivals the stars in brightness, is something almost celestial.

3. **Ka-tzetnik often speaks of the prisoners of Auschwitz as if they were simply body parts. In the section called "Inside," for example, the prisoners are called "necks," while in "Dawn in Auschwitz" they are repeatedly referred to as "eyes." What effect does the author achieve by referring to the prisoners in this way?**

The roomful of necks in the section entitled "Inside" suggests animals waiting to be slaughtered: "Necks stretched out. To the slaughtering knife on high." The prisoners are, of course, looking at the ceiling in expectation of being gassed by the sprinkler pipes overhead, and the overriding image is a collection of headless necks. In "Dawn in Auschwitz" the author speaks of "ten thousand pairs of eyes" that represent many kinds of people, ranging from "lords of wealth" to "delicate spirits" to "careworn shopkeepers." Because the prisoners cannot exchange words with each other, their eyes have become the main instruments of communication. For this reason, the author reduces each man to a pair of eyes.

4. **Ka-tzetnik recalls several members of his family by describing the remnants that are left after their death. How does he use these remnants to characterize his father and sister?**

Ka-tzetnik's father has become a pair of shoes with heels that "were never crooked." With this brief description, the author characterizes him as a man who was straight and honest in his dealings. Ka-tzetnik's sister has become a "rectangular bale" of golden hair that was used to make a blanket. With this gruesome description, the author laments the loss of his sister's loveliness and the perverse way her remains were packaged and sold.

GUIDELINES FOR ASSESSING STUDENT WRITING

Imagine that you are a publisher who is planning to publish an illustrated edition of *Star Eternal*. The artist who will do the illustrations needs guidelines about how they should be drawn. Choose one section that you would like to see illustrated. Then write a letter to the artist explaining what should appear in the illustration. Be sure to explain the mood you want to create in the illustration. You might also want to make suggestions about the use of color, if any, and the style of drawing (detailed and realistic or simplified and stark, for example).

The main purpose of this assignment is to give students practice in writing clear instructions, with enough descriptive detail to communicate the situation and mood effectively. Students who select the more graphic sections, such as the march to the bathhouse or the shower scene, will need to tell the artist approximately how many people should be in the scene and will need to describe their facial expressions, physical condition, and surroundings. Those who select the more abstract and reflective sections in "Wiedergutmachung" might describe the mountain of shoes or some other remnant of the murdered Jews. Alternatively, they might decide to illustrate a scene from before the war, such as one showing the mother braiding the sister's long golden hair. In this case, they will ask the artist to create a peaceful, pleasant scene that contrasts with the other grim, brooding illustrations.

AHARON MEGGED

The Name

SUMMARY

"The Name" begins by describing the monthly visits of a young couple, Raya and Yehuda, to Raya's grandfather. The old man lives alone with his memories of the German slaughter of an entire village of 20,000 Jews. Among those killed were the grandfather's son and a grandson named Mendele. During every visit the old man annoys Raya and Yehuda by having them read a long lament he has written for the village and by talking repeatedly about Mendele, who was a talented and promising boy.

When the grandfather learns that Raya is expecting a baby, he sends a message through Raya's mother that the child should be named Mendele if it is a boy. Raya and Yehuda refuse, claiming that the name carries connotations of a past they want to forget. The grandfather pays a personal call on the couple and makes a moving appeal to them not to let the names and memories of the past disappear without a trace, but to no avail. When their son is born, he is named Ehud.

A month later Raya and Yehuda take the baby to visit the old man, who pointedly ignores him. After a strained conversation, the couple decides to leave. When they get outside, Raya bursts into tears, realizing that her son will have no connection to past generations but will be, in a sense, "an orphan in the world."

GUIDELINES FOR DISCUSSION QUESTIONS

1. **What would you have done about the baby's name if you had been in Raya and Yehudi's position? Why?**

   Responses to this question will depend partly on students' attitudes toward family traditions and partly on their feelings toward Grandfather Zisskind, who is largely a sympathetic figure, though perhaps not sympathetic enough to win over students who place a very high premium on individual freedom. Some students may suggest a compromise position, such as using Mendele as the baby's middle name. At any rate, the discussion should engender interesting variations on the age-old conflict between social unity and individuality.

2. **What indications are there at the beginning of the story that Grandfather Zisskind relies strongly on traditions?**

Whenever Grandfather Zisskind receives visitors, the events of the day are completely predictable. The long-established routine begins with "three cautious knocks" on the door, continues to the tea and preserves, and finally ends with the reading of the lament for the slaughtered Jews. The grandfather's ritualistic tendencies, even during a casual family visit, suggest that he relies strongly on tradition.

3. **What is the symbolic significance of Grandfather Zisskind's wall clock, which is mentioned several times in the course of the story?**

The clock has stopped and remains fixed in time, rather like the grandfather, who forgets recent events but remembers "down to the smallest detail" the events of many years ago. The documents that commemorate the main cause of Grandfather Zisskind's fixation, the slaughtered Jews, are stored in the clock. In a sense, then, the clock, like the old man, has stopped moving forward and has fastened itself around one central event from the past.

4. **How does Grandfather Zisskind's behavior change when he finds out that Raya is about to have a child? How do you explain this change?**

When he hears about the baby, Grandfather Zisskind leaves his apartment for the first time and seems to be restored to his former pleasant self, turning his thoughts to the future rather than to the past. For him the baby clearly represents new hope, a sense of continuation, and even a resurrection of Mendele.

5. **What does the grandfather mean when he says to Yehuda, "You're finishing off the work which the enemies of Israel began"? How does his repeated phrase, "Not a trace," change meaning in the course of the story?**

According to the grandfather, the enemies of Israel killed the Jews physically, and Raya and Yehuda are doing their part to kill all remembrance of them. When Grandfather Zisskind first uses the phrase, "Not a trace," he is referring to the obliteration of the Ukrainian village and the murder of its inhabitants. The last time he uses it he is referring to the obliteration of their names and their memory.

6. **At the end of the story why does Raya regard her baby as an "orphan"?**

Raya and Yehuda had both tried repeatedly to include the baby in the conversation during their visit with Grandfather Zisskind, but he made it clear that he did not intend to recognize the child. At this point Raya realizes that the baby is "orphaned" from his ancestral roots, that he will have no ties with his people or with their history.

GUIDELINES FOR ASSESSING STUDENT WRITING

Select an established tradition that you would like to see preserved. It could be a holiday tradition such as fireworks on the Fourth of July or trick-or-treating on Halloween. Or it could be a special tradition that is observed in your family or community. Imagine that someone or some group is trying to eliminate the tradition. Write an essay defending the tradition and explaining its importance to the participants.

Students may select traditions as light-hearted as birthday celebrations or as serious as religious observations. Their strategy for defending the tradition will vary, of course, depending on its purpose and its degree of seriousness. Students should try to move beyond the let's-have-fun rationale to a recognition of shared values or a sense of social cohesiveness.

THE KORAN

SUMMARY

Surahs 81 and 82 both describe the end of the world and the Day of Judgment with cosmic images of destruction and chaos. Not only is the earth destroyed but also the sun, stars, and planets, which all come crashing down. The righteous, however, "will be in delight," though the nature of their reward is not presented in any particular detail. Surah 112, a short chapter only four lines long, invokes Allah as the only God and asserts that he is the primary cause of everything, since he was not born or made by anyone else.

GUIDELINES FOR DISCUSSION QUESTIONS

1. What impression do you think the first two surahs were intended to have on readers or listeners? Why do you think so?

The major impact of these two surahs is to impress the reader with the power of Allah and to inspire fear of the consequences of living a sinful life. Almost the entirety of each passage is devoted to images of destruction, with only a few images of hope presented. Students may contribute other impressions as well.

2. What images do the first two surahs have in common? What message do they deliver?

Surahs 81 and 82 deliver terrifying messages about the Day of Judgment, emphasizing punishment and destruction. At the same time, they both remind people of the power of personal choice. Surah 81 says, "Then every soul will know what it hath made ready," while Surah 82 asserts that "a soul will know what it hath sent before it." The images used in these surahs are also quite similar in that they both describe the toppling of the entire universe: suns, stars, planets, seas, and land.

3. What attributes (qualities) of Allah are emphasized in these selections from the Koran?

The compassion of Allah appears in the first-line invocations, which are always the same throughout the Koran. The absolute authority and power of Allah are set forth in Surahs 81 and 82. In Surah 112

Allah is presented as a Being that people long for ("Besought of all") and also as the first cause of everything—Someone neither born nor made by anything else.

4. Surah 81 offers a clue about the special reward that awaits the righteous. What is that reward?

In line 13 of Surah 81 there is a reference to a garden that will be "brought nigh" at the same time that "hell is lighted." Presumably the reward will involve an afterlife in a garden setting.

GUIDELINES FOR ASSESSING STUDENT WRITING

Compare the message and the images of Surah 82 to those set forth in the following verses, taken from the fourth chapter of Malachi in the Old Testament:

For, behold, the day cometh, that shall burn as an oven; and all the proud, yea, and all that do wickedly, shall be stubble; and the day that cometh shall burn them up, saith the Lord of hosts, that it shall leave them neither root nor branch.

But unto you that fear my name shall the Sun of righteousness arise with healing in his wings; and he shall go forth, and grow up as calves of the stall.

Obviously the general theme of these two passages is the same, the punishment of the wicked, and there is a shared emphasis on burning as the specific method of punishment to be used. In spite of these similarities, students should recognize that the image clusters vary somewhat. The Old Testament passage essentially leaves the earth intact, with sinners compared to burning plants that are destroyed root and branch, while the righteous are allowed to prosper like "calves of the stall." The passage from the Koran involves destruction that is cosmic in scope, with Allah destroying the physical universe and relegating both the wicked and the righteous to some other place.

AL-JAHIZ

Flies and Mosquitoes

SUMMARY

In this brief, anecdotal account, Al-Jahiz defends flies by demonstrating that they have two good qualities. First, they can be dispensed with easily by providing a source of light, toward which they will invariably fly. Secondly, Al-Jahiz is convinced that they eat mosquitoes. He bases his conclusion on an observation made by a man named Muhammad, who noticed that whenever the door to his sleeping quarters was left open and the curtains left up during the day, almost no mosquitoes entered to bother him during his afternoon nap. Muhammad believes that the presence of flies, which are attracted to a room with plenty of light, accounts for the absence of mosquitoes. He concludes that the flies must have entered and eaten the mosquitoes.

GUIDELINES FOR DISCUSSION QUESTIONS

1. **Al-Jahiz seems to accept the reasoning of Muhammad, son of Jahm, when he concludes that flies must eat mosquitoes. Do you find Muhammad's experiment and conclusions convincing? If not, why not? Can you think of a better way to find out the truth?**

   The conclusion that flies eat mosquitoes is not a sound one. Muhammad notices that mosquitoes are not present in his room during the day when flies are present. He even subjects this observation to repeated experiments that seem to confirm his theory that mosquitoes will not be found when flies are present. However, even if this is true, there are other explanations. Perhaps mosquitoes dislike the bright light that attracts flies and therefore avoid the room at such times. Muhammad did, in fact, report that when the door was closed and the curtains pulled, the mosquitoes tended to cluster in the room. At such times, of course, flies would not be present since they dislike darkness.

   One way to test the theory that flies eat mosquitoes is to enclose a known number of flies in a room with a known number of mosquitoes and see if the mosquitoes begin to disappear. If possible, it would be good to actually observe the room for a prolonged period of time to try to see mosquito consumption in action. Students may have other suggestions for setting up an experiment.

2. What are the fly's "two good qualities," according to Al-Jahiz?

According to Al-Jahiz, the fly's two good qualities are (1) the ease with which it can be driven out of the house simply by darkening the room and (2) its tendency to eat mosquitoes.

3. This essay, which was written to glorify the fly, is similar to several ancient fables in which an insignificant creature proves its worth, such as Aesop's tale of the lion and the mouse. Usually such stories have a moral. Do you think that this essay has a moral, either directly stated or indirectly suggested?

Responses to this question will be partly a matter of opinion. Some students may see the essay simply as an informative piece of writing on fly behavior. There is some evidence, however, that Al-Jahiz is presenting an underlying moral about the value of accidental discoveries and the necessity of being open to new and unexpected evidence. Muhammad slept well only when his precautions were ignored, and he had the sense to exercise his curiosity about this ironic situation and not just his annoyance at the slaves. As a result, he made an important discovery. Students may be able to see other possible morals that can be derived from the essay.

GUIDELINES FOR ASSESSING STUDENT WRITING

Choose an animal that is often detested, such as the snake, rat, spider, alligator, shark, or bat. After doing some research, write an essay entitled "In Defense of the _____," in which you present the good qualities of that animal. Your defense should be based on actual facts. (If you have had first-hand experience with any of these animals, you may use your personal observations as evidence too.)

These defenses should be based on factual information derived mostly through research. In some cases, this information may be supplemented by actual observations if students have pets such as rats or snakes. The defense strategy may be built around the fact that the animal is indirectly beneficial to humans, as in the case of insect-eating creatures. Or the strategy may be based on qualities the animal possesses that are inherently admirable quite apart from any effect on humans. The alligator's parental devotion is an example.

OMAR KHAYYÁM

The Rubáiyát

SUMMARY

Of the 100 quatrains that FitzGerald translated, 34 appear here. (The original Persian poem has almost 1,000 quatrains.) All are self-contained units expressing Omar Khayyám's search for meaning, the disillusionment resulting from his failure to find answers, the relentless march of time and destiny, and his advice to enjoy earthly pleasures while there is still time.

GUIDELINES FOR DISCUSSION QUESTIONS

1. Fatalism is the belief that humans have no free will, that they are like puppets controlled by an outside force. Would you characterize this poem as fatalistic? Why or why not?

Students can easily make a case for *The Rubáiyát* being a fatalistic work. The poem is filled with references to such predestined things as the "yet unfolded Roll of Fate" (quatrain 98) and the "Moving Finger" (quatrain 71). In addition, the images in quatrains 68 and 69 portray human beings as characters in a shadow show and pieces on a checkerboard, in both cases equating them to objects under the control of an unnamed Manipulator. On the other hand, students may point out that humans obviously have some small degree of choice, or else the poet would not be giving advice about how to live. In a few cases, he even suggests that one can overcome some of the predetermined events laid out, as in quatrain 80: "Thou wilt not with Predestined Evil round / Enmesh, and then impute my Fall to Sin!"

2. To what is the sun being compared in the first quatrain? What event is being described?

In the first quatrain the sun is compared either to a hunter causing animals to flee or to a warrior causing the enemy to flee. The fleeing figures in this metaphor are the stars, which are "scattered into flight" with the sunrise. The event being described is dawn.

3. What is the "battered Caravanserai" in quatrain 17? Which other quatrains make use of journey metaphors?

The "battered Caravanserai" is earthly existence, through which all creatures pass briefly as if visiting a traveler's inn. Journey metaphors can also be found in quatrains 64, 80, and 97.

4. According to Omar Khayyám, what effect do learning and religion have on one's life? (See quatrains 27, 28, and 65.)

Learning and religion have absolutely no effect on one's life. Various metaphors are used to communicate their ineffectiveness, such as "Wind," "Stories," and going out "by the same door," i.e., making no impact at all.

5. In quatrain 13 what is meant by "take the Cash, and let the Credit go"? In which other quatrains can you find the same idea expressed?

The expression "take the Cash, and let the Credit go" means that one should enjoy the immediate pleasures that are available and not yearn for those that are out of reach, whether "Glories of This World" or some kind of afterlife ("the Prophet's Paradise"). If students are not familiar with the *carpe diem* (seize the day) theme that is so widespread in literature, now might be a good time to introduce it. Quatrains 7, 11, 21, 24, 42 and 77 also express this theme.

GUIDELINES FOR ASSESSING STUDENT WRITING

Quatrain 17 is filled with images from the medieval Middle East. Using the same rhyme scheme—*abaa*—rewrite this stanza with images drawn from modern American culture. Try to preserve the original idea expressed in the poem.

The student's main task is to create a rhyming quatrain expressing the brevity of life, even for people in high and powerful positions. The student will need to create a cluster of current images to replace the caravan inn, portals, and the sultan. Below is an example:

Consider this hotel, on every floor,
How many travelers passed through each door:
Executives with credit cards, cell phones,
Just one brief day, and then they're seen no more.

Given the highly restrictive rhyme scheme and the difficulty of the assignment, student quatrains should be judged leniently, or perhaps just shared.

RUMI

Poems

SUMMARY

These five poems all focus on spiritual matters and are intended to offer inspiration. "Remembered Music" and "The Truth Within Us" both emphasize the intuitive basis of mysticism by suggesting that a certain amount of human knowledge is inborn. "The Evil in Ourselves" is a fable demonstrating that the evil we see in others is often a reflection of our own tendencies. "The Soul of Goodness in Things Evil" argues that every false or evil act contains a degree of truth or virtue. "The Progress of Man" traces human development from plant to animal to human being to heavenly being.

GUIDELINES FOR DISCUSSION QUESTIONS

1. "The Evil in Ourselves" is half fable and half explanation of the meaning. Do you think the fable would be better without the explanation, or does the explanation provide a satisfying conclusion?

The "moral tag" at the end of a poem, once a common occurrence, has, of course, fallen out of favor in the twentieth century. Nevertheless, the resurgent interest in such things as proverbs and wisdom literature may indicate a renewed interest in direct moral statements. Students are likely to express various opinions on the explanatory portion of this fable, some appreciating the clarity while others are annoyed by the preaching.

2. What is the "remembered music" in the poem by that title?

Because Rumi sees the presence of God in all things, he believes that there is a universal spirit, which is symbolized in this poem by music. All individuals possess this spirit, which lies deep in human memory, waiting to be activated. Thus, the universal spirit can be "remembered" through meditation and love for God.

3. In "The Truth Within Us" what does the Sufi mean when he says, "The signs [of God] I behold within; / Without is naught but symbols of the Signs."?

In "The Truth Within Us" Rumi expresses the view that God is within us and can be reached directly through contemplation. The orchard and other parts of creation are only indirect manifestations of God. Meditation, then, is a better way to achieve unity with God than by observing the beauties of nature.

4. **What idea is being presented in "The Soul of Goodness in Things Evil"? What three kinds of metaphors are used in the examples? It has been said that mystics like Rumi helped promote a spirit of tolerance. How might this poem be viewed as a plea for tolerance?**

In this poem Rumi points out that bad deeds are often inspired by a desire for goodness. The three images used in the poem relate to money, food, and religious quests. By asserting that false and evil deeds contain a grain of truth and virtue, Rumi is discouraging absolute judgments against any human act and encouraging caution and tolerance.

5. **Trace the various stages of development of the human soul as they are outlined in "The Progress of Man." How did Rumi seem to view death?**

The stages of development are plant, animal, human being, and heavenly being, each stage representing a definite elevation. Since this world is only a "sleeper's dream" and a "vain illusion," death is a welcome escape to an "everlasting home."

GUIDELINES FOR ASSESSING STUDENT WRITING

1. **Throughout history humans have been variously viewed as basically good, basically evil, or simply blank pages for experience to write upon. How do you think Rumi viewed human nature? Give evidence from the poems in this section.**

Students can make a strong case for Rumi's viewing human nature as essentially good. The poems "Remembered Music" and "The Truth Within Us" both attest to the innate wisdom and godliness inside each individual. Even "The Soul of Goodness in Things Evil," though it describes evil deeds, seems to argue for the basic goodness of people hidden away somewhere. If students focus strongly on "The Evil in Ourselves," they may decide to make a case for human nature being viewed as essentially bad. However, this fable can also be read as a caution against rash judgments and an exhortation to try to see the good in others. The important thing is not the viewpoint adopted by students but their skill in expressing and supporting these views with evidence from the poems.

2. **In "The Soul of Goodness in Things Evil" Rumi acknowledges that good and evil often seem to be inseparable. Using the same title, write a personal experience narrative in which you demonstrate how a bad experience also brought about something good.**

These narratives, since they are personal and highly individualized, will follow no predictable pattern. Students should demonstrate something beneficial emerging from an unpleasant experience— perhaps a discovery of unknown powers of endurance or a new appreciation of the support of friends and family.

HAFIZ

The Divan

SUMMARY

The three odes of Hafiz shown here all display the merging of pain and pleasure that generally characterize his poetry. Odes 1 and 5 are love poems, while Ode 8 presents individual stanzas that are variations on the theme of sorrow and the mitigating circumstances that make it bearable.

GUIDELINES FOR DISCUSSION QUESTIONS

1. **Do you think Ode 1 is strictly a love poem, or does it seem to be a symbolic poem describing a religious experience? Defend your answer.**

   Either one of these responses could be defended. The references to "prayer" and "God's image" could be taken literally or simply as an indication of how much the poet worships the beloved. The lines that complain about the unseen beloved ("Unto mine eyes a stranger, thou that art / A comrade ever-present to my heart") could be a reference to the invisible God or to a human lover who is far away. Students will probably find other lines that lend themselves to two interpretations.

2. **Hafiz's love poems often contain examples of hyperbole (figures of speech involving great exaggeration). In Ode 5 find several examples of hyperbole.**

   In the first stanza the poet claims that he will remain on his beloved's threshold until "dust shall cover me," clearly an instance of hyperbole. In the second stanza he writes that his "breath is narrowed down to one long sigh." In the third stanza Hafiz insists that his love will endure beyond death, burning so hot that "the smoke rises from my winding-sheet." In the last stanza he describes his heart as covered with "countless wounds from which the red drops start."

3. **Ode 8 is a series of variations on a theme. Each stanza presents a different situation, but the underlying idea is the same. What is the idea that connects these five stanzas?**

The connecting idea in Ode 8 is that sorrow abounds in the world but that there are compensations. Each stanza addresses a different kind of sorrow, from the pain of separation from loved ones and ignorance of life's meaning to the pain of death.

4. Hafiz brings his own name into the final stanza of all three of these odes. What impression do you get of his general situation in life from these personal remarks?

In the final stanza of Ode 8 Hafiz speaks of being "persecuted" by his enemies, of being "chained in poverty," and of having lost his beloved, who has "turned and fled from out my door." Clearly the circumstances of his life were not particularly happy. In Odes 1 and 5 he dreams of receiving some acknowledgment, " a robe of honor and a harnessed steed" in the first case and "praise" to accompany his name in the second.

GUIDELINES FOR ASSESSING STUDENT WRITING

1. For one day keep a journal noting examples of hyperbole that occur in everyday conversation. (Example: "When I saw the chemistry test, I almost died.")

The result of keeping these journals will probably be a list of dozens of hyperbolic expressions, making students aware that American slang is filled with such figures of speech.

2. Imagine that you are the beloved of Hafiz in Ode 5. Respond to Hafiz's proclamation of love with a letter explaining your reaction to his images and to his description of his feelings. Are you flattered or annoyed by the ridiculous exaggerations? Feel free to be as humorous or serious as you wish in this letter.

Some students may decide to respond sympathetically to the obvious hyperbole in this ode, while others may want to satirize Hafiz' extravagant style of expression. Whatever the tone of these letters, students should make specific references to the poem and its language when they respond.

TAWFIQ al-HAKIM

The River of Madness

SUMMARY

This play is set in a royal court in an indeterminate time and place. As the play opens, the king is speaking with his vizir, who informs him that everyone in the kingdom had been drinking from a local river that causes madness. The only rational people left are the vizir and the king. They discuss possible solutions but, with the physicians and other experts reduced to a state of madness, the situation seems hopeless. Furthermore, the people of the kingdom all see the king and the vizir as the mad ones and regard themselves as sane. They are beginning to murmur and conspire against a king whom they judge to be insane. In the final scene the king and the vizir, realizing that they are just "two grains of sand" trying to contend with an ocean, decide to drink the river water.

GUIDELINES FOR DISCUSSION QUESTIONS

1. In this play the king makes a monumental decision that can never be reversed. Do you think he was justified in drinking the river water? Do you think you would have done the same thing?

Some students will no doubt feel that reason is useless if no one will listen to it and that the king and the vizir might as well capitulate to popular demand and drink the water. Others might maintain that the king and the vizir should preserve their integrity and keep fighting for the sanity of the kingdom, even though success seems extremely unlikely.

2. When the king and queen talk, they misunderstand each other completely. What is the cause of the misunderstanding?

Both the king and the queen speak of their great suffering on account of the disease (meaning the other person's disease), and both of them interpret these words to mean that the other person is aware of his or her own affliction.

3. The subtitle calls *The River of Madness* a "symbolic play." Explain the symbolism. (What ideas are represented by the king, the river, and the queen?)

The play is a warning against conformity, suggesting that the prevailing majority view may in some cases be a crazy view. The king represents the voice of reason and sanity; the river represents the majority view (once reasonable but now turned crazy); the queen is the voice of conformity.

4. **An old proverb states: "Everyone is crazy except me and you, and sometimes I wonder about you." To what extent does *The River of Madness* reflect this view?**

The River of Madness supports this view, which implies that madness is a tricky thing to define and often ends up being simply another name for the minority view. Although the king and the vizir are the only remaining sane people, each of them is worried that the other will "go over the edge" and join the other mad people in the kingdom.

GUIDELINES FOR ASSESSING STUDENT WRITING

The king and the vizir in this play both conclude that they will be in danger if they do not join the other people in their madness. Try to recall a period of history when exercising reason might put an individual in danger. Then imagine that you are planning to write a play about this time period based on *The River of Madness*. Write a letter to a publishing company summarizing your play and explaining its theme. Your purpose is to get the company interested in publishing the play.

Students will need to choose a time of mass hysteria, such as the Salem witch trials in colonial America, the Holocaust in Europe, the McCarthy era in the United States, or the Soviet purges in Russia. During these times the prevailing, or "official," view bordered on craziness while the voice of moderation was regarded with deep suspicion and often stigmatized as treasonous. Students should describe the character(s) representing the voice of reason, the nature of the prevailing "craziness," and the outcome. Students having trouble with the assignment might need to do some research on the time period before they begin.

THE MAHABHARATA

Savitri's Love

SUMMARY

Savitri, the beautiful and wise daughter of a king and queen, is sent on a journey by her parents to find a young man to marry. A year later she returns with the news that she wishes to marry Prince Satyavan, who lives a humble life in a jungle cottage since his blind father was deposed from his throne. The king consults with his counselor, who strongly advises against the marriage on the ground that Satyavan will die in a year. Savitri, however, insists that she can love no other, and the wedding takes place. Savitri and Satyavan then live together happily in the cottage with Satyavan's parents.

When a year has passed, Satyavan sets off into the jungle to cut wood, and Savitri, knowing that this is the day of his death, insists on coming. Late in the day, Satyavan falls to the ground with a pain in his head and dies. When Yama, the god of death comes to take away his spirit, Savitri follows him through the jungle, saying that she must go where her husband goes. Impressed with her courage and loyalty, Yama grants her any wish except the soul of her husband, and she asks to have her father-in-law's sight restored. They continue their dialogue, and Yama is so impressed with her wisdom that he grants her another wish. She then asks that her father-in-law's kingdom be restored. As they continue talking, he is impressed with her compassion and grants still another wish. At this point she asks to be allowed to bear Satyavan's children, and Yama at last restores the prince to life. Returning home, Savitri and Satyavan find that the old king has regained his sight and that the tyrant who captured his throne has been overthrown.

GUIDELINES FOR DISCUSSION QUESTIONS

1. Savitri is presented as the ideal of Indian womanhood. What special qualities make her a flawless wife? Do you think Savitri would be considered an ideal wife in our society today?

Savitri's most impressive quality, of course, is her devotion. Knowing that Satyavan has lost his kingdom, must work hard to support a blind father, and will die in a year, she still does not hesitate to bind herself to him. Other admirable qualities include her willingness to do manual labor in spite of her royal upbringing and her compassion for the old king, who is the beneficiary of her first two wishes. A few students may find her service to her father-in-law and her desire to be "the mother of noble children" a bit quaint, but Savitri is definitely not a subservient woman. She trusts her own judgment and is capable of persuading others, as when she insists on an unpromising marriage and later insists on accompanying Satyavan into the woods. Her courage in confronting Yama and her ability to persuade him to restore her husband's life are certainly not the qualities of a subservient woman. With a very few exceptions, Savitri's attributes are likely to be admired in the modern world just as they were in the ancient one.

2. Although Savitri is beautiful, no men come to seek her hand in marriage. How do you explain this?

It seems that Savitri's seriousness and wisdom tend to intimidate young men, and so they do not come courting.

3. What characteristics does Prince Satyavan have that attract Savitri? Would you say that this is a case of opposites attracting or similarities attracting?

Interestingly, the qualities of Satyavan that Savitri mentions as particularly attractive to her are mainly qualities of light-heartedness and playfulness. When she defends her choice of a husband, she says that he is "full of laughter" and that he is skillful at riding horses and painting pictures of them. Satyavan does, of course, have more serious qualities as well, but the fact that Savitri mentions these particular attributes suggests that this is a case of opposites attracting each other.

4. How would you describe Yama, the god of death who appears in this story? Does he behave the way you would expect a god of death to behave?

Yama is a rather surprising figure for a god of death in that he is flexible, reasonable, and definitely ready to negotiate. Most traditional figures of death are depicted as silent, grim, and relentless in carrying out their task.

GUIDELINES FOR ASSESSING STUDENT WRITING

Savitri is clearly an idealized portrait of a wife. Choose another role—such as friend, teacher, parent, or coach—and present a portrait of a character who plays this role perfectly. The character may be either fictional or actual.

Students may wish to describe an individual of their acquaintance who serves as a sound role model, or they may wish to create a fictional personality. In either case, the description should have plenty of supporting details to round out the portrait, and the student's concept of the ideal friend, teacher, parent, or coach should emerge from the finished portrait.

BHATTA SOMADEVA

The Confidence Men

SUMMARY

"The Confidence Men" is a folk tale about two con-artists, Madhava and Siva, who decide to fleece a greedy Brahman priest named Sankara. Hearing that Sankara has a beautiful daughter and immense wealth, the two tricksters set out for his city. Siva takes up residence in a deserted temple, where he soon gains a reputation as a holy man. Madhava decks himself out as a nobleman and sends gifts to Sankara, along with a message saying that he would like help in making the acquaintance of the king. Sankara, impressed with the gifts, invites Madhava to stay with him. Madhava then requests permission to keep his jewels in Sankara's safe, spreading them out on the table to dazzle his host. Not knowing that they are fakes, Sankara enthusiastically agrees.

A short time later Madhava pretends to be deathly ill and asks Sankara to find him a holy man who is worthy to inherit the jewels. One of Madhava's attendants, acting on instructions, suggests Siva. The greedy Sankara visits Siva and tries to convince him to accept the jewels and rejoin society, thinking that he will be able to dupe this gullible holy man into sharing his profits. Siva says that he might be persuaded to rejoin society if he could find a good woman to marry. At that point Sankara offers his daughter, and the wedding takes place, with Siva receiving a large dowry of gold and silver. A short time later Siva asks for half of the jewels, but "reluctantly" agrees to accept a large amount of gold instead. Madhava, of course, "miraculously" recovers and shares in the profits.

Sankara eventually discovers that the jewels are worthless and takes the two con-artists to court. The judge, however, convinced by the smooth talk of the con-artists that Sankara was the one who initiated the deal and that neither Siva nor Madhava knew that the jewels were counterfeit, exonerates them.

GUIDELINES FOR DISCUSSION QUESTIONS

1. **With whom did your sympathies lie as you read this tale—the confidence men or their victim? Explain why.**

Responses may vary, but most readers of rogue tales such as this tend to side with the trickster. If this turns out to be the case, ask students why they place their sympathies on the side of wrongdoing. Perhaps readers simply enjoy seeing a clever and complex plan carried out successfully. Students may have other explanations to offer.

2. One of the clever strategies underlying the hoax of Siva and Madhava is to make Sankara believe that he is the trickster rather than the one being tricked. How do the confidence men convey this impression?

Madhava and Siva never seem at all eager in their negotiations with Sankara. In fact, they often display reluctance, giving their victim the impression that everything that transpires is actually his idea. However, they constantly manipulate the situation so that Sankara's next move will be obvious. For example, when Siva is offered the jewels, he turns them down, knowing that Sankara will then try to persuade him. When Sankara tries to persuade him to accept them and live in society, he reluctantly says that he will first need to find a wife, knowing that Sankara has a beautiful daughter. When Sankara offers his daughter, Siva reluctantly agrees, knowing that he will receive a rich dowry, and so on. Sankara thinks that he is calling the shots, but it is the seemingly reluctant Siva who is in control.

3. How does the author prevent the reader from identifying too strongly with Sankara, the victim of the hoax? Why is it important to control the reader's response in this way?

The author prevents the reader from feeling much compassion for Sankara by depicting him as a greedy and dishonest man. Repulsive physical descriptions, such as "Sankara Swami's eyes bulged like two huge balls," also contribute to his negative image. It is important for Somadeva to keep readers alienated from Sankara if they are to enjoy the hoax.

GUIDELINES FOR ASSESSING STUDENT WRITING

Imagine that your school wants to produce "The Confidence Men" as a play. The director has divided the action of the story into the five acts shown below and has invited you to write one of them. Select the act that interests you the most and begin by describing the setting. Then write a script for the dialogue that will take place. (If the act contains more than one scene, you will need to describe each new setting.)

Act I: Siva and Madhava review their situation and agree to try their luck with Sankara in the city of Ujjayini.

Act II: Siva establishes his reputation as a holy man.

Act III: Madhava worms himself into the good graces of Sankara.

Act IV: Sankara, believing that Madhava is about to die, strikes a deal with Siva.

Act V: Sankara discovers that the jewels are worthless and brings the two con-artists to court.

This is an ideal assignment for collaborative group work. The class could be divided into five groups, each of which is responsible for writing and producing one act. If time permits, the individual groups could also be responsible for creating stage settings and costumes for their particular act. The play could be presented either as a live-action drama or on video. Students should demonstrate that they understand the setting of each scene, as well as the nature and motivations of the characters.

RABINDRANATH TAGORE

My Lord, the Baby

SUMMARY

"My Lord, the Baby" is the story of an old servant named Raicharan, who has served a family of well-to-do judges for many years. Having raised a boy named Anukul to manhood, he is tending his master's toddler-aged son when the story opens. The little boy disappears while Raicharan is wading through the mud to pick a flower for him, and it seems likely that he has drowned in the rapidly moving river nearby. Stricken with grief and guilt, Raicharan leaves the household and returns to his village the next day.

A year later Raicharan's wife gives birth to a son and dies. Raicharan observes some of the same antics in his son as he did in the little master he tended, and he concludes that this child, whose name is Phailna, must be a reincarnation. He devotes himself to the child, buying him fine possessions and a good education, while he himself nearly starves in the process. When he runs out of money, he decides to pay a visit on Anukul and his wife, who have never succeeded in having another child. He tells them what he has come to believe—that Phailna is actually their son, whom he stole many years back. Not understanding how Raicharan thinks and taking his words literally, Anukul banishes him from the household. Phailna, exhibiting the same cool judicious approach as Anukul, suggests that Raicharan be given a monthly allowance, since he is now too old to work. When the money is sent to Raicharan's village at month's end, however, he is nowhere to be found.

GUIDELINES FOR DISCUSSION QUESTIONS

1. **How do you feel about Anukul's decision to send Raicharan away? Was it foolish, harsh, or justified under the circumstances?**

   If Anukul actually believed that Raicharan kidnapped his son, then sending him away from the house is not a particularly harsh punishment. If he did not believe it, then it is very harsh, since it means depriving an old loyal servant of his livelihood. Students may wish to debate the issue of what Anukul actually believed. Whatever the case, they should come to realize that Anukul's and Raicharan's ways of thinking are so different that they cannot communicate at this crucial time. Clearly Anukul's abilities as a judge fail him when they matter the most.

2. **Why does Raicharan think that his son Phailna is the reincarnated little master?**

Because Phailna was born shortly after the little master's death and because he had certain traits possessed by the little master (such as walking with a toddle and saying "Ba-ba and Ma-ma"), and also because Raicharan believes his wife did not "merit" a child, he concludes that the baby is actually Anukul's dead son. Raicharan's traditional religious beliefs about the transmigration of souls, in combination with his failure to notice that virtually all babies toddle and say "Ba-ba and Ma-ma," lead him to this erroneous conclusion.

3. **If Raicharan really believes that his son is the "little master," why does he wait twelve years before giving him back to Anukul?**

Raicharan has sold his land and has deprived himself of food for years on his son's account, but after twelve years he finds himself completely out of money and about to lose his job. His son, who seems to be quite a demanding child, keeps complaining about his clothes and wanting more money. It would seem that Raicharan finally decides to take him to Anukul in order to secure a good future for him. Raicharan does not, however, expect to be cut out of the picture.

4. **In what ways does the young Phailna already show signs of developing into a judge? How does Raicharan feel about these budding judicial tendencies?**

Phailna's magisterial tendencies can be seen at their strongest in the final scene. Upon learning that Anukul is supposedly his "father," the boy's first thought is that he has been "cheated all this time of his birthright." When he finds out that Raicharan is being sent away, he does not respond with any emotional attachment to the man who has sacrificed so much for him, but coolly suggests that the old father figure should receive "a small monthly pension." His judicial thinking is clearly a shock to the old man, who "did not utter another word" after hearing his son's pronouncements.

5. **Tagore creates two sets of characters representing extreme positions. Raicharan typifies the traditional Hindu orientation, while Anukul typifies the cool professional rationality of the Western world. How does Tagore seem to feel about each of these orientations? Give evidence for your answer.**

This is a difficult question, and students may need some help in coming to terms with the author's position. Tagore is actually demonstrating the inadequacy of both these modes of thinking—the traditional Hindu and the secular rationalist. Raicharan's views about reincarnation lead him to faulty conclusions about the identity of his own son. His self-denial causes him to deprive himself while indulging his son, thus giving Phailna the mistaken impression that Raicharan is his servant rather than his father.

Anukul's reasonable views, however, also contain pitfalls. He is incapable of understanding Raicharan's claim that the situation was an act of God and sees this claim in silly legalistic terms (putting the "blame on God's shoulders"). Although he has known Raicharan all his life, he has no understanding of the old man, nor does he seem to recall the servant's desperate grief and guilt when the child disappeared. More importantly, he appears unable to ask the probing questions that would bring the truth to light. At a time when judicial skills would seem of paramount importance, he either cannot or will not exercise them. The extreme positions represented by both men, then, are shown as untenable. Tagore is perhaps demonstrating his enduring belief that a blend of Eastern and Western thinking is necessary.

GUIDELINES FOR ASSESSING STUDENT WRITING

The ending of this story involves an extreme case of misunderstanding, even though Anukul is a judge who is supposed to be able to unravel the truth. Imagine that Raicharan has been brought to court for kidnapping Anukul's son. You have been appointed to be his defense attorney. Write a script showing what questions you would ask Raicharan in front of the court and how he would likely respond. Finish your script with a short closing speech that will convince the court that your client is an honorable and innocent man.

The questions should give Raicharan the opportunity to explain that the child was "stolen" only in the sense that his soul was reincarnated in Raicharan's son. This belief is what leads the old servant to say, "It was not I who did it. It was God." The defense should also draw heavily on Raicharan's exemplary behavior throughout his life in terms of his dedication to Anukul, the little master, and Phailna. The circumstances surrounding the disappearance of the little master might also be mentioned—the fact that Raicharan was seen desperately searching for the baby and the fact that he was clearly grief-stricken when the child did not turn up. Witnesses might attest to the fact that Raicharan's wife did indeed bear a son and that the boy is about a year younger than the little master. There are probably other angles that students could explore as well.

DHUMKETU

The Letter

SUMMARY

The main character of this story, called simply "Old Ali," is a lonely man who visits the post office early each morning in expectation of receiving a letter from his daughter Miriam. His daughter has not written since she got married and left town five years ago, but Ali lives on the hope that she will. His frequent visits have made him a familiar and comical figure at the post office, where he is often teased for his pointless persistence. One day he comes to the post office looking ill and asks to have all future letters delivered to his grave. Then he disappears.

A few months later the postmaster, who had been particularly annoyed by Ali's daily presence, experiences a crisis with his own daughter, who lies ill in a distant town. He eagerly awaits a letter giving news of her condition, but no letter arrives. Just then he spots a letter for Ali. By this time the postmaster's harsh views have been softened by his own pain, and he decides that he will personally hand the letter to Ali. When he hears a knock on the post office door, he invites Ali in and offers him the letter. Noticing an "unearthly" light in his visitor's eyes, however, the postmaster shrinks back, and the visitor disappears. Learning from his assistant that Ali has been dead for three months, the confused postmaster sits down to await news of his daughter.

GUIDELINES FOR DISCUSSION QUESTIONS

1. Do you think the postmaster really saw Old Ali's ghost? If not, what did he see?

This question is somewhat open to interpretation. Either the postmaster actually saw Ali's ghost or else his thoughts were so focused on Ali that his mind conjured up a vision. No matter which interpretation prevails, the general impact is the same. The postmaster has learned about human pain from his own recent experiences and is now eager to compensate for his past unkindness to Ali.

2. How does the first sentence of the story serve as a foreshadowing of Ali's situation?

In the first sentence of the story the author describes the stars in the dawn sky as if they were hanging on to their glow as long as possible, just as humans hold on to happy memories as their lives draw to a close. This description anticipates the situation of Old Ali, who is trying desperately to hold on to his relationship with Miriam, the only light left in his life.

3. **What is the author's purpose in describing Ali's past fascination with hunting? How does this segment relate to the theme of the story?**

The hunting segment is brought into the story to demonstrate how human awareness can change after one has experienced misfortune. Ali used to enjoy hunting, but his separation from Miriam opened his heart to the pain he was causing animals when he left them "bereft of their parents." The general insensitivity of people to anything they have not personally experienced is a major theme of the story, which is dramatized more fully in the postmaster's change of attitude after his daughter's illness. The hunting segment, then, serves as a preparation or foreshadowing of the main events.

GUIDELINES FOR ASSESSING STUDENT WRITING

Imagine that you are one of the postal workers who see Old Ali every morning. You are disturbed by the situation and have decided to try to persuade Miriam to write to Ali. Compose a letter in which you politely explain the old man's behavior and try to convince her to write to her father.

Students should describe Ali's daily visits to the post office and his longing to receive a letter from his daughter. They might also mention his declining health. The letter should make a diplomatic and persuasive appeal to Miriam to ease the old man's worry and loneliness by writing to him.

ACHINTYA KUMAR SEN GUPTA

The Bamboo Trick

SUMMARY

Narrated by one of the spectators at a small shabby fair, this is the story of an elderly Indian, starving and desperate, who attempts to make a living by twirling his sons on the end of a bamboo pole. As the story opens, the narrator has encountered the old man, whose name is Mantaj, with his crying and terrified younger son. The boy does not wish to perform the trick, and his father is trying to coerce him to climb the bamboo pole. At that moment the boy's older brother appears and volunteers to do the performance. His stomach and face are covered with terrible cuts and sores, which are the result of an accident during his last performance.

The narrator is upset by the boy's wounds and the starved appearance of the family, but he stays to watch the trick. As the boy is being twirled, Mantaj slips, and the boy plunges to the ground. At first he appears to be dead, but eventually a heartbeat is detected, and he is taken to a charity hospital. Knowing that he will have to perform next, the younger boy begins crying again, protesting that he will fall and die. Having received no money for the performance, Mantaj looks grim and silent. He does not respond to the child's cries, but takes him by the hand and walks on.

GUIDELINES FOR DISCUSSION QUESTIONS

1. **Imagine that Mantaj has been accused of child abuse for his treatment of his two young sons. You have been asked to testify in court. Would you defend him or speak against him? Explain your reasoning.**

   Certainly Mantaj's exploitation and endangerment of his sons qualifies as child abuse, but students may wish to weigh the father's behavior against the dire circumstances that drive him to such desperate measures. Some students may see the father's behavior as justified by these circumstances. Other students may see Mantaj's behavior as unjustifiable under any circumstances.

2. How does the opening description of the fair prepare the reader for the story of Mantaj and his sons? How would you describe the mood of this story?

The fair is obviously a very squalid one that is attended by poverty-stricken people. The uncompassionate stance of the fairgoers and their refusal to give the starving Mantaj any money for his flawed performance might be disturbing to the reader, but the destitute atmosphere of the place makes their attitude somewhat understandable. The mood of the story is clearly one of strong pathos. (Students will use their own descriptive words.)

3. The narrator of this story is also one of the spectators at the Gajan fair. What function does he serve in the story? How are his reactions different from those of the other spectators watching the bamboo trick?

The narrator of "The Bamboo Trick" functions as a newcomer to the fair, someone who must have everything explained to him. This device allows the author to inform the reader of the various happenings by having the other spectators inform the narrator. He differs from the other spectators in that he is sympathetic toward the starving man and his terrified child, while the others simply want to be entertained. It is the concerned narrator who communicates the terrible pathos of the situation.

GUIDELINES FOR ASSESSING STUDENT WRITING

The officials at the Gajan fair have asked you to create an advertising brochure for the event. They plan to pass out these brochures in the town of Gajan. Your task is to describe the attractions of the fair, including Mantaj and his bamboo trick, in a way that will draw crowds.

It will not be easy to make this pathetic fair sound inviting, but students should make the attempt by describing the food (papadams, popcorn, and mangoes), the clay toys, and the baskets for sale. The bamboo trick should be presented as an exciting climax to the event, and students should include a description of the high-speed twirling of the bamboo pole with the death-defying child balanced at the end.

MULK RAJ ANAND

The Gold Watch

SUMMARY

In this story Sharma, a minor Indian employee of a British company in colonial India, is surprised when the owner of the company, Mr. Acton, stops by his work station to announce that he will be receiving a gift the following Monday. As Sharma thinks about the news, his surprise gradually turns to dread. Mr. Acton is not a cordial man, and Sharma knows that something is afoot. His curiosity is so intense that he breaks with protocol by running after Mr. Acton as he leaves the building after work in order to ask what the gift might be. He learns that it is a gold watch from London.

Sharma broods all weekend, knowing that a gold watch usually means retirement. He is not scheduled to retire for another five years, and he is riddled with worry about the future. When he returns to work on Monday, he finds that his fears are confirmed. Mr. Acton presents him with an inscribed watch, telling him that the company is "increasing the efficiency of the business" and that he is sure Sharma would "like to retire." Distressed and unable to voice a protest, Sharma accidentally drops the watch. Mr. Acton picks it up and ushers him out the door. On his way home Sharma discovers that the watch has been broken, but he reminds himself that in the future he will not "need to look at the time very much."

GUIDELINES FOR DISCUSSION QUESTIONS

1. Do you approve of Mr. Acton's method of telling Sharma about his forced retirement? If you were in charge, how would you have communicated this news to Sharma?

No doubt most students will disapprove of Mr. Acton's tactics in dismissing Sharma. He leaves his employee to stew in uncertainty for several days and then mentally bullies him by claiming that he knows Sharma would "like to retire." He also adds insult to injury by reminding Sharma that the company could have found someone with "better qualifications." Students are likely to offer a variety of alternative methods. (Remember that retaining Sharma is not an alternative. Students have been given the task of forcing him into retirement.) Some possible ways of taking the personal sting out of the retirement decision include (a) giving him several weeks' advance notice (b) making a ceremony of the watch presentation, with an opportunity for other employees to express their appreciation or give parting gifts, and (c) expressing regret at the decision rather than making it sound like a blessing.

2. What do the scenes involving Sharma's wife and son show about the kind of man he is?

The scenes that take place at Sharma's home demonstrate that he is indeed a man with "nobility of soul and fundamental innocence," as he is described at the beginning of the story. He tries to spare his family the pain that he is enduring by keeping up a cheerful front. When his son asks for his silver watch, he generously gives it to him, even before he has the gold watch in hand. His wife notices that he is not "in his usual mood of accepting life evenly," an observation implying that Sharma is generally very easy to live with.

3. What seems to be the author's attitude toward the British presence in India? Give evidence to support your answer.

The author does not present a positive view of the British colonists and their "anonymous, smooth-working Empire." They are cold and condescending toward the Indians who work for them, and their feelings are always hidden behind a façade. In fact, Sharma's first clue that something alarming is about to happen is the fact that Mr. Acton smiles. The employees have learned over the years that "the detached faces of the white Sahibs" do not display their genuine feelings. A smile, then, is probably a way of covering up something unpleasant rather than an expression of pleasure. The impersonal and officious manner in which Sharma is dismissed, of course, is emblematic of the formal and rather heartless ways of the British colonists.

4. What does Sharma plan to do after his retirement? How do you know?

The last sentence of the story indicates that Sharma has no choice but to return to his father in the town of Jullundhur in the Punjab, apparently a rather backward place where people do not use watches or make appointments.

GUIDELINES FOR ASSESSING STUDENT WRITING

Pretend that you are an employee at Henry King & Company. You have decided to circulate a petition asking Mr. Acton to give Sharma back his job. Begin with the words, "We, the undersigned, do respectfully request that Mr. Sharma's position at Henry King & Company be restored." Then present your reasons in a paragraph or two.

If you are artistically inclined, you might prefer to draw a cartoon showing Mr. Acton's dismissal of Sharma, which you will pin on the company bulletin board. This cartoon should communicate the employees' feeling that the dismissal was unjust.

The petition might point out Sharma's unfailing loyalty, his long-term service, and perhaps the fact that proven performance is more important than academic matriculation.

Students who decide to attempt the cartoon should show the imperial manner of Mr. Acton in contrast to the abject Indian clerk. They might translate this contrast into physical terms by showing Mr. Acton puffed up to twice his normal size by his sense of his own benevolence and by showing Sharma as a small, cringing figure. The caption should demonstrate Mr. Acton's condescension in some way.

HAN-SHAN

Cold Mountain Poems

SUMMARY

The Cold Mountain poems express the poet's sense of oneness with nature in the remote area where he has chosen to live. Other human sentiments are also expressed, such as his sadness at separation from friends and family, his melancholy thoughts upon encountering ruins, and his longing for spring.

GUIDELINES FOR DISCUSSION QUESTIONS

1. **Lu Ch'iu-yin, the man who collected the Cold Mountain poems, speculates that the poet was ecstatically happy with his hermit-like existence. Judging from the poems, would you say that Han-shan was completely content on Cold Mountain, or did he seem to have moments of regret?**

   Responses will vary somewhat. Although Han-shan seems to be generally content with his chosen way of life, he clearly has moments of despondency. Poem 9 expresses his loneliness and longing for spring, Poem 53 expresses his regret at being separated from friends, and Poem 218 voices a complaint that others don't understand or respect his way of life. Some students may conclude that he seems generally satisfied in spite of these occasional drawbacks, while others may decide that he is not particularly content.

2. **In Poem 3, why is the road to Cold Mountain described as "funny"?**

   The road is funny (or laughable) in the sense that it hardly qualifies as a road. Anyone taking the "road" must constantly try to determine where it actually is. The trail is finally so indecipherable that "form asks shadow where to."

3. **In Poem 131 what is the meaning of the last line: "to lie in the stream and wash out my ears"?**

   The poet has been describing false starts and misguided efforts that he is now leaving behind him. The expression "wash out my ears" probably means to clear away all the old thoughts and to unclutter the mind so that he can start fresh on Cold Mountain.

4. Poem 205 expresses some of the satisfactions of living on Cold Mountain. Explain what Han-shan means when he says, "I can roam the whole galaxy from here."

Han-shan is speaking of letting his thoughts roam free and yielding to the natural flow of things so that he can achieve union with the forces of the universe.

GUIDELINES FOR ASSESSING STUDENT WRITING

Imagine that you are publishing a new edition of Han-shan's poems and have decided to write a preface for the book. Your first sentence will be the following: "Nothing is known about Han-shan, but from his poems we can infer a few things about the place he lived, why he lived there, and how other people in the area regarded him." Finish the preface, writing one paragraph for each of these three points.

It is fairly clear from the poems that Han-shan lived in a very remote mountainous area with plenty of clear streams and quite a cold climate. (He mentions snow and ice.) He has chosen this area because it provides the solitude, peace, and sense of space that helps him to feel at one with the universe. As for the other people who occasionally see him, Poem 218 indicates that they are wary of him and may even think he is crazy. Students will need to develop these three paragraphs with details drawn from the poems.

LI PO

Poems

SUMMARY

These tender, reflective poems treat the subjects of love, music, and friendship. "A Bitter Love" and "A Sigh from a Staircase of Jade" hint at disappointed love, while "A Song of Ch'ang-kan" is an understated tale of fulfilled love addressed to an absent husband from his young wife. "On Hearing Chün the Buddhist Monk from Shu Play His Lute" is a sensuous description of the associations conjured up by hearing lovely music. "Parting at a Wine-Shop in Nan-King" dramatizes the pain of parting from friends as well as the pleasure of old friendships.

GUIDELINES FOR DISCUSSION QUESTIONS

1. "A Bitter Love" and "A Sigh from a Staircase of Jade" both center on a forsaken woman. How is her pain revealed in each poem? Which of the two treatments do you prefer?

In "A Bitter Love" the woman's pain is demonstrated mostly through a description of her facial expressions (her "troubled brow," her tears), and the cause of her trouble is stated directly in the last line. "A Sigh from a Staircase of Jade" is much more indirect in its approach, as the woman's expressions and feelings are not mentioned. Instead the poet relies on background objects to suggest the futility of her wait and her state of mind (wet shoes, staircase cold with dew, autumn moon). Student preferences, of course, will vary.

2. In the poem "On Hearing Chün the Buddhist Monk from Shu Play His Lute" what happens to the speaker of the poem when he hears the music of the lute?

The music of the lute conjures up natural images such as the sound of pines and brooks. The lute music and the music of nature become inextricably mixed in the listener's mind, creating a feeling of harmony with the universe.

3. In "A Song of Ch'ang-kan" the speaker never directly expresses her love for her husband. How is it revealed in the poem?

The young wife's love is revealed by her sharp memories of her husband and their developing relationship, by her desire to wait for him "unto death," by her offer to meet him no matter how far the distance, and by her belief that their love will endure after death ("no dust could ever seal our love").

4. **How does Li Po suggest the passage of time in "A Song of Ch'ang-kan"?**

The passage of time in this poem is so relentless that it permeates almost every line. The speaker keeps up a running chronology of her age as the relationship develops, starting in early childhood and, by suggestion, moving beyond death. In addition, she indicates the passage of time since her husband left by tracking the natural and seasonal changes that are taking place around her—the spreading moss, falling leaves, and mating butterflies, for example. The unfolding of the days and years is central to the poem and produces a sense of eternity.

5. **"Parting at a Wine-Shop in Nan-king" might be described as a bittersweet poem, since the speaker feels a mixture of pleasant and unpleasant sensations. Explain the two kinds of feelings that are blended in this poem.**

The bitterness in this poem springs from the fact that the friends must part, while the sweetness springs from the knowledge that their friendship is strong and enduring.

GUIDELINES FOR ASSESSING STUDENT WRITING

Pretend that you are the husband who received the message expressed in "A Song of Ch'ang-kan." You would like your wife to know that you are on your way home. Write her a letter communicating your plans and your feelings.

Responses will vary widely, but students should construct a letter that is tender and appreciative. The letter might mention some of the couple's shared history, as well as familiar objects that constitute their home and surroundings (the watch tower, the west garden). It would also be good if the letter would acknowledge the wife's offer to come meet her husband at Chang-fêng Sha. Students should demonstrate that they understand the general nature of the relationship and should draw their specific details from the poem.

TU FU

Poems

SUMMARY

All of the poems in this section focus on personal experiences of Tu Fu that involve loss. "On Meeting Lu Kuêi-nien down the River" tells of an acquaintance whose fortunes changed abruptly when he lost his position at court. "Remembering My Brothers on a Moonlight Night," "A Night Abroad," and "On the Gate-Tower at Yo-chou" describe scattered friends and the general rootlessness of Tu Fu's life. "A Hearty Welcome" and "To My Retired Friend Wêi" present hospitality scenes that are marred by poverty and a sense that the friends may never see each other again. The losses of war are described in "Night in the Watch-Tower" and "A Song of War-Chariots." The poem entitled "A Drawing of a Horse by General Ts'ao at Secretary Wêi Fêng's House" lavishes praise on a beautiful drawing of horses but also bemoans the loss of the glorious days when the Emperor T'ai-tsung paraded these majestic horses.

GUIDELINES FOR DISCUSSION QUESTIONS

1. **What would you say is the theme or message of the poem entitled "On Meeting Li Kuêi-nien down the River"?**

The theme or message of this short poem is the uncertainty of life. The man who is the subject of the poem was once a respected court musician, but now he is reduced to sitting under a tree watching life pass him by. The falling petals reinforce the passage of time.

2. **In "Remembering My Brothers on a Moonlight Night" how do the season and time of day reinforce the poet's message? What does the speaker mean when he says, "How much brighter the moonlight is at home!"?**

The setting of the poem, a night in autumn with frost approaching, reinforces the bleak mood of the speaker and the sense that everything is dwindling and dying. The moon, of course, is not really brighter at home; this "observation" merely dramatizes the speaker's yearning to return home.

3. **In "A Night Abroad" and "On the Gate-Tower at Yo-chou" what attitude toward his travels does Tu Fu express? How is the setting**

in "A Night Abroad" appropriate to the comparison in the last two lines?

Tu Fu is thoroughly sick of his travels, tired of being alone and feeling adrift in the universe ("I can see heaven and earth endlessly floating"). The poet is sailing on the river, and he compares himself to a bird living by the water. The bird (a sand-snipe or sandpiper) must, like him, constantly flit from place to place.

4. **"A Hearty Welcome" and "To My Retired Friend Wêi" express the pleasures of hospitality, but both poems are weighed down by a tone of sadness as well. What is the cause of the sadness in each poem?**

In "A Hearty Welcome" the social gathering is marred by the poverty of the host, who can "offer . . . little." "To My Retired Friend Wêi" is a more complex poem that is tinged with sadness because the friends are keenly aware that time has gotten away from them, that they are growing old, that many of their friends are dead, and that they may never see each other again.

5. **What are the reflections of the speaker in "Night in the Watch-Tower"? The last line of the poem is not in the original Chinese version. Why do you think the translator added it? Do you prefer the poem with or without the last line?**

The speaker of the poem is reflecting on the frenetic activity of the world and how it all comes to nothing in the long run. (Even the great generals "are dust.") The last line, added by the translator, is an attempt to capture the poem's general thrust for Western readers, who are accustomed to having details synthesized and themes made more explicit. Opinions about the effectiveness and necessity of the final line will vary.

6. **Tu Fu obviously feels tremendous admiration for the artist in "A Drawing of a Horse by General Ts'ao at Secretary Wêi Fêng's House," but the drawing inspires other thoughts as well. What other reflections are expressed in the poem?**

In addition to extravagant praise for the artist, the speaker of the poem also expresses great admiration for the magnificent imperial horses, with their "high clear glance, the deep firm breath." The last eight lines of the poem express sorrow and regret that these powerful and beautiful creatures are gone, along with the glorious emperor who owned them.

7. **In "A Song of War-Chariots" how does the poet indicate that the war has been going on a long time? Why does he conclude that "to have a son is bad luck"?**

The first indication that the war has lasted a long time is the fact that the young men who were drafted into the army at fifteen now have white hair. The other indication is the poet's reference to the "new ghosts . . . wailing there now with the old" (line 34). The speaker claims that sons are "bad luck" because they will eventually be consumed by the war effort and buried, while daughters will stay nearby.

8. **Li Po once remarked that Tu Fu had grown extremely thin and joked that he "must have been suffering from poetry again." In fact, Tu Fu's poetry does express quite a bit of misery and suffering. Judging from the poems you have read, do you think Tu Fu's experiences and subjects are genuinely sad, or does he just like to wallow in pain, as Li Po humorously implies?**

Most students would probably agree that losses caused by war and separation are genuinely painful subjects, but opinion may be divided about the amount of misery caused by such subjects as a man who no longer plays music at court ("On Meeting Li Kuêi-nien down the River") and the disappearance of the emperor and his horses ("A Drawing of a Horse by General Ts'ao at Secretary Wêi Fêng's House"). Help students to see that it is not specifically the man or the horses but the general sense of uncertainty and awareness of relentless change that cause the sadness.

GUIDELINES FOR ASSESSING STUDENT WRITING

Almost all of the poems shown in this section are based on Tu Fu's personal experiences. Imagine that you are Tu Fu and that you keep a journal of your experiences so that you can write poems later. Writing one journal entry for each poem, describe the experience and the thoughts that might have occurred to you as you encountered each situation.

In each journal entry students should clearly explain the situation and present some of the reflections that occur in the poems. Previous classroom discussion, of course, will be beneficial. Below is a sample journal entry for "On Meeting Li Kuêi-nien down the River." You might wish to share it with students if they are having trouble getting started.

Today as I was walking along the river, I saw an old acquaintance of mine, Li Kuêi-nien. Several years ago he was a celebrated musician and a great favorite of the emperor, enjoying the pleasures of the court and the high regard of everyone there. Now he has fallen from favor and sits alone and friendless. I watched the petals falling from the trees around him and was reminded of how quickly things change, both in nature and in society. Our lives may seem secure, but they are filled with uncertainty.

PO CHÜ-I

Poems

SUMMARY

"Lao Tzu" is a sardonic poem about the founder of Taoism, who claimed that "those who know are silent," but also wrote a book. "The Red Cockatoo" draws a satirical analogy between the speaking bird who is shut away in a cage and learned men who are placed under restriction. The two personal poems about Golden Bells, the poet's small daughter, are restrained expressions of love and grief over her death. "Chu-ch'ēn Village" describes a remote village that embodies all that is simple and good in the world and contrasts it with Po Chü-i's complicated and frustrating life.

GUIDELINES FOR DISCUSSION QUESTIONS

1. Who are the targets of satire in "Lao-tzu" and "The Red Cockatoo"? Which attack do you consider more serious, and why?

In "Lao-tzu" Po Chü-i pokes fun at Lao-tzu for his claim that "those who speak know nothing" and that "those who know are silent" and points out that this philosopher wrote a book (and therefore, presumably, knew nothing). "The Red Cockatoo" is a sharply satirical poem that draws an analogy between a bird with a special gift of human speech and the learned and talented men of the empire. Both are shut away in cages, the bird in a literal cage and the educated men by virtue of being pressed into service for the empire. Opinions may vary about the relative seriousness of these two satires, but most students will feel that the attack on Lao-tzu is relatively mild and humorous, while the attack in "The Red Cockatoo" is more urgent and pointed.

2. In the poems "Golden Bells" and "Remembering Golden Bells" what kind of a parent does Po Chü-i seem to be? How does he try to banish the pain he feels after his daughter's death?

Po Chü-i seems to be a rather reluctant father who, in the first poem, focuses on the sacrifices of parenthood rather than on its pleasures. Under the surface, however, he is clearly being drawn toward his daughter, as evidenced by the fact that he seems to notice everything she does. When she dies, his grief is understated but obviously sincere. He tries to banish the pain by recalling the years before she was born.

3. What is the poet's attitude toward the place he describes in "Chu-ch'ēn Village"? What does the village seem to represent to him?

Po Chü-i views the village as an ideal place to live, mainly because it is remote from "Government affairs." The villagers live in a prosperous, close-knit community that they never have to leave. They are not drafted into the army or forced to travel from post to post to make a living, as are those who serve the vast government network. They are born into a family trade and have a comfortable position in their community, where they are known and accepted all of their lives.

4. How is the life of the poet different from the life of the villagers in Chu-ch'ēn Village?

The speaker in the poem, who is Po Chü-i himself (he does not tend to use *personas*), is constantly forced to scramble for government posts and to travel "without pause." He is cut off from his family and friends, and his life is fragmented into separate and irreconcilable pieces. Toiling at tedious official tasks and deprived of human companionship, he longs to live a more natural, simple life like the people in Chu-ch'ēn Village.

GUIDELINES FOR ASSESSING STUDENT WRITING

The Welcoming Committee of Chu-ch'ēn Village has appointed you to create materials for the new residents of the community. Design and write a pamphlet that will present the features of Chu-ch'ēn and the special benefits of living there. Divide your pamphlet into categories with separate headings.

There are abundant details in the poem that students can draw from as they construct their pamphlets. The village appears to be a prosperous place, with plenty of mules and oxen packing the streets and surrounded by fields of hemp and mulberry trees. The villagers frequently gather to dine on white wine and roasted fowl and live to a ripe old age. In addition to their physical and economic well-being, the villagers are fortunate enough to live in a simple community where political intrigue is absent and where their role is clear and uncontested. The fact that the village is too remote to be of interest to Government officials is also a benefit.

The description above is not a definitive compendium of benefits by any means, and students will likely find other details of life in Chu-ch'ēn Village that they wish to present. The pamphlets should be logically divided into separate sections, such as Physical Setting, Job Opportunities, Leisure Activities, Community Values.

LU HSÜN

The Widow

SUMMARY

In this sad tale the narrator, who has returned to his native village for the New Year celebration, meets a former servant woman of his uncle's household on the street. The servant, who goes by the name Sister Hsiang-lin, has been reduced to begging for a living. She recognizes the narrator and, knowing that he is educated, suddenly asks him if there is life after death. Perplexed but not wanting to throw her into despair, he answers that there probably is. She then asks him if there is also a hell, and he waffles but finally says there might be. That evening he learns that she has died.

Thinking back on everything he has heard about Hsiang-lin, the narrator tries to understand what led her to ask that question. Shortly after coming to work for the household, she was kidnapped by the mother of her dead husband and forcibly married to another man. Two years later she was widowed again and left with a small son, who was carried off and killed by a hungry wolf. She returned to her old place of employment but could not recover from her grief over her son, and her work suffered. Her bad luck led the villagers to conclude that she was an evil person. One of them told her that she would surely go to hell, where the lord of hell would saw her in two, giving half to each of her husbands. Eventually she was fired from her position and forced to go begging.

At this point the narrator's thoughts are interrupted by firecrackers and other sounds of the New Year celebration. He puts aside his melancholy thoughts and is swept up in the festive mood that permeates the village.

GUIDELINES FOR DISCUSSION QUESTIONS

1. The narrator of the story says that his uncle is "very moral and righteous." Do you agree with his assessment of Uncle Four? Explain your reasoning.

Uncle Four is undoubtedly an upright man when judged according to traditional standards of social conformity. Students whose definition of "moral and righteous" includes some degree of compassion, however, are likely to fault him on his cold treatment of Sister Hsiang-lin. When he first meets her, he is reluctant to hire her because "he did not like the idea of widows." After her forcible second marriage and widowhood, he unaccountably calls her "a bane against morality" and orders that she not be allowed to touch anything in connection with the ancestral sacrifices. Later he throws her out on the street when her personal suffering affects the quality of her work. Finally, he is offended that she would die at such an inappropriate time.

2. Who is the narrator of the story? What kind of a person is he? How does he differ from the other villagers?

The narrator of the story is the young nephew of Uncle Four. He is a scholar who has been away from the village for some time and is undoubtedly more sophisticated than the other villagers. His interest in Hsiang-lin's situation indicates that he is concerned with finding the truth beneath the surface, and his confusion over her question suggests that he is skeptical about religious matters. His uncle's annoyance with him probably springs from the fact that he appears to be a more progressive thinker than the conservative old man.

3. What is the purpose of the rather long introduction before the story of Sister Hsiang-lin begins?

The introduction prepares the ground for the story that follows by presenting the traditional and somewhat superstitious household where Hsiang-lin once worked and by establishing the significance of the New Year celebration. In addition, the unexpected meeting between the narrator and Hsiang-lin in the introduction piques the reader's curiosity about the main character.

4. Why is Sister Hsiang-lin eager to know about the afterlife? What motivates the narrator to answer her questions as he does? Do you think his answers contribute to her death?

Hsiang-lin is eager to know about the afterlife because she has been terrified by an unkind villager, who predicts that she will end up in hell. This villager tells her that the lord of hell will saw her in half and give a piece to each of her husbands. She is hoping that the narrator will tell her that there is no afterlife. Mistaking her intent, however, and believing that she wants assurance of an afterlife, he gives her that assurance. It is quite likely that this dreadful news contributes to her death.

5. The story begins and ends with the New Year celebrations. Why do you think the story was placed in this particular time setting?

The New Year celebration, with its festivities and hope for the future, stands in stark contrast to Hsiang-lin, who is a perpetual outsider in this community.

GUIDELINES FOR ASSESSING STUDENT WRITING

Imagine that you are a journalist who has observed the recent events in the Chinese village of Luchen and knows all the details of Sister Hsiang-lin's story. You have been asked to write an article on the position of women in this part of China. Using plenty of concrete details, present your observations on this subject.

Students who read carefully can ferret out a number of details indicating that women are not accorded much respect in Luchen, beginning with the incidental remark that "only the male members of the family participated in the ceremony." The most overwhelming piece of evidence, of course, is the manner in which Hsiang-lin is married against her wishes. Mrs. Wei's words make it clear that this practice is widespread: "Any bride will make a scene; but all one has to do is bind her up, stuff her into the sedan. . . ." The fact that Hsiang-lin's in-laws receive money for this marriage transaction makes it seem akin to being sold as property. Students should offer ample evidence and occasional quotations in their articles.

MAO TUN

Spring Silkworms

SUMMARY

"Spring Silkworms" describes the arduous task of raising silkworm cocoons, focusing on the extended family of Tung Pao, an older man who was once fairly prosperous but whose family is now in decline. The complex and delicate process is explained at length and the precariousness of the workers' livelihood is dramatized. In this particular year, the weather is good and the silkworms prosper, but the workers learn that the silk factories are not buying cocoons because of the war effort. Unable to pay the debts they incurred to feed and raise the worms, the members of Tung Pao's family lose a piece of their land and find themselves sinking deeper in debt.

GUIDELINES FOR DISCUSSION QUESTIONS

1. How would you characterize the peasants in this story who raise the silkworms?

The peasants portrayed in the story are all extremely hard-working and somewhat superstitious, as evidenced by their visits to fortune tellers, their reliance on signs such as the number of leaves sprouting from garlic, and their avoidance of any individual (such as Lotus) who has had bad luck.

2. How do the first two paragraphs of the story establish Tung Pao's age and income level without any direct statements?

In the first paragraph Tung Pao's poverty is indicated by the fact that he has to pawn his winter jacket before he can get a spring jacket. In the second paragraph his relative age is shown by the remark, "Even the weather is not what it used to be!" A young man would not be expected to speak in such a manner.

3. What does the secondary plot, concerning Lotus and Ah Dou, contribute to this story?

The secondary plot involving Lotus and Ah Dou humanizes the story, revealing some of the folkways and conflicts that might typically develop among the peasants who raise silkworms.

4. The author of "Spring Silkworms" devotes a great deal of space to describing the actual process of raising silkworms. What might be his purpose in doing so?

The rather detailed presentation of silkworm farming is necessary to demonstrate the precarious existence eked out by the workers. Even in a year when weather conditions are favorable and everything goes right, there are still unpredictable market forces that can suddenly sabotage the workers' livelihood for an entire year. Mao Tun clearly is seeking to engender understanding for these workers.

GUIDELINES FOR ASSESSING STUDENT WRITING

Imagine that you are a talk show host and that Tung Pao has agreed to appear on your show to discuss the job of raising silkworms. What questions would you ask him? How would you expect him to answer? Write a script for the show, providing both the questions and the answers.

The script should demonstrate an awareness that a successful crop of silkworm cocoons comes about only after a long chain of events has taken place. One glitch anywhere along the line, including unfavorable weather, and the crop is likely to fail. The talk show host should, of course, find out something about this process. The host might also want to ask about peripheral matters such as the process of borrowing money or the effect of foreign goods.

LAO SHÊ

The Last Train

SUMMARY

"The Last Train" introduces a cast of characters who are traveling by train on New Year's Day. The author begins by presenting their rather vacuous and self-centered conversations. Then he describes in detail how a fire, which was started by a cigarette in the second-class car, spreads wildly through several cars on the train, killing all the occupants. (The fire spreads quickly because of some fireworks being carried on board.) The haphazard investigation that follows results in the firing of an innocent waiter and the conclusion that "the fire could not have started in the second-class carriage."

GUIDELINES FOR DISCUSSION QUESTIONS

1. **In this story the author tends to create characters by giving them a single trait or topic of conversation. How does he characterize the waiter ("the boy"), Mr. Chiao, Little Tsui, and Mr. Chang? In general, would you say that the characters are pictured as sympathetic or unattractive?**

   The waiter is characterized by his repeated complaining about having to work on New Year's Day, Mr. Chiao by his snobbery about having a free pass, Little Tsui by his addiction to opium, and Mr. Chang by his frequent comments about the train being too hot. The characters are, without exception, unattractive. The author is clearly not trying to work up any sympathy for the characters in this story.

2. **The fire in this story is presented in such a way that it seems to have thoughts and emotions of its own. Reread the paragraph that begins, "The fire had discovered a new colony . . ." and describe the "feelings" of the fire.**

   The fire is described as "mad with joy," and its tongues of flame are said to be "dancing." At an earlier point in the story, the flames are compared to "streamers," as if this were a party scene. The paragraph ends with the strange statement, "It was a lovely cremation," probably an expression of the fire's "feelings."

3. Do you think the investigation of the fire was handled competently? Why or why not?

The investigation is strikingly incompetent, and its conclusions are totally false. To begin with, it takes the inspector fifteen days to arrive, and he then proceeds to spend three more days attending "official receptions." When the haphazard investigation finally begins, it reveals that the fire could not have originated in the second-class car because no tickets were sold for this car. The fact that free passes were issued for this car is completely overlooked, as is the fact that this particular car was totally burned out when it arrived at the station, indicating that the fire had started there. Finally, the inspector, whose investigation has revealed virtually nothing, arbitrarily decides to lay the blame on a waiter.

4. What is the purpose of the short conversation between the waiter and his wife at the end of the story? How does this conversation reinforce the theme of the story?

This conversation demonstrates that the silly waiter is still concerned about the fact that he had to work on New Year's Day, while his wife is only concerned about her dinner being burned. All of the characters in this story are encased in their own selfish worlds and oblivious to anything else. The people at the station who see the burning train pass through, for example, simply shrug at the tragedy and play mahjong. They even conclude that everything is "right with the world." The theme of social indifference and corruption is reinforced at all levels of society, from the higher levels, represented by the inspector and the tribune, to the lower levels, represented by the waiter and his wife.

GUIDELINES FOR ASSESSING STUDENT WRITING

Imagine that you are a television newscaster who has been assigned to report on the mysterious train fire that occurred on New Year's Day. You have seen the remains of the train, talked to some people who were at the station, and received the inspector's report. There are, of course, no living witnesses who can tell you how the fire started. Write the news report that you will deliver on television.

The news report should objectively communicate the known facts—the condition of the train when it arrived, the number of casualties, and perhaps some statements from witnesses at the station. The report should also present the inspector's conclusions, though an objective newscaster will report them without endorsing them.

THE HYAKU MONOGATARI

Hōichi the Earless

SUMMARY

"Hōichi the Earless" is the tale of a blind and talented musician who resides in a Buddhist temple with a priest. One evening Hōichi is visited by a stranger who bids him come and perform for a high-ranking individual and his noble attendants. Hōichi accompanies the stranger and performs in an unknown place, which appears to be filled with people. They ask him to recite the tale of the battle at Dan-no-ura, which he performs skillfully, causing great emotion in the listeners. The next evening he is again fetched by the stranger, but this time his absence from the temple is noticed. The priest sends some of his attendants to find Hōichi, and they locate him playing his instrument in the cemetery. It seems that he has been playing for the spirits of those who died in the battle at Dan-no-ura.

When the priest hears about the situation, he is alarmed and convinces Hōichi that he must not go again. Writing holy texts on Hōichi's body to protect him, the priest instructs him not to move or answer the voice of the spirit who comes to fetch him. When the spirit arrives, Hōichi follows instructions. The priest has forgotten to write holy texts on his ears, however, which are visible to the spirit as a result. The spirit tears off Hōichi's ears to take back with him. Hōichi, who is now safe from the spirits of the dead, gains fame throughout the land and receives visits from many noble people. Eventually his fame makes him a wealthy man.

GUIDELINES FOR DISCUSSION QUESTIONS

1. **What was your first impression of the supernatural beings that Hōichi entertained? (Did they seem benevolent or threatening?) Was this impression later confirmed or modified?**

   At first the spirits seem benevolent, requesting only music and responding with sensitivity and appreciation. Later the priest informs Hōichi that they intend to take possession of him and that they will tear him apart. Some students may be skeptical about the priest's advice and may doubt that these gentle souls would cause any harm. By the time the visiting spirit tears off Hōichi's ears, however, it is patently clear that the priest is right.

2. How does the first paragraph foreshadow the main episode of the story?

The first paragraph, in a description that seems to be nothing more than literary hyperbole, contends that Hōichi's music is so lovely that "even the goblins could not refrain from tears." As it turns out, this statement is no figure of speech, but is quite literally correct.

3. What hints are given that Hōichi might be dealing with supernatural forces?

The stranger who comes to fetch him has an iron hand and seems to be dressed in full armor, which is a bit strange. As they near their destination Hōichi is aware that they pass through a large gateway, which he does not remember existing in any part of the town except the memorial area.

4. Which part of Hōichi's recital do the spirits in the cemetery find especially moving? Why?

The spirits in the cemetery are especially moved by the part about Nii-no-Ama jumping to her death with the imperial infant in her arms. The individual requesting the performance, as it turns out, is the spirit of this imperial infant, Antoku Tennō.

5. What long-term benefits does Hōichi receive from his strange experience?

Although Hōichi loses his ears, his experience with the spirits is, in a sense, a blessing in disguise since it brings fame and wealth his way.

GUIDELINES FOR ASSESSING STUDENT WRITING

Imagine that you heard Hōichi's performance in the cemetery and have decided to write a review of it for the *Amidaji Times,* a local newspaper. Evaluate the performance, explaining its special strengths.

The review of Hōichi's recital should, of course, be extremely positive, praising both his singing and his playing. Hōichi seems to have the ability to make the *biwa* imitate sounds in the real world. It is mentioned at one point in the story, for example, that he can make his instrument sound like "the straining of oars and the rushing of ships, the whirr and the hissing of arrows." Students might mention these special effects in their reviews.

SEAMI

The Damask Drum

SUMMARY

In this classical Noh play, an old gardener catches a glimpse of a young princess and falls in love with her. Hearing of his infatuation, the princess sends word that a drum hangs from a laurel tree. If the gardener beats the drum and the sound is heard in the palace, she will appear before him. The gardener beats the drum, but no sound is produced because the drum is covered in damask. In despair, the gardener drowns himself. Shortly afterward, his ghost appears and torments the princess with the constant beating of the drum.

GUIDELINES TO DISCUSSION QUESTIONS

1. **The princess in *The Damask Drum* decides to discourage the old gardener by humiliating him. What do you think is the best way to discourage unwanted attention? Can it be done without cruelty?**

Students are likely to mention a variety of indirect tactics, such as ignoring the interested person and hoping that he or she "gets the message." They may also suggest telling the individual directly that they are not interested in a relationship. Both of these approaches will inevitably result in disappointment on the part of the rejected person, but they can be done without deliberate cruelty.

Any method involving humiliation or tricks is an act of intentional cruelty. Students should see that the princess chose an extreme method for making her point.

2. **How is this Noh play different from most of the American or European dramas you have seen or read?**

Students should be able to note a number of differences between Noh drama and the realistic drama that is typical of most modern American and European theater; for example, poetic language, lack of stage directions, presentational style (in which characters acknowledge the presence of the audience), and so on. For students who have not yet read any Greek drama, the presence of the chorus may be a new feature. Some students may also comment on the general lack of fast action and the air of tranquility that pervades the Noh drama. Help students to see that the total effect of these elements is to create an experience that encourages contemplation.

3. It has been said that Seami's plays often create a sense of eternity by emphasizing (a) the quick passing of time and (b) the insignificance of human life. Select several phrases or statements from the play that demonstrate these themes.

Some of the more significant phrases and statements from the play that demonstrate these themes appear below:
- . . . as a white colt flashes / Past a gap in the hedge, even so our days pass.
- . . . Goal of his dewdrop life
- It was yesterday, and it is today.
- The days had left their marks, / Coming and coming, like waves that beat on a sandy shore . . .
- I was driftwood in the pool . . .
- The wind passes, the rain falls . . .

4. Seami is known for his skillful use of figurative language. Discuss the meaning of the following figures of speech:
- **The damask drum is called "the voiceless fabric of pride."**
- **The ghost of the gardener says, "I spent my heart on the glimpse of a moon that slipped / Through the boughs of an autumn tree."**
- **As the princess is being tormented by the ghost, she cries, "By what dire seed this harvest sown?"**

The implications of the three figures of speech are indicated below:
- The damask that covers the drum is "voiceless" because it produces no sound, and it is a "fabric of pride" because of its associations with royalty and aristocracy. Some students may be able to extend the meaning of this phrase by observing that the princess, who is also covered in damask, is voiceless in the sense that she cannot respond decently to a human being in need.
- The moon is a reference to the beautiful and elusive princess that slipped from the old gardener, who is compared here to an "autumn tree." (He has almost reached the end of his life.)
- The princess is asking what terrible cause ("dire seed") has produced this unfortunate result ("harvest"). She is referring to the punishment being inflicted upon her by the gardener's ghost and is asking what she has done to deserve it.

5. In what way does "the punishment fit the crime" in this play?

The princess, who humiliated the gardener by asking him to produce sound from a silent drum, is repaid by being subjected to the constant beating of that drum. She is possessed by the ghost of the gardener, who is doing just what she asked him to do.

GUIDELINES FOR ASSESSING STUDENT WRITING

1. **Write a paragraph describing either the pain of rejection or the annoyance of being pursued by an unwanted suitor. Use figurative language to describe your feelings. Try to use related images. The sample below, for instance, draws all its images from the sea:**

> I needed him as much as a fish needs water, but he needed me about as much as a fish needs a pair of shoes. When I realized how things stood, I felt like a fish left gasping on the seashore.

Any kind of imagery is appropriate to this exercise as long as it conveys the pain or annoyance in a vivid way. The images chosen should all relate to the same subject area. A student who starts out by comparing a pesky admirer to a mosquito that will not go away, for instance, should not shift ground and suddenly compare him to a rubber ball that keeps bouncing back. You might want to explain the problem of the mixed metaphor at this point. (Example: "*Once you have set sail, it is disastrous to try to change horses.*" The sailboat metaphor here conflicts with the horseback metaphor.)

2. **Write a short one-act play about a disappointing experience that a high school student might have. Try to introduce some of the characteristics of Noh drama, such as its contemplative mood and a character who functions as the chorus. Use plenty of figurative language to express the disappointment of the main character. Resolve the situation by showing some kind of justice done.**

The one-act play could, of course, focus on any one of a variety of subjects such as a personal relationship or a failure to make the team. Students should emphasize the inner thoughts and feelings of the main character rather than any overt action, and these thoughts should be expressed through imagery to some extent. If the play includes someone functioning as the chorus, this character should summarize the situation and help the characters to communicate their feelings. Students should demonstrate that they understand the sparseness, the quietness, and the contemplative nature of the Noh play.

HAIKU

SUMMARY

Like most haiku, the ones in this collection tend to focus on miniature scenes in a fleeting moment of time. The subjects are usually natural phenomena that include insect life, birds, plant life, waterfalls, and the sky. A few human-centered haiku show people laboring at their daily tasks in a natural setting.

GUIDELINES FOR DISCUSSION QUESTIONS

1. Why do you think the Japanese haiku has become such a popular form of poetry?

Responses to this question are speculative and will probably vary widely. The intensity and extreme compression of the poems are no doubt part of the appeal. The theme of the inter-relatedness of things is generally attractive in an ecological-minded age. The idea of capturing a fleeting moment in a tiny "snapshot" is, of course, popular. And perhaps the apparent simplicity that invites amateur poets to "try their hand" is also an appealing feature of haiku.

2. What are the most common subjects of these traditional haiku?

Natural scenes and objects are by far the most prevalent subjects. Very few of these haiku contain human beings, and only one ("The Great Buddha at Nara") can be said to center on a human-made object.

3. Explain the witty hyperbole (exaggeration) in the haiku entitled "Persistence."

The poet jokingly claims that the cicada sang so loudly that it eventually blew itself out of the shell.

4. Unable to reproduce the Japanese 17-syllable pattern in the English translation, the translator of these haiku has imposed structure in another way. What technique has he used to give the poems a structured pattern?

The most common pattern imposed on these poems is an *aba* rhyme scheme (first and third lines rhyme). Alliteration and assonance are also occasionally used ("clouds come").

5. It has been said that the haiku often expresses hidden hopes in small things. Which of the haiku in this collection fit this description?

This may be a discussible point, but the most obvious examples are "Clouds," "The Sun Path," "The Sound," and "Contentment in Poverty."

GUIDELINES FOR ASSESSING STUDENT WRITING

Choose an academic subject or a school-related activity that is part of your life right now. Write two haiku that capture the essence of this subject or your feelings about it. Follow the syllabic requirements for the haiku (5-7-5).

By selecting subjects that are personally familiar, students will avoid the temptation of writing haiku that are merely thinly disguised clones of the Japanese haiku in this collection. The results should be judged leniently, as long as they conform to the syllabic requirements of the haiku. This exercise also lends itself to group work.

SHIGA NAOYA

Seibei's Gourds

SUMMARY

"Seibei's Gourds" depicts a 12-year-old boy's consuming interest in collecting gourds, which he preserves and polishes. His father is annoyed by Seibei's behavior but does not at first actively interfere. One day Seibei is caught polishing a gourd in school, which is confiscated by the enraged teacher and given to a porter. When Seibei's father hears the news, he smashes his son's entire collection of gourds.

Sometime later the special gourd that was given to the porter is sold for a large sum of money and the buyer, recognizing its value, resells it for even more money. Seibei becomes engrossed in painting, but his disapproving father again tries to discourage him from his artistic pursuits.

GUIDELINES FOR DISCUSSION QUESTIONS

1. What words would you use to describe Seibei? Were you able to sympathize with his rather unusual interest in gourds?

Students will probably remark on Seibei's persistence and quiet confidence in the face of strong disapproval. Some students might also mention his surprisingly mild-mannered acceptance of the harsh treatment he receives from the adults in his life. He eventually gives up his gourds and takes up painting with no feelings of bitterness toward his teacher or his father, who have sabotaged years of careful work.

2. What is the purpose of the short scene at the beginning of the story in which Seibei mistakes a man's bald head for a gourd?

This short, amusing scene demonstrates Seibei's complete obsession with gourds. They seem to be uppermost in his mind wherever he goes.

3. What kind of gourds does Seibei like? What does this say about his artistic taste?

Seibei's preference for plain gourds probably indicates that he has excellent taste, since true artistry tends to be marked by simplicity. While his father and others are only impressed with bizarre and showy gourds, Seibei bypasses the glitzy ones and zeroes in on real quality.

4. Explain the unintended irony in the words of Seibei's father, who shouts, "When you don't know what you're talking about, you'd better shut up!"

Seibei's father is speaking contemptuously to someone whose judgment about gourds is unerring. Seibei probably cannot articulate any "artistic principle." His knowledge is intuitive, and so he simply looks at a gourd and "knows."

5. What does "Seibei's Gourds" seem to imply about the place of an artist in society?

The story implies that artists have an uphill battle and that they must face continual prejudice. Often the artistic impulse is so strong, however, that a gifted individual simply cannot stop, and this seems to be the case with Seibei.

GUIDELINES FOR ASSESSING STUDENT WRITING

Think of an interest, preference, or pastime that you have that is not understood or respected by some of your acquaintances. First write a letter or E-mail message from your acquaintances' point of view, explaining why this seems like a strange pastime. Then write a response from your own point of view, explaining the value of this pastime.

The first of these message is the more challenging, since students will need to sympathize with the opposing point of view well enough to present it lucidly. The second message, which presents the defense, should be clear, convincing, and as specific as possible about the benefits of the student's chosen pastime.

TANIZAKI JUNICHIRO

The Thief

SUMMARY

"The Thief," which is narrated from the first-person point of view, is the story of four roommates at a preparatory school. One evening they are discussing a string of thefts that have recently occurred at the school. It becomes clear from the discussion that one of the boys, Hirata, suspects the narrator of being the thief. Acutely conscious of his inferior social and economic status, the narrator feels stigmatized and obsesses over the incident. When he finds out later that some of the proctors also suspect him, he offers to move out so that his roommates will not feel ashamed to be living with him. His other two roommates stand by him and say they will fight the false accusation. As the story draws to a close, the narrator steals money from Hirata's drawer and is caught by him. He confesses that he has been a compulsive thief for a long time. The carefully presented first-person narration has misled the reader into thinking that this victimizer is actually a victim.

GUIDELINES FOR DISCUSSION QUESTIONS

1. Did you suspect the narrator of being the thief before it was revealed? If so, what made you suspicious?

Some students' suspicions may have been aroused by the fact that the narrator keeps speculating about what he would think or do "if he were" the thief. Statements such as, "No matter how vicious a thief I might be, I could never steal anything from Nakamura" are bizarre at best.

2. What is known about the narrator, other than that he is a thief?

The narrator is the son of a poor farmer and is attending school on scholarship. He is acutely aware of the social distance between himself and most of the other students. He is also keenly aware of his underdeveloped physique, describing himself as "skinny and pale and high-strung." In general, he seems to live with a strong sense of his own inferiority.

3. **The narrator claims that he did his best to warn his friends "in a round about way" and that he even tried to protect them by offering to move out. Do you think he was trying to warn and protect them, or did he have another motive?**

Students may have different observations on this point. There are some clues in the narrator's tangled psychology suggesting that his openness with his friends is merely a ploy to disarm them. He says, "If I were a prudent, clever thief—no, I mustn't put it that way—if I were a thief with the least bit of conscience and consideration for other people, I'd try to keep my friendships untarnished." He corrects himself in this sentence, but his slip-up is revealing. He is trying to convince himself that he cares about his friends, but his caring behavior is perhaps part of being a "prudent, clever thief."

4. **How would this story have been different if it had been told from the point of view of one of the other boys?**

The tightly controlled point of view creates suspense and surprise. If the story had been told by an innocent person, the surprise element would have been much weaker. The reader simply does not expect a narrator to engage in deliberate falsehoods, and so the surprise is that much greater.

GUIDELINES FOR ASSESSING STUDENT WRITING

The personality and character of the narrator are the center of interest in this story, but his three friends also emerge as individuals. Select one of these three minor characters and describe his personality. Support your description with details and quotations from the story.

The most difficult character to get a handle on is Hirata. It is not clear whether his hostility springs from genuine insight into the narrator's flaws or whether it is simply class prejudice. Students may adopt either of these stances as long as they give specific evidence from the story. Nakamura is a loyal, fair, and extremely judicious character who never accepts anything on hearsay, certainly a better friend than the narrator deserves. Higuchi is a bit more gossipy than Nakamura, but students may not pick up on this trait. On the whole, he is a decent character. The most important task is for students to support their observations with concrete examples drawn from the text.

AKUTAGAWA RYŪNOSUKÉ

Hell Screen

SUMMARY

"Hell Screen" is the story of a great artist named Yoshihide, who is ordered by the Lord of Horikawa to paint a screen showing the circles of hell. Thoroughly dedicated to his art, Yoshihide always tries to arrange a direct observation of anything he paints. He is so unscrupulous in his pursuit of perfection that he puts one of his apprentices in chains and has another one attacked by an owl in order to get a detailed view of bodies writhing in agony. He is determined to the make the hell screen as realistic as possible.

Yoshihide has a beautiful fifteen-year-old daughter who lives at the palace where the Lord of Horikawa resides. The artist, though generally unfeeling toward other people, loves his daughter deeply. As the artist works feverishly on the hell screen, his daughter is growing more and more distressed at the palace, presumably because the lord is making sexual advances.

One day Yoshihide pays a call on the lord and asks if he will arrange to burn a carriage so that the artist can benefit from the sight. The lord agrees, and they gather a few days later for the burning. Just as the fire is lit, the carriage curtains are parted to reveal Yoshihide's young daughter chained inside. The lord is apparently taking revenge on her for rebuffing his advances. Overwhelmed with grief and terror, the artist runs toward her, but the flames are already starting to consume the carriage and its occupant. The artist's distress suddenly turns to joy as he observes the flames doing their work. Within a month he has finished the hell screen, which is so realistic that viewers say it makes them hear "dreadful cries." Then he kills himself.

GUIDELINES FOR DISCUSSION QUESTIONS

1. How would you describe the narrator of "Hell Screen"? Do you agree with his self-description: "I have always been a stupid person and unless something is absolutely plain I cannot grasp it"? Why do you think Akutagawa created a narrator like this?

The narrator is certainly naïve, and his assessment of himself as "stupid" may not be far from the mark. Though faced with abundant evidence, he cannot comprehend that Yuzuki is being pursued by the Lord of Horikawa but claims that his overtures to her are "nothing but kindness." One of the benefits of having an obtuse narrator such as this one is to create mystery and uncertainty about what is actually going on at the palace. The reader's curiosity is aroused by this technique. Another benefit is the creation of subtle irony as the narrator continually misinterprets the obvious.

2. Why are the stories of the two apprentices to Yoshihide included (one almost bitten by a snake, the other attacked by an owl)?

The two apprentice stories obviously demonstrate the cold and unfeeling nature of the artist, but they serve a more important purpose as well. These episodes reveal Yoshihide's obsession with having direct models for his paintings. In this way they foreshadow the terrible scene in which his daughter will serve as the artist's model.

3. How do you account for the fact that Yoshihide stood "joyfully watching the death of his daughter"?

Yoshihide is not joyful about the death of his daughter, of course. His artistic sensibilities are so keenly aroused by the flames and the rare view of the girl in torment that he momentarily loses sight of the fact that his own daughter is dying in agony.

4. Explain the role of the monkey in this story. What purpose does he serve?

The monkey, whose name is Yoshihide, is a contrast to the other Yoshihide, the artist who is Yuzuki's father. The human Yoshihide, as it turns out, is less human than the monkey, who, oddly enough, plays the father role to Yuzuki better than her actual father. The monkey watches over Yuzuki when she is sick and acts as her protector when she is being molested by the amorous lord. Finally, the monkey is the only individual at the burning scene who exhibits real compassion for the dying girl. He demonstrates his loyalty by making the ultimate sacrifice, giving up his life to die with her. The artist's failure as a human being is dramatically revealed by the devoted monkey, who steps into his shoes.

5. At the end of Section 6 of the story, the narrator tells us that the hell screen eventually caused Yoshihide to take his own life. Then he says, "I may have told the wrong end of the story first." Why did the author give us a glimpse of the ending at this point?

The intriguing remarks made by the narrator "out of sequence" pique the reader's interest. One naturally wonders what is meant by remarks such as "this hell he pictured was the hell that he . . . was one day to fall into."

6. What would you say is the main theme or message of this story?

The main theme of the story relates to the temperament and personality of great artists. The author implies that such artists, haunted by a terrible compulsion to achieve artistic perfection, eventually lose their basic humanity and their ability to relate to people.

GUIDELINES FOR ASSESSING STUDENT WRITING

Analyze Akutagawa's likely attitude toward one of the following: (1) artists (2) members of royalty (3) animals. Your observations should be based on how these individuals are depicted in "Hell Screen." Support your observations with specific examples.

In order to write a responsible and scholarly essay on Akutagawa's attitudes, the student would, of course, need to examine more than one story. The present assignment, though a definite shortcut, has value as an inductive exercise and gives the students practice in gathering evidence. Based on "Hell Screen" alone, students would have to conclude that (1) artists are emotionally maimed people, (2) members of royalty are decadent power abusers, and (3) animals can sometimes outdo humans in their capacity for loyalty and love. All conclusions would need to be fully supported with details from the story.

IBUSÉ MASUJI

The Charcoal Bus

SUMMARY

In "The Charcoal Bus" the unnamed narrator returns to Japan after World War II and boards an old broken-down bus that he used to ride before the war. He notices that the bus has been painted and the windows repaired, but it still runs on charcoal. The narrator recalls a previous experience on the charcoal bus that occurred during the war and recounts it. On that occasion the engine would not fire, and so the passengers got out and began pushing. The driver became angry when he noticed that a young couple in the back of the bus had not gotten out to push. He began to argue with them and ended up punching the man in the face.

After four miles of pushing, the group reached a crossroads. At this point many of the passengers decided to abandon the charcoal bus and take a "proper bus." As the story ends, the driver is tinkering with the engine and the conductor is turning the blower. They still believe that they can make the bus function.

GUIDELINES FOR DISCUSSION QUESTIONS

1. On the basis of the story, how would you describe the situation in wartime Japan?

The charcoal bus seems to be an allegorical symbol of Japan. The serious delays and breakdowns of the bus indicate that the country is functioning inefficiently and that the leadership is incompetent.

2. Why do you think the characters in this story are all unnamed?

Characters are often unnamed in allegorical works because they are not intended to be individuals but to be representatives of ideas, social groups, or political forces.

3. What is the allegorical significance of the fact that, after the war, the bus has been painted and the windows repaired but it still has to run on charcoal?

After the war the bus was spruced up and made to look presentable. However, it still runs on charcoal, an undependable source of energy.

The implication is that the political and social changes in Japan are only surface changes and that the underlying structure is as inefficient as ever.

4. **What is implied by such remarks as "the purgees are all coming back into favor" and "reverence had been unfashionable for some time after the war but was now gradually coming back into favor"?**

These comments suggest a basic instability in the Japanese political and social system. Individual leaders quickly fall from grace and are later restored. Social values are subject to constant change. Even something as perennial as religious faith goes in and out of fashion during these volatile times.

GUIDELINES FOR ASSESSING STUDENT WRITING

1. **Do some research on Japan during World War II and in the years shortly afterward. Then write an essay explaining the specific allegorical details in "The Charcoal Bus." (Who might the bus driver and conductor represent? What do you think the young married couple represent? What about the old farm couple?)**

Student's individual interpretations of this story are less important than their success in uncovering historical facts that seem to "fit the case." The bus driver who was removed from his position but likely to be reinstated might be Yoshida Shigeru, who was arrested for resisting the war effort but later became Prime Minister. Students might also see him as Emperor Hirohito. The passengers who labor to push the bus and who get nothing for their efforts are either the Japanese people in general or the Japanese soldiers. The honeymoon couple and old farm couple probably represent the contrasting attitudes of the younger and older generations. (The younger people are less willing to dedicate themselves obediently to the state.)

2. **Write a short allegory of your own that demonstrates a mishandled situation. Your main allegorical symbol should not be a bus or any other vehicle.**

There are an unlimited number of approaches to this assignment. Students should invent characters, objects, and situations that clearly represent ideas or social forces. Some students may wish to work in groups and to present their allegories to the class in the form of skits.